POWER, POWERLESSNESS, AND THE DIVINE

— 3 April 1998 —

For Professor Migliore,
My mentor and friend.

With great appreciation—

Cindy

Scholars Press

Studies in Theological Education

Christian Identity and Theological Education   Joseph C. Hough, Jr./
John B. Cobb, Jr.

Vision and Discernment: Charles M. Wood
An Orientation in Theological Study

The Arts in Theological Education: Wilson Yates
New Possibilities for Integration

Beyond Clericalism: Joseph C. Hough, Jr./
The Congregation as a Focus for Theological   Barbara G. Wheeler
Education

The Education of the Practical Theologian: Don S. Browning/
Responses to Joseph Hough and John Cobb's   David Polk/
Christian Identity and Theological Education   Ian S. Evison

Piety and Intellect: The Aims and Purposes   Glenn T. Miller
of Ante-Bellum Theological Education

Religious Studies, Theological Studies
and the University-Divinity School   Joseph Mitsuo Kitagawa

The President as Educator:
A Study of the Seminary Presidency   Neely Dixon McCarter

Power, Powerlessness, and the Divine
New Inquiries in Bible and Theology   Cynthia L. Rigby, editor

POWER, POWERLESSNESS, AND THE DIVINE
New Inquiries in Bible and Theology

edited by
Cynthia L. Rigby

Scholars Press
Atlanta, Georgia

POWER, POWERLESSNESS, AND THE DIVINE
New Inquiries in Bible and Theology

edited by
Cynthia L. Rigby

© 1997
Scholars Press

Library of Congress Cataloging in Publication Data
Power, powerlessness, and the divine : new inquiries in Bible and
    theology / edited by Cynthia L. Rigby.
        p.   cm. — (Scholars Press studies in theological education)
    Includes bibliographical references.
    ISBN 0-7885-0422-3 (alk. paper). — ISBN 0-7885-0423-1 (pbk. :
alk. paper)
        1. Power (Christian theology) I. Rigby, Cynthia L. II. Series.
    BT738.25.P69   1997
    230—dc21   97-42124
                                                            CIP

Printed in the United States of America
on acid-free paper

Contents

⌘

PART I
Method and Content

PART II
Conceptual-Theological Reflections

Prologue

⌘

In November 1990, the Executive Committee of the Lilly Endowment made a generous grant for the "Project of Bible and Theology." The present volume collects the final product of "Power, Powerlessness, and the Divine"—one of the working groups of this Project, chaired by Michael Welker and William Schweiker.

The Project of Bible and Theology was dedicated to the goal of providing a forum which could help to overcome the fragmentation of theological studies by bringing into conversation areas of specialization which too frequently have no vital contacts with each other. During its four-year duration, the Project developed two primary centers of activity.

(1) The Project assisted in the formation of three working groups whose members agreed to pursue a topic of significance in joint work which extended over several years. Members of each working group represented most areas of theological studies, but there was in all groups a preponderance of specialists in contemporary theology and in biblical studies. Each working group consisted of 10–12 active participants who met together, submitting to each other their proposals about the selected topic, engaging in extensive dialogue about their varied positions, and developing their own views of the subject in the course of long and repeated dialogue. The idea behind this aspect of the Project was to provide the opportunity for a representative group of scholars in different areas of theological work to engage in substantive, collaborative work on a single theme. The hope was to find new avenues through which the fragmentation of theological education might be addressed by engaging in joint theological efforts.

(2) The Project provided the means for an annual plenary meeting to which approximately 120 scholars of all theological disciplines were invited. Between 55 and 65 persons participated in each of three annual plenaries. The agenda for each of these plenaries was set by one of the three working groups, who presented their papers, along with reports about the methods employed in their common research, for discussion by the plenary participants. Reactions by a larger group of colleagues to the

vii

proposals of one working group could then be taken into account in reworking individual contributions.

The Project of Bible and Theology was, from its inception, guided by a Steering Committee who initiated the planning, supervised the implementation, and contributed constant adjustments in the course of the Project's four-year history. The membership of the Steering Committee evolved over a period of time, and some of its members served only for a limited time. But thanks are due to all of them for the vital assistance they gave to the Project. They are: Lisa S. Cahill, Ronald H. Cram, John R. Donahue, Paul D. Hanson, Patrick D. Miller, Andrew Purves, Sharon H. Ringe, Katharine Doob Sakenfeld, and Michael Welker. The undersigned, who served as Director of the Project, owes special thanks to two other persons who accompanied the Project from its inception and who gave a great deal of time and care to its work: Charles M. Wood was appointed evaluator of the Project on behalf of the Lilly Endowment, and Cynthia L. Rigby served as assistant to the Project and organizer of the annual plenary.

Without the constantly encouraging support of Craig R. Dykstra, Vice President for Religion of the Lilly Endowment, no part of the Project of Bible and Theology could have been accomplished. All of us involved in the Project thank him and the Executive Committee of the Lilly Endowment for their help.

Ulrich W. Mauser

Preface

⌘

Commitments to justice, mercy, and wholeness can lead one to dance with unexpected partners. Such has been the case for members of the "Power, Powerlessness, and the Divine" working group, a sub-unit of a project funded by the Lilly Foundation designed to encourage interaction among biblical scholars and theologians. In spite of differences in disciplinary background and habits of mind, this group quickly discovered common ground in our unwillingness, perhaps even our inability, to discuss the relationship of biblical studies and theology without respect to the real-life crises of contemporary societies, including the social breakdown, the struggles for power, and the anguish caused to human life by these realities. The desire to do justice to the interweaving of the three arenas of Bible, theology, and contemporary society—each a complex context in itself—required both a focal point that could provide *coherence* to a multi-leveled analysis and a prism that could refract the issues in all their *complexity*. Coherence and complexity were discovered in our common reflection on the theme that gives this book its title: power, powerlessness, and the divine.

In a scholarly interchange that lasted over a period of three years—usually around seminary tables and in conferences, but sometimes on a dance floor; always creative, regularly contentious—a collective movement of thought emerged that informs the essays in this volume and that, we believe, may offer a new possibility, indeed a new paradigm, for biblical and theological work in the contemporary world. In the first chapter, this new paradigm of inquiry will be explained in detail, even while the book as a whole is its best representation. *In nuce,* it is a paradigm founded on acts of imagination embedded in given social, technological, and natural environments. The paradigm rests on the simple but important belief that human beings are always engaged in the on-going task of world-making. What is most fundamentally under inquiry for us is the way social worlds come to be, the distortions that permeate these worlds, and the capacities of persons, communities, and traditions to refashion their worlds in less distorted and oppressive ways. And we here most fundamentally respond to this inquiry with the assertion that human beings perform our world-creating tasks, not only by applying overt power and technologies, but also, significantly, by symbolic and metaphoric means. The analysis and critique of "world" must, then, include analysis and critique of these imaginal acts and their real-life effects. The work of biblical and theological study provides means to reflect on the dynamics of world-making, or social construction, in a critical way. But also, constructively, the plumbing and combing of these fields can—sometimes but not always!—provide the intellectual and imaginal resources for reconstruction of our own damaged and distorted worlds.

Principles Guiding Our Work

Because a detailed exposition of this paradigm is provided in the first chapter, this preface will merely indicate some of the movements each of us has provided to this work in terms of five principles which govern the shape of our discourse—its choreography, if you will.

The first and most apparent of these guiding principles is our theme of power, powerlessness, and the divine. The kind of reflection found in this book is content-driven inquiry. We selected a topic fundamental to virtually every aspect and avenue of the cultural worlds we seek to understand, a topic that invites consideration of values, social structures, and frameworks of meaning. Both the scope and essential quality of this topic allow for the complex, multi-perspectival analyses that are at the heart of the essays. Yet we also, in a sense, deconstructed the theme precisely by means of these analyses. As the reader will discover, "God" is for us paradoxically both a stabilizing and de-stabilizing symbol, while power and powerlessness operate in dialectical tension, neither valued systematically over the other.

The second analytical principle is found in our interdisciplinary, multi-layered approach to social/cultural analysis. Our topic required an approach involving the examination, from a variety of disciplinary angles, of systems whose many layers compose societies and cultures. Given this complex approach to religious reflection and cultural criticism, these essays are constituted by various combinations of historical, literary, psychological, and theological inquiry.

Third, members of the group have had a common interest in reflection that takes seriously not only the issue of socio-cultural context but also the systemic distortions inherent to any and all contexts. Our interest in the how and why of social construction and distortion is manifested in the analyses of social and cultural worlds found in each essay, especially with regard to problematic aspects of those worlds that create, intensify, of reinforce injustice. Such problematic aspects are often so embedded in their social/cultural contexts that they are virtually invisible. We understand, moreover, that the most invisible of all distortions are those embedded in a culture's symbol system, the realm of its world-constituting imagination, including its religious imagination and its theology. It is this realm that lies at the heart of our enterprise.

For this complex approach to religion and culture is at the same time deeply theological in nature, and the effort to do theology—a theology in dialogue with the biblical traditions—constitutes the fourth unifying principle of our project. As a theological project, however, the attempts to understand the relationship of God to a suffering world included in this volume move well beyond the bounds of conventional systematic theology and academic biblical studies. We understand theology as an activity of critically interpreting and imaginatively construing the world. Thus, as noted, we struggle to understand and evaluate many dimensions of human life and social construction, along with their distortions, including the distortions of theology. But our interest in making a world where healing and justice are possible leads us not only to critique but also to engage in constructive theological reflection. Members of this group shared a dedication to intellectual rigor in this reflection, but with deep understanding of the role of imagination in the enterprise of world making. In this dance, the Bible was our constant though (paradoxically) ever-changing partner. While we found it as needy of critique as all our human efforts to speak of God—and indeed, in some cases, as irredeemable—we also found within it a rich (because diverse) fund of imaginal resources and a fundamental structure of self-critique that, we argue, should inform all theology.

Finally, and in a sense in summary of the preceding four points, the members of this project sought to create a methodological shift that maintains respect for the often-difficult tensions of diversity and difference in texts and social contexts and, at the same time, transmutes them into creative, nontotalitarian forms of inquiry and understanding. Our concern is to provide a paradigm of research that can address the real complexity of both biblical texts and social situations without loss of conceptual coherence and, conversely, avoids purchase of clarity at the cost of ignoring the complexity and diversity of texts and contexts. These are the twin errors that, we believe, have haunted modern biblical studies and theology. Through our interdisciplinary research, we attempt to contribute to a new form of theological discourse—including biblical interpretation—that respects complexity while, at the same time, articulating a coherent theological vision.

Summaries of the Essays

The essays are divided into three major sections, corresponding to the three points of reference in our inquiry into the relationship of theology, Bible, and world. Each group is followed by a response prepared for the conference in which they were presented.

I

The first group, then (part II of the volume), contains papers whose points of entry are questions of a conceptual-theological nature.

Michael Welker argues that, because of the lack of center in contemporary social existence, moral communication in the face of global dangers finds little or at least insufficient practical resonance even among those to whom it is directed. He combines this cultural criticism with critique of two theological models that attempt to address the situation, finding Küng's approach to be too authoritarian and Tracy's mysticism to be constructively inadequate with respect to the post-modern context with which Welker is concerned. Welker's own constructive proposal is a biblical theology that stimulates and promotes self-criticism and creative communication by providing access to the diverse biblical traditions, with their differing *Sitze im Leben,* as a pluralistic continuum of experience. The moral perspective is one that is value-laden but not Olympian. It is worked out by Welker in terms of the dialectic of God's power and powerlessness manifested in biblical allusions to God's Spirit.

Catherine Keller's essay explores the systemic distortions encoded in the doctrinal assumption of omnipotence as it culminates in the vision of the Apocalypse of John. She finds here a view of power that is at best dominative, at worst annihilating, and in which even the image of powerlessness presupposes its dominative opposite. But, Keller further argues, even recent progressive constructions of power—whether in liberation theology, feminism, Foucauldian post-structuralism, or process theology—still either presuppose a win/lose dynamic or leave the presupposition untouched by their vagueness. In the attempt to formulate a coherent account of power without sacrificing either the complexity of multiple voices or the ambiguity of a Foucauldian analysis—systematic enough to counter the systemic distortion under investigation—she moves to a relationalist counter-apocalypse.

Cynthia Rigby addresses the problem of belief in a transcendent God, a belief that tends to produce systemic distortion by repressing human agency and fostering a sense of passivity and powerlessness among the oppressed. Offering counter-examples of instances in which belief in divine transcendence empowers resistance to oppression, she draws on the discourses of theology, exegesis, and psychology to suggest when and why such belief empowers rather than not. Rigby proposes criteria, based on Metz's and Welch's concept of "dangerous memory," by which variants of this belief can be assessed. She argues that Psalm 22, by articulating the psalmist's memory of both blaming and trusting in God, shows how the perception of powerlessness can be transformed to one of power. In this case, human power is realized precisely when and because one believes in a subject-God who has the power to liberate.

William Schweiker explores the moral ontology of post-theistic technological society to show how it is defined by a concentration of access to and enhancement of power which systematically distorts any understanding of moral value. Considering how and in what ways the biblical traditions offer resources for overcoming this destructive power and distortion in a theory of value, he links biblical thought to contemporary moral outlook by means of an analysis of the moral ontology of the Tower of Babel story in Genesis 11:1-9. Schweiker discloses in this mythic construal of reality the view that the basic human problem is not that of the exercise of power in the creation of civilization, but, rather, fidelity to a power which grounds and limits human power (the divine), a problem endlessly examined throughout the biblical texts. He thus poses the systematic problem of how to think about life at the level of the connection of power and value and suggests that the biblical texts taken in their diverse strata seem truer to the complexity of the moral space of life than the conceptual and axiological reductionism of modern theology and philosophy.

II

The second group of essays (part III of the volume) contains papers that address relations of power and powerlessness in diverse social-historical and experiential contexts.

Drawing on the work of Alice Miller and Nel Noddings, *Rita Nakashima Brock* engages in a feminist deconstruction of the patriarchal family, the site of our earliest experiences of the systemic distortions of power abuse and the poisonous pedagogy that justifies it. She then turns this lens on the ethical terror which results when theology replicates this pedagogy to justify a powerful God inflicting suffering on "his" powerless children. Brock demonstrates the theoretical and practical dangers of focusing on the extremes of the powerful, malevolent abuser and the innocent, powerless victim. Using Ruddick's model of maternal thinking, she argues instead for a paradigm of taking responsibility for the use of power by those caught in-between levels of power, as exemplified by the mother. Jeremiah 31:15-22 poetically illumines this paradigm with its images of divine and human mothers, replacing an ethics of retribution with one of a surrounding power that overcomes the power of death by risking its embrace.

Kimberly Parsons Chastain juxtaposes Job, Girard, and clinical literature on childhood sexual abuse to illuminate the multiple ways that a scapegoat mechanism functions to protect the "truth" of a patriarchal social system against the challenges of family sexual violence. A major concern is to expand the focus from the relational dyad of Job and God, or victim and abuser, to the larger social matrix in which abuse occurs. Chastain thus concentrates on the role of witnesses, exemplified by Job's friends, whose encounter with this trauma typically eventuates either in denial of the victim's experience or demonization of the perpetrator (as in Girard's rejection of the God who answers Job). In either case, a systemic distortion occurs, reproduced socially and theologically, that restores coherence to the witnesses' meaning system at the expense of the victim. Healing, both of the victim and of the theological system, can only occur when the victim is allowed an authentic choice in her relationship to God and abuser, and is vindicated by witnesses willing to sacrifice coherence in favor of justice.

For *Paul Hanson,* the figure of the Servant of the Lord in Second Isaiah serves as a lens to reflect on the empowering and disempowering uses of tradition both in the ancient context of Israel's Babylonian Exile and today. Tradition, he argues, entails a dialectic of continuity and creative engagement that is manifest in the prophet's paradoxical call to remember and *not* remember the things of old. That memory serves the liberating God of the exodus while rejecting the royal power that had identified itself with the divine. The new vision that shifts the eternal promise to David to the people as a whole and that shifts the locus of political power to a foreign Messiah culminates, Hanson argues, in the figure of the Servant who suffers without guilt and establishes justice without force. The Servant does not, however, model acquiescent suffering, but rather a relational empowerment deriving from a God who values justice over hierarchy. The Servant also, then, typifies a relationship to Scripture marked not by the "fundamentalist transfer" of easy answers, but rather an active partnership with God for justice.

III

The last group of essays (part IV of the volume) explores relations of power and powerlessness in biblical materials and in their various receptions in the tradition.

Claudia Camp analyzes the impact on women's power of the metaphor of Wisdom personified as woman (Sophia), both in the ancient context of the book of Proverbs and in recent debate about its feminist appropriation. She employs metaphor theory as a bridge between the enterprise of understanding the Bible's theology, which is often metaphorically expressed, and that of constructing theology from the Bible, a task in which the appropriators of Sophia are actively engaged. Metaphor theory is also useful in disclosing what is suppressed by powerful manipulations of language, in this case the close connection between woman wisdom and her "negative" counterpart in Proverbs, the so-called strange woman. Camp argues that the dialectic of wise and strange, center and margin, must be embraced to understand the nature of either power or the divine.

Burton Mack explores the relation between power, purity, and innocence in the symbolic construction of the social worlds of Judaism and Hellenism as these two cultural streams converged in the Christianity of the first century. He shows how this connection, when focused christologically in the narrative imagination of the Gospel writers, emerges as a systemic distortion within the text itself, a distortion with a continuing and debilitating influence on contemporary Western society. Specifically, Mack argues that the Jesus narrative collapses the symbols of purity and power (which had been held in tension by the Jewish temple-state) and combines them with the Greek ideal of the martyred innocent. The result is a myth involving a series of violent reciprocities that will end in an imagined—and longed for—apocalypse. Mack finally reflects on the construal of power in our Christian culture through presenting a profile of the American hero in comparison with Mark's portrait of the Christ. He articulates the difficulties in theorizing the role of power in society, given this mythic legacy of violence and victory.

Like Mack, *Vincent Wimbush* also engages in an attempt to analyze more accurately the present by means of a better understanding of the symbolic world of the past. His foil is Harold Bloom's recent characterization of fundamentalist, individualistic American religion as "irretrievably Gnostic." In contrast to Bloom's method of comparing concepts, ideas, and language, Wimbush looks (in the mode of Ninian Smart) to the more comprehensive cross-cultural framework of the history of worldview. Specifically he examines the complex of attitudes, behaviors, and rhetorics categorized as *contemptus mundi*, which forms a part of many different cultures of Greco-Roman antiquity and beyond. Not mere other-worldliness, *contemptus mundi* involves a coming to power through speech that problematizes the world and its systemic distortions in order to gain ground for the rethinking and reframing of existence. Ancient Gnostics, Wimbush argues, would share little of the "world" with Bloom's Americans: the latter would be considered far too worldly, far too unwilling to level and sustain radical critique against culture and society, to qualify for membership in Gnostic circles.

Conclusion

The contributors to this volume have attempted to wrestle with several issues, each one extraordinarily difficult in itself. We have attempted to establish a working relationship between the academic sub-disciplines of theology and biblical studies in a way that is fully respectful of their variant interests and methods. We have attempted to do, or at least lay the groundwork for, constructive theology in conversation with a variety of critical theories. We have undertaken analyses based on explicit value positions while at the same time holding ourselves and each other to the highest degree of intellectual rigor within our capabilities. And we have endeavored to make a difference in the real world by means of our intellectual pursuits. In sum, we have sought to articulate our understanding of the complex coherence at the heart of human life.

Rita Nakashima Brock
Claudia V. Camp
William Schweiker

Acknowledgments

⌘

This volume is the product of several years of conversation and academic labor. The work of our group was made possible in large measure by a grant from the Lilly Foundation to the Project of Bible and Theology directed by Professor Ulrich Mauser of Princeton Theological Seminary. We wish to extend our special thanks to the Lilly Foundation and also Professor Mauser for their constant support and encouragement of our work. Our work was also supported by Heidelberg University (*Wissenschaftsforum*) and special grant funding through the German Government. While meeting in Germany, we were able to test our ideas with European scholars, a testing which enriched each scholar's thought and the word of our group as a whole. We extend our thanks to our European colleagues and also to the University of Heidelberg for its hospitality. We owe a special debt of gratitude to David Jobling, David E. Klemm, Flora A. Keshgegian, and Patrick D. Miller for their willingness to engage our work. Their responses were initially given at the conference on Bible and Theology at which these papers were presented in public forum. In the true spirit of collaborative research, these individuals engaged our work in ways which isolated insights and oversights missed by the group itself. It is for these reasons that we have published the responses here, and in doing so continue the collaborative enterprise of biblical-theological inquiry. We thank each of these scholars. Finally, the members of the group wish to thank William Schweiker and Cindy Rigby for their administration of the group.

Part One

— METHOD AND CONTENT —

⌘

1

A New Paradigm of Theological and Biblical Inquiry

William Schweiker and Michael Welker

⌘

Introduction

The work collected in this volume is part of a larger movement among theologians and biblical scholars aimed at reassessing the relation of biblical studies to theological reflection. Indeed, the theme of "Bible and Theology" signals for some a creative advance in interdisciplinary research dedicated to the integration of historical inquiry, textual interpretation, and theological reflection. But for other scholars, the theme "Bible and Theology" designates a constellation of problems rather than an easily identifiable research agenda. This was the judgment of many of the participants in the working-group on "Power, Powerlessness, and the Divine" that fostered the research presented in the chapters of this book. From the outset, it seemed to some of us that all possible forms of dogmatism and biblicism concealed themselves behind the title "Bible and Theology." Yet other members of the group noted that this title can hide not only authoritarian forms of theology, but also liberal types of "integration theology" aimed at "retrieving" the Bible for our time under the rubrics of contemporary thought. This form of "retrieval" too often misses the power and insight of the biblical texts in their difference from contemporary mores and life.

As an interdisciplinary group we have come to see that each of these approaches (dogmatism, biblicism, liberal theology) challenges the possibility of developing new paradigms of scholarly work on the Bible and its role in addressing basic concerns. In spite of the radical divergences between these forms of thought, in each case one finds the attempt to articulate the "unity" or "essence" of complex traditions through a reduction of the complexity to one root metaphor, basic concept, or idea.[1] Persons commonly speak of "the" Bible or "the" Christian tradition, thereby effacing the radical complexity of these textual and historical realities. It is this reductionism that has rendered biblical and cultural traditions opaque to us, and also, often in concealed ways, distorted reflection on questions of pressing need in a world deeply influenced by the biblical traditions. We have sought to fashion a non-reductionistic paradigm of theological and biblical inquiry.

What provides coherence to the inquiries presented in this book is our focus on an issue of grave human importance in our time, namely, the relation between power and powerlessness in a world dominated by types of oppression, technological patterns of thought and value, and the legacies of distortion that characterize our histories. The essayists have attempted to address basic issues of how we are to think about these matters in a way informed by the diverse texts and traditions associated with biblical texts and their reception in Western societies. The resulting paradigm of collaborative research touches basic conceptualities and scholarly methods with respect to a pressing problem of our time.

The purpose of this chapter is to clarify this new research paradigm as well as to introduce basic concepts and themes found throughout the remainder of the book. This will also allow us to isolate the underlying conceptual and methodological issues in biblical theological inquiry. Let us begin by specifying in more detail basic themes and ideas found in the book as a whole.

Themes and Ideas

The theme of this book is power, powerlessness, and the divine within diverse social contexts. This topic is of obvious importance. And in one respect, we all have some idea, however vague, of what is meant by power, powerlessness, and even the divine. We daily experience or

---

1   This point has been made by various scholars. For instance, Elisabeth Schüssler Fiorenza draws a distinction between, on the one hand, "archetypal" ideas of the text that seek to isolate *the* essence of the text, and, on the other hand, "prototypical" ideas of the text open to the internal complexity and also diverse receptions of the scriptures. See her *Bread Not Stone: The Challenge of Feminist Biblical Interpretation* (Boston: Beacon Press, 1984).

witness the exercise of power; we know the powerlessness of those who suffer. More than ever before, we live in an age of human power—the power to control the environment, to alter the genetic structure of species, to foster new modes of communication. These developments have made our planet into a global village composed of wildly diverse communities. It is also the case that we live in a world of powerlessness where most people on this planet are hungry and have little capacity to direct and shape their own lives. Finally, we live in an age of the resurgence of the religions and also traditional ideologies around the globe. Religious beliefs about what God requires of persons often drive individuals and even nations in how they exercise the power at their disposal. Power, powerlessness, and the divine signals, then, a constellation of issues that enables one to examine the texture of current life. It draws on ideas that are in some way understandable to all of us.

While the theme of this book is understandable to all of us, it is not at all clear that we have an adequate grasp of what is meant by power, powerlessness, or the divine. The meaning of these ideas seems to slip and slide whenever we consider them in detail. What is power? Who is powerful? What does it mean to be powerless? How is God powerful? Can God be powerless? The questions seem endless. In order to help us reflect upon and also address these matters, the essays collected in this book take an indirect approach. Rather than trying to focus directly on the nature or function of power and powerlessness, the essayists focus on a reality in which power, powerlessness, and religious belief meet and interact, namely, the reality of human societies. By focusing on the activity of social construction, or world-making, we have sought to understand and evaluate power and powerlessness with respect to beliefs about the divine.

Thus, the concern of this book is to isolate the resources, if any, the biblical texts hold for identifying, understanding, and changing social existence. This means that each essay must undertake (1) an analysis of some real social context, (2) engage the biblical text(s), and (3) clarify how that movement of thought between text and social context is to be made. Central to each of these "steps" of reflection is the connection between beliefs about the divine and ideas of power and powerlessness within social construction. Given this fact, we need some purchase on these basic ideas beyond the vague notions we have of them based on experience. With these definitions in hand, we can then clarify the way in which previous approaches to the relation between Bible and theological reflection manifest problems the essays seek to avoid.

By "social construction" all we mean is that human beings continually face the great task of social life, that is, the demand to form cultures and civilizations to meet the necessities of life and to answer the human drive for meaning. Human beings are profoundly "worldly" creatures in the sense that to be human is to exist in some socio-cultural world and to contribute to the continuation or destruction of that world. In the process of world-making, human beings are also fashioning their personal lives. None of us come into the world whole. Every person must in some way and to some degree fashion her or his life and character. These are of course rather general claims. They say nothing about *particular* forms of social existence or forms of personal identity. Indeed, the task of the essayists is to explore distinct social worlds and forms of personal life with an eye to the relation between power, powerlessness, and the divine within them. In the course of this examination, we learn a good deal about the difference between social worlds, their meaning systems, how they are structured, and also patterns of authority and value.

We have also tried to isolate two interrelated forms of distortion which beset the work of social construction. There are, first, what we have called "systemic" distortions. These are distortions which function within the subsystems of the social order (economy, legal system, moral codes, media). Related to this are "systematic" distortions. By this term we mean the distortions operative in the meaning system of a society, its cultural products, and also in patterns of thinking about human life and society. By focusing on world-making, our research must, therefore, cross through the analysis of cultural meaning systems (the beliefs and values which shape a society's way of life), examine social structures (the institutions and relations which constitute the social order), undertake psychological inquiry (forms of personal identity formation) and, finally, engage in religious reflection. It is this multi-perspectival approach that we believe is unique to the paradigm of inquiry proposed in this book. We will return to this point in greater detail below. Yet the fundamental assumption of this volume is that the activity of social construction is important for understanding questions of power, powerlessness, and the divine.

The difficulty is that even with an indirect approach to power, power and powerlessness can be understood in a variety of ways.[2] In fact, the essays collected here draw on various conceptions of power in order to understand texts and social contexts. Conceptions of power range from understanding it ontologically, that is, as a claim about being, to political definitions of authority and ideas about charismatic leadership. More specifically, the scholars represented in this book distinguish between domination, or "power-over," from patterns of mutual empowerment, or "power-with," and the ability to act or be a cause in the world, "power-to." Power-over is usually linked to claims about political authority and also domination. An understanding of

---

2   See Christine Firer Hinze, "Power in Christian Ethics: Resources and Frontiers for Scholarly Exploration" in *The Annual of the Society of Christian Ethics* (Washington, D.C.: Georgetown University Press, 1992), 277–90.

power as the "power-to" centers on the capacity of an agent, community, or event to act and cause things to happen. "Power-with" designates patterns of mutual empowerment where authority and the capacity to act are shared among persons and communities: authority is not dependent on domination but persuasion; action is collaborative rather than centered on individuals. Power has diverse meanings and the varieties of its meanings will be found in these essays simply because what is under examination is the complexity of forms of power and powerlessness in diverse social and interpersonal contexts.

Within this diversity of meanings of power we can nevertheless isolate a common, shared idea of power crucial to the argument of the chapters. Generally, the authors understand power as the ability to respond to, influence, and shape reality. As the feminist ethicist Beverly Wildung Harrison notes, power "is the ability to act on and effectually shape the world around us, particularly through collective action and institutional policy."[3] On this account, not only individuals but also collectives, ideas, and values can have "power." The power of ideas, values, persons, and institutions is increased not simply through domination or collaboration, but through enriching and rendering more complex the capacity to respond to, influence, and shape reality. Ideas about domination (power-over), ability (power-to), and relational power (power-with) are merely diverse ways in which the capacity to respond to, influence, and shape reality is found in social existence. Indeed, the claim of these essays is that the activity of social construction, that is, the formation of meaningful and viable worlds, is itself a profound expression of power. Through world-making, human beings respond to, influence, and also shape reality.

The principle concern of the essays collected in this book is to isolate, analyze, and enhance those events in which dominating and destructive forms of power (power-over) give way to creative forms of power (power-to, power-with) in social and personal life. Further, the essays seek to show the ways in which beliefs about the divine have been linked to power as domination as well as power as creative transformation of social existence. We want to address from theological, social, and textual perspectives the forms of systemic and systematic distortion that permeate social life. The wager of the authors is that there are resources internal to the biblical texts to aid in recognizing destructive forms of power and for articulating a new

---

3   Beverly Harrison, *Making the Connections: Essays in Feminist Social Ethics* (Boston: Beacon Press, 1985), 290 n. 5. As Larry Rasmussen notes, "Power in its most elemental, vital sense is simply the 'power to,' the power of agency, human and non-human agency alike, in the vast web of this miracle called life, itself the expression of God's life." Larry L. Rasmussen, "Power Analysis: A Neglected Agenda in Christian Ethics" in *The Annual of the Society of Christian Ethics* (1991), 9.

vision of our social world. At the deepest level of reflection, the essays present in this book are charting the connection between world-making, the divine, and how we *think* about social existence.

We have now specified the basic theme and distinctive focus of this book, clarified some basic concepts, and also noted the methodological pluralism to be found among the essayists. We want next to elaborate in more detail the connection between reflection, social construction, and theistic belief. This is important for understanding the new paradigm for biblical-theological inquiry, since it bears upon the way in which we undertake disciplined reflection on power, powerlessness, and the divine. By clarifying this point, we will also be able to isolate problems in previous ways of specifying the relation between Bible and theology.

Problems in the Relation of Bible and Theology

The most basic problem facing those who seek a new paradigm for relating Bible and theology becomes clear when we compare the hermeneutical methods of traditional Christian theology with the patterns of thinking in other biblical religions, especially Judaism. This comparison illuminates the inner-dynamics of much Christian theological-biblical reflection even as it exposes an enduring problem and challenge to theological reflection. An important, clear critique of the very idea of biblical theology has been presented by the Harvard Jewish scholar Jon D. Levenson. What is his argument?

In his article "Why Jews are Not Interested in Biblical Theology," Levenson criticizes not only the "marked anti-Semitism" found in much of the classical work of the early Protestant exegetes that is still often associated with "Biblical Theology."[4] Levenson also rejects every form of theology that seeks to prove or articulate one form of thought or thematic connection as *the* form and system of biblical traditions. He criticizes all so-called biblical theologians who work out *one* theme (e.g., reconciliation, covenant, divine lordship, God's holiness, liberation, etc.) as *the* content of the biblical traditions. In Levenson's judgment, "the effort to construct a systematic, harmonious theological statement out of the unsystematic and polydox materials in the Hebrew Bible fits Christianity better than Judaism because systematic theology in general is more prominent and more at home in the church than in the yeshivah or the synagogue."[5]

---

4   Jon Levenson, "Why Jews are Not Interested in Biblical Theology" in *Judaic Perspectives on Ancient Israel*, edited by J. Neusner, et al. (Philadelphia: Fortress Press, 1987), 281 ff. Also see D. Ritschl, "'Wahre', 'reine,' or 'neue' biblische Theologie?: Anfragen zur neuren Diskussion um 'Biblische Theologie'" in his *Konzepte, Ökumene, Medizin, Ethik* (München, 1986), 111ff.

5   Levenson, 296.

From this perspective the enduring problem and challenge of Christian thought is the attempt to provide a coherent account of the diverse and polycontextual biblical materials. Not only is the Bible composed of diverse texts, but those texts—and even strata in particular "books"—are contextualized within divergent social and historical contexts. Given this wide diversity, how, if at all, can one read the Bible as a coherent whole? What is the principle of unity? Here we must note that implied in Levenson's criticism of the task of articulating the thematic or conceptual unity to the Bible is a particular conception of "system." The criticism is based on the assumption that to think coherently or systematically requires that the scholar reduce the complexity of the textual material to a unity through *one* concept, idea, root metaphor, or theme.[6] Admittedly, this is a widely held assumption. For instance, Christian theologians have long fastened on the idea of covenant, or justification by faith, promise-fulfillment, or some other single idea or concept in order to specifying *the* unity of the biblical texts. We can now call this a "mono-systematic" approach to thinking; coherent thinking, on this account, requires the reduction of complexity to some more fundamental unity that explains and/or is represented in the actual complexity of life, texts, traditions, and experiences. The reductionism in this approach leads to what we will call below the poverty of theory. What is needed are more internally complex theories and systems. We need paradigms of scholarly research that coordinate a manifold of approaches to texts, traditions, and societies.

Against the "impulse to systematize among Christians,"[7] Levenson stresses "the stubborn Rabbinic resistance to losing the particular in the general."[8] He cites Susan Handelman's book *The Slayers of Moses.* She writes that one of "the most interesting aspects of Rabbinic thought in its development of a highly sophisticated system of interpretation based on uncovering and expanding the primary concrete meaning, and yet drawing a variety of logical inferences from the meaning *without* the abstracting, idealizing movement of Western thought."[9] Handelman's point seems to be that the operative hermeneutical method found in rabbinic thought is at once highly differentiated, and thus not reductionistic, and yet is also "systematic" in

---

6   On the epistemological and hermeneutical depth of this problem see William Schweiker, *Mimetic Reflections: A Study in Hermeneutics, Theology and Ethics* (New York: Fordham University Press, 1990), esp. ch. 1.

7   Levenson, 296.

8   Levenson, 298.

9   Susan Handelman, *The Slayers of Moses: The Emergence of Rabbinic Interpretation in Modern Literary Theory* (Albany: State University of New York Press, 1982), 19. Levenson wants to attribute this tendency of Western systematic theology to *the* Western form of thought.

the sense of providing the means to reflect on the coherence of complex textual phenomenon. In agreement with Handelman's basic intent, Levenson writes that "the search for the one great idea that pervades and unifies the Hebrew Bible is unlikely to interest Jews."[10]

Thus, the problem facing anyone who seeks a new paradigm for relating Bible and Christian theology centers on the relation between the complexity of the texts and traditions in question and the drive for reflective coherence found in traditional hermeneutical methods. The criticism is that theological reflection is reductionistic in that it specifies the principle of coherent thinking through a single, simple "great idea." This is why Christian theologians have often spoken of a "canon within the canon." A "great idea," say, for instance, justification by grace through faith alone, provides the principle, the measure or "canon," for identifying the unity of the Bible and also its canonicity for faith and life. But even that is not all. This "great idea," the canon in the canon, is taken in traditional Christian thought to identify not only the *meaning* of the text, but, much more, the unity of thought and reality itself. Read from its "center," the Bible is revelatory of the ultimate nature of things. To think the great idea (the canon in the canon) is nothing less than to think the very meaning of reality. The "world" is inscribed within the logic of the "great idea" encoded in and expressed through the diverse biblical materials. This act of inscription has been the basic aspiration and central task of much traditional Christian biblical-theological reflection.

The criticism of this hermeneutic strategy is now widely voiced in the academy. It has been made by feminist theology (traditional theology effaces the experience of women through a reductionistic systemization of experience), contextual forms of theology (that is, traditional theology in trying to specify *the* structure of worldly existence and the divine denies the deeply social character of human life), and process and hermeneutical theologies (that is, the conception of 'being' and its relation to 'God' in traditional theology not only effaces the question of the meaning of being but negates the internal relation of God and world). The same point is made by post-structuralist thinkers who speak of the loss of "metanarratives" as defining the postmodern age and the current rejection of modern forms of reductionism centered on the human subject—the thinking 'I'—and unified philosophies of history. In all of these cases, the criticism of inherited patterns of biblical-theological thinking centers on the relation that can and ought to obtain between the complexity of phenomena (experience, traditions, texts, societies, etc.) and methods of thinking. This criticism seems basic to the host of positions now called postmodern; it is, in large measure, shared by the authors represented in this book.

---

10   Levenson, 298.

After the loss of an all-integrating form of thought or unified theme, after the "great idea" and the dream of "the" system, is there still a subject matter that runs through the biblical traditions? Can we think systematically and pluralistically at the same time, or, is systematic inquiry always reductionistic? These questions have played a central role in recent discussions of Bible and theology. Indeed, much of the research that has taken place under the programmatic rubric of "Bible and Theology" has clearly distinguished itself from the kind of traditional positions presented and criticized by Levenson and others. Recent scholarship takes the Bible as an "astonishingly pluralistic library with traditions accumulated over a period of more than 1500 years."[11] It also seeks consciously to be interdisciplinary and pluralistic in its approach to the material. This has meant taking seriously the various biblical traditions in their concrete differences within distinct *Sitze im Leben*. Finally, scholars have insisted on the fact that there are distortions not only in the history of reception in church history and ancient culture, but already the biblical traditions themselves can and often do offer distorted and confused perceptions of the divine and reality.[12] In other words, the criticism of reductionist interpretive methods has been voiced by scholars interested in the relation of Bible and theology.

The present volume must be seen as part of this larger scholarly enterprise that is self consciously pluralistic, interdisciplinary, and seeking to address honestly the distortions and possibilities found in these traditions. The research agenda proceeds from a complex and differentiated engagement with the manifold witnesses to the divine, to understandings of self and world, and to social, cultural, and moral expectations found in traditions. However, reaching this judgment about the project we have undertaken has exposed yet another set of problems for the authors. These difficulties center on the connection between claims about God and patterns of religious thinking. They center, in other words, on the great idea of Christian theology (God's relation to the world) and the attempt to inscribe reality within the biblical narrative of God's dealing with the world. What does this mean?

Granting the complexity of biblical traditions and cultural contexts, two basic problems have presented themselves to us in the course of our work. The first problem is the pervasive assumption that because of the complexity of traditions and social contexts it is impossible to develop a coherent, that is, systematic, mode of thought equal to the complexity of our subject matter. Given the poverty of reductionistic systems, many postmodern thinkers simply reject all

---

11   Heinz Schürmann, *Gottes Reich-Jesu Geschick* (Leipzig: St. Benno-Verlag, 1983), 246.

12   See James Barr, *Biblical Faith and Natural Theology* The Gifford Lectures for 1991 (Oxford, 1993), 208ff.

attempts to develop coherent paradigms of thought and research. They advocate *ad hoc* patterns of thought concentrating on forms of local-knowledge and the practices of particular communities. Let us call the problem this first option poses to the very possibility of developing a new paradigm of biblical-theological inquiry *the challenge to reflective coherence*. The second and related problem is that the scholar or theologian, under the pressure to develop coherent proposals for actual life, orders the complexity of material into a thematic constellation in ways that merely repeat the problem of reductionism at a new, more subtle level. This ordering is either through overly formalized modes of thought based on vague theological ciphers or a rhetoric of progressive moralism. Let us call the problem this second option poses to our undertaking *the challenge to reflective complexity*. In our context, then, the double challenge to scholarly work is how to achieve a balance between coherence and complexity and thereby to avoid reductionist modes of thought or *ad hoc* accounts of traditions, texts, and communities. Let us explain this double challenge in more detail.

Traditions, Contexts, and the Poverty of Theory

The Bible represents "an astonishingly pluralistic library with traditions accumulated over a period of more than 1500 years." It seems obvious that there is *no single* progressive direction through the entire length and breadth of these texts. These texts have also been part of an "astonishingly pluralistic" historical reality of thousands of years. And, in fact, the constellation of texts and histories designated by "the biblical traditions" now exists within a world reality in which roughly one-third of humanity defines its religiosity with respect to those traditions.[13] For good and ill, the biblical texts and traditions have deeply impressed themselves on what we can call "world culture" or "world ethos." At the level of texts, history of reception, and current contexts, we confront an overwhelming complexity characterized by divergent forms of mutual interrelationship that shapes current life. In the face of this fact, are the only options simply to turn, on the one hand, to the particularities of distinctive communities and their forms of local-knowledge, or, on the other hand, to insist on a universal perspective? Our situation is a shared planetary space composed of diverse, often competing, communities and traditions. We must think about the coherence and the complexity of our situation, emergent forms of life, and also diverse histories.

---

13   See David Barrett, *World Christian Encyclopedia: A Comparative Survey of Churches and Religions in the Modern World A.D. 1900–2000* (Oxford:Oxford University Press, 1982).

The authors represented in this book have sought to reflect upon this situation with respect to the question of power and powerlessness. We have placed the question of understanding the biblical texts and also theological discourse within the reality of social life. The question of 'God' is then posed as a second-order reflection arising from inquiry into these power matrices in social construction. We conclude that the rather impressive power of a tradition to shape for good or ill global reality is not understandable in terms of one principle, one form, or one simple content that supposedly designates a power (call it the divine) operative aside from other actual social powers. Of course, classical theism and other forms of theology in Western societies that produced a transcendent personality, such as the christological concentration of much 20th century theology, often sought to designate this "power" operative in the world. These theological positions did so with respect to a massive symbolic center, a lordly figure, that specifies the interrelation between traditions and contexts in terms of domination. That is to say, 'God' was conceived as a unifying, dominating power necessary to explain historical and social reality. 'God' was the principle of any form of systematic thinking; 'God' was *the* great idea. To think the being of God—whether given in reason or revealed in the Bible—is, then, to think the overarching and dominating coherence and unity of reality. This idea of God thereby articulated and backed one conception of power—power as domination. It was often specified symbolically through patriarchal and militaristic imagery; God is sovereign Lord, for instance.

On seeing this point, we better understand the real depth of the methodological problems noted above and the pervasive sense in postmodern discourse of the poverty of theory. Systematic thought can be reductionistic, and, furthermore, this conceptual strategy is often wedded in classical theism to the question of power. In classical theology and its impression on Western thought, the act of thinking about God is in fact to conceive of the unity of all that is, the coherence of reality, from the perspective of a dominating power operative outside of relations to other social powers. The act of thinking and a specific conception of power (domination) become wedded in much (but not all) classical theism. The canon within the canon, accordingly, centered on how this 'God' acts on the world witnessed to by the biblical texts. All of reality is to be inscribed within the narrative logic of this God's dealing with the world. We judge that this theistic form of systematic thinking leads to reflective coherence but at the cost of reflective complexity.

In this light we must ask: Is the agenda of a theism of domination implicitly or explicitly found in the biblical texts? Do the diverse traditions and texts of the "Bible" warrant and inform the conceptual enterprise of isolating a dominant power as the unity of thinking? Is it necessarily the case that any attempt to think the coherence of complex phenomena—like the biblical traditions in their social contexts with respect to our world situation—devolves into an assertion of dominating power that falsely orders the very complexity we seek to understand? Manifestly, many contemporary thinkers answer yes to these questions. They take this to define the limits of classical theism and also the poverty of theory. Accordingly, the postmodern move in theology and biblical studies has often been to turn to the welter of particular texts, traditions, and contexts as if these are self-explanatory, and, further, to celebrate the flux or play of experience and language as supposedly generative of meaning. And in reaction to this move, other scholars, usually identifying themselves with the modern, Enlightenment project, have tried to reassert the demand for generalized strategies for validating cognitive and moral claims. Thus, the twofold challenge to reflective coherence and complexity is played out in the academy as the clash between modern and postmodern forms of thought.

The issues behind this debate over postmodernism cover a wide array of problems. How are we to think about the patterns of interdependency that constitute our world situation in order to address the real, concrete problems facing us? Additionally, how are we to think about those particular texts, traditions, and contexts in terms of their beliefs about meaningful life? More profoundly, what is the connection between power and thinking, a connection often seen in how God has been understood in Christian thought? These questions seem difficult to address if one simply insists, as many "postmoderns" do, on the poverty of theory, or, conversely, if one flatly rejects, as many "moderns" do, any pluralistic sensibility. Caught between these extreme positions, scholars interested in addressing pressing human problems have been forced into what we now judge to be false forms of coherence.

The purpose of this volume is not simply to abandon theory, but, rather, to challenge the basic connection between power and forms of thought found in much traditional reflection. We have done this so that we might (1) avoid reductionistic accounts of texts and social contexts while (2) having the means to provide a coherent account of complex social and textual phenomena. The authors have undertaken reflection on a manifold of traditions and social contexts by using manifold scholarly methods. We might call this "a many-to-many-through-many" relationship of Bible and theology. Bible and theology are not related as if they represent unified entities. Rather, the many and divergent strands of thought found in the "Bible" are related to the full complexity of our social reality through the use of various interpretive methods. We have attempted to avoid the covert connection between power and systematic reflection while nevertheless hoping to articulate the coherence of complex traditions.

Is this agenda an impossibility? Are we finally left with an either/or: either we forego all concern for systematic reflection in the name of particularity, or we seek once again the "great idea," the unified system? This question is not merely academic in nature. In a time of global interdependence when diverse and divergent cultures must interact amid increasing economic conflict and ecological pressure, does the scholar have anything to say about the meaning and direction of life? It is in light of these matters that we can understand prevalent forms of thought and why our working-group diverges in important respects from each of them. While offering genuine insights, these options finally offer false forms of coherence in thinking about traditions, texts, and social contexts.

Traditions and Contexts: False Coherence

Thus far we have noted two fundamental challenges to current academic work: the challenge to reflective coherence, and the challenge to reflective complexity. In the face of these challenges, theorists over the course of this century have in fact developed *formal* patterns of thought on the level of hermeneutics, cultural theory, and social critique that are compatible with the complexity of traditions, texts, and cultural realities. Thinkers have developed the formal means to examine the polysemic nature of texts to present a world of meaning (hermeneutics), the social order and its divergent cognitive claims (discourse theory and communication ethics), and even the emergence of increasing complexity within the natural world (new physics). These developments have had grave impact on contemporary theology in terms of theories about language, understanding of the status of cognitive claims, and even claims about God and the natural world. Granting those developments, it is still the case that we have not developed rich *material* and *contextual* forms of thought. This lack is seen in the two most dominant forms of theological reflection given genuine pluralistic sensibilities.

First, highly developed postmodern and postliberal theologies rightly begin hermeneutically with the *material* levels of texts, narratives, traditions, and contexts but then reduce these to *formal* constructs through vague ciphers of integration (e.g., Ground of Being; Ultimate Point of Reference, God as "model," the Bible as "narrative," the "mystical and political"). A single cipher is drawn from complex materials or imaginatively constructed by the theologian and then taken theologically as the principle for understanding worldly existence. This means that discourse about the divine is symbolically designated or practically postulated as the unity behind the diversity of the world or supposedly rendered forth in "narrative" as *the* form of biblical discourse. These forms of thought deeply influenced by the developments in hermeneutics, social theory, and even physics noted above manifest a pluralistic sensibility in that they do not assume a unity simply given within the biblical texts or diverse cultural forms. Nevertheless, these positions do specify the *theological task* as articulating that unity through concepts, images, symbols or in ecclesial practice. Second, forms of reflection arising out of sensitivity to the *contextual* nature of all thought and life seldom go beyond a rhetoric of progressive moralism. The coherence of theological thinking is not specified into terms of its ground, point of reference, or discursive form, but with respect to a specific socio-moral agenda theology ought to serve (e.g. liberation, Christian identity, ecological and global responsibility). In doing so, there is a failure to see how any form of discourse and any moral agenda is transmuted and variously understood within complex, highly differentiated social systems.

The first theological response to pluralism reduplicates the problem of reductionism at the level of ideas and discursive forms (symbols, images, models of God, narrative) and thus effaces the material reality we seek to understand. This second response never reaches beyond the social-political context other than through appeals to a moral-political agenda that is quickly lost given the way complex social systems function. In both of these theological options there has not been a successful response to the need to enhance reflective complexity along with reflective coherence. Because of this, the biblical texts and traditions either become irrelevant in theologies driven by the need to isolate an ultimate ground, the texts are reduced to a discursive form used to foster Christian "identity," or they are co-opted within a specific moral agenda and thus reduced to hollow rhetoric given the hard facts of social life. Is it any wonder that the rubric "Bible and Theology" would spark aversion and suspicion by thinkers aware of the shortcomings of these modes of thought?

The perception that we are searching for a new paradigm of thought is widely held. For instance, Cornel West has recently noted the demand for a "nuanced historical sense" and "subtle social analysis" that are to communicate and evolve, but do not indoctrinate social commonalities and moral-political projects.[14] The insights of the currently dominant forms of thought must be acknowledged. But in the face of the challenge posed by "Bible and Theology" what lies beyond moralistic appeals, vague ciphers, or older forms of reductionism? We identify the current demand for a new conceptual model and method of

---

14   Cornel West, *Prophetic Thought in Postmodern Times: Beyond Eurocentrism and Multiculturalism*, vol 1. (Monroe, ME: Common Courage Press, 1993).

reflection as the search for a *multi-perspectival social critique*.[15] By this we mean a pluralistic method of thought aimed at understanding, isolating, and overcoming distortions in the social world(s). This form of reflection cuts against a long history of thought noted above that is mono-systematic (reductionistic, non-pluralistic) in specifying the structure of thinking, and orders moral and metaphysical material from a top-down perspective. The purpose of this book is to redeem interdisciplinary work aimed at articulating common thematic structures that will not prevent access to particularity or order the material from a top-down perspective.

We have come to believe that a *culture of difference* is itself a necessary context for multi-perspectival inquiry. The very nature of an interdisciplinary research group (1) must be characterized by diverse thinkers who work inductively, or "bottom-up", in particular context(s) but with respect to a shared thematic concern (power, powerlessness, and the divine), (2) the process of interdisciplinary work must be self-conscious about the methodological and conceptual problems facing this work, and (3) there must be a willingness by all to reconsider and reconceptualize organizing themes in light of the process of scholarly exchange among diverse perspectives. These concerns have directed the labors of our working-group so that the process of our deliberations have been part of the subject matter in question. In this respect, we have attempted to enact a new paradigm of interdisciplinary work that centers on *material* and *contextual* considerations without loss of the question of how to think systematically about complex phenomena. The coherence of our work is found in the critique of social distortions arising out of the relation of power and powerlessness.

Toward a Paradigm of Interdisciplinary Work

Thus far in this chapter we have attempted to isolate the problems that beset the enterprise of "Bible and Theology" with respect to (a) religious traditions and the forms of rationality they involve, (b) connections between systematic thinking and domination found in much, but not all, traditional theism, and (c) dominant trends in current thought that either do not escape or do not grasp the depth of this problem. We have also (d) stated the aim of this book as enacting a paradigm of interdisciplinary work designated as a "multi-perspectival critique" of the human activity of social construction. Examining the theme of "power, powerlessness and the divine" within a project on "Bible and Theology" has then forced our group into a line of inquiry that reaches

---

[15]　We understand "critique" here in the constructive sense of the art of distinction.

well beyond the usual rubric of such work. It has forced us to consider how it is we think about the divine, power, and powerlessness in a way that does not reduplicate longstanding problems.

The organizing purpose of the book and of all of the individual essays is to explore patterns of power and powerlessness, their criticism and transformation in diverse strata of the biblical texts and cultures and also in Western thought and culture. We tried to incorporate multiple perspectives on this question and thereby sought to better understand the place, if any, of biblical and theological discourse and practice in these complex social processes. In order to further a *material-contextual* and yet *systematic* mode of thinking, we initially bracketed the usual debates about methodology in religious studies in order to examine the complexity of biblical discourse about power with respect to our own moral, political, and religious situations. The outcome of this inquiry has been to refashion how one ought to think and speak of the divine. How is this so?

The discovery that orients our inquiry is the appearance of an explosive tension at work in the human activity of world-making, manifest within the interfaces of complex textual and social phenomena. This "explosive tension" was between powers of domination and other powers working for the transformation of these patterns of domination. These other powers—often depicted in terms of powerlessness or strangeness—were readily designated by the biblical texts as the divine. Amid instances of these "explosive tensions" we thus found examples of the emergence of novel forms of world-making that were rid, or at least sought to rid themselves, of basic distortions. Based on this finding, the essayists have been moved to ask: What happens if we take the explosive tensions present in the contextual and material levels of traditions, texts, and social contexts seriously for reflection on power, the divine, and even systematic thinking? In this light, we judge that 'God' cannot be conceived (1) removed from the conflicts and processes of transformation in social reality, or (2) through the systematic reduction of complexity to a single principle or "great idea." Discourse about the divine is defined with respect to understanding and explaining emergent social processes, the very dynamics of world-making, in which oppressive and destructive relations of power and powerlessness are legitimated, criticized, or transformed. Moreover, power must be understood within these complex explosive tensions when domination confronts "other forces" in the emergence of new forms of life. What differentiates the divine and the demonic, legitimate and illegitimate forms of power, is then the extent to which a power matrix respects and enhances the emergence of just forms of life. The emergent forms of just social construction are nothing less than disclosures of God. Discourse about God is, then, to be undertaken by sustained attention to the details and dynamics of world-making. In this way our theological agenda radicalizes previous forms of the theology of culture, a form of inquiry aimed at the religious depths of human cultural activity, into reflection on world-making itself.[16]

This paradigm of biblical-theological reflection seeks, then, to move reflection on power and powerlessness from a theism of domination and control to a consideration of the transformation of distortions in social reality as the basic datum for claims about God and God's action. We understand this agenda to arise out of our reflection on the material-contextual resources of texts and traditions even as it bears on systematic and formal dimensions of reflection. All of the authors chose analogous problems in cultural and biblical traditions, problems that we have designated conceptually as "systemic" and "systematic" distortions.[17] These concepts allow us to specify those powerful forms of thought, value, and belief about human life, community, and culture that appear to be unquestionable and even life enhancing in a specific society, but, in fact, are destructive, detrimental to life, deceptive, and socially poisonous with respect to the viability and flourishing of actual life. In this respect, the biblical texts and their historical contexts become a resource for understanding and explaining deep patterns of distortion in Western history as well as providing means to reflect upon overcoming those distortions. Thus, "Power, Powerlessness, and the Divine" designates not only the title of this book. It also expresses how we understand the forms of distortion and their transformation that the research paradigm seeks to understand, critique, and, in the case of transformation, to further.

The connections among power, powerlessness, and the divine are interpreted by the scholars whose work is found in the pages of this book in view of very different problems, biblical traditions, and scholarly methods. In this respect, the essays taken as a whole represent a "many-to-many-through-many" approach mindful of systemic and systematic distortions to the question of power, powerlessness, and the divine. Yet the title of this volume also seeks to designate an explosive tension that

---

16   For an early attempt to specify this agenda see William Schweiker, "To Dwell on the Earth: Authority and Ecumenical Theology" in *Worldviews and Warrants: Plurality and Authority in Theology*, eds. William Schweiker and Per M. Anderson (Lanham: University Press of America, 1987), 89–112. More recently, see Michael Welker's account of "realistic theology" in his *God the Spirit*, translated by John F. Hoffmeyer (Philadelphia: Fortress Press, 1994). We should note that our conception of theology differs from recent proposals for a "world theology" (W.C. Smith; J. Hick) and also for a "global ethic" (H. Küng). Our focus is on world-making, and not simply the diversity of religions in the world, and, ethically, on understanding, judging, and overcoming forms of distortion rather than merely articulating general principles of right action.

17   We have used this term rather than "ideology" in order to clarify the connection between value-systems and patterns of thought and also to recognize the fact that any form of thought and belief is, at some level, an ideology.

in specific ways is real and important within biblical traditions, the history of Western thought and life, and our contemporary world. We have dared to argue that the problem of identifying and overcoming social distortions focused on the connection of power, powerlessness, and the divine—while not denoting *the* meaning of the text—at least provides a way to reflect coherently on diverse materials and contexts. This is the answer we propose to the challenge raised by Levenson, Handleman, and other critics of biblical-theological reflection. We have made this argument mindful of the material, contextual, and formal dimensions of interdisciplinary work in our time. Insofar as that is the case, the chapters of this book also meet the dual challenge to reflective coherence and complexity. It remains the reader's task to assess the adequacy of our proposal by engaging the contribution of each author.

Conclusion

In this chapter we have attempted to specify the most basic moral-religious concern of a new paradigm of biblical-theological inquiry and the reasons for our apprehension about the usual understanding of the enterprise of "Bible and Theology." Additionally, we have sought to clarify how reflection on that very apprehension has led us to seek a new direction for research and also better to understand the connection between power and systematic thinking within theistic traditions. Finally, we have specified how we have refocused the question of the relation between Bible and theology in terms of distortions and possibilities in social construction as the context to explore the relations among power, powerlessness, and the divine.

It is our hope that the work collected in this volume will be a catalyst to further discussion on the relation of Bible and theology. More importantly, we hope that biblical scholars, theologians, and all concerned persons will seek to understand the problems and possibilities of the great task of world-making which befalls human life. Insofar as that task is undertaken, then our intellectual resources and energies will be rightly focused on matters of pressing importance even as we will come to understand better the world in which we live in all of its fragility and promise.

2

The Ambivalence of Power in Early Christianity

Gerd Theißen

⌘

Religious faith is not only confronted with power, but it is power with some ambivalent effects. Faith not only motivates people to admirable altruism, but to excesses of inhumanity. Religious beliefs not only motivate people to resolve conflicts, but also hinder the solution of social and political conflicts as a result of fanaticism (as in Northern Ireland, Cyprus, the Middle East, and India). Religion contains both blessing and curse. Whoever interprets religious traditions professionally takes responsibility for turning the dangerous power of religion into blessing, whenever this may be possible. This also requires uncovering the ambivalent function of religion where it appears to be a mere blessing. Research into religion must not be controlled by a "myth of innocence" as if it were an entirely beneficial faith which we just had to free from its estrangements, distortions and perversions. Religion as such is as ambivalent as power itself. And religion is all the more ambivalent if religion is dealing with power.

I shall try to show this by using early Christianity as an example—a tradition which motivates my living and thinking. I wish to conceal neither this nor my opinion that even in the beginnings there was a dark shadow, a certain tragedy.

In the first part, I shall present (very briefly) the theoretical framework whereby I shall examine the correlation between religion and power in early Christianity. In the second, I shall show how dealing with power is at the center of the synoptic Jesus tradition. The third part of my essay will show how this is continued within the early Christian *kerygma* —now within a new code of a mythical story of Jesus told in the Pauline and Johannine scriptures.

The real story of the first Christians will be my topic of part four and will be juxtaposed with the narrative and mythical story of Jesus. The problem is this: Why do we find so much in early Christianity's *real* history which is promised to be overcome by that *narrative* and *mythical* story? How can this contradiction be explained? Finally, I would like to explain how we can deal hermeneutically with this contradiction today.

I. Conflict and Integration: On Some Theoretical Requirements for Analyzing the Relationship of Religion to Power

Society and history can be viewed in the light of two contradicting theoretical models: theories of conflict and theories of integration. Conflict theories claim that history is a distribution struggle for chances and prospects of living. Above all, three goods are objects of this distribution struggle, namely, rulership, property, and education. All three can be understood as variants on power—as "coercive", "utilitarian", and "persuasive power" (A. Etzioni). While on the one hand the rulers conflict with the ruled, on the other hand there are also conflicts between co-existing groups including kinship groups, different peoples and cultures. Religion accompanies this distribution struggle over power, providing bases that fuel the fight over legitimacy. In all pre-industrial societies both the claims of the rulers and the claims of the ruled, both repressive and rebellious power, are legitimated by religious beliefs and symbols. Power is always characterized by asserting itself against the resistance of others; supported by religion, power turns into authority, into legitimate power. One function of religion is to legitimate power.

Such conflict theories increase one's awareness of distribution struggles. But they explain insufficiently the great human ability of cooperation. This is the actual topic of integration theories: history and society are continuous attempts to establish cooperation of people within a framework of a reliable social order (within a "Nomos"). It is within this order that human beings can compete for control, property, and education, but they can also exchange all these goods. It is the great task of society to control antinomic tendencies which are threatening the social order. This control happens by distributing value and not-value, merits and demerits (with according sanctions). In the ancient pagan societies it was a matter of honor and shame, in Judaism and Christianity a matter of purity and impurity or sin and salvation, in our secular society it is often just a matter of health and neurosis; but it is always a matter of some sort of "transgression." In fact, if there is an order or a "nomos" there is also violation, aberration and infringement. Hence, within an integration theory, society is again determined by a distribution fight, but it is a fight for distributing guilt, for the definition of transgression, and for blaming certain people and groups. Again, it is a distribution fight between those ruling and those ruled. Outsiders and strangers are usually the "unlawful" from the outset.

In my opinion, both approaches are necessary, although I am afraid I am not able to integrate them into a single comprehensive theory, for they refer to different aspects of social life which in some societies are organized in different institutions—namely, where a political and a religious system either compete against each other or work fairly independently side by side. The political system then deals primarily with resolving conflicts, the religious with upholding rules and order. In fact, both tasks overlap. Both systems have to deal with conflict and integration, because both systems are systems of power.

In the Judaism of New Testament times, we find a tendency towards a sophisticated institutionalization of the two basic social tasks. The political system distributed power and property. It worked with the help of Jewish client-rulers and Roman provincial officials. The religious system distributed purity and impurity, sin and salvation. Both overlapped with each other over education; education associated with the political centers (the royal courts) competed with a religious education in the shape of scribes. Both systems often worked together, but often also against each other. The tension between them even found expression in eschatological dreams. Some Jews expected only a single (royal) Messiah. But he was supposed both to fulfill the priestly task to hallow his people before God and to expel impurity from the country (PsSal.17). Others expected a royal and a priestly Messiah simultaneously—the priestly exercising the real power (as can be seen in the Qumran scriptures).

II. The Synoptic Jesus and His Dealing with Power

How did Jesus deal with this double system of political and religious power? I shall not attempt to examine the historical Jesus' conduct, but that of the "narrative Jesus"—viz., the Jesus of the synoptic gospels. This synoptic Jesus performs two public symbolic acts in Jerusalem which show a double conflict with the political and the religious systems alike, namely, his entry into Jerusalem and his cleansing of the temple.

Jesus' entry into Jerusalem is motivated by messianic expectations. Jesus riding in on a donkey creates the expectation of him bringing

David's kingdom. This king is the counter-image of a powerful king—irrespective of whether the vision of a powerless king of peace riding on a donkey, according to Zechariah 9:9, has dominated the story from the very beginning or whether the Old Testament text interpreted it secondarily (Mtt. 21:5/John 12:15). What is indisputable is that this is the beginning of a conflict with the political system which will later lead to Jesus' execution as the "King of the Jews."

Jesus' cleansing of the Temple, however, is a symbolic act which shows a conflict with the religious system. It is again interpreted according to the Old Testament. The Temple shall be opened for the Gentiles; it shall become a house of prayer for all peoples (according to Is. 56:7). Its function of separating pure from impure, Jewish from Gentile, is challenged. The prosecution before the Sanhedrin later confronts Jesus with his temple prophecy—that prophecy which very likely gave meaning to his prophetic symbolic action.

Jesus' double conflict with the political and religious systems of power is indicated by a double symbolic act, by a double charge before the Sanhedrin (firstly, temple prophecy and secondly, messianic claims) and by a double "trial" before a religious and a political forum. This double conflict is not an accidental end, but the consequent result of Jesus' entire working and preaching as it is told by the synoptics.

Dealing with the Political System of Power According to the Jesus Tradition

The entry into Jerusalem shows that the expectation of a "royal rule" which Jesus brings in the name of God is the reason for the conflict with the political system of power. In the center of Jesus' preaching is the *basileia tou theou*, the proclamation of a final intervention of God in history in order to create salvation. Thus, proclamation of a transcendental power is the central idea. The very idea is not a new one, but Jesus' semantic connections *are* new. They give a new meaning to this central metaphor of his preaching.

In my opinion, the connection of the metaphor of the kingdom with the metaphor of the father is crucial. We only find them connected in a few words, but these words are in a central position, namely, in the Lord's Prayer. "Our Father, hallowed be thy name, thy kingdom come," the text reads (Luke 11:2). Further, the kingdom and the father are related in the word on not worrying (Luke 12:30f.), in the words on the small flock to which the Father has given the kingdom (Luke. 12:31), and the Lukan version of the logion on the Twelves (Luke. 22:29). The fact that there are but few direct connections between the two metaphors still derives from their independence in the tradition.

Wherever Old Testament and early Jewish texts talk about the kingdom of God (e.g. about God's *malkut* or *basileia*), they are also referring to the kingship of God. The king imagery is differentiated as matter (kingdom) and person (king). It is precisely this double shaping of the king imagery that is missing in the preaching of Jesus. Its factual variant (the kingdom of God) appears with striking frequency in the words of Jesus; its titular variant, however, is almost entirely missing. We find an exception to this rule, in Matthew 5:35, where Jerusalem is called the city of the "great king." In the parables, one encounters a king as conventional metaphor for God only in the secondary texts. This becomes evident when parallel versions of the parable are compared (cf. Mtt. 22:1ff. to Luke 14:16ff. and Luke 19ff. to Mtt. 25:14ff.) or when the *kyrios* title in the parable is considered in relation to the king's title (compare Mtt. 18:23 to vv. 27, 31, 32, and 34).

In short, the king metaphor as a title is dropped by the Jesus tradition and the kingdom metaphor is expanded. It leaves an empty space. This leads to the question: Whose kingdom is coming? And the answer is: it is the kingdom of the father. And that means that this father's sons (and daughters) have a privileged position in that kingdom. They participate in his power. They belong to the ruling family.

Consequently, the king title is associated more strongly with human beings than with God in the Jesus tradition, and more with ordinary people than with actual kings. In particular, the king's title is concerned with the issues of control, wealth, and education; with "coercive," "utilitarian," and "persuasive power."

A ruler's authority is shown by his ability to collect taxes and tributes. Jesus once used the parable of the king's sons in order to account for the disciple's freedom from the temple tax. He asks, "The kings of the earth—of whom do they take custom or tribute? Of their own children or of strangers?" (Mtt. 17:25). Being king's sons, the disciples are freed from compulsory tributes.

Kings have riches at their disposal. But God is going to care for his children so that they have less need to worry than did king Solomon about his clothes (Mtt. 6:25ff.).

Wisdom is ascribed to kings, especially to king Solomon. The disciples have access to such royal wisdom, too. Even more, listening to Jesus' preaching they are better off than the Queen from the South who came from the ends of the earth in order to listen to king Solomon's wisdom (Mtt. 12:42).

The poor and ordinary people do not benefit from the power of God's royal rule by just becoming citizens of his empire. They belong to its royal family. When Jesus blesses the poor, asserting that "theirs is the kingdom of God," this has to be understood literally. In short, the poor exercise "power" in God's kingdom. They do not belong to the powerless any more. However, their power is a particular kind of power; whoever wants to be the first shall be prepared to be the last (cf. Mark. 10:42ff.). There is an analogy to this humane ideal of power: the Macedonian king Antigonos Gonatas, (influenced by Stoic philosophy) supported the theory that kingship was an *endoxos douleia*, an honorable form of slavery.

Where God's rule shows its first effects—as in Jesus' preaching—people are not supposed to experience a change of power in the sense that subjects of this world turn into subjects of God's rule. In fact, they are supposed to participate in the power of God's rule. They shall become little kings themselves—or better, members of the *familia dei*. That is why we often find fragments of ruler ideals and upper class ideals applied to ordinary people in the Jesus tradition: a "downward transfer of upper class values," as I once put it.

Dealing with the Religious System of Power According to the Jesus Tradition

The religious system does not only distribute power by distributing property and means of coercion (although it always uses such means); it gives power by its various closenesses to the center of holiness which is re-established by religious rituals again and again. The separation of sacred and profane, pure and impure, sin and salvation, good and evil is essential to establishing such an order—at least in Judaism and Christianity, where ethics are an integral part of the religious system. Personal power is exercised by the priests in the religious system; they control the temple, perform the rituals, and define what is pure and what is impure. Everyone else participates in their power through sharing religious knowledge about the holy and the profane and about good and evil, particularly the scribes in Palestine.

The Jesus of the Synoptics defends his cleansing of the temple—his symbolic attack on the center of the religious system—by referring to the baptism of John. Jesus' authority to challenge the temple cult (whatever aspect of the temple cult he might have been challenging) and the legitimacy of John's baptism are factually connected, although this connection is not explicit (Mk. 11:27ff.). In fact, if the baptism is the crucial condition for God's forgiveness of sins, this calls the function of the temple in question without a critical word being uttered, for the temple is the place where God grants the forgiveness of sins. Forgiveness comes by means of the scapegoat ritual on Yom Kippur for the entire people, by means of atonement and expiatory sacrifices for every single person. That there is a fundamental tension behind this conflict with the temple is, I think, shown by the saying about the pure and impure as well as traditions concerning the remission of sins.

The Markan logion on "pure and impure" (Mk. 7:15) is an indicative aphorism. It does not ask for a certain conduct. It says, "There is nothing outside a person that can defile that person by going in." Because no specific rule of conduct is derived, this aphorism can be understood as an enigma saying (or a "parabole") which has to be explained. Even if one is convinced that it is impossible to separate the pure and the impure, one can still adapt one's behavior to conventional purity norms. Jesus, for example, declares a leper pure—but requires that he ask a priest to declare him pure officially (Mk. 1:40f.). The Mark 7:15 aphorism is thus too unclear to exclude post-Easter debates about the actual consequences of not being pure (and therefore might date back to the historical Jesus). The crucial point for us is that this reading of the logion challenges the axiom which is ordinarily considered to be fundamental to all purity regulations. This axiom says that one can distinguish pure from impure things by external features. Rejecting this axiom is indeed questioning the religious system of power. Thinking accordingly means that one is already—in his heart of hearts—beyond that dualistic system.

The same is true for the tradition of the remission of sins. Forgiveness of sins is granted to the paralyzed. The story (Mk. 2:1ff.) does not understand these words as indicating that God has forgiven the sick man's sins, but as remission of his sins by Jesus himself. Only this interpretation makes sense of the accusation of blasphemy. Such is the remission of sins preached by Jesus in his parables. Such a remission of sins he is demonstrating by living in table-fellowship with tax-collectors and sinners; in fact, he invites everybody to forgive the sins of others (Mtt. 6:12, 14f.). All these forms of remission of sins have one thing in common: they are independent from the temple. They are, in fact, even independent from baptism, the ritual which was connected to the remission of sins by John the Baptist.

At least one point follows clearly from this interpretation. Jesus' preaching negates the definition of power of the religious system which dichotomizes between sin and salvation, pure and impure. Sometimes he directly calls it into question. The most obvious implication is that a new understanding of the relationship between sin and salvation must be sought. Salvation is granted not to the pure, but to the stigmatized and marginalized.

In summary, the narrative Jesus of the synoptic gospels confronts the political system of power with a conception of political power which promises to the powerless access to power in the *familia dei*. He also opposes the religious system of power by introducing a new distribution of sin and salvation; the target group of salvation is indeed those stigmatized by the religious system in force. Both features of the narrative Jesus quite certainly go back to the historical Jesus. Both are closely connected to the expectation of the imminent kingdom of God.

It is here, however, that we face a problem. Jesus wants those who used to be subject to political and religious control to participate in divine power. His proclamation of the *basileia* is the offer of a *symbasileia* for the poor and for outsiders. But this divine power is supposed to prevail without any exertion of force or pressure, as harmlessly and non-violently as the growing of seed. This divine power does not face any human resistance. The emperor is not God's enemy. It has to face mythical resistance, though. The *basileia* asserts itself against Satan and demons.

We touch upon an *aporia* here which is inherent in any use of power, namely, "Power corrupts and absolute power corrupts absolutely." For power has to assert itself against resistance *per definitionem,* therefore it is always in danger of becoming inhumane. In the Jesus tradition, this problem is shifted to a mythical area. Satan is defeated. Nobody need sympathize with him when his resistance is being broken. It is being broken by curing human beings.

The non-violent *basileia* did not come, however. But this proclamation of the *basileia* continued to have an impact—by attributing a new status to human beings in a symbolic universe rather than by the transformation of the real world. Nevertheless a few disciples did withdraw, within the real world, to a marginal way of life. The main change that did occur in the "here and now," then, was the establishment of new communities.

In fact, something crucial had changed for these new communities. Although the *basileia* did not come, Jesus was raised from the dead; he was part of divine power. The executed one became ruler of the world. His name was above all names. The beginning of a fundamental, radical change had already happened, although *we* can only notice the change of a religious belief. Our question now is: How do the first Christians cope with the conflict inherent in any kind of power?

III. The Kerygmatic Christ and Dealing with Power

Was it not the case that the development of Christian belief from the synoptic to the kerygmatic Christ of the Johannine and Pauline writings neutralized, to some extent, the opposition of divine power against human power-structures? The story of the synoptic Jesus took place on earth—under the real circumstances and conditions of power of those days. On the other hand, the story of the kerygmatic Christ was the story of a heavenly figure that was pre-existent, whose earthly existence was only an intermediate stage on the way to final exaltation. However, there was one thing that was especially interesting for Paul about this intermediate stage: the crucifixion. Beginning with the cross, Paul develops a theology in which the dynamics of opposition against political and religious power-structures are still alive. To some extent, he even radicalizes this opposition.

The Pauline Christ

Let us again go through the three goods for which the historical distribution struggle competes: power control, property, and education (or wisdom). My proposal is that Paul is questioning the distribution of these goods by unfolding his kerygmatic image of Christ—although to varying degrees in relation to each of these three.

Power has always surrounded itself by divine splendor, whether rulers were regarded as *epiphane* gods, as natural or adopted sons of God, or as the chosen ones; in any case, they were surrounded by a divine aura, a *doxa*, a "glory" that gave them legitimacy. Early Christianity gave this aura to a crucified one and withdrew it from the rulers of the world: "None of the rulers of this age understood this [the divine wisdom]; for if they had, they would not have crucified the Lord of glory [the *doxa*]" (1 Cor. 2:8). The crucified one is thus the "Lord of glory." He is surrounded by the aura which befits the power. According to the hymn of Philippians 2, he renounced this "aura" in order to take on the most humble social position, that of a slave and of the criminal who is executed on a cross, in order to be then appointed to the universal ruler above all powers. Whatever the early Christians might have said to convince their society of their loyalty to government and rulers, their commitment to Jesus led them to question the absolute legitimacy of the rulers.

The issue of property is also connected with Paul's story of the kerygmatic Jesus, although it fades in importance when viewed in light of the synoptic tradition. One can observe a shift in interest here. When Paul tries to get support for Jerusalem's early Christian community, he conjures up the kerygmatic Christ as a model. "For you know what Jesus Christ, our Lord, did," writes Paul, "He, though he was rich, yet he became poor for your sakes, so that by his poverty you might become rich" (2 Cor. 8:9). The pre-existent one exposed himself to the "poverty" of earthly life. It is here that the distribution of wealth and poverty is questioned in a mythically coded way—with concrete consequences for mutual human support.

Finally, Paul writes one of his greatest texts on the issue of education or wisdom. The kerygmatic Christ's fate, especially his crucifixion, shows how people perceive the wisdom of God as foolishness (1 Cor. 1:18ff.). That is how human wisdom and education is interpreted in relative terms. They were not able to perceive God's message in the crucified one. This also has real consequences. There were only a few educated people in the Christian community, none with the right to exalt themselves by boasting of their wisdom.

The kerygmatic Christ expresses his critical view on power, property, and education—a view not different from the synoptic Jesus. God himself takes on powerlessness, poverty, and foolishness in Christ—and thus de-legitimizes the distribution of power, property, and education in society. It is striking that Paul connects all this to his *theologia crucis*. However, in this context it is a *theologia crucis* without any soteriological interpretation of death in the sense of a dying "for us." The cross is the foundation for salvation here because it expresses a change in the standards of power, property, and education. God chooses the powerless, the poor, the uneducated—this is the message of the cross.

In addition, Paul unfolds another *theologia crucis* in which the death "for us" is central—in a soteriological interpretation in the narrow sense. Of course, he does not make a great distinction between the *theologia crucis* as radical re-evaluation of all values and the *theologia crucis* as new distribution of sin and guilt.

Unlike that which is true in the case of the synoptic Jesus, St. Paul's concern is not to challenge the exclusion of stigmatized ones from Jewish society, but to overcome the separation of Jews from Gentiles. Paul grew up with the conviction that all pagans are sinners (Gal. 2:15). The wrath of God is on them (cf. 1 Thess. 1:10; Rom. 1:18ff.). Paul's turning to them via his mission to the Gentiles presupposes that their terrible transgressions are objectively atoned for, before they even realize it. With the help of the atoning death of Jesus, pagan sinners can turn into chosen ones, the non-people into the people of God. That is why Jesus' expiatory death is so important for Paul (as for the entire Pauline sphere, that is, the Gentile mission). Paul employs cultic imagery in communicating this message. In Romans 3:25, he probably pictures Jesus' expiatory death as a replacement of Yom Kippur (which is disputed among scholars). In any case, he regards this expiatory death as a precondition for the openness of salvation to the pagans. The crucial point is that Paul thereby wants the expiatory death of Jesus to be more than a replacement of traditional means of atonement. Traditionally, atonement is always a *re*-placement of a disturbed order or a disturbed relationship. Atonement confirms the order whenever a rule is contravened. St. Paul had a different view. If the sinless Jesus atones, that means something is wrong with the very order (and the relationship to God) that required such an atonement. A revision of that order (especially of the Law) is necessary, and Paul does this in some concrete areas, specifically, where the Law made the separation of Jews and Gentiles insuperable, in circumcision and meal laws. Paul is also interested, however, in a fundamental change of the role of the Law itself (although exegetes disagree about the nature of this change).

We are now able to summarize this passage. Paul's kerygmatic Christ confronts the political system of power with a redistribution of control, property, and education. He also confronts the religious system of power with a radical redistribution of sin and salvation. The pagans, previously excluded as "sinners," turn into chosen ones, the non-people into the people of God. The old order which caused such exclusion is being (partly) revised. All this is coded in a mythical language of images.

We face the same problem, however, as we did with Jesus' preaching. The crucial changes have already taken place in a mythical act covering earth and heaven alike; this certainty relieves the pressure to realize them within the "real world." The problem is focused even more sharply. In the early Jesus movement, those who prepared themselves for the coming *basileia* can give up their ties and follow Jesus. With St. Paul, the expectation is that each person remain in the circumstances and conditions in which the call of the Gospel initially met him or her. The slave shall remain a slave until his or her liberation—not least so as not to jeopardize his or her imminent freedom (1 Cor. 7:21). The same goes for all Christians. They are all supposed to subordinate themselves to the state and to the government—for they know, in any case, that their redemption, their "setting free," is imminent (Rom. 13:1ff.; also cf. 13:11). That is why they are able to respect state and government not only out of conformity, but also out of conviction. Although a revolutionary view on power is "coded" in the christological pictures of Pauline theology, it has a conserving and stabilizing effect on everyday life.

The Johannine Christ and Dealing with Power

How is power understood in the Johannine writings? It is known that the Johannine Christ is a kind of synthesis of the synoptic Jesus and the Pauline Christ—a divine figure walking on earth. The exalted becomes transparent in the earthly Jesus.

The Johannine writings also show the re-evaluation of political power. Jesus' crucifixion is presented as condemnation by Pilate following a politically-motivated accusation by the Sanhedrin. The political context of Jesus' humiliating death appears in this otherwise spiritually-oriented gospel clearer than elsewhere. It is Jesus' humiliation by his execution, though, which is re-interpreted as exaltation (ὑψωθῆναι) and glorification (δοξασθῆναι). The powerless one has come back to God through his crucifixion and was thereby victorious over the "ruler of this world;" his resurrection gives him every right against this ruler, who is the Satan. The Satan—the ruler of this world—is connected in the Gospel of John with the real rulers of the world, i.e., with the Romans and their allies. For Satan is active through Judas through whom he is able to command a Roman cohort and the soldiers of the Temple aristocracy.

Even more instructive for us is the re-evaluation of religious power. The Johannine Christians have experienced one of their most severe sanctions, namely, excommunication. They react by forming a radical new distribution of sin and salvation. It is not they, the excommunicated ones, who represent the unholy and satanic, but the Jews who excommunicated them. In the gospel of John, we find a drastic anti-Judaism born out of the traumatic experience of excommunication—with disastrous consequences in the history of Christianity. Again, the mythical world is activated in order to relieve the aggressive impulses. The gospel of John puts it clearly: the killing of Jesus and the excommunication of the first Christians are not acts the Jews would have committed as free children of Abraham. They obeyed an alien power. They followed impulses alien to them, impulses originating with the ruler of this world—and thus consistent with the factual world rulership. Because they swore their loyalty to the emperor, Jesus had to die. An excommunicated community is groping to excuse the community which excommunicated them. They reason that it was only in a state of estrangement that the enmity between Jews and Christians could develop.

It would be unfair to blame the Johannine Christians for the later consequences of the Johannine anti-semitism; let us rather ask to know the real consequences of the Christian faith in those days, and let us assess them in a realistic way. A change of society was out of reach for the first Christians; they only had the freedom to structure things within their own communities. Hence, let us compare the narrative and the mythical story of Jesus to the real story of the first Christians.

IV. The Real Story of the First Christians and How They Dealt with Power

The real history of the first Christians did not come up to the aims which were inherent in the story of the synoptic, the Pauline, and the Johannine Christ, although the criticism of power continued to have an effect.

The life of the Pauline community is characterized by the model of a charismatic community. All members have a special gift, a certain talent; everyone has a charisma, each of them a task to fulfill. However, all to soon, the communities developed internal structures of power that exclude an integral group from leading offices: women.

Certainly, the communities developed an admirable system of mutual support. However, they did not part with the ugliest form of possession, the possession of human beings. Slavery was humanized, but not abolished, within the boundaries of the community. The Christian faith was used to motivate Christian slaves to become even better slaves.

Certainly, one refused to rule above others by means of religious knowledge. The Gnosis which promised its followers a superiority to ordinary Christians was rejected in principle. But the flourishing pseudepigraphy (that is, faking scriptures) of early Christianity shows that the communities were manipulated by means of putative authentic and old traditions (and the literary ability to fake epistles)—although with the clearest conscience.

Certainly, the community offered remission of sins to everybody. The religious system which distributes sin and salvation is open to people from all cultures and traditions, but at the same time, new groups become stigmatized—especially the group of origin, the Jews. An early Christian anti-semitism with disastrous consequences in later history is disseminated in many scriptures.

All this is not just inconsistency of theory and practice, scripture, and life. It is inconsistency in the old scriptures of Christianity as such—inconsistencies which were canonized in the course of canonization. The canonic New Testament is a *corpus mixtum*, a holy scripture with unholy elements. I have mentioned just a few examples of such "unholy" elements: namely, exclusion of women, stabilization of slavery (also by its humanization), the fakings, anti-Judaism. One could add more.

The contradiction between motives critical to power and rulership in the narrative and mythic story of the Christians, on one side, and the power structures within their own communal life, on the other side, calls for an historical explanation and, finally, a hermeneutical reflection.

The historical explanation has to answer the question, how can it possibly happen that a life characterized by the usual power structures could develop thoughts as critical to power as those contained in the Jesus story? This is to be explained. The accommodation of the early Christians to the usual conditions of life need not be given the same degree of attention.

Today, I am afraid, I can offer only an historical explanation which is a variation of an older theory, i.e., the theory of itinerant radicalism. Radicalism flourishes in marginal minorities which undertake to transform their deviant behavior into charismatic authority in relation to bigger groups. Or, more concretely: Jesus and his first followers—Paul and his collaborators—were itinerant preachers and traveling missionaries. They lived a deviant life style without the ties of a *stabilitas loci*, a family, or ordinary work (which Paul did only sporadically in order to secure his independence). Distant from ordinary life, they were able to develop values and ideas which transcended ordinary life in their radicality. The cynics of pagan antiquity are comparable. They also expressed social criticism by their life style. But they remained isolated figures without bonds to a community.

The synoptic Jesus cannot be understood apart from consideration of the historical Jesus and his deviant life style. Similarly, the Pauline Christ is closely connected to the Apostle's eccentric life style. However, both Jesus and Paul show not only a radicalism contrary to life, but also moderate exhortations in wise doses (especially Paul). Both preach to groups who lived and wanted to live within ordinary bonds. Charisma—that is, authority without support by formal institutions—presupposes both. On the one side, deviance from ordinariness gives charismatics that divine aura which propels their inexplicable influence. On the other side, they are able to radiate into everyday life, communicating their values to ordinary people.

There is a contradiction between deviant behavior and moderate practical imperatives from the very beginning. One cannot view one as original and the other as secondary. But the elements of conformity are strengthened in the course of the development of a charismatic community. In early Christianity, we can observe two developments of literary history accordingly: the revising of the Jesus tradition and the development of the Pauline tradition. The development of the Johannine tradition remains a special case.

The Jesus tradition was revised by the gospels so that they could serve as a foundation for the life of local parishes. The concept of the imitation of Christ, for example, was expanded so that it was not only valid for homeless itinerant charismatics. All Christians could regard themselves "imitators," "followers," and "disciples" of Jesus.

The authentic Pauline epistles, however, are supplemented by pseudo-epigraphic epistles. The bulky features of the image of Paul are eclipsed. In Ephesians the disruptive fighter and polemicist turns into an apostle of internal peace for the community; in the pastoral epistles, the ascetic is against asceticism, and the representative of a charismatic community order turns into an ideologist of the church office.

Johannine literature chose a third way. Here we find a spiritualized image of Jesus created for a small circle of "friends of Jesus" who know that they are different from parochial Christianity. There remains a bit of the old radicalism in the spirit and in the truth, but only by giving up concrete terms.

V. Conclusion

Thus far we have been concerned with historical explanations. How to deal with the New Testament today is a different question, as we understand more and more that it is a *corpus permixtum*—a holy scripture with unholy elements and aspects. The ambivalence of power found expression in it.

Let me unfold my thoughts concerning the hermeneutical question within the frame of a mythical picture. Let us imagine the best scholars of the world are in a heavenly academy in the end of all days. They receive the order to create a valid canon out of all the texts of the world. I am convinced the Bible would belong to this canon, although in a changed form, or better, in a revised and further developed form. And I ask myself, which principles will lead the heavenly scholars for their canonic edition? My considerations would be these:

(1) The Old and the New Testament are not opposed in the sense of promise and fulfillment; they are, rather, both the "Old Bible" which is fulfilled together in the revised "New Bible." Put differently, the New Testament and Old Testament together is read as the book of expectation, as the document of a development which goes beyond the New Testament. The Old Testament used to be read as the "unfinished project" of a religion with an external center beyond its own boundaries. The New Testament can be read similarly, that is, as evidence of an unfinished project. This approach corresponds to the New Testament's own self-understanding. Let us consider, for example, the promise of the paraclete who will lead into all truth, or the expectation of the coming *Parousia*. Even more importantly, this approach corresponds to a reading of holy texts which is trained by the Old Testament. In sum, the New Testament is read through Old Testament eyes as a testimony to an ever-growing expectation. The two testaments might have different names. The Old Testament would be called the First Testament, the New Testament, the second. Both would be fulfilled only eschatologically, having then a transformed shape which differs form their present shape.

(2) Criteria for reading the Bible are generalization and universalization of traditions. The texts are developed beyond themselves in a way which makes them accessible to everyone— especially to those two communities which have always been bearers of the bipartite canon, i.e., Jews and Christians. This generalization and universalization of traditions is the crucial event of the New Testament. However, it corresponds to the Old Testament expectation that once all peoples shall acknowledge the truth of God, they shall no longer teach one another (Jer. 31:34). Knowledge of God is equally accessible to all. The New Testament is enthusiastically convinced that this expectation had already been fulfilled in its own age—the messianic age (Heb. 8:8– 12; 10:16–17). However, it is still an unfulfilled expectation. Put simply, the Old Testament is here read through New Testament eyes.

(3) I would like to mention a third principle. Both Testaments are recorded as remembrance—including their problematic parts and messages, this also as remembrance of the suffering caused by religious faith. Without remembering these sufferings—especially those of others—there is no freedom to go forth into the future.

Somebody could now say this is an utopian program. Such a reading of the Bible does not stand a chance. I think such a reading of the Bible has been the secret program of biblical hermeneutics since theology was disturbed by the great unrest emerging in the days of the Enlightenment. This unrest continues to plague us today. Any sermon is an attempt to develop concrete texts so that the word of God will be heard in valid kind. However, one can also better understand much of theology if its struggle for an understanding of the Bible is considered to be a very special attempt—an attempt to seize the historical text of the Bible not only in its distance, but also to develop it towards an "eschatological" biblical text. It is true that this secret program of many approaches to biblical hermeneutics is probably not acceptable for many, when openly supported. Such a reading entails an evolutionary biblical understanding which regards any text in relation to its potential for meaning that is to be developed out of it—meaning that directs us toward a canon of truth which is inaccessible to us, toward the full and final truth to which only God has access.

Part Two

—CONCEPTUAL-THEOLOGICAL REFLECTIONS —

⌘

3

God's Power and Powerlessness
Biblical Theology and the Search for a World Ethos in a Time of Short-lived Moral Markets

Michael Welker

⌘

We had agreed to describe *Sitze im Leben* in which biblical-theological orientation in general, and in particular the recognition of the connection between God's power and powerlessness, are meaningful for human beings of our time. I have selected the following experience and problem: *In the face of global dangers, moral communication finds little or at least insufficient practical resonance among those to whom it is directed.*

Many human beings in different contexts of experience suffer under the depressing consciousness of the powerlessness and ineffectiveness of moral appeals (including moral appeals brought into circulation by the mass media!) directed against obvious global crises, dangers, and threatening catastrophes. Why does the force of worldwide moral appeals not suffice to stop the financial exploitation of the Third World through interest payments, even after renowned bankers have publicly considered canceling debts as a realistic possibility? Why does the force of public moral appeals not suffice to put the brakes on logging the tropical rain forests? Why does the force of such appeals not suffice to stop French nuclear experiments and to shut down highly insecure Russian atomic reactors in order to prevent a second Chernobyl? Why is what we call "public morality" not strong enough to reverse the dynamics of progressive criminalization, drug abuse, child abuse and other developments uniformly perceived as curses? Why is it that "public morality" is not strong enough even to put a recognizable damper on those developments?

Certainly there are numerous possible ways to answer this question. In what follows I would like first to call attention to the phenomenon of the market constitution of morality. I would also like to draw attention to the related decomposition of moral communication in our societies, as well as to the acceleration of the rate at which that decomposition occurs.

Next I shall discuss two prominent religiously-inspired attempts of our day to counteract this development. At issue are Hans Küng's search for a "world ethos" and David Tracy's attempt—normative in a more subtle way—to "name the present." Küng's approach, though surely unintentionally, is in fact authoritarian and hierarchical. Tracy's conception is emergent and mystical. I shall attempt to show some of the fundamental difficulties to which these two approaches lead.

Taking up the intentions of Küng and Tracy, in the final section of my reflections I shall call attention to the strength and the promise of religious communications which consciously orient themselves in relation to biblical traditions, with an eye toward decoding and reshaping the "implicit axioms"[1] which still inform or even direct our moral discourses. Precisely the normative potential in the biblical traditions—which lies in the connection of God's power and powerlessness—can render theologies of *metaphysical one-upmanship* (or theologies of the 'I'll go you metaphysically one better' style) superfluous and can help answer the open question concerning the *revelatory potentials and communicability* of the "prophetic-mystical" alternative described by Tracy.

In the Face of Global Dangers, Moral Communication Finds Little Practical Resonance Among Those to Whom It is Directed

Among the realizations which have practically ceased being disputed, at least in the intellectual disciplines, is the insight that

---

1   Cf. Dietrich Ritschl, *The Logic of Theology: A Brief Account of the Relationship Between Basic Concepts in Theology.* London: SCM Press, 1986, esp. Part I: Regulative statements (implicit axioms). "The methods of guidance which for an individual or a group see to it that thought and language can be examined and action guided can be called 'regulative statements' (= implicit axioms). They are not necessarily and in every instance statements actually formulated in language, but they lose their value as guidance if they completely escape formulation. On the other hand there is a danger of formulating them with excessive haste in an undesirable fixed form and thus often with a superficial and trivial content." Ibid., 108ff.; see also M. Welker, "Implizite Axiome: Zu einem Grundkonzept von Dietrich Ritschl's 'Logik der Theologie,'" in W. Huber et al., eds., *Implizite Axiome: Tiefenstrukturen des Denkens und Handelns,* Festschrift für Dietrich Ritschl (München: Kaiser Verlag, 1990), 30ff.

contemporary societies are distinguished from earlier societal forms by the fact that contemporary societies' most important subsystems are *functionally differentiated*. In these societies areas like economy, politics, law, religion, and family each have tasks which are undeniably important "for the whole society." That these areas are functionally differentiated means that they seek to optimize their tasks, and *must* seek to optimize them, by becoming increasingly capable of standing on their own over against the other subsystems. Although they all fulfill an indispensable task for "the whole," each subsystem optimizes its own function by developing a specific code and specific modes of procedure. Thus society does not possess a middle, a center, an apex, or an ultimate goal. Society is not a readily surveyable whole which admits of being regulated by one code. Instead, society is polycentrically organized and can be understood and described only by taking account of its polycontextual constitution. A plurality of publics conducts not "the discourse," but the diverse discourses of this society. And these publics obey different interests in and laws of development and optimization. Therefore their discourses are partially incomprehensible or inaccessible to each other. Each of the publics has only a limited capacity to resonate to the communication addressed to it by the others. If they are compelled to communicate, either there is only a mutual reception of "static,"[2] or the contents are so highly abstracted and so thoroughly trivialized that they hardly if at all influence real forms of experience and patterns of behavior.

Yet because these publics partially overlap, and because concrete human beings can and do simultaneously belong to different publics, the situation as described is difficult for *common sense* to comprehend. Common sense advances the argument that every human being is in some wise a private citizen, in some wise educated, in some wise a consumer, in some wise informed by means of mass media, etc. How can it be claimed that "the" general public is a fiction? How can it be claimed that the idea that societal developments can be accurately regulated through appeals to this public and to "the subject" is an illusion, except in extreme cases? The situation as described is also difficult for a religion to comprehend which has claimed jurisdiction over "the most important," "the whole," "the central," "the first and the last." Religion and common sense are always trying to use some new *tour de force* to combat the unmanageable multiplicity of definitions (mostly implicit) of "the first and the last," "the most important," "the central," and "the whole"—definitions which do not admit of being ordered according to

---

2   Cf. N. Luhmann, *Ökologische Kommunikation: Kann die moderne Gesellschaft sich auf ökologische Gefährdungen einstellen?* (Opladen: Westdeutscher Verlag, 1986); M. Welker, "The Self-Jeopardizing of Human Societies and Whitehead's Conception of Peace." Niklas Luhmann on his 60th birthday, *Soundings*, LXX 1987, 309ff.

the scheme of parts and whole. Hans Küng's attempt, which will be examined below, is but a current example of this type of *tour de force*.

The capacity to communicate about the whole, about reality, about society, and about social life eludes not only common sense and religion, but also moral sensibility. For each societal subsystem a different morality predominates. The *criteria according to which recognition is given or withdrawn* (i.e. the criteria of moral communication) are different in family life than in the economy's process of communication. They are different in politics than in intellectual life. To be sure, there are regions in which the boundaries are blurred. To be sure, there are extreme situations which temporarily generate the illusion of "societal unity." Yet there are no blanket homogeneous and universal conditions for the gift of or the withdrawal of respect. They are established according to each particular system of reference. They take their distinctive coloration according to each particular cultural situation and societal form. On top of that they vary relative to specific groups. This allows great flexibility in the change of "fundamental moral positions." The rapid displacement of the parameters of moral markets is clearly seen when one merely casts a backward glance over the last two or three decades in North America and Europe, not only with regard to sexual morality, or with regard to expectations and commitments concerning the carrying out of familial roles, but also in relation to many other "basic" positions and attitudes.

The processes in which the conditions for the gift of and the withdrawal of respect are established are continually readjudicated by relatively large groups of affected persons. For each of these processes the relative duration and the "half-life" admit of very poor prognostication. Spectacular integrative power does not necessarily argue for long duration. The "thousand-year *Reich*," for example, endured for only twelve years, and internal morale collapsed shortly after the beginning of the war. Persistent public criticism does not argue for a lack of effectiveness; the morals attached to the much-decried technological ideologies of our century seem to have great staying power. Multiform emergent presence does not argue for predictability and clear recognizability; in politics and education there is ongoing puzzlement both concerning the susceptibility to crisis of the moral potential of the civil rights movements and concerning that potential's capacity for regeneration. On the whole we still know little about the laws for the construction and decay of moral markets, little about the genesis and the structure of the processes in which human beings reciprocally influence each other not only by somehow establishing expectations of each other, but also by correlating the fulfillment and disappointment of these expectations with respect and with the withdrawal of respect. It does indeed seem to be the case that under the conditions of "post-modernity" the decomposition and recomposition of moral markets are accelerated. That reinforces the helplessness of religion, common sense, and moral communication over against "the public" and "the state of the world."

Although in principle it is hardly possible to think of a theme which can not be moralized, all attempts to grasp "the whole" or to address in fact "the" individual turn out to be dead end streets. They run into various moral restrictions and prejudices. Political or economic or intellectual or judicial or familial or group-specific considerations, considerations which are correlated with gender, race, nation and social status, require specific moral options or accommodation to specific moral expectations. This conditions a relative regional solidity which blocks individual dispositional freedom. But it also leads to tensions over against demands which aim at "the universal," "the whole," "the state of the world," and dominant crises defined in a seemingly transperspectival manner. The solidity of the binding to specific moral markets is definitely not of such a nature that it could remain immune to displacements in the so-called *Zeitgeist*, to economic changes, to intellectual trends and fashions of style, to career changes, changes in age, etc. Moral markets undergo mutation and positions of individuals within them are displaced. Even when specific parameters hold constant, the way in which fundamental options are grouped undergoes realignment. It is thoroughly comprehensible that in this situation the "danger of a vacuum in meaning, values and norms" (Küng) would be invoked. It is thoroughly comprehensible that in this situation theologians would set out on the "search for a fundamental universal ethos" and would undertake the attempt to uncover a fundamental universal ethos of all world religions which would put an end to the unmanageability (*Unübersichtlichkeit*) of moral markets, to their practically unpredictable transformations and to their reciprocal blockages.

Hans Küng's Hierarchical-Authoritarian Attempt to Ground a "World Ethos"

Hans Küng's "project world ethos" begins with clear diagnoses of crises.[3] He formulates these diagnoses in the form of questions

---

3   The passages quoted in this section are taken from Küng's "Towards A World Ethics of World Religions: Fundamental Questions of Present-day Ethics In a Global Context," *Concilium* 1990/2: *The Ethics of World Religions and Human Rights*, eds. H. Küng and J. Moltmann, 102–119. They overlap with similar reflections that he offers in: *Projekt Weltethos*, (München: Piper Verlag, 1990); "Die Funktion der Religion zur Bewältigung der geistigen Situation: Versuch einer zeitgeschichtlichen Analyse," in *Wissenschaftliche Theologie und Kirchliche Lehre, Pannenberg-FS*, ed. J. Rohls and G. Wenz (Göttingen:

addressed to the different societal systems of reference. He asks: Why shouldn't human beings lie to, deceive, and steal from fellow human beings? Why should politicians resist corruption? Why should the businessperson set limits on his or her greed for profit? Why shouldn't the embryo researcher develop a commercial reproductive technique? Why can't a people, a race, a religion hate and bully a people who are different or who believe differently? Küng first diagnoses a crisis of orientation which makes it hard for human beings to know "what the basic options are which should help them make the daily minor or major decisions in their lives, what preferences they should follow, what priorities they should set themselves, and which role-models they should choose" (Küng, 103). It is obvious that Küng's concerns are about the crisis of orientation in pluralistic societies shaped by the mass media.

He too casually blocks out the crisis of orientation brought by totalitarian structures, e.g. states, which attempt to develop a uniform "morality" across society and which know how to indoctrinate human beings in a corresponding manner, or at any rate attempt to do so. In any case it is with a certain astonishment that we must recognize that in Küng's opinion we have never seen, "at least in Germany and Japan," "scandals in the world of politics, the economy, unions and society" on such a scale as in the present absence of orientation (Küng, 104). Part and parcel of this one-sided focus on order is Küng's prediction that "with increasing glasnost and perestroika, we shall ultimately see exactly the same signs of a lack of orientation, not only in the [former] Soviet Union but also in Catholic Poland. . . ." (Küng, 104). Against this background Küng poses the large and open question: "What is the relation of modern democracy to morality?" Küng notes the "dilemma" that the modern democratic state "cannot decree precisely what meaning life should have and how it should be lived; it can not prescribe any supreme values and ultimate norms" (Küng, 105). On the other hand Küng asserts that "without a minimal basic consensus on particular values, norms and attitudes there is no possibility, either in a smaller or a larger community, of living together in a manner which befits human dignity. . . ." (Küng, 105).

It is worth remarking that Küng sets up his answer in such a way that the die is already cast before he takes recourse to religion. He describes the "necessary fundamental consensus" as "the main

---

Vandenhoeck, 1988), 138ff; "Dialogfähigkeit und Standfestigkeit: Über zwei komplementäre Tugenden," *Ev.Th.* 49 (1989): 492ff. Parts of my critique were published under the title: "Hans Küng's *Projekt Weltethos*. Gutgemeint— aber ein Fehlschlag," *Evangelische Kommentare*, 6 (1993): 354–356; cf. Hans Küng, "Nicht gutgemeint— deshalb ein Fehlschlag. Zu Michael Welkers Reaktion auf 'Projekt Weltethos,'" *Evangelische Kommentare*, 8 (1993): 486ff. and M. Welker, "Autoritäre Religion. Zur sachlichen Prüfung von Küng's 'Projekt Weltethos,'" *Evangelische Kommentare*, 9 (1993): 528f.

direction" and as "the goal." For Küng that "necessary fundamental consensus" is the answer to "the desire to cling to *something*, to rely on *something*...to follow some kind of guideline...to possess *something like* an underlying ethical orientation" (Küng, 106; emphasis mine). On the basis of these vague formulations one could object that human beings naturally both choose some "ligatures," some kind of binding ties and some kind of criteria in each particular case, and reach partial agreements about their choices. These objections make clear the problem which preoccupies Küng: the limited scope, the instability, and the rapid change of guiding criteria. But that means that little is gained by invoking "binding ties" if their durability, the depth of the "fundamental consensus," and the stability of the goal are not given—in Küng's terms, if the "main direction" is withheld.

The fact that his concern is with precisely this problem is shown by comparing his reservations to the "retreat" of recent philosophical ethics "to the customary practices of different lifeworlds and forms of life" (Küng names A. MacIntyre, R. Rorty, M. Foucault and R. Bubner as representative figures.). But towards that philosophy which, like Küng, is concerned with "the grand whole," he assumes a different attitude. Into the lap of that philosophy he tosses the problem of how "pure reason [should] decide between true and illusory, objective and subjective, acceptable and reprehensible interests" (Küng, 110). A *religiously* grounded ethos is in Küng's opinion apparently released from that worry as well as from the vague concern over whether one can "therefore meet every danger of spiritual homelessness and moral waywardness with pure reason" (Küng, 111; similarly *Projekt Weltethos*, 66).

Küng thinks that the "*unconditionality* and *universality* of ethical obligation" (Küng, 113) are religiously grounded on the basis of a very simple insight, indeed a simple idea. This simple idea is "the primal ground, the primal support, the primal goal of humankind and the world which we call God" (Küng, 114). Readers are almost sure to respond with the following questions. How is "that primal ground, that primal support" or "that primal goal" in a position to prevent the specific crisis situations described above? How does the "primal ground, primal support and primal goal" enable us to distinguish "between true and illusory, objective and subjective, acceptable and reprehensible interests"? Does the "primal ground, primal support and primal goal" enable us to counter "every danger of spiritual homelessness and moral waywardness"? If so, how? Such questions initially run up against the arid assurance that the "primal ground, primal support and primal goal" presents a "transcendent authority," (Küng, 113) and that on the basis of this "primal support, primal ground and primal goal" religions can speak with "absolute authority" (Küng, 114). The few moves which Küng makes towards more precise determination of the absolute authority of religion are frightening. It is frightening when Küng informs his readers: "religions have means of shaping the whole of a human being's existence—and this will be tested by history, adapted to a particular culture and given concrete form in the individual case" (Küng, 114).[4] This general recourse to the positivity of the psychic and social *power* of religion is particularly frightening in a country which has experienced a religiosity which was fully corrupted both politically and morally. Coming from the mouth of a man who has let his public identity and impact be characterized by chronic critical engagements with authoritarian styles of religious leadership, such a statement provokes the return question whether religions do not also possess the means to *deform* the entirety of a human being's existence, and to do so in a way which is "historically tested, culturally adapted and individually concretized"!

At first glance this question does not seem to leave Küng at a loss. He repeatedly emphasizes that he is concerned with religion which serves "the *humanum*," religion in which theonomy and autonomy are set in the "correct" relation, as Küng's Tillichian formulation puts it (Küng, 118). The modern ethos and modern reason are to take part in the project "world ethos" in a formative and engaged manner in spite of the relativism strikingly described by Küng and in spite of their ultimate failure to establish a secure foothold for themselves. But by invoking autonomy as a criterion for distinguishing between religiosity which forms existence and religiosity which deforms it, Küng finds himself holding precisely the same difficult ball which he had initially tossed in the lap of the philosophers and the general culture. Everything which Küng piles on the shoulders of philosophical positions and of a culture devoid of orientation can now be tossed back in the lap of his abstract religiosity—in order to diagnose the same dilemmas. The "primal ground, primal support and primal goal" invoked by Küng oscillates between a carte blanche for an authoritarian religiosity and, to use a phrase of Hegel's, a "pliable material upon which any and every arbitrary invention can impress itself."[5] The fact that Küng has been compelled to make his peace with arbitrariness is shown when he concludes by informing his readers that "an ethic[6] is concerned in the last analysis not with a variety of theoretical frames of reference but rather with what should or should not be done, quite practically, in life as it is lived" (Küng, 118). Since the "primal ground, primal support and primal

---

4   Cf. the German original: "Religionen besitzen Mittel, um die ganze Existenz des Menschen zu formen—und dies geschichtlich erprobt, kulturell angepaßt und individuell konkretisiert." *Concilium* 26, 161; compare with *Projekt Weltethos*, 78.

5   G. W.F. Hegel, *Grundlinien der Philosophie des Rechts*, Philosophische Bibliothek 124a, (Hamburg: Meiner, 1955), 16.

6   In my terminology, an "ethos."

goal" can come to have either a life-promoting effect or a demonic one, and since mere autonomy can not distinguish between "true and illusory, objective and subjective, acceptable and reprehensible interests," the final remedy can be distinguished from the deplored initial situation only on one condition. That condition is that people be prepared to place their hope and trust in what—N.B.!—the "leaders and teachers" of the great religions will do with—N.B.!—"all the means and possibilities at their disposal" to propagate and to execute the project "world ethos" (Küng, 116).

At one point Küng seems at first glance to be successful in breaking through relativism, or perhaps the religious camouflage of relativism. This occurs when he sees a convergence of the great religions not on the basis of the "primal support, primal ground and primal goal," but "in absolute agreement in some basic ethical imperatives" (Küng, 116). According to Küng these imperatives are: "Thou shalt not kill the innocent. Thou shalt not lie or break promises. Thou shalt not commit adultery or fornication. Thou shalt do good." (Küng, 116). Yet it is not difficult to show that precisely the process of determining who is "innocent," what is "sexual immorality" and what is "good" is in an extreme measure dependent upon the particular moral market in question. That is all the more true of the question of how to stabilize promises in a rapidly changing global situation and social reality.[7]

David Tracy's "Mystical-Prophetic" Vision of the Present and of the Future[8]

David Tracy has developed an approach that stands in opposition to Hans Küng's conception,[9] which is undoubtedly, albeit involuntarily, authoritarian and hierarchical. As human beings seek help and support, religions are not to operate upon them with "absolute authority" on the basis of a "primal support, primal ground and primal goal." Still more clearly, religions are not to operate upon them through "leaders and teachers" and, in certain cases, "with all the means at their disposal." Such an attitude towards the operation of religion includes an unclarified and internally contradictory relation to autonomy, which leaves autonomy to oscillate between the positions of modern and pre-

---

7   Küng himself casts light upon two of the problems of consensus which emerge with regard to these "imperatives" (*Projekt Weltethos*, 98ff).

8   The following quotations are taken from: David Tracy, "On Naming the Present," *Concilium* 1990/1: "On the Threshold of the Third Millennium," 66–85; see also: D. Tracy, "Approaching the Christian Understanding of God," in *Systematic Theology: Roman Catholic Perspectives*, Vol.1, ed. F. Schüssler Fiorenza and John P. Galvin (Minneapolis: Fortress Press, 1991), 131 ff.

9   Küng's venture can be characterized in Tracy's terms as "neoconservative."

modern consciousness. Tracy clearly describes the tension in which the thought of Hans Küng, among others, moves. He sees that tension as a conflict between the "modern" emphasis on the autonomy of the subject and the "pre-modern" longing for "the return of the repressed traditional and communal subject" (Tracy, 66). At the same time Tracy is open to relativistic positions of "post-modern" consciousness, noting that for the post-moderns "at their best, the hope of the present is in the reality of otherness and difference" (Tracy, 66).

Tracy has an acute perception that "modern" theologians (an identification he explicitly applies to Hans Küng) could easily further a situation in which they "will be tempted quietly, even unconsciously, to retreat to social-evolutionary scenarios which secure modern centredness at the price of illusion for self and destruction for others. They will be tempted to hear others only as projected others— projections of their present fears and anxieties, hopes and desires" (Tracy, 82). Tracy develops his vision over against the moderns, over against the fundamentalist and neoconservative anti-moderns who seek to reverse societal development, and over against the post-moderns, "proud and ironic in their centrelessness" (Tracy, 82). Over against all these, Tracy develops a vision which takes up the "best forms" of the post-moderns and attempts to direct them out of their "proud and ironic centrelessness" under the impetus of liberation theologies: "Where, in all the discussions of otherness and difference of the post-moderns as well as the moderns and the anti-moderns, are the poor and the oppressed? These are the concrete others whose difference should make a difference. For through them the full and interruptive memory of the Gospel is alive again among us. In their prophetic speech and their liberating actions lies hope for the true time of the present before a judging and saving God. In their actions, historical subjects act and speak . . ." (Tracy, 82).

Tracy's "naming of the present," his description of currently valid developments of paradigmatic weight and paradigmatic worth, can be described as a *post-modern perception of an emergent development of polycontextual liberation movements*. In these liberation movements the subjectivity of modernity is concretized and transformed in a plurality growing out of diverse experiences of suffering. At the same time the emergent development may very well awaken hope for the "working of a different reality" and offer a future equivalent for the object of "pre-modernity's" longing. Post-modern, modern and pre-modern impulses and developmental tendencies reciprocally transform each other in this polycontextual community of the poor and oppressed. Tracy explicitly names the "various and, to be sure, often conflicting theologies of liberation" as bearers of the reality which he perceives (Tracy, 83). This reality aims at a new "world ethos," but not on the basis of a "primal ground, primal support and primal goal" determined and mediated by teachers and leaders. Rather the reality sketched by Tracy moves toward a new "world ethos" in a polycontextual and emergent manner from a multiplicity of concrete experiences of suffering and liberation.

At issue is a radically polycentric movement with centers in "Latin America, Asia, Africa, Eastern and Central Europe" and in "the African American theologians, the native American theologians, the communities of Christian feminist and womanist theologians throughout the world" (Tracy, 83). In and from this polycentric movement Tracy sees an ecclesial public developing which can be identified as the "global Church" because in the Spirit of Pentecost it "promise[s] liberation for all" (Tracy, 83).

Tracy terms the theology emerging in this movement "mystical-prophetic" theology (Tracy, 83). In that designation the expression "mystical" comes across as externally imported and tacked on. On the basis of the biblical traditions and of regard for the working of God's Spirit, the characterization of this emergent community as a community of "prophetic" communication makes good sense. But the aptness of the term "prophetic" is matched by the difficulty one has in understanding why at this point Tracy explicitly employs the concept of "the mystical," burdened as it is with various associations of subjectivism, cognitivism and elitism.

To be sure, the communication processes of the polycentric community of the poor and oppressed are difficult to grasp. But should we invite indeterminacy with the expression "mysticism"? It is also difficult to grasp Tracy's hope, oscillating between positions of modern and anti-modern consciousness, that "a new historical subject in the Western centre itself [could] emerge after the death of the modern subject" (Tracy, 82–83). Should mysticism bridge the gap between modern subjectivism and pre-modern religious attitudes? Is something like a "postponed neoconservatism" or a vague hope in somehow reshaping modern consciousness the light at the end of the tunnel of mysticism? In pluralistic societies the pressure is intense to muster forms of experience and of thought which are simple, easily rendered plausible, yet extremely flexible and capable of generating a high degree of integration. Gordon Kaufman's "God as ultimate point of reference" or Küng's "primal ground" can be regarded as reactions to that need. The interest in mysticism seems to move in this same direction, although on a more demanding level, since it includes transcendental stances.

Yet this interest in mysticism, which seems to be enjoying new life in regions of recent North American Catholicism, lies below the level of Tracy's pluralistic approach. At least in the undeveloped forms so far exposed[10]—it blurs the differences between positions of post-modern,

---

10   It would be important not only to name but also to specify traditions and positions which in theology and praxis were able to combine prophetic and mystical spirituality in communicable and revelatory ways.

modern and anti-modern consciousness. It threatens to drag back into indeterminacy the "prophetic" will to express and expound a position, the "prophetic" readiness to take a stand and to assume responsibility. Without further clarification and qualification, it threatens to individualize and to empty the spiritual and ethical processes, which Tracy tries to "name."

We must therefore ask what alternative there is to a concept such as "mysticism" which covers over or even consecrates the fact that it is very difficult to reveal or lay hold of the processes of emergence accurately described by Tracy. I think that the placement of self in contemporary polycentric experiences of suffering and hopes for liberation must not be lost in mystical indeterminacy. The revelatory power of the prophetic can also, on the basis of polycentric concreteness, be capable of communication, assume solid form, and lead to a new, common religious language, vision, and form of life. The recognition of the connection in the biblical traditions between God's power and powerlessness allows us to speak of God and God's action without a metaphysical back-up, without invoking an authoritative primal support, primal ground, and primal goal meant to stabilize hierarchies. This approach makes it possible, to cite Tracy yet once more, to renounce the "desire for totality" which is "the concealed wish and death-dealing fate of modern reason" (Tracy, 78–79). It makes it possible to do this without sliding off into the indeterminacy of the "radically apophatic tradition" (Tracy, 78) in which totalizing and particularizing forms can merge indiscriminately into each other.

Epistemic Connections and Forms of Communication on the Basis of "Biblical Theology"

Since the 1980's a "new" biblical theology has been developed.[11] This biblical theology disassociates itself from all earlier attempts to read out of the biblical traditions—perhaps to read into them—a single form or a single theme (e.g., reconciliation, covenant, Kingdom of God, God's holiness, etc.) as "the form" or "the content" of those traditions.[12]

---

11   Limiting myself to the academic realm, narrowly construed, I name as examples only the series and "instituted" forms: *Overtures to Biblical Theology*, edited by W. Brueggemann and J. Donahue S.J. (Philadelphia: Fortress Press), the *Jahrbuch für Biblische Theologie* (Neukirchen-Vluyn: Neukirchener Verlag, since 1987); the "Frederick Neumann Symposium on the Theological Interpretation of Scripture" (Princeton Theological Seminary; annual event since 1986). See also Elisabeth Schüssler Fiorenza, *But SHE Said: Feminist Practices of Biblical Interpretation* (Boston: Beacon Press, 1992).

12   J.D. Levenson rightly criticizes this conventional form in: "Why Jews are Not Interested in Biblical Theology" in: J. Neusner et al., *Judaic Perspectives o n*

Instead the new biblical theology adopts a consciously "pluralistic" approach. It takes up and takes seriously *the diverse biblical traditions with their differing "Sitzen im Leben"*—traditions whose experiences of God and expectations of God evince *both continuity and discontinuity, both compatibility and an absence of any direct possibility of mediation.* This theology assumes from the start that no human experience has "God in Godself" at its disposal, but rather that God's revelation mediates itself in a multiplicity of human testimonies to God's presence.

Since these are human testimonies, they are in each case threatened by distortion, error, falsehood, the thirst for power, and the attempt to make oneself look good. But insofar as these testimonies point to God's revelation and to a humanity destined for justice and freedom, they can in manifold ways reciprocally challenge and strengthen each other, and can lead to clearer knowledge of God and of the reality intended by God.

This new theology critically engages not only metaphysical and politico-ideological totalizations. It also attempts to lay bare the patriarchal, class-based, imperial, and militaristic ideologies and forms of thought which permeate the biblical traditions themselves. Finally, in this theology the development of a sensibility for *differences and discontinuities* of these traditions is hardly less important than the interest in continuities and forms of unity.

In contrast to the metaphysical "primal ground" or to the "abysses" of mysticism, here we have a pluralistic continuum of experience which stimulates and promotes self-criticism and creative communication. This continuum of experience aids in perceiving relative continuities and discontinuities between different political, social, moral and psychic realities. It allows the differentiated and differentiating identification of diverse present, future, and past stances of consciousness, as well as definitions of multiple "presents." It demands complex critical engagements and communication between these varied realities. It allows different forms of common sense to locate themselves in different ways. It allows critical engagement and reciprocal fertilization between these different forms of common sense. It allows for multi-systemic cultural and social critique and for the perception and stimulation of creative emergent processes.

An apparent weakness of this pluralistic continuum lies in the fact that it does not attain the Olympian standpoint of metaphysical totalizations and "ultimate" points of reference from which can be generated the ultimate and final worldview.[13] Nor does it attain the

---

Ancient Israel (Philadelphia: Fortress Press, 1987), 281ff; cf. D. Ritschl, "'Wahre', 'reine,' oder 'neue' biblische Theologie? Einige Anfragen zur neueren Diskussion um 'Biblische Theologie'" in D. Ritschl, *Konzepte. Ökumene, Medizin, Ethik. Gesammelte Aufsätze*, (München: Kaiser Verlag, 1986), 111ff.

13   Cf., in this volume, Vincent Wimbush, "*Contemptus Mundi* Redux: The

indifference of moral markets. This pluralistic continuum has specific forms and contents, albeit with a high degree of complexity and far removed from all one-dimensionality. And some of these forms and contents function as "implicit axioms." In this way the pluralistic continuum is—again in highly complex forms—"value-laden" in both positive and negative ways. Therefore sensibilities must be developed for the limits and biases of those who communicate on the basis of this continuum of experience. It encourages the development of what Cornel West describes as "a nuanced historical sense" and "a subtle social analysis."[14] Yet, at the latest in a more radically "postmodern" culture than today's, this supposed weakness could prove to be a strength. If the constant development of sensibility for limits and biases were carried through, it would not impede communication with other great religious traditions and with secular forms of consciousness, but would rather improve it.

On the one hand, the secret and unintentional absorption of foreign ways of thinking by metaphysical, moral, prophetic, mystical and other "fundamental" positions which are only *apparently* neutral would have to be exposed and limited in a more radical way than has previously been done.[15] On the other hand, bridges would have to be established between the *contents* of the different complexes of traditions and experience—likewise more clearly than has happened previously. The apparently more comprehensive and more fundamental commonalities which were imputed with the help of highly abstract forms and of ultimate referents which existed only in the realm of linguistic mystification would have to yield to specific sets of questions about content in boundary situations and relations of proximity uncovered by investigation.[16]

Politics of an Ancient Rhetorics and Worldview": "Christianity is fundamentally a proliferation of social formations inspired by *contemptus mundi* as worldview."

14   Cornel West, *Prophetic Thought in Postmodern Times: Beyond Eurocentrism and Multiculturalism*, Volume I, (Monroe, Maine: Common Courage Press, 1993), 3ff.

15   Cf., in this volume, Catherine Keller, "Power Lines." Keller offers several disclosures of hidden apocalyptic forms in theological modes of thought and practices, which are widely appreciated and still badly needed.

16   Cf. John Polkinghorne, *The Faith of a Physicist: Reflections of a Bottom-up Thinker*. The Gifford Lectures for 1993–4, (Princeton, NJ: Princeton University Press, 1994), 4ff.: "We have learned so often in our exploration of the physical world that 'evident general principles' are often neither so evident nor so general as one might at first have supposed. Many theologians are instinctively top-down thinkers. I do not deny a role for such ambitious intellectual effort. I am merely wary of it and wish to temper its grand generality with the questionings that arise from the consideration of particularity."

This new biblical-theological approach intends anything but a "neoconservative" securing of what has been acquired in the past. It is not the intention to secure perduring narratives from the past, not to mention an overarching "metanarrative" (Lyotard), which would have the right to expect a hearing whenever and to whomever it was told. The concern of this new biblical theology is instead to open access *to a continuum which guides spiritual experience and prophetic communication in a multiplicity of emergent processes.* This continuum makes it possible continually to test key points of view—although not arbitrary ones—by placing them in the center of experience and communication particular to each concrete case. Indeed, this continuum compels such placement and testing. This process of placement and testing calls into question theologies of one-upmanship as well as theological conceptions which could be called "theologies of absorption."

It compels us to take our leave of many familiar conceptions of God's power and of religious confrontation with that power or participation in that power. It compels us to take radically seriously the connection between God's power and powerlessness. It compels us to come down from the mountain and out of the clouds in order to inquire after God's presence and God's effectiveness, posing our questions from many concrete and authentic contexts of experience, and from the problems of finding common wavelengths of communication which both burden and enrich those experiences.

God's Power and Powerlessness

The connection of God's power and powerlessness provides a starting point not only in terms of content, but also formally, structurally, existentially, and hermeneutically. This starting point is not dictated simply by the requirements of our pluralistic cultures after the collapse of the continuum of reality and rationality, and in the midst of a multiplicity of moral markets. The connection of God's power and powerlessness is intrinsic and essential to many biblical traditions. It is essential in a context of traditions whose paradigmatic *Sitze im Leben*, formative at a basic level, are to be sought in acephalous societies without king, acropolis, bureaucratic staff, or power of military enforcement. Yet not only the pre-state and anti-state genesis, but also the internal constitution of a people which understands itself as liberated slaves and strangers reflects the essential connection of God's power and powerlessness. The *paradigmatic public*, cultically constituted, gives a continually-renewed anchoring to the consciousness that God, the God of the Exodus, essentially acts out of powerlessness and oppression, of weakness and of collective helplessness. To this corresponds the frequent promise, in the mercy laws and in the prophetic traditions, of God's particular partiality specifically for the weak. To this corresponds above all *God's presence in God's Spirit.*

Beginning with the earliest witnesses to whom we have access, the working of God's Spirit is perceived as an action upon or in the midst of a ruptured, threatened community which in and of itself can not generate capacities or strategies for deliverance, successful interaction, or communal action. God's Spirit characteristically acts in and through emergent processes which transform communities that are either powerless or disparate and which are either potentially or actually in conflict. The notion of the "pouring out" of the Spirit shows with particular clarity the way in which a plurality is led to emergent community. The Spirit of messianic promise works out of and in the midst of a plurality of international hopes for justice, mercy, and knowledge of God. The tensions present in this international public are considerable. Yet the working of the Spirit does not remove this international and multicultural differentiation, as is evident not only in the Pentecost story but also in earlier events. Instead, the relative powerlessness in this plurality is a condition of the possibility of bringing justice, mercy, and knowledge of God (the intentions and functions of "the law") *to a greater fullness.*

Homogenization and simple hierarchical constructions do not go hand-in-hand with the bestowal of God's countenance and the pouring out of God's Spirit. This becomes particularly clear in the promise of Joel, which is then taken up in the Pentecost account: the pouring out of the Spirit leads to pluralistic and prophetic openings of access to experiences of God and of the reality intended by God. The unimpeded presence of God's countenance is attendant upon precisely this plurality. In precise correspondence to this fact, according to chapter 42 and other passages in Isaiah, the promised bearer of the Spirit *does not use the typical political and moral forms for acquiring power and loyalty. It is out of public powerlessness, indeed out of public misunderstanding and public contempt, that the promised bearer of the Spirit gathers God's people as a community not structured along the lines of a single hierarchy.*

This community is not simply an ensemble comprised of conceptions of the world and religious schemes of totality which are in part compatible with each other and in part incompatible. This community is upheld by faith in the revelation of God's *justice* and in the connected promise that justice will be realized for human beings. This justice gains material reality not only in the community's relation over against God, but also in its relations among human beings. In this dynamic it is again God's partiality for the weak, oppressed and marginalized which serves as the source of unwavering processes for the generation of order and reality, as well as for the transformation of reality.

For this renewal of the relationships of human life, orientation toward the suffering Messiah and the crucified Jesus of Nazareth is an initial experience. But this orientation fails if it is not seen in the context of the legal traditions and the promises of the Spirit embedded in the biblical traditions.[17] It degenerates at least into an incomprehensible, abstract principle which can be turned back to authoritarian uses. In the context of the legal traditions and of the promises of the Spirit, which can function as "implicit axioms," it becomes clear that it is proper to the orientation on the suffering Messiah and on the crucified Jesus of Nazareth to release specific, formative experiences which are capable of communication, but which above all are situated in various socio-political and other contexts of life. At issue are experiences which challenge and instruct us to grasp the salvific connection of God's power and powerlessness in our own contexts of life, to experience that connection and to let others experience it.

Such communication of the connection of God's power and powerlessness can counteract authoritarian hierarchical constructions, be they intentional or unintentional. It can also counteract intentional and unintentional escapes into indeterminacy in the face of situations which overwhelm moral and communicative resources.

---

[17]   Cf. Rita Nakashima Brock's and Catherine Keller's critique of the religious use of the dualism, "powerful parent/ powerless child."

4

Power Lines

Catherine Keller

⌘

God then,
encompassing all things, is
defenseless? Omnipotence
has been tossed away, reduced
to a wisp of damp wool?

- Denise Levertov,
"Mass for the Day of St. Thomas Didymus" (excerpt)[1]

I

1. "**G**od of Power and Might" rings out at a key moment in the liturgy, indeed the revised version, of my own tradition. During our weekly communion service I ritually wince as we perform this tautology of domination. Why the overkill? Why not "power and love," I wonder; are they afraid we might miss the point? The assumption of omnipotence, despite or perhaps because of the variety of persuasive alternatives now available, continues to dominate Christian imaginations. Its

---

1   From *Candles in Babylon,* by Denise Levertov (New York: New Directions Publishing Corporation, 1982).

unconsidered implications mingle misleadingly, indeed dispiritingly, with the best of intentions. Let me suggest that it holds us captive to the 'bad faith' of a systemic self-deception. To heal itself, theological power-rhetoric requires a moral account of the character of this power and therefore of "power" itself—i.e., of the matrix of meanings we *mean* when we deploy power-language.

Within this essay, I consider a set of converging lines of inquiry. Each of these reflections on power, represented by liberation, feminist, postmodern and process thought respectively, raises telling questions for any theo-ethical reconstruction. It is so much not that these perspectives add up to a correct doctrine of power, but that they together may empower a set of practices. These practices, which cannot be designated apart from their own contortions into theory, constitute an on-going if spasmodic struggle within theological education and religious reformation. This struggle takes place at the theological intersections of various social movements marking the so-called "end of modernity." The familiar litany whereby we attempt to keep conscious our social context or location (our race, gender, class, nation, religion, species, etc.) evokes, however awkwardly, a new self-consciousness of power-relations. For what is a "social location" but a site of interacting social forces and resistances, of powers and counter-powers?

Any reflection about power is at the same time an act of power—an exercise of influence within a matrix of relations, itself demanding accountability. The present inquiry participates in the theological reformation motivated by a penitentiary Christian awareness of the field of structured power relations in which we move, live and are. The biblical case with which I will engage happens to be the book of Revelation, a work honestly obsessed with power and counter-power, with imperial domination and divine revolution. It can be said to mark the limit, the outer edge (*eschatos* indeed) of any Christian rhetoric of power and may thus illumine certain edges of the present discussion.

2. As Michel Foucault especially has shown, western discourse commonly reifies power, imagining it as a kind of commodity that one might "have" more or less of, distribute or monopolize. Simply put, power is a matter of more or less, win or lose. Presumably, therefore, God could also "have" this power limitlessly, to preserve in omnipotence, share in freedom, or empty in incarnation. Christian faith, whether in power or out of it, has found it irresistible to load the metaphor of divine power with every sort of hope for paternalistic intervention. These hopes draw their apocalyptic tenor from Hebrew despair in the face of centuries of imperialist intervention and elite betrayal. The prophetic expectation of a historical end to the causes of suffering, requiring the full collaboration of the people, eventually

exaggerates into an end-time hope for supernatural intervention.[2] At the *eschatos*, everyone will see who had "had" the power all along.

The desired divine interventions, however, have a habit of failing. Jews, recognizing that the Messiah is yet to come, and even Christians, realizing that the first coming only opened up the need for the second, implicitly acknowledge this disappointment.[3] But in the meantime human powers stand ready to assume a god-like stance of dominance: god-like only according to the standards of power by which God fails. Hence a kind of vicious theo-secular cycle of power whirls its way through history. The more the powers of dominance succeed, the more God fails; the more God fails, the more the powers of dominance fill the vacuum. The dominative model of divine power prepares the way for modern secularist uses and knowledges of power, mechanizing its operations and rendering one set of beings powerful and all other sets proportionately powerless. In other words, assuming the dominative-possessive view of power invariably sets God up in an abusive relationship to the world. An alternative model will then hold up neither an all-powerful divine parent nor a powerless child-victim as paradigms of salvation, recognizing such figures as complementary poles in the historical cycle of abuse. The abuse of power, collectively entrenched with the preconscious and well-nigh universal repetition-compulsion sometimes called original sin, can be seen at every level of the social orders dominating the planet. During these last decades of the millennium, this "seeing" takes on the visionary character of an *apokalypsis*—an unveiling of intimate abuses and planetary assaults against the social fabric of creation, a dis/closing which seems unprecedented, potentially liberating precisely for its "powers of horror."[4]

3. So one might ask first of all—how does reflection on divine power and powerlessness illuminate the political and economic power driving the contemporary world-order? The collapse of the Soviet empire alleviated the threat of a nuclear apocalypse for the time being, yet it also relieved capitalism of any counterbalancing ethos. The manichean dualism of monolithic modern powers, which repressed local tensions, has balkanized into a postmodern pluralism of wars: the repressed returns, and it is legion. The ecological end-time tribulations continue unimpeded, and everywhere the gap between the affluent and

---

2   Paul Hanson, *Dawn of the Apocalyptic* (Philadelphia: Fortress, 1975/79).

3   For a theologically cogent and recent account of this convergence of deferral, cf. Jürgen Moltmann, *The Way of Jesus Christ: Christology In Its Messianic Dimensions* (San Francisco: Harper & Row, 1990).

4   Julia Kristeva's *Powers of Horror* (New York: Columbia Press, 1982) lightly but recurrently links apocalypse with her analysis of the fascinating and repelling "abject."

the destitute deepens into abyss. These threats are too big to think about
for long; the brain numbs into progressive truisms, warmed by the glow
of a lingering self-righteousness. But right now we hardly hear of new
strategies, let alone effective examples, of resistance to the man-made
apocalypses of the end of this millennium. Powerlessness, or rather, the
sense of it, appears then as a dire social problem, threatening democracy
in the U.S. and socializing masses of young people into futurelessness.
And if the unveiling of incest and other primordial violations be figured
in, it is not surprising that generations of children grow up expecting
ever more grown up levels of the abuse of power.[5] Perhaps this is why
we see so little long-term—mature—resistance to the systematic
annihilation of social and terrestrial viability. Expectation, and thus
apocalypse, proves self-fulfilling.

4. Spirituality, or the practice of faith, seems to offer some kind of
antidote to the sense of powerlessness, allowing people to live in dignity
and community, and sometimes in hope and joy, no matter what. But
when does it do more than allay the *sense*? When does it actually
empower social—"structural"—change of the causes of suffering? This
is a way of asking: what difference does and can "God" make for social
justice? That is, which conceptualizations of divine
power/powerlessness serve as theological reinforcements of the status
quo, and which might activate, like yeast, the rising of the
commonwealth of God—the social movement toward socially
cooperative, economically just, ecologically sustainable, and emotionally
vital communities? Which theological perspectives help to heave power
into consciousness and hold it there long enough to affect our practices?
For instance, what kind of symbiosis of spiritual and socioeconomic
practices do they stimulate? And can one articulate theological
alternatives to *dominative* power in such as a way as to demand from
them a certain empowerment nonetheless?

The failure of the omnipotent God has normally been disguised by
some sort of eschatological deferral. Yet this failure has been revealing
itself throughout modernity—even before Bonhoeffer—as a matter of
human responsibility. Of course theology today may continue quietly to
reinforce the oppressive arrangement of powers. Or it may help to
unravel the hidden theological justifications of world-power. It will do
so, I submit, to the degree that it points those paralyzed by the politics of
power to power sources to which they *already* have access. "The poor,"
says Marta Benevides, the Salvadoran activist-theologian, "do not need

---

5   For the interaction of violence against children with apocalyptic
protestantism and the cultural expectation of mass doom, cf. Philip Grevin, *Spare
the Child: The Protestant Roots of Child Abuse*, (New York: Knopf, 1991).

to be empowered. They already have power. They need to recognize and release it."[6]

What is this power? Let me suggest that there is implicit in her argument an alternative understanding of the very nature of power. If those who appear powerless claim this power, they do not fail—even when particular projects do not succeed. Their kingdom is not of win/lose.

II

1. Liberation theology, in its prophetic evocation of Exodus imagery, economic and class analysis, and the postcolonial imperative, has exposed the complicity of traditional piety with the ecclesial hierarchy in maintaining the powerlessness of the poor. At the same time it mobilizes liberative biblical imagery with which to empower resistance to domination. The relatively powerless popular collectivity, the *anawim*, appear as the locus of salvation in history—but after all only because they, with Moses, undergo "conscientization," organize to become "persons" rather than "nonpersons," "subjects of history"—that is, agents, powers, rather than mere objects of the manipulation of oppressive forces. Yet God's power does not in the formative Exodus story add up to much beyond voices and magic, burning bushes and pillars of flame. Even in the mythical imagery, God does not precisely "do" it for them: God is the inspiration behind their own historical struggle. Thus the discovery of the "others" of history, the "people," "is made only in a revolutionary struggle that questions the existing social order in its very roots and insists on the involvement of popular power in the construction of a society of genuinely equal and free persons."[7]

When liberation theology becomes theologically implicit, however, it invokes divine power vs. the oppressive powers: God's own "option for the poor" apparently assures an ultimate victory. Thus the model of power is apocalyptic, pitting one mode of dominance against another—for the sake of hope and justice. True, its apocalypticism lacks all interest in a vindicating vengeance or an eternal damnation of the oppressors (though justice certainly entails judgment, as in the current need for "truth councils"). "It is interesting to note the absence of the apocalyptic evocation of the judgment and punishment of 'enemies' in the eschatological language of the base Christian communities" writes Jose Miguez Bonino.[8] Those at the liberation base often express the need to liberate the oppressor as well.

---

6   From a lecture at Drew University, November 1993.

7   Gustavo Gutiérrez, *The Power of the Poor in History* (Maryknoll: Orbis, 1983), 37.

8   ". . . The celebration of future freedom, the overcoming of exploitation and

What sort of divine power is at work? Liberation theology, especially in its classic early manifestations, invests in the "promise" of the God of Moses, the liberator. Jesus also came to deliver (Luke 4:16–2), and left us with a renewed eschatology: "thus all theological categories are intertwined, finding their full sense in the promise of the coming of the Reign of God and in the coming of the Son of Man... The promise of the Coming opens the historical process to its future dimension."[9] Or: "Human history is in truth nothing but the history of the slow, uncertain, and surprising fulfillment of the Promise."[10]

But if history is "nothing but" this teleological fulfillment, then how "uncertain" can it be? Is it just an uncertainty as to how, not as to whether? At the same time this sentiment voiced early by the founder of Black liberation theology seems at least more consistent: "The victory over evil is certain because God himself has taken up the cause of the oppressed, promising today what was promised to Israel while they were yet slaves in Egypt."[11]

Certainly as the decades of unmet promises roll by, liberation theologians increasingly avoid making the promise into a guarantee. "This faith-hope relation is not an escape from reality: on the contrary our hope in the final victory breaks the fatalism which is resigned to evil as our final destiny. Our hope affirms that, to be coherent, a militant attitude is necessary, an attitude that shows solidarity with the suffering, trusts in the victory over evil, and includes faith in the resurrection and in life which is indeed inseparable from faith in the creation."[12] Within the context of nearly unlivable present life, the appeal to the victorious future may sometimes be the only way to inspire a hope that in turn activates the agency of the oppressed. Yet the balancing act of liberation theology remains precarious: to affirm at once something very like a divine omnipotence ultimately in control of history, while making clear that the "way things are" does not reflect the will of God; to stimulate trust that something powerful will support their efforts, while working to liberate oppressed Christians from the paralyzing fatalisms of faith and culture. The inconsistency of the appeal to an extrinsic, patriarchal Power and the power of the people to sustain their own liberative practices creates dangerous tensions. Perhaps what

---

hunger, the victory over death and pain are celebrated in song and prayer. But there is scarcely a mention of the future of the enemy beyond their defeat." Jose Miguez Bonino, in *The Future of Liberation Theology*, eds. M. Ellis and O. Maduro (Maryknoll: Orbis, 1989), 127.

9   Gilberto Da Silva Gorgulho, "Biblical Hermeneutics" in *Mysterium Liberationis*, eds. I. Ellacuria and J. Sobrino (Maryknoll: Orbis, 1993), 129.

10   Gustavo Gutiérrez, *A Theology of Liberation* (Maryknoll: Orbis, 1973), 92.

11   James Cone, *God of the Oppressed* (New York: Seabury, 1975), 99.

12   Ofelia Ortega, *Ec. Rev.* Vol. 41 #4 10/89, 89.

Jon Sobrino calls the "praxis of the Reign of God" resolves the contradiction.[13] This eschatological—indeed, quite unabashedly apocalyptic—praxis is also "new life in the Spirit," who is the cipher of an alternative power to "the powers of the world."[14]

So far liberation theology lends more theological assistance to clarifying the power relations between human classes than between God and humanity. As to God, it helps more in articulating the commitments and the values, the "option" of God, than the character or feel of divine power. Perhaps this is as it should be. Yet even if liberation theology seeks laboriously to shift attention from ultimate redemption to present struggle, the sense of endless deferral, of failure not just of utopia but of improvement, haunts the movement—like that of the early Christians— after a couple of decades. Power language regarding God and the Reign must be faced more directly. Otherwise power—in both rhetoric and reality— remains locked up in the dualisms of domination and oppression, requiring a dubiously homogenized Subject of history—"the People", "the Workers," "the Poor," in the case of Latin America. And besides, or rather, precisely to the point, the dualism undermines too many potential solidarities—such as those with women within the oppressed group and with the indigenous peoples or peoples of diverse racial identifications. In the interval following the collapse of the communist alternative (and its fiscal support of people's movements), female and indigenous protest spiritualities may be of life-or-death significance in redefining and sustaining the struggles which liberation theology accompanies.[15] As one indigenous Salvadoran woman analyzes the situation, even the liberation theological attempt to "empower" subjects in history is misguided. "We do not need to be empowered; we need to be enabled."[16] The rhetoric of power as something God "had" and will surely "use" for the sake of "his" people

---

13   "In the last analysis, what liberation theology says is that the Reign of God is to be built in history—together with other human beings, hence the radical ecumenism of the concept of the Reign of God—and that, in the light of faith, we see ourselves to be on the road, as we accomplish this partial construction, to the definitive reign of God." —Jon Sobrino, in "Central Position of the Reign of God," *Mysterium Liberationis* (Orbis: Maryknoll, 1993), 386.

14   "Evangelization in the power of the Spirit, shown in the practice of love for neighbor, establishes the meaning of the journey of a people redeemed vis-à-vis the future." —Da Silva Gorgulho, 143.

15   Cf. the work of Latin American and African American women theologians (i.e., Ivone Gebara, Ana Maria Tepedino, Delores Williams, Katie Cannon), but also of theorists of gender, development, and third-world issues such as Vandana Shiva.

16   Marta Benevides thus refers to the developing NGO consensus around the language of "enabling environments" for developing nations and their impoverished populations.

works analogously to that of the "empowerment" by some who "have" it of those who do not.

2. Feminist theology goes a long way with the liberation hermeneutic, but finally requires a more radical transformation of the notion of power itself. Feminist theory and practice have from the outset expressed dissatisfaction with moral dualisms and therefore also with the dualism of "good-powerless-victimized women" and "patriarchal-powerful-abusive men." Such a construction of power readily foments the passion to turn the table: to grab maximum power in order to defeat the powerful at their own game. Indeed, women seem (like Christians in general) queasy at the impurity of power.[17] Partly this is our lingering victorian myth of our own higher nature. But this also emanates from a legitimate awareness that the terms of power-language are themselves corrupt. A third way, beyond both the glorification of our powerlessness and the pragmatism of our politics, has always been emerging. Let us call it the way of feminist relationalism.

Certainly no theology emerging out of any sector of the women's movement will glorify "powerlessness" as an alternative to "power." Such an opposition appears simplistic in its dualism, and dangerous in its sanction of the way of the victim. Rather than pitting revolutionary power against the unjust powers—the power of the Other clashing heroically, often onto martyrdom, against the power of the Same—it lifts up an altogether different kind of power. In theology it exposes the root of the worship of Power, analyzing all the relationships of dominance, beginning with that of the classical deity, as arranged in a hierarchy of subjugations—of women, of children, of people of color, of animals and earth. Thus the powerlessness inflicted by patriarchy upon women becomes key to the entire panoply of powers. Patriarchal power apotheosizes itself primordially in its construction of divine power. Feminist theory seeks to reconceive the function and the quality of power: distinguishing "power over" from what is variously called power to, power with, empowerment, transformative power, or erotic power.[18]

Feminist theory raises into consciousness the psychosocial matrix of relationships through which energy and influence—power—flow; and at the same time the ways in which the distortion of relationship into dominance dams up the power and turns it against relationship itself. Of course dominance is itself nothing other than a form of relationship. Power thus conceived seems to overcome the classical

---

17 As Marilyn French's massive analysis of power exemplifies.

18 Especially Rita Nakashima Brock, *Journeys by Heart: A Christology of Erotic Power* (New York: Crossroad, 1988) and Carter Heyward, *Touching Our Strength: The Erotic As Power and the Love of God*, (New York: Harper & Row, 1989).

divisions between the subject and the objects of action—it washes out any fixed boundaries, demanding rather the constant reconfiguration of subjects in relation to each other's fluid margins. Power appears as nothing more and nothing less than the dynamic of relations—liberating or abusive, nurturing or deadening, proliferating or constrictive. How does a normative distinction between dominative and decent power insert itself into this implicit feminist ontology? The high value accorded by women theorists to *mutuality* provides the basis for distinguishing between dominative and ethical relations—the ethic of "accountability," "solidarity" and "right relation."[19]

The earliest biographical—if not historical—rehearsal of human identity plays itself on the stage of gender formation. The first historical and personal training in domination takes place as the infliction of "manhood" on males: psychoanalytically and in some macrohistorical sense as well, boys traded the relational world of mother for the power of the father; girls became experts in relationship by forfeiting a claim to the public world.[20] Extraordinary exceptions seem to have remained just that, like utopian religious leaders Anne Lee of the Shakers; or Jemima Wilkinson, who after an illness in the early 19th century was reborn as "the Universal Publick Friend," formed an egalitarian community and refused all gender references for herself, including the pronoun "she." Their accomplishments have been hushed up as aberrations who prove the rule.[21] The processes of gender formation are now however evolving at an extraordinary rate globally. Yet the discursive and political history of power remains indelibly androcentric.

The image of divine power as the absolute agency in the universe, the subject to whom (for Barth at least) we are all objects, undergoes transformation accordingly. The appeal to a merely transcendent Father, Savior or Liberator as an agency outside of but intruding into human history seems to feminist theology an old case of projection—but a projection in which Feuerbach and Freud are themselves still entangled.[22] Thus theism has continued to feed on images of dominative power. The projection of dominative power onto the God of the

---

19   Perhaps first articulated with clarity by Beverly Harrison, *Making the Connections*, (Boston: Beacon, 1985); cf. more recently Ada María Isasi-Díaz's definition of "solidarity" as "the praxis of mutuality" in the "kindom of God"["Solidarity: Love of the Neighbor in the 1980's," in *Lift Every Voice*, eds. S. Thistlethwaite and M. Potter Engel (San Francisco: Harper Collins, 1990)].

20   Cf. my early attempt to read a larger swathe of patriarchal history through the limited modern analysis of Nancy Chodorow and other psychoanalytic object-relations theorists in *From A Broken Web* (Boston: Beacon, 1986).

21   Cf. Sharon Betcher, unpublished essay, Drew, 1993.

22   For they could not imagine an alternative image of divine power, and therefore in all honesty had to jettison the object of theology—while conveniently retaining the patriarchy of public power.

patriarchs legitimated their own dominative power over their subjects: women, children, servants, slaves, workers, the darker ones, and ultimately all the creatures of the earth. Feminism provides a growing series of perspectives upon the theological interrelationships of these modes of domination.

The intimate theological interlinkage of dominativity with masculinity exercises a massive historical momentum, which feminism, womanism, and other women's and profeminist voices have effectively interrupted here and there.[23]

Yet in feminist theory and theology the nature of power itself, as distinct from its functions, remains still inadequately illumined, and therefore too readily recursive to our own apocalyptic temptation: to the dualisms of gender. These, like the binaries of liberation theology, may be necessary for the initial disclosure of power abuse, but then become too readily sealed into the internal monism of the 'privileged oppressed' group (i.e., the pseudo-homogeneity of "Woman"—belying the intersecting dimensions such as race, culture, class, religious practice, etc.). Note that all dualism involves a double monism: that of the privileged Subject on the one side, the objectified Other on the other— which for feminism takes the form of our overgeneralized rhetoric of "patriarchy." Then we too are in danger of reifying our power, as some sort of essence of relationality, that is, as the possessive power of a particular unity of subjectivity, a kind of "gynergy" or "cronepower."[24] While we are struggling to formulate a relational and agential subjectivity, resort to a unitary female Subject—either as a collectivized Sisterhood or a gender genus instantiated individually—self- deconstructs more quickly than the modern individual One.[25]

For the sake of the wider sisterhood we dream of but as white feminists tend to undermine, wishful thinking and the apocalyptic habits of monistic dualism must be gently replaced. Instead let us cultivate strategic sensitivities to the ambiguous ebb and flow of power in our bodies and our souls, our social networks and our religious institutions. This sensibility is gradually providing the material criteria for a reconceptualization of power itself. Hence feminist theory will be

---

23   Male voices have also interrupted. Cf., for example, David Blumenthal's *Facing the Abusing God: A Theology of Protest* (Louisville: Westminster/John Knox Press, 1993) and Glen Mazis, *The Trickster, The Magician & The Grieving Man* (Santa Fe: Bear Press, 1993).

24   Mary Daly, *Gyn/Ecology* (Boston: Beacon, 1978)—a source of marvelous prophetic metaphor, metaphysically brimming over into a Daly-speak which loses liberating power only as it takes itself too essentially.

25   Cf. poststructuralist feminist critiques of identity politics: J. Butler, I. Young, S. Benhabib. Afro-American women's critiques of feminism's white sisterhood, however, precede and dovetail with this postmodern critique—cf. esp. bell hooks, Delores Williams.

indispensable to any theo-ethical attempt to reconstruct the subjects of power as interactive agencies rather than separate agents: agencies not of mere sisterhood but of the "kindom."[26]

3. How *is* power actually working itself out in and among us? How do we feel it, embody it, institutionalize it, recognize it, claim it, deny it, repress or suppress it, resist, release or recycle it? What *is* it? Is it, as Michel Foucault displays it, the subtle, all-pervading force of social control? For him power is not something merely concentrated in top-heavy institutions and downward-flowing hierarchies. This is his great insight. It has nudged progressive scholarship away from its dream of a just state, a centralized power of distributive goodness. Power "is never localized here or there, never in anybody's hands, never appropriated as a commodity or a piece of wealth. Power is employed and exercised through a net-like organization." He defines power fundamentally as a "relation of force." That is, rather than a static, exchangeable something, it is a function of relations and "only exists in action."[27]

Exploring the modern link between knowledge and power, Foucault has shown how especially in the last two hundred years, an epistemic imperialism has been at work—not only in the bourgeois establishments of knowledge/power, but also in the revolutionary reactions. Both imply monisms in which one dominant or resisting subject engages in the binary struggle with its "other." He tries instead to ramify resistance into multiple sites of dissent. Thus his work is highly influential upon the most recent wave of critical theory and feminist philosophy. He abjures us to "conduct an *ascending* analysis of power, starting, that is, from its infinitesimal mechanisms, which each have their own history, their own trajectory, their own techniques and tactics, and then see how these mechanisms of power have been—and continue to be—invested, colonized, utilized, involuted, transformed, displaced, extended, etc. by ever more general mechanisms and by forms of global domination."[28]

Feminists often criticize Foucault for undermining the possibilities of altering this endlessly ramified monolith of Power.[29] He does avoid identifying his analysis with any political program (which would have had as its options in his context a variety of Marxism or of anti-Marxism). Yet he illumines the way in which power—unlike force—cannot be discerned apart from the attempts to subvert it. "Where there is power, there is also a resistance, and yet, or rather consequently, this

---

26   Cf. Isasi-Díaz.

27   Foucault, *Power/Knowledge* (New York: Pantheon Books, 1980), 98; 89.

28   Ibid., 99.

29   Cf. Nancy Fraser, *Unruly Practices: Power, Discourse and Gender in Contemporary Social Theory* (Minneapolis: University of Minnesota Press, 1989).

resistance is never in a position of exteriority in relation to power."[30] But beyond this power to resist, to affirm the freedom of one's difference, what is the condition of the possibility that the internalized and encompassing Power could be *effectively* resisted? "Power appears to him as ever expanding and invading. It may even attempt to 'annex' the counter-discourses that have developed."[31] Though Foucault cannot be read consistently on this matter, his "Power" has a quasi-demonic flexibility—not unlike the Pauline "Principalities and Powers"—and so can corrupt in advance any organized resistance. But biblical powers and principalities are only conceivable from the perspective of a somehow efficacious grace. Such grace has no possible equivalent beyond mere resistance in Foucault. And resistance in itself does not lead to transformation. For this we would need to explore an alternative power.

Shunning alliance with the purported "essentialism" of "standpoint" or "identity" politics, poststructuralist theories contribute to the needed self-critique of any social movement or voice of protest. It is helping to challenge the dogmatic certainties and fixed boundaries as arbitrary and counter-productive. The danger of unconsciously recapitulating the terms of power, inscribed as they are on our bodies and souls by the subtle machinations of "carceral" society, the internalized "panopticon" by which we are socially controlled, can only be resisted by its continual deconstruction. But the stylish avoidance of "identity," indeed of any position or positivity, ultimately precludes any subject of history and so makes the conceptualization of agency, makes it difficult for postmodernism to propose another path of power, and possibly impossible to theologize one.

Certain feminist appropriations of Foucault prove especially enlivening, for they have effectively criticized his own androcentrism and raised clearly the question of the locus of this resistance. Sandra Lee Bartky, for instance, examines the notion of "modernization of patriarchal power" not just in Foucault's "docile body" but especially— and as reinforced by Foucault's gender blindness—in the creation of the "feminine" body. Examining the concrete rituals and advertisements of cosmetic culture—in diet, exercise, make up, dress and gesture—she suggests that "images of normative femininity...have replaced the religiously oriented tracts of the past."[32] The embodiment and the internalization of the regimes of female subjection now obviate any

---

30   Michel Foucault, *The History of Sexuality, Vol. 1: An Introduction*, trans. R. Hurley (New York: Vintage Books, 1990), 95.
31   Nancy Hartsock, "Foucault on Power," *Feminism/Postmodernism*, ed. Linda J. Nicholson (New York: Routledge, 1990), 167.
32   Sandra Bartky, *Femininity and Domination* (New York: Routledge, 1990), 80.

main outside oppressor. In late modernity, as we celebrate our new freedom and motility, we do "femininity" to ourselves. This parallels the deceptive modern freedom of individual "rights." (This critique also checks the feminist temptation to romanticize the revelatory body.) In the western carceral society, a broadly self-incarnating power of social control may take the place of authoritarian surveillance. Theologically we might consider how incarnation thus takes the place of incarceration in "inscribing power in our bodies." Yet incarnation also provides clues to resistance—and beyond resistance, which is never enough, to *persistence* in the face of tediously disseminated, commodified, free market abuse.

Still, in order to attend with political and spiritual care to the manifestations of power, to its abuses and its resistances, we need a better grasp of what it is—of what kind of force we are trying to address, resist and turn around. Liberationists show the distortion of relations into "class" and "race," feminism into "gender," and postmodernism into a field of microrelations in which all such constructs continually reinscribe the status quo. To get at the intimate junctures of the powers which shape us, the material loci where political, psychosocial, imaginal and spiritual power intersect, clash, confuse and recombine, it may yet be useful to engage some kind of wider description: that is, what *is* power that it so pervades our moment to moment existence? Where in it would the divine element be? Both questions have been rendered illicit by postmodern protestations of ontotheology. Still, the academic prohibition against the ontological imagination—a prohibition forging together quite unconsciously the heritage of protestant orthodoxy and common sense empiricism along with postmodern anti-orthodoxy—may obstruct the sort of vision of interrelatedness which might allow us to trace the connections and differences between our incessant experiences of power.[33]

1. It is at this point that consideration of the metaphors of divine power, rendered politically cogent by feminism, seeks a wider base. Whitehead and the tradition of process theology contributes to this discussion a helpful distinction between the divine final causation and the effective or mechanical causes which operate within the material world. I follow Whitehead in his understanding of all such metaphysical language as a series of "metaphors mutely appealing for an imaginative leap."[34] In other words, process theology which remains true to its

---

33 Feminists and postcolonial voices have effectively exposed the danger of a depoliticizing elitism at work in poststructuralist taboos. For an especially helpful inside critique of the postmodern "anti-essentialism" and its contested political implications, cf. *The Essential Difference*, eds. Naomi Schor and Elizabeth Weed (Bloomington: Indiana University Press, 1994).

34 Alfred North Whitehead, *Process and Reality*, eds. David Ray Griffin and Donald W. Sherburne (New York: MacMillan Free Press, 1978), 4.

originative spirit does not deductively describe 'the way things are' but rather imaginatively mimics what they may be like.

God in this view does not, cannot, exercise direct effective causation, as envisioned in all interventionism. God operates by influencing very subtly, when at all—offering a "lure" to the free self-realization of creatures, but not controlling the outcome.[35] Rather, by virtue of being in reciprocal relationship with the deity, we are part of God as we are part one of another. However, to participate in God means to partake in the divine vision of the possible—a source of possibilities abstract in themselves and only relevant as goads to actualization, rather than a donor of programs, plans and interventions. But Brock rightly questions even the persuasive power of the divine lure as so defined, for persuasion again implies a deity who knows best and like a caring but controlling parent or effective politician tries to get us to do the right thing. She suggests that the model of persuasion does not present a radical alternative to the controlling power of what Alice Miller terms "poisonous pedagogy." Daddy still knows best—even if this is a nice liberal daddy.[36] I would suggest that this lingering impression of divine dominance does not jibe with the radically interactive ontological dynamism of process philosophy, nor certainly with the non-literalism of the philosophical source. The system is therefore capable of self-correction on this score: the theology is no more static than its deity.

I find that the process grasp of power as the ubiquitous energy of relationship remains invaluable, as does its understanding of divine power as neither omnipotent nor impotent but different. In church-oriented contexts in which the rhetoric of a "personal God" remains the only currency in which to challenge the assumption of a controlling omnipotence, I recur continually to the language of the divine lure. The visualization of the divine in terms of "divine eros" or "appetitive wisdom" still provides one of the most honest theologies extant for imagining any sort of distinctive divine agency. In other contexts one may advocate perhaps a non-agential ground of being, for instance, or an exhaustively immanent divinity; yet these lack the normative edge, the ethical *eschatos*, of a purpose will to mutuality arising from the very heart of things.

A self-critical process theology still provides the least evasive pastoral response to the classic question of theodicy: why does God 'let' all these bad things happen? God does not. God does not 'cause' events

---

[35]   For good introductions to process theology, cf. John Cobb and David Griffin, *Process Theology: An Introductory Exposition* and Marjorie Suchocki, *God, Christ, Church* (New York: Crossroad, 1992), which works better in the classroom.

[36]   Cf. Brock, *Journeys By Heart*.

in the world to happen, good or evil. Traditional theology discerns the divine will in every tragedy, every abuse, and therefore implicitly or explicitly blames God or the victim. If God is not in control, neither God nor the victim can be blamed.[37] Responsibility is thus recirculated to human agents using their relative freedom against the background of cosmic indeterminacy. The one we call God can then symbolize the healing, limiting, redeeming valency in things—the relation of the relationships that allow life to renew itself. Freed of the onus of classic omnipotence, what we call God no longer takes the rap for history. Cast in the role of the controlling Providence of our world, God fails horribly, unless hedged around by all sorts of untestable eschatological promises. As the luring, loving Spirit of the creative process of the universe, however, the divine neither succeeds nor fails in any final sense. Win/lose is not the point. The process is open and shared.

The process ontology of relations allows us to continue to claim power, indeed shows power as the path by which relationship occurs: I become part of you, and in that way, apart from any intentions I might have to persuade or coerce you, who I am becomes a causal force in who you become at that moment. This is willy nilly completely and irreducibly reciprocal. Such a vision helps to provide a crucial conceptual basis for the ethics of mutuality, which otherwise might strike one as a piece of feminine romanticism or communitarian nostalgia. If our theo-ethical relationalism is not somehow backed by a descriptive account of the constitutive character of relations, it will not hold up well against the complementary pulls of collectivism and individualism.[38] From the relationalist perspective it is the *denial* of relationships as internal to what we are, rather than the relatedness itself, that allows relationships to be shaped into modalities of dominance, that renders us vulnerable to manipulation, that exposes us to social control and the quest for militant messiahs—i.e., to the vicious cycle of divine failure and human dominativity.

For the notion of a redemptive powerlessness has not transformed power but abdicated and abreacted it. Yet relational power is still after all a power powerless on its own—for it does not exist in isolation from its embodiment in relations. It is therefore a power, which, when true to itself, lacks the ability to stop or intervene or control. But human power tends to operate in abstraction from and denial of this surrounding haze of relations. In this view, divine power is not the same as any human

---

[37]   Cf. David Griffin, *God, Power and Evil: A Process Theodicy*, (Philadelphia: Westminster Press, 1976).

[38]   Process theology does not hold a monopoly on theological relationalism: Buber moved in the same direction, and in Christian theology both Pannenberg and Moltmann have focused relationships anthropologically and ecologically, as well as in trinitarian terms.

powers and must be distinguished theologically, precisely in its difference.

The depth of being that is God, which spews up relevant fragments of an infinite vision of the possible, refers us immediately to the mutual attunement of all beings. In some sense that very attunement can be identified as the Holy Spirit: "love itself," in one of Augustine's trinitarian analogies. Yet as an active agent of and within the mutuality, God is always at once affecting and affected (in the process theological interplay of "primordial" and "consequent" natures) in the relation to human and nonhuman worlds. Power is not unilateral but always already generated in mutuality. We mediate this Spirit to each other, and we may maximize the mutual immanence driven by this power—the power by which the gifts of the self and other are together released into realization. We have always also the option to manipulate and destroy. Does God?

III

1. Creation and annihilation have spelled out the Alpha and Omega of divine omnipotence. If God is both Creator and Destroyer, then mutuality recedes into a sentimental dream-world. Let us briefly struggle with a biblical test-case of the constructive theology so far implied. Certainly that text most obsessed with power, the extraordinarily influential *Apocalypse* of John, seems to affirm that God destroys in order to create and therefore first created in order to destroy. And that when God creates, even as the creator of the New Creation, God creates out of a nothing—therefore with an absolute, unlimited, dysrelational power. In the Book of Revelation the attributes of God and Christ are almost exclusively metaphors and evocations of power— king of king and lord of lords, sovereign judge, the messianic revealer who promises to share power with the obedient ones—ones who therefore partake in the imagery of dominance: "He who conquers and who keeps my works until the end, I will give him power over the nations, and he shall rule them with a rod of iron, as when earthen pots are broken in pieces, even as I myself have received power from my Father. . ." (Rev. 2:26f). As Foucault would lead us to suspect, divine power is here conceived as supremely concentrated in the hands of One, and therefore able to be exercised from above and shared or withheld at will. It thus mirrors the power it depicts as demonic, the power of the "Whore of Babylon" concentrated in the upper reaches of the social order.

Apocalypse paints the vision of divine power and demonic power slugging it out to the cosmic grand finale, implicating the entire creation in the binary struggle, and culminating in the urban-architectural New Jerusalem. There and then, most of what we call nature, including the ocean and the sun, finitude and ambiguity, will have been destroyed forever; and all that was evil, that was corrupt, that was not properly aligned with the ultimately triumphant Power, is if not destroyed then consigned to eternal torture, to the glory of God. This picture represents a fairly accurate projection of the clashing powers of dominance. The ultimate wish of the dominated minority represented by John is precisely to have God, as ultimate wielder of Power-Over, not just fight on their own side but utterly and violently smash the persecutors, to lend those who have been victims the power and riches of kings for a "millennium," and finally to free them from all mortal limits for habitation in the new heaven and earth.

Early in John's ecstatic vision, a heavenly voice announces the one worthy to open the scrolls of the fate of the world: "Behold, the Lion of Judah" [5:5] But what was announced orally is belied visually: the one who appears is a Lamb. This bizarre vision-lamb—"having seven horns and seven eyes, which are the seven Spirits of God" bears the pre-Christian symbolism of sacrifice, "as having been slain." It may be as D. H. Lawrence has it, a case of "a lion in lamb's clothing." The Christian religion of love, he suggests, here shows its true hand—or rather it gives way to the raw will to power.[39] Yet one might also argue that the inconsistency reveals a struggle between the temptation to return to the standard, dominative Power and the visionary renunciation of theocratic fantasy. For the sacrificed lamb can suggest the willingness of the divine to go down with us into our worst suffering (not therefore to *will* it).[40]

I suspect both are true. The vision recurs to an image of radical vulnerability, of a tormented death somehow and strangely redeemed in the realm of pure possibility—of the "heaven" of the apocalyptic seer.[41] Yet this is the very image which has been since so heavily laden with the culture of the powerless victim, an image which readily constellates its own dominative opposite. Hence the voice-over expresses a dangerous new will to power among those Christians badly frustrated by their sense of disappointed powerlessness. The voice summons out of heaven a new breed of macho messiahs. The voice overpowers the vision.

---

[39]   D.H. Lawrence, *Apocalypse* (New York: Viking, 1982).

[40]   By contrast, Ron Farmer, developing a process hermeneutic, suggests that the vision mode very significantly had preceded the oral interpretation: he reads a "basal lure"—the Whiteheadian divine vision—into a non-deterministic vision of suffering, redemptive love (unpublished manuscript).

[41]   Cf. Michael Welker, *Die Universalität Gottes und Die Relativität der Welt*, (Neukirchener-Vluyn: Neukirchener Verlag, 1981).

I contend elsewhere that the Book of Revelation carries a unique charge in western history.[42] It is a text of power: both *about* power and itself *exercising* power. Indeed Foucault's use of Nietzsche's *wirkliche Geshichte*—though misleadingly intended as an anti-teleological/anti-apocalyptic and at the same time anti-historicist argument—helps to illumine the inconstant but effective inscriptions of power communicated by the Book of Revelation.[43] John of Patmos has articulated not only the frustrated will to power of the repressed and the oppressed, in Lawrence's Nietzsche-like reading. Theologically, John deals with the failure of Christ's resurrection to bring on the messianic kingdom. He has also expressed just aspirations to a radically new economic and political order. He has envisioned a massive power of world destruction, to be sure; but the text itself does not in any simplistic sense identify the content of the seals with God's will, nor can a literalist end of the world be derived from the mythopoeic visions and voices of the text. Certainly for John of Patmos, as for many Jews and early Christians, the distinction between the inevitable consequences of human history and the will of God remains subtle.

Yet the lethal implications of the expectation of a final overpowering of the planet only become possible after Constantine—and their literalization only as the work of high modernity. That is, only after the power of Christendom moves to fill the aching void expressed in John's vision—the void of the failure of the God of power and might—do the horrors of the self-realizing prophecy really get moving. The crusades, the conquest of the Americas, the arrogance of modern progress—all will empower themselves through the apocalypse myth of power. Yet the resistance to dominative power will also emanate from the same apocalyptic-millennialist myth, differently interpreted.[44] Where there is power, there is resistance. Or let us say, the power to resist. And, as John continually admonishes his beleaguered community, to persist.

2. Still, political revolutions have tended, along with the God of the Apocalypse, to fail. Yet much occurs in and around them that does not, that breathes another power. These alternative moments in-spire themselves as much through other sources, constituting what I have termed a "counterapocalypse" to express a vision neither apocalyptic nor anti-apocalyptic. The counter-apocalyptic trajectory exemplified,

---

42   Cf. *Apocalypse Now and Then: A Feminist Guide To the End of the World* (Boston: Beacon Press, 1996).

43   Cf. *The Foucault Reader*, ed. Paul Rabinow (NY: Pantheon Books, 1984), 76ff.

44   E. Bloch, N. Cohn, C. Hill and others have traced major western revolutionary movements to the renewal of the apocalyptic imagination in the early medieval period.

for instance, by Jesus' parables have not inscribed themselves in our history, our bodies, our relations and our discursive practices with anything like the power of the Apocalypse [45]

Both apocalyptic and counterapocalyptic elements appear in the first three of the four theoretical perspectives mentioned above—liberationist, feminist, and even, against its own will, postmodern, binary oppositions of their own deconstructive dis/closures of the prior worlds vie with their own more processive-relational tendencies. But this is why they are more socially radical perspectives than process, which is non-apocalyptic as to beginnings, endings and the exercise of power, but nonetheless disclosive.

Now, ironically, the apocalyptic hermeneutic has made itself indispensable—if only because the biblical apocalypse has been so effectively distorted into religious and secular literalization that our global situation is, all too literally on many fronts, apocalyptic. Forgive the oracular density of that claim. I do not thereby blame Christianity itself for the unprecedented and perhaps unsurvivable level of genocide and ecocide its accompanying culture has unleashed. But it has at minimum created a perilous anticipation of global destruction and therefore a tolerance and perhaps even an eagerness. I wish in this context only to call theologians to responsibility for the apocalypse habit: a prophecy of doom which has proved paradoxically both self-fulfilling and self-transforming. For one finds in the emergence of millennialist utopian movements also a resistance to the inevitability of doom, an empowering resistance that is dialectically also *internal* to the self-fulfillment of the text in history.

3. I have suggested that the metaphor of divine power as relational power is a more helpful, if less dramatic, alternative than that of the divine powerlessness—itself a radical and innovative idea, of which the crucifixion has been the primary symbol. Articulating this death as the powerlessness of a suffering God has definitively challenged the age-old assumption of Omnipotence. Moltmann's christocentric patripassionism (by any other name. . .) has opened up a 'crucial' space for reconceiving divine power as empty of controlling omnipotence. Yet traditional glorification of the *theologia crucis* (of which his recent work is hardly guilty[46]) may too readily encourage self-sacrifice, martyrdom and victimization on the part of those already marginalized.

In the forcefield of self-revealing relations, the Roman instrument of execution symbolizes the dominative powers over which Jesus did *not*

---

45   Cf. John Dominic Crossan's *The Historical Jesus* for an account of Jesus' divergence from the Baptist's apocalypticism (New York: Harper, 1991), 227ff.
46   Cf. Jürgen Moltmann, *The Way of Jesus Christ.*

triumph. But neither can he be said to have failed.[47] The disclosure of divine immersion in human suffering, and thus of the *possibility* that the powers of injustice could be ultimately overcome, suggests neither divine powerlessness nor divine all-power. It hints rather at the slow and halting process of awakening to the alternative power evoked by the parables and the Sermon on the Mount: the transformation of our vulnerable relatedness into an unbounded field of mutuality—the "commonwealth of God." This is the power of a love-centered justice. Perhaps the evanescent, heterogeneous vision-experiences we call "resurrection" have been reduced to a bizarre proof of Omnipotence in the eyes of classical theism. But the resurrection accounts suggest something more subtle, something more like an indomitable spirit unleashed by the love-ethos: if a body is crushed for its fidelity to the struggle for love, the spirit it embodied will return to in-spire new bodies, new con-spiracies of loving life.

4. Systematically speaking, we might well outgrow the apocalyptic deadlock of a triune theology of omnipotence, impotence and their dispiriting co-dependency. To what? Perhaps to a counter-apocalyptic dynamic of potentiality, incarnation and eros? Indeed, perhaps even to omnipotentiality, omnicarnation and omnirelationality? It is then proper, as even Augustine recognized, that both the first and second persons partake of the third; only the third—as Spirit, or Love—is biblically identified with God *tout court*. Despite such efforts as the *filioque* clause to inhibit the free circulation of the spirit in nature and history, pneumatology whispers an intuition into the subtler powers of the universe.[48]

Relationality gives potentiality the life with which it seeks experimentally, wildly, nondirectively, to actualize itself within the spontaneous relations of all creatures with each other and with the spirit. Spirit, like relationship, is not necessarily "holy." Yet relatedness itself, like spirit, is not therefore an empty concept. No more, that is, than "cosmos" or "being" have been at other times—and as early Christianity declared "world" itself, or "being" itself, intrinsically good—despite its profound implication in "sin"—so we may declare relationship *ontologically* but not yet *ethically* good. Without this distinction the anthropocentric morality which limits relationships to humans and human-like beings dominates. The ecological relatedness of which the fabric of life spins itself was good before people were around to declare it such, or to destroy it. And only within this larger ecological

---

47   Though perhaps Albert Nolan's claim that the Jesus movement, as an attempt to circumvent the apocalyptic forces of imperial oppression, did fail—did not attract enough people to itself to prevent it becoming a tool in the hands of that very empire. Cf. *Jesus Before Christianity* (Maryknoll, NY: Maryknoll/Orbis Books, 1976/92).

48   Jürgen Moltmann, *The Spirit of Life* (New York: Harper, 1993).

realm of relations does the eschatological prefiguration of the realm of God—the "kindom of God"—become possible today.

At the same time, *right* relation is only possible to humans inasmuch as it fulfills the criterion of *mutuality*.[49] But right relation is predicated upon attention to relationship—i.e., the awareness of the subject of its own profound inextricability from its matrix and thus its endless debt. The debt can finally only be paid with the grace which perpetually heals the wounds of dysrelation and renews our potentialities—hence our potencies. But then these relational powers are continually released, transformed by our intersubjective agency, into the solidarity of shared potencies.

The power of mutuality is not likely to win. Mass crucifixions continue, as the martyrology of the theologies of the two-thirds world illumine. On the other hand, what if increasingly organized and growing masses of designated "losers"—and of those with the option to "win" who seek to release power to the service of those who do not— *recognize* the bankruptcy of the win-lose paradigm? Perhaps this is happening. Cynicism does not appear as the only option. The love of justice and the justice of love have not been and will not be defeated. They do have a chance to realize themselves socially—not absolutely, not permanently, not triumphantly, but with the dauntless vulnerability of the Spirit of life. The lines of dominative power only realize the good when they meet in their endlessly deferred *eschaton;* the lines of relational power, more like fibers in a web than railroad tracks to the horizon, intersect and energize communities of support and struggle already. This latter strategy does not await a Messiah astride His white horse, leading hoardes of final angels. But it will nurture the delicate and nonetheless messianic power of awakened relations.

---

[49] Cf. Carter Heyward's classic definition in *Touching Our Strength: The Erotic as Power and the Love of God* (San Francisco: Harper & Row, 1989).

5

Someone to Blame, Someone to Trust
Divine Power and the Self-Recovery of the Oppressed

Cynthia L. Rigby

⌘

My God, my God, why have you forsaken me?
Why are you so far from helping me, from the words of my groaning?

O my God, I cry by day, but you do not answer;
and by night, but find no rest.

Yet you are holy, enthroned on the praises of Israel.
In you our ancestors trusted;
they trusted, and you delivered them.
To you they cried, and were saved;
in you they trusted, and were not put to shame
—Psalm 22:1–5[1]

Bill and I exchanged looks of dismay as the young Caucasian man who called himself "a traveling evangelist for the Lord" told story after story about how God had intervened in his life and declared that he was to go and proclaim Truth to others. Our Filipino friends measured their expressions of respect as he proceeded to tell them what was right and what was wrong, and how they could be sure that God would be on their side: chastity, patience, tearful strugglings over sinfulness . . .

---

1   All biblical citations are taken from the NRSV, unless otherwise indicated.

79

resistance to low wages and government interventions was not on the list.

One of our favorite tasks was to visit the "Under the Bridge Community," a group of sixty or so families who "squatted" on land they did not own. The children's favorite songs were "Peace Like a River" and "Father Abraham Had Seven Sons" because they loved the hand motions and body movements that went along with them. The women sat in their *sari sari* windows, selling sticks of gum and solitary cigarettes, amused at the spectacle of a white couple hopping around with the children. Later, Juli told us about his latest business prospects. He had been up since dawn, trying to get a job driving a motorella[2], and was now thinking that he would buy and sell used jewelry, if he could find enough capital to get started. "Hey, Bill and Cindy," he said in his joking, serious voice, "do you think God will let me improve myself this time?"

In the lobby of the national office of the United Church of Christ in the Philippines we read through the banner displaying the names of the sixty-six church members who had been gunned down so far that year, some by the military and others by the New People's Army. God did not want this to happen, a friend told us, a gleam of anger and determination in his eye. God wants us to teach the oppressed that God is on their side so that they will be empowered to resist.

Statement of the Problem & Approach[3]

Belief in a transcendent God—a God who is distinct from human beings and in some sense has the power to influence human circumstances—sometimes impedes human agency and sometimes compels human beings to act. Why can such a belief have such opposing effects? When does belief in a transcendent, powerful God render human beings relatively powerless, and when does such belief affirm and intensify the power of human agents?

Feminist theologians are rightly alarmed by unbalanced emphasis on divine transcendence in traditional dogmatic conceptualities, pointing out that such beliefs are often associated with fostering human powerlessness and "faintheartedness."[4] And yet to insist that transcendent beliefs must be eliminated if human power is to avoid being

---

2   A motorcycle outfitted with side-seats for passengers.

3   I credit William Greenway, with whom I have discussed this subject over a period of years, for initially articulating the problem in terms of the relationship between *belief in a transcendent God* and *human agency*.

4   Cf. Rita Nakashima Brock's *Journeys By Heart: A Christology of Erotic Power* (New York: Crossroad, 1991).

jeopardized is not to take into account those cases in which belief in a transcendent God and the flourishing of human power go hand-in-hand. Oppressed people,[5] in order to continue in their daily struggle, often rely on a God whom they relate to as a distinct subject who has the power to liberate. And these beliefs can be affirming of their integrity as subjects, of their agency in relation to the events of their lives.

In this essay I will explore one possibility for how belief in a transcendent God functions in a way that is empowering for such people. I will argue that oppressed individuals are often enabled to resist oppression and to live more humanly when they feel free to blame[6] and to trust[7] a God who they distinguish from themselves,[8] a God who they believe has the power to liberate. I will attempt to show that belief in a transcendent God is not necessarily inhibitive of human agency, that there are times when it actually propels individual actions and communal movements for social justice because it enables human beings to "remember" their subjectivity in relation to their life-events. In the terms of "power, powerlessness, and the divine," I will argue that while belief in divine power *can* foster human powerlessness, there are times when such belief actually promotes the realization of human power.

After offering a more detailed description of the problem at hand, I will draw from theological literature and a biblical text in order to paint a picture of how oppressed persons tend to view God and God's involvement or lack of involvement in human history. Following Delores Williams,[9] I will note that belief in a transcendent God is evident in seemingly contradictory statements that often emerge out of oppressive experiences: (1) First, it is presupposed in the declaration

---

5   The reader should note that I am attempting to explore an observation I have made about the religious experience of "the oppressed" in general. I recognize that such generalizations can be risky; the religious experience of all oppressed people is certainly not alike. And yet I do want to consider what seems to be a central element of religious experience as it is reflected in the lament Psalms of the Bible, in squatters' communities in the Philippines, among African American communities in New York City, and in the families of those who have suffered chronic economic hardship in the churches where I have worked: they cry out to God for abandoning them and they trust that God ultimately will help.

6   I am understanding "blame" to mean "to find fault with; to put the responsibility on" (*Webster's*); to complain, accuse (*American Heritage English Dictionary*).

7   I am understanding "trust" to mean "belief in the... justice of another person or thing" (*Webster's*); to rely on, place hope in (*American Heritage English Dictionary*).

8   This is primarily what I have in mind when speaking about "transcendence." The emphasis is not on God's distance from the world, but on God being *other than* the world.

9   Cf. Delores Williams, *Sisters In The Wilderness* (Maryknoll: Orbis, 1993), 21.

that "God does not liberate," a declaration that might take the form of blaming God for not exercising God's power to liberate; and (2) Second, it is seen in the proclamation that "God liberates," a proclamation which reflects a level of trust that God can still act powerfully in relation to the oppressive situation. The power exercised by those who are identified as the powerless when they candidly declare that "God liberates" or that "God does not liberate" is especially evident in Psalm 22, as I will show.[10]

In part two I will discuss the concept of "dangerous memory" as it is understood by J.B. Metz and Sharon Welch, arguing that "remembering" is fundamental to the working of human agency. While belief in One who is transcendent and powerful often functions to thwart the work of memory, I will attempt to show that there are ways in which belief in a transcendent God can support the work of memory, empowering people to recognize their selfhood in relation to the events of their lives. I will demonstrate, through considering Psalm 22, how the belief that "God is a liberator" works in conjunction with memory. I will argue that the psalmist's *blaming* and *trusting* of the liberator-God actually enables him (or her[11]) to understand himself as a subject in relation to his (and the community's) experience of oppression and empowers him to act in ways that resist oppression and promote liberation. Because belief in God as a distinct subject allows the psalmist to "remember" where he stands in relation to the events of his life, his understanding of how God liberates is actually transformed.

Finally, I will conclude in part three by setting criteria for self-recovery derived from the discussion of dangerous memory in dialogue with insights gleaned from examination of Psalm 22 in order to make the case that belief in a transcendent God can foster the self-recovery of the oppressed.

---

[10]   This essay is not concerned with making a case for God's guilt or innocence in relation to oppressive realities, but rather with the nature/breadth of the response to these circumstances by oppressed people of faith in their particular *Sitze im Leben*.

[11]   Because Psalm 22 is traditionally ascribed to David, I will use the male pronoun in referring to the speaker. This is not to imply that these words would be any less likely to be uttered by a woman. It is in fact that case that women from oppressed contexts might be more likely to resonate with the words of the psalmist precisely because they have been, traditionally, the "oppressed of the oppressed" (cf. Williams, chapter 1). There is some evidence in the Midrash on the Psalms that the words we find in Psalm 22 were actually spoken by Esther during the three days that she fasted for her people [cf. John H.P. Reumann, "Psalm 22 at the Cross: Lament and Thanksgiving for Jesus Christ," (January 1974): 56], so associating these words with the experience of women is not without precedent.

I. Divine Power: Disempowering or Empowering?

> *Many bulls encircle me,*
> *strong bulls of Bashan surround me;*
> *they open wide their mouths at me,*
> *like a ravening and roaring lion.*

> *I am poured out like water,*
> *and all my bones are out of joint;*
> *my heart is like wax; it is melted within my breast;*
> *my mouth is dried up like a potsherd,*
> *and my tongue sticks to my jaws:*
> *you lay me in the dust of death.* — Psalm 22:12–15

Many feminist theologians argue that traditional notions of transcendence must be rejected if we intend to work whole-heartedly toward the transformation or replacement of oppressive power systems. Notions of a divinity who exists outside of our experience and has the power to alter our circumstances only distract us from the task at hand: namely, doing the work of social liberation. Waiting on God to do the work for us "someday... if we just remain patient" is the theme song of the oppressor, who does not want to deal with the discomfort inherent to movements of resistance and solidarity.[12] We will be able to live joyfully only when we rid ourselves even of the "vestiges... [of] divine transcendence,"[13] only when our power is derived from communal memory rather than from a paternalistic promise that preserves the present crisis, Sharon Welch convincingly argues.

Welch, among others, implies that belief in a transcendent God who has the power to intervene in human circumstances can be problematic for the oppressed (1) because it can relegate the possibility for change to the hands of God, leading a person to "give up" working for liberation, and (2) because it can prevent the oppressed person from being open to "the work of dangerous memory" and ultimately from recognizing herself as a subject in relation to the events of her life. These two problems are closely related, for it is the recognition of one's subjectivity that empowers one to persevere as an agent.

Oppressed persons and communities very often "give up" when they are pressured by those in positions of power to believe in a God of two worlds: this one and the next. This world is the less important one,

---

12   While oppressors are primarily interested in avoiding discomfort *to themselves*, it has been my experience that there are many "kind" oppressors who sincerely cringe at the thought that others (e.g., their own daughters or wives) might be repressing a great deal of pain.

13   Sharon D. Welch, *A Feminist Ethic of Risk* (Minneapolis: Fortress, 1990), 111.

the one in which they are tested for patience, and endurance, and cooperative capacities. The next world is the one in which they will no longer be hungry, or unequal, or shot down by the military in the middle of the night. One of the more blatant manifestations of this troubling theology is the strong implication that liberation of the body might need to be forgone in favor of redemption of the soul.[14]

In addition to fostering passivity among the oppressed, belief in a transcendent God often serves as an "escape" for those who benefit from the power structures themselves, so that they never feel challenged to resist these structures. Those who function as oppressors in society are already apt to rationalize their participation in the status quo by arguing, logically enough, that they are not directly responsible for the circumstances of the oppressed and that it would be impossible, anyway, to eliminate such conditions entirely. Transcendent conceptualities can function to ease the suspicion that such attitudes should be scrutinized by suggesting that, somehow, God will work things out in the end, i.e., in the second of the two worlds. Such a framework for understanding the relationship between God and human history has shunned the question marks of worldly existence, choking off any honest grapplings with the relation of God to human history that attempt to penetrate its boundaries.

If transcendent beliefs always influenced the oppressed and the oppressor in ways that stifled human agency, it would be reasonable for those whose fundamental concern is human liberation to view them as inherently oppressive and therefore unacceptable. The experience of the oppressed, however, often speaks otherwise. With this in mind, I turn to two contemporary examples of people who are empowered by belief in a transcendent God to continue struggling for liberation. The first is the community of African American women; the second is a woman from the Philippines.

The Liberator Who Doesn't Always Liberate

In the experience of many African American women, Delores Williams notes, God has the power to liberate human beings but does not always exercise this power.[15] While God assisted Hagar in enabling her to *survive*, Williams points out, survival is not equivalent to liberation. God did not rescue Hagar from being abused in the home of

---

14   To illustrate this phenomenon: When my husband and I were living in Mindanao in 1989, we were asked by a wealthy Filipino businessman—a man who was heavily influenced by American missionaries—to lead a weekly Bible study for the employees of a department store he owned. The requested topic: "Why God Doesn't Want You To Join A Union"!

15   Williams, 148.

Sarah or from the abuse of being expelled from the household and sent into the desert. Rather, God comforted Hagar within the context of these abusive situations.

From the perspective of the lived experience of the African American woman, God liberates the oppressor (the Hebrew) and does not liberate the oppressed (the non-Hebrew), according to Williams.[16] Further, Williams observes that, even when "God liberates" the *oppressed*, "God does not (always) liberate" the *oppressed of the oppressed* (176).[17] And yet the experience of those whom God has not liberated is not simply that God has abandoned them. Despite their complaint that God has failed to liberate, Williams explains, "the design and character of the means of the struggle are governed by black women's communication with God through prayer, by their faith in God's presence with them in the struggle, by their absolute dependence upon God to support resistance and provide sustenance."[18] Black women still trust and rely upon that God who has failed to liberate, and it is precisely their interaction with God as a subject, in the context of the divine/human relationship, that empowers them to resist oppression. Williams is so insistent on the importance of this point that she ends her book by reminding us that, though

> The greatest truth of black women's survival and quality-of-life struggle is that they have worked without hesitation and with all the energy they could muster... in the final analysis the message is clear: they trusted the end to God.[19]

---

16 Williams, 148.

17 Williams, 176. Williams points out that, although theologians such as James Cone are correct in describing God as "a God of liberation, who speaks to the oppressed and abused and assures them. . . divine righteousness will vindicate their suffering. . ." this is not the whole story (144). Men and women—the oppressed of the oppressed—are also *not* liberated. Williams implies that this fact is more likely to be noticed by black women than by black men because women, by virtue of their sex, *are* the oppressed of an already-oppressed race.

The idea that women read the biblical account differently in this way from men, and even from male liberation theologians, is central to feminist hermeneutics. Along these lines, Schüssler Fiorenza explains that "liberation theologians emphasize that the God of the Bible is on the side of the oppressed and impoverished. . . (while) feminist theologians do not find an explicit feminist-critical principle in the Bible" [*Bread Not Stone: The Challenge of Feminist Biblical Interpretation* (Boston: Beacon Press, 1984), xxi]. Womanist and feminist theologians, then, might be particularly apt to describe the religious experience of the oppressed in terms of the tension between "God liberates" and "God does not liberate."

18 Williams, 176.

19 Williams, 238–239.

In this essay I am interested in the phenomenon, clearly evident in the work of Williams and others, that those whom God does not liberate seem better equipped to act in relation to their life-experiences when there is not a gap between the way they experience life and the way they talk about God. Those who have a conceptuality in which they feel free to blame and to trust in the God in whom they believe seem to be able to muster the energy to survive, unlike those who are pressured to accept and to wait and to not use any of their own critical or interpretive powers. Hagar could choose whether to blame or to trust God, whether God was a "God who sees" or a God who had abandoned her. Because she was able to assess the quality of the events of her life in relation to this subject-God, she was able to know herself in relation to these events, and in this knowledge gained strength to continue the struggle for survival.

The Filipina woman who prays and has faith and credits God for continued existence seems to believe that God has the power to do something to preserve and even to improve her life. When she says, "God liberates," she reflects an understanding of the divine/human relationship that allows for God's involvement in human history. As the writer of Psalm 22 looks back into history and identifies God's action on behalf of his ancestors, so this woman has seen that God *can* liberate. For example, she might explain that, in the Edsa Revolution of 1986, God liberated the Filipino people from the tyranny of Ferdinand Marcos. Or she might understand the volcanic eruptions near Subic Bay, which contributed to the closing of the U.S. military bases in 1992, as "acts of God" in which it is particularly evident that "God liberates."

This woman might at other times say that "God does not liberate." Perhaps she feels pressure to work as a "hospitality girl" (a prostitute) in order to feed her children or watches her son get gunned down in the middle of the night or sees the lists of mail-order brides that are distributed to the male American and European tourists. In saying that "God does not liberate" in reference to her situation as a Filipina, the woman has not changed in her understanding of the relationship between God and the world. God is a liberator, but God has not liberated. The Filipina woman might cry out with the psalmist, "Why have you forgotten me?" At the same time, she would likely remind herself to trust in God, who she believes still has the power to liberate her from the oppression of the enemy. And through it all, there would be a tone in her voice that was very matter-of-fact, because she is describing the way her life is. God does not liberate, but God liberates. We do not have rice, but we hope to have a feast day soon, as we did before. And she would keep on working as she explained what her life was like.

Now that we have noted these instances in which the agency of oppressed persons is fostered rather than inhibited by belief in a transcendent God, it is imperative that we look more deeply at exactly what understanding of God and God's transcendence is operative.

The Immanent Transcendence of the Liberator

To freely describe one's circumstances in the terms "God liberates" and "God does not liberate" is to reflect particular understandings of who God is and how God relates to the world. When someone blames God for not helping or cries out to God for help, she or he is revealing a conceptuality that encompasses some notion of divine transcendence as well as divine immanence. Such a person might conceive of God not only as present in and through the situation in such a way that she or he is able to survive. God is also understood to exist outside of the oppressive experience itself—as someone who is present with us but not confined by the painful circumstances; as a distinct entity who has the power to affect change and to empower the powerless; as an overseer of justice in relation to whom an oppressed person can recognize her or his victimization.

Such a conception of the God/human relationship is evident, for example, in the writings of Aracely de Rocchietti, a Methodist pastor in Uruguay. In her article, "Women and the People of God," de Rocchietti discusses the situation of the "Church in Latin America" in terms of the tension between "two dimensions . . . wretchedness and hope."[20] In describing the religious life of her people, de Rocchietti notes that injustice is an historical and ever-present reality (thus, wretchedness ensues). At the same time, however, justice is understood to be "an historical constant" (so hope is still operative). Further, central to de Rocchietti's understanding is the conviction that God is both transcendent and powerful, offering us the "certainty of future salvation."[21]

A counter-example may help to clarify the type of belief in transcendence that I am trying to make a case for in this essay. When I refer to an oppressed person's belief in a transcendent God, I have in mind an understanding that is not descriptive, for example, of that of Alida Verhoeven, whose essay "The Concept of God: A Feminine

---

20 Aracely de Rocchietti, "Women and the People of God," *Through Her Eyes: Women's Theology from Latin America,* ed. Elsa Tamez (Maryknoll: Orbis, 1989), 97. While there is not a direct parallel between de Rocchietti's "wretchedness"/"hope" polarity and the polarity "God does not liberate"/"God liberates," both reflect the tension that exists between ongoing oppression and liberation from oppression in everyday life experience.

21 de Rocchietti, 101.

Perspective" is found in the same volume as the de Rocchietti essay.[22] Verhoeven, a native of Holland who is a Methodist minister in Argentina, holds that "the Presence of Creative-Recreative Spiritual Force, the source of Life and Love, is like an ongoing movement, an ebb and flow that moves in growing waves that wash over everything."[23] This is a beautiful image of the divine immanence, but is not sufficient in and of itself to describe the God of Hagar, the Filipina woman, or the psalmist. Such a God cannot be blamed or trusted in such a way that oppressed individuals and communities can recognize themselves as subjects in relationship to this God and subsequently in relation to the circumstances of their lives.[24]

I am focusing, rather, on conceptualities which make a clearer distinction between God and the world than Verhoeven makes; a transcendence that is *more than,* e.g., Carter Heyward's understanding that God is the *"transcending . . .* 'power of mutual relation'"[25] or Nancy Frankenberry's description of the "something more" that we experience in our living.[26] With Kathryn Tanner, I am considering the strength of models that avoid "psychological identification with God,"[27] arguing that "understanding oneself as a creature. . . [fosters] the sense of oneself as possessing a value independent of a demeaning social status"[28] which can empower one to recognize one's agency and participate in acts of resistance.

This view of transcendence, however, does not come at the expense of an appreciation of the divine immanence. Fundamental to

---

22   Interestingly, all but one of the contributors to *Through Her Eyes* are working with conceptualities that maintain a strong view of transcendence. The one exception—Verhoeven—also happens to be a native of a European country rather than a native of the third world. This points toward the possibility that belief in a transcendent God might tend to be empowering in the context of e.g. impoverished communities in the third world and disempowering (because it serves as an "escape" for the more wealthy) in the context of economically advanced nations.

23   Alda Verhoeven, "The Concept of God: A Feminine Perspective," in *Through Her Eyes,* 54–55.

24   This is not to suggest that one can recognize that one is a subject in relation to the oppressive events of one's life only if one believes in a transcendent God, but that belief in a transcendent God can serve, rather than detract from, the work of self-recovery.

25   Carter Heyward, "Crossing Over: On Transcendence," *Our Passion For Justice* (New York: The Pilgrim Press, 1984), 243-247.

26   Cf. Nancy Frankenberry, *Religion and Radical Empiricism,* (New York: SUNY, 1987).

27   Kathryn Tanner, *The Politics of God: Christian Theologies and Social Justice* (Minneapolis: Fortress Press, 1992), 234.

28   Tanner, 230.

the freedom that the African American woman and the Filipina woman and the psalmist experience is the conviction that God is near, that God is accessible enough to be spoken with about the realities of human living. To overemphasize the "distance" between God and the world would be to preclude blaming God as a possibility and to foster a "trust" in God grounded more in fear than in authentic recognition of God's presence in human history.[29] Such understandings depict God not only as power-full or influential, but as having all the power, as virtually unconditioned by the world, and as therefore beyond human challenge or human decision. This is a God whose immanence, when it is noticed, is seen as a great, self-sacrificing favor because it is known that this is not what God is *really* all about. This is the God of patriarchy, the God who knows best, the God we cannot *choose* to trust but cannot dare to blame as we patiently endure our sufferings. This is the kind of transcendent conceptuality that squelches human agency, that inhibits the work of social justice.

I have offered contemporary examples of when belief in a transcendent God promotes human agency, and I have clarified what is meant by "transcendence" in such a conceptuality. I turn now to a biblical example of this phenomenon in which the statements "God liberates" and "God does not liberate" take the shape of trusting and blaming God.

Living In the Tension: The Psalmist

Religious experience marked by the tension between the belief that God is a liberator and the oppressive realities of worldly existence is powerfully portrayed in many of the lament psalms (e.g.: 13, 35, 38, 42, 44, 90), particularly by the writer of Psalm 22. Psalm 22 is comprised of two major sections, with verses 1–21a characterized primarily by the complaints of the innocent sufferer ("God does not liberate") and with 21b–31[30] devoted to praise for God's apparent intervention in the sufferer's life ("God liberates").

While the complaint section is composed primarily of observations that God has not liberated, integral to the development of the psalmist's argument are recollections of God's liberative acts and reliance on God's continued power to liberate. Reumann notes, in fact, that this

---

29 Karl Barth, for example, is often considered by feminist theologians to overemphasize such distance. While it is clear that he argues that the transcendence of God must be understood prior to consideration of the divine immanence (cf. *CD* II/1 §28.3), he also has a strong view of the divine immanence, arguing that God is also "conditioned by the world" (cf. *CD* II/1, 303).

30 I will discuss the second section of the Psalm more fully in part III of this essay.

section is made up of three laments (vv. 1–2, 6–8, 12–18) interspersed with "assertions of trust and confidence" and petitions.[31]

The nature of the sufferer's complaints in verses 1–21a clearly reveals that he conceives of God as having the power to liberate, while he conceives of himself as relatively powerless. The psalmist describes himself as dehumanized, scorned, despised, mocked (v. 6)[32], threatened (v. 13), and prey to various physical afflictions (vv. 14–15). He believes God has the power to answer his cries, to deliver him from trouble, and to vindicate him in the eyes of the people. But up to verse 21a, the psalmist has not experienced a divine response. The psalmist blames God for not exercising God's power to liberate on his behalf. "Why have you forsaken me?," he asks. Why have you not helped? Why have you not answered my cries? "*You* lay me in the dust of death," he accuses his God (v. 15, my emphasis).

In addition to the evidence in the complaints themselves, the psalmist's reflections between complaints reveal that he understands God to be a liberator even as he blames God for not liberating. Though you have not answered my cries by night or by day, he prays to God, "yet you are holy" (v. 3). Though you have not honored *my* pleas, he implies, "In you our ancestors trusted. . . and you delivered them" (v. 4, my emphasis). And even though you are not responding to my needs at this particular point in my life, "Yet it was you who took me from the womb" (v. 9). Even as he is blaming God, it is apparent that it is still in God that the sufferer places his hope for deliverance. Even though God has not liberated God has the power to liberate.

In verse 21 a drastic shift occurs. While up to this point the primary emphasis of the psalmist has been that God does not liberate (even though God *can* liberate), the emphasis is now on the fact that "God liberates." Something has happened, in the middle of verse 21, that has moved the psalmist from a posture of complaining to a posture of praise. His understanding of God's involvement in his life has changed. Further, while the complaining psalmist understood himself to be powerless in relation to the silent God, the praising psalmist understands himself to have powers of speech, material resources, and prophesy. While some might argue that the psalmist is empowered precisely because God has answered the psalmist's prayers and intervened by altering his circumstances, I will argue that his blaming, praising, and petitioning lead him into a new understanding of faith which affirms human power as well as the power of God.

---

[31]　　John H. P. Reumann, "Psalm 22 at the Cross: Lament and Thanksgiving for Jesus Christ," *Interpretation* 28 (January 1974): 44.

[32]　　Note that, while the people mock the psalmist for his convictions in verses 7–8, they do not blame God for not liberating. They, in contrast to the psalmist, do not hold the conviction that "God is a liberator."

I will return to the question of this shift shortly, but it will be helpful, first, to discuss the empowering process itself. How is it that a person who understands herself as powerless can come to realize that she or he is power-full? Memory must do its liberating work, as we will see below.

II. Self-Recovery and Belief in a Transcendent God

> *On you I was cast from my birth,*
> *and since my mother bore me you have been my God.*
> *—Psalm 22:10*

In this section I will draw upon the work of Sharon Welch and Johann Baptist Metz to introduce the concept of "dangerous memory" and to explain how it enables victims of oppression to survive and to continue to work for liberation. I will explain how "dangerous memory" compels those who are oppressed to understand themselves as subjects in relationship to the events of their lives, and how this self-discovery empowers human beings to act in relation to the events of their lives. I will reiterate the claim that, while traditional notions of divine transcendence often serve to impede this process, Psalm 22 demonstrates that there are cases in which belief in a liberator-God and the work of dangerous memory are mutually supportive.

"Dangerous Memory" And the Discovery of the Self

According to Sharon Welch and J.B. Metz, escapist notions of hope prevent people who live in an oppressive context from realizing their agency. Reliance on a transcendent God who will liberate us "someday" *hinders* rather than *propels* the work of social justice and must be rejected outright. Where, then, should the powerless turn if they are to actualize their power as agents? An alternative to such "hope," argue Metz and Welch, is dangerous memory itself.

"Dangerous memory" encompasses the re-membering and "re-construing"[33] of oppressive events from the past and/or the present which are often forgotten or not acknowledged because the pain they elicit can be threatening to one's very survival. Dangerous memories are dangerous not only because they are painful, but because they demand — in a powerful, overwhelming, transforming, liberative voice—that injustice be acknowledged and dealt with. Such demands emerge out of

---

33   Catherine Keller, *From a Broken Web: Separation, Sexism and Self* (Boston: Beacon Press, 1986), 193.

the oppressed person's profound self-discovery: she has experienced the joy of living humanly that comes with recognizing herself as a self, and will resist anyone or anything that tries to take this joy from her.

Remembering. Many of us were carefully, though subtly, trained to forget certain life experiences. Dwelling upon situations of suffering is generally discouraged "in our advanced social systems," writes Metz, because "suffering is pictured as insignificant, ugly, and better kept out of sight."[34] Those memories which "make demands on us" and on others are the ones which we are most encouraged to repress by people who, at least according to the standards of our society, are more powerful than ourselves. These are the "dangerous memories."[35] They are dangerous to those who are oppressed, in part, because they are a reminder of the pain and hurt that has been suffered. They are dangerous to those who oppress because they threaten the power of the oppressor. When those who are oppressed have dangerous memories, they become enraged and begin to resist their oppression; such a dynamic disturbs the lives of both oppressed and oppressor.

Dangerous memories are especially painful for those who have been victimized. Because we desire to protect ourselves, to avoid the potentially destructive power of pain, we forget that events of suffering have even occurred. While repression of a particular memory might help us temporarily to survive in the midst of an oppressive situation, such repression is not ultimately healthy. Whether we consciously realize it or not, memories of past (and ongoing) oppression exist in the very fabric of our being, and they affect who we are. According to Metz, forgotten incidences of oppression can serve to threaten our selfhood, the realization on the part of the oppressed individual of his or her subjectivity.

Such a loss of memory is tantamount to a loss of freedom. When we do not understand ourselves as subjects in relationship to the events of our lives, we do not recognize our capacity as agents, and are therefore in bondage to our circumstances. Metz puts the matter quite succinctly, noting that "the enslavement of men [and women] begins when their memories of the past are taken away. . . All forms of colonialization are based on this principle."[36] When the oppressed of the third world recognize that their national identity has been stolen by first world colonists, they gain the freedom to reclaim this identity. When African-American individuals remember the history of the slave trade, they are empowered to resist the racism which still plagues them.

---

[34]   Johann Baptist Metz, *Faith in History and Society* (New York: Seabury Press, 1980), 105.

[35]   Metz, 109.

[36]   Metz, 110.

The freedom that comes with remembering is not a freedom from pain. On the contrary, the experience of liberation involves embracing that deep pain that has too long been ignored. According to Welch, the nature of being truly human, the joy of participating in the fullness of life, is to feel, at times, the pain of suffering.[37] Alice Miller argues, similarly, that through his or her experience of pain, the individual is able to come to identify her or his "true self," the self that has been "buried" or hidden behind the "thick prison walls" of the false self that the child needed to create in order to receive love. Such self-discovery frees us quite literally to be human, to feel the pains and pleasures connected with the events of our lives.[38]

Reconstruing. Remembering a past event does not consist simply of recollecting the "facts" surrounding place, time, and characters involved in a specific historical moment. The emotions and reactions of the oppressed individual are also of critical importance. Most important of all, perhaps, is how the oppressed individual lays claim to the historical facts that she or he remembers.

The importance of understanding oneself as a subject related to the historical facts of one's life is demonstrated in the story of a woman who knew "intellectually" for over a year that she was a victim of incest. She could recount all the historical details, but she did not experience healing. It was not until after she realized that "This was about me!" that she was able to benefit from the healing power of memory.[39] In actuality, this woman did not "remember" her pain until long after all the facts had been gathered.

In light of the difference between recounting historical facts and remembering events of the past, Keller makes the distinction between "reconstructing" and "reconstruing" a past event. While reconstructing the past aims at discovering what is "literally true *of* the past," reconstruing the past is concerned with "implications... (that) may be true *to* the past.[40] Citing the work of Herbert Marcuse, Metz similarly suggests that "remembering. . . is a way of relieving oneself from the given facts, a way of mediation that can momentarily at least break through the omnipresent power of the given facts.[41]

It is the imagination which allows us to grapple with the facts of history in a way that is healing. Metz argues that the power of imagination inherent to memory is so connected to the invoking of

---

37   Welch, 93–94.

38   Alice Miller, *The Drama of the Gifted Child: The Search For the True Self*, Trans. Ruth Ward (Chicago: BasicBooks, 1980), 113.

39   Ellen Bass and Laura Davis, *The Courage To Heal* (New York: Harper & Row, 1988), 79.

40   Keller, 90.

41   Metz, 193.

compassionate feelings and action that the "memory of suffering" itself "brings a new moral imagination into political life, a new vision of others' suffering which should mature into a generous, uncalculating partisanship on behalf of the weak and unrepresented."[42] One does not remember past and present incidences of suffering and oppression without remembering in the same moment that people should not be treated in such an unjust manner;[43] every individual is a subject who should be respected. Realizing what *should be* rather than what *is* pushes our memory into the future. We are empowered, in our rage and in our hope, to "remember" this future possibility in our compassionate and resisting actions.

I have shown how remembering is essential to the actualization of human power. Before I discuss the shift in the psalmist's perception of his power in light of this discussion, arguing that belief in a transcendent God can bolster the work of memory, I will reiterate the potential hazards to self-recovery that are frequently posed by belief in transcendence.

The Endangered Self

In the terms of dangerous memory, transcendent conceptualities inhibit self-recovery when they recommend belief in an all-powerful God whose actions, by definition, can *only* be liberative. When the conviction that "God is a liberator" functions to squelch authentic responses to oppressive circumstances, when it holds within it the condition that life events be interpreted in light of the fact that God *always* liberates, serious impediments to healthy self-awareness abound. In a system in which human faithfulness is implicitly assessed on the basis of how able a person is to recognize this liberation despite seemingly oppressive surroundings, the oppressed are not encouraged to face up to the horrific nature of what is really going on around them. Responses such as crying out, blaming, and becoming angry are discouraged because they are less faith-full, making it difficult for those who have been victimized to recognize themselves as subjects in relationship to their life-events. And it is not only blame which is disallowed; in a dogmatic conceptuality in which trusting God is the only option, authentic trust is actually not possible. Genuine trust can only emerge when one person freely decides that the other is trustworthy.

---

[42]   Metz, 117–118.

[43]   Thus the importance, for example, of "Remembering Auschwitz." According to Richard Rubenstein, the memory of Auschwitz must be preserved in order for the Jewish people to maintain a posture of solidarity and resistance, in order that they will never be victims again [Cf. *The Cunning of History: The Holocaust and the American* Future (New York: Harper & Row, 1975, 68–72)].

In a framework in which God is understood only to liberate, the realization that God has not liberated is extremely dangerous. This is because such realization entails not only that oppressed individuals and communities will suddenly have to work through pain they have repressed; they will also have to do so without the certitude that justice will inevitably be done in the end. The oppressed who have been lulled into passivity by colonialist notions of transcendence naturally tend to deal with the pain of their victimization by minimizing its importance. When efforts for liberation seem to be failing, they might console themselves with the belief that it is the next world that matters, not this one—resigning themselves to wait patiently for the promised "Day of the Lord."

Such resignation does not characterize the psalmist, even though he clearly believes in a transcendent God who has the power to liberate. Why is this the case? I will discuss the psalmist's re-membering, his shift from understanding himself as powerless to seeing himself as power-full, in an attempt to address this question.

Blaming and Trusting In Psalm 22: The Self In Relation To God

The psalmist's understanding of his relationship to God enables him to recognize his self-hood in relation to the events of his life and in this to be empowered to act on behalf of himself and his community. The psalmist's perception is that his relationship to God involves two distinct subjects who each have a conscious commitment to the other. In vv. 1–21a, he prays to, pleads with, and praises the God who he understands to exist in some way outside his circumstances with the power to intervene and make things right. As a close friend reflects on the history of relationship with one who suddenly seems to be distant, or a lover reassures herself with evidences of her partner's commitment when intimacy is not at its peak, so the psalmist reminds himself and God of the closeness they have shared. "On you I was cast from my birth," the psalmist remembers, "and since my mother bore me you have been my God" (v. 10). God has claimed the psalmist and the psalmist has claimed God, the psalmist believes, and God has a responsibility to honor this mutual commitment. Given his perception of intimacy, it is no wonder that the psalmist feels forsaken when God does not respond to his cries. Carroll Stuhlmueller notes that the "persistent and emphatic I-Thou sequence" in verses 1–10[44] creates a "dramatic effect" which

---

44   Following the Masoretic delineation, Stuhlmeuller notes these verses as 2–11 [Cf. "Psalm 22: The Deaf and Silent God of Mysticism and Liturgy," *Biblical Theology Bulletin* 12 (July 1982)].

reveals the depth of the psalmist's pain and loneliness when God is silent.[45]

Because he lives his life in relationship to a God who he believes to be a liberator, the psalmist has a basis upon which to ascertain that he is being violated and that this should not be. Without someone to blame, to plead with, to convince, to trust—without someone to interact with and turn to and before whom to identify that he is hurting—how would the psalmist have been in touch with the fact that he (and his community[46]) is suffering unjustly? Fundamental to our capacity to critique is the recognition of where we stand in relation to the oppressive circumstances. As Kathryn Tanner notes, when belief in a transcendent God is in place "a divine standard stands outside those [corrupted] happenings of human life to prompt their critical appraisal.[47] I am arguing, further, that the oppressed can critique—and resist—only when they recognize that *they* are being violated by such "corrupted happenings." The psalmist's consciousness of himself as a subject in relation to the subject-God enables him to "remember" that he is a subject in relation to the oppressive circumstances of his life and in this to recover his power as an agent of change.

It is because he recognizes himself as a subject in relation to God and subsequently in relation to his context of oppression that the psalmist has power even when he perceives himself to be powerless. Though he portrays himself as lonely, ignored, ostracized by society, persecuted by "bulls, dogs, and evildoers" and physically afflicted, the psalmist has enough strength and self-confidence to confront God on his own behalf. Because he feels free to blame God for not liberating and to challenge God to liberate, he is able to utilize the vehicles of pleading and argumentation in finding voice as a subject.

While the power of the psalmist is evident in the very development of his petition, the sufferer of the first 21 verses clearly does not at first recognize his power and so does not direct it toward transformative actions. In fact, he perceives himself as powerless to change his circumstances apart from God's intervention. By contrast to the groaning, blaming, ostracized psalmist of 1–21a, the psalmist of 21b–31 is full of praise, interacting with members of his community about what God has done, exhorting others to praise God, reaffirming his vows, feeding the poor, prophesying about the universality of God's reign and,

---

45   Stuhlmueller, 88.

46   Evidence that the psalmist is speaking on behalf of his community, which is probably also struggling with the same oppressive circumstances, is seen most clearly in the last ten verses of the Psalm, where the psalmist speaks "in the midst of the congregation" to his "brothers and sisters" (v. 22), fulfilling his vows in the context of the "great congregation" (v. 25), reassuring them that the Liberator-God will liberate.

47   Tanner, 122.

in short, "living for [God]" (v. 29). This is quite a shift in the psalmist's self-perception and activities. He moves from believing he has less power than the dog (v. 20), to exercising his power to lead in the context of his worshipping community (vv. 22, 25).

The psalmist accounts for this shift in his attitude and actions by explaining that: "[God] did not hide [God's] face from me, but heard when I cried to [God]" (v. 24). The intimacy of their relationship has been confirmed. The psalmist no longer feels abandoned by God, who he credits with hearing his cries and rescuing him "from the horns of the wild oxen"[48] (v. 21). It is at this point that the psalmist discovers the power to be a public speaker (vv. 22 & 25), the resources to keep his vows (vv. 25–26), and the vitality of a prophet (vv. 27–31).

What is it about the interaction of the subject-God with the subject-psalmist that leads the despised, mocked, dying sufferer to become a contributing member of his community who is brimming with praise, health, and prophetic words of encouragement? Hogg attributes this change to "some divine restorative event;"[49] Mays discusses the psalm in terms of "before" and "after" God's action in answer to the psalmist's prayer.[50] The NRSV translation of verse 21b, following the Masoretic text, might lead one to believe that God finally responded to the pleas of the sufferer in such a way that the circumstances of the psalmist were transformed.

According to Davis, Stuhlmueller, and Tostengard, the change in the psalmist's tone probably did not occur because there was a punctiliar event—i.e. between 21a and 21b—in which God dramatically intervened. Rather, it is the psalmist's growing awareness of the desperate nature of his situation that leads him to move, in 21b ff., to "a new kind of speech" founded on "a future" that does not seem likely,

---

48   Reumann explains that there is some ambiguity surrounding the question of how verse 21 should be properly translated. While the Masoretic text reads "'and from the horns of the wild oxen *thou hast answered me*' ('*nîthanî*). . . . moderns have usually emended to "*nîyathî* 'and from the horns of the wild oxen (save) *my afflicted (soul)*" (44). Despite this difficulty, Reumann argues that the Masoretic text reading may be used if 22:21b functioned as a "'salvation oracle,'" or "divine response to the [psalmist] . . . delivered by a priest at the temple" (44). Evidence that 21b functioned in this way is seen in the progression of the passage itself, Reumann explains. It would account for why the psalmist is suddenly able to turn to praise, and why it seems that a "cultic situation" (including a meal and a sacrifice) follows. "The key to the text problem is thus assumption of a *tôdah* or "thanksgiving" offering and ceremony" (44).

49   William Richey Hogg, "Psalm 22 and Christian Mission: A Reflection," *International Review of Mission* 77 (April 1988): 243.

50   James L. Mays, "Prayer and Christology: Psalm 22 as Perspective on the Passion," *Theology Today* 42 (October 1985): 325.

given the oppressive circumstances against which he is struggling.[51] The psalmist realizes, in essence, that his paradigm for faith has failed. Trust has not given way to deliverance, as it did for his ancestors; cries have not led to salvation.

Davis argues that "imaginatively engaging" the psalm as a poetic text which is a literary unity inclines one toward such an interpretation (95). The "initial accusation of neglect. . . shows how completely the old *mythos* of salvation has broken down" (97). The dangerous memory that "God is implicated in suffering as much as in deliverance" eventually leads the psalmist to "account himself as already dead . . . [cut] off from any inherited hope of salvation" (v. 15; p. 98). As the desperation of the psalmist grows, the "images of imminent death become more savage... but, strangely, the assurance of the demand also grows in strength (99). Davis explains the progression in the psalmist's tone leading up the transformation:

> The first petition is formulated negatively: 'Do not be far away.' Then the psalmist switches to positive imperatives—'save me, deliver me'—and finally to a perfect verb (*nîtanî*, 'you have answered me,' v. 22), indicating that rescue is a certainty, if not already accomplished.

Davis concludes, on the basis of this reading of the passage, that "it is. . . the petition itself, envisioning and calling forth God's new action in the present desperate situation, that opens up the possibility of praise" (99).[52]

Speaking about this in the terms of "dangerous memory," the petition is able to open up new possibilities for the psalmist precisely because it is the creation of the "imaginative capacities" inherent to the psalmist's "remembering." The psalmist remembers that he is a subject in relation to the oppressive circumstances of his life. Through blaming and trusting in God—both of these actions are integral to the psalmist's petition—the psalmist eventually "forces a break with the past (98-99). While this break is so painful that it leads the psalmist to speak with images of death, it is at the same time full of hope and power. The

---

51   Ellen Davis, "Exploding the Limits: Form and Function in Psalm 22," *Journal for the Study of the Old Testament* 53 (March 1992): 99. All further references to Davis' work will be indicated parenthetically in the text.

52   Interestingly, while Davis clearly attributes the dramatic shift in the psalm to the development of the psalmist's understanding of the way God acts rather than to an act of God, it is the more traditional translation of verse 21 to which she subscribes. "The Masoretic text of v. 22b is both legible and effective," she writes, concurring with Kirkpatrick's statement that the "broken phrasing [is] 'a singularly bold and forcible construction'" (99).

imaginative capacities of his remembering ultimately push him to envision a new paradigm, a paradigm in which he is a power-full agent filled with compassion for others and a sense of possibility for himself.

Central to this shift is the psalmist's recognition that he "has the privilege and the responsibility of mediating the relationship between God and others (101). While in the first 21 verses of the psalm the psalmist is isolated not only from God but also from other people, having no energy beyond his own miseries to alleviate the suffering of others, a shift from private to public, from struggling alone to struggling in community, and from being viscerally focused to having eyes for the needs of others as well marks the transformation of the psalmist. "Private lament in the face of God's hiddenness is caught up in a faithful, corporate cry for help."[53] The poetic strategy of building in emotional intensity continues in the praise section as communal memory gives way to joy;[54] the vision expands to include brothers and sisters, the congregation, the afflicted, all the nations of the earth, the dead, and all those who will live in the future.

While Davis does not use the language of "subjectivity" in discussing the changes in the tone of the psalmist, she clearly believes that the petition—comprised of both blaming and trusting—is the vehicle for evolution in the psalmist's perception of his relationship to God, and the relationship of God to the events of his life. While the psalmist believes that "God is a liberator" throughout the course of this psalm, his understanding of how this Liberator-God interacts with the world broadens significantly. In the past, the psalmist's only hope was that God would intervene, would "break in" from the outside, in such a way that his circumstances would be changed. His role—the human role—in this process was simply to call God to action. But God did not act in the way that the psalmist expected, if we concur with the interpretation of Davis, Tostengard, and Stuhlmueller. The silence of God, coupled with the psalmist's growing self-awareness in the remembering and reconstruing process, leads to a new understanding of the way in which God interacts with the world. The psalmist praises God for deliverance even though oppression still surrounds him. He is empowered by his conviction that God *will* liberate, which replaces his lament that God has not liberated, to join in the work of liberation. He will no longer wait for God, but will work for liberation.

This raises a critical question. If God did not in fact intervene by changing the psalmist's circumstances, why did the psalmist stop blaming God after verse 21? Is the nature of the psalmist's transformation such that he comes to understand God as so powerful that God is beyond human questioning? Has the psalmist decided that he

---

53   Sheldon Tostengard, "Psalm 22," *Interpretation* 46 (April 1992): 170.

54   Davis, 100–101.

does not have the right or the power to declare that "God does not liberate"? Are we not to learn from the change in the psalmist's tone that God is present even when God appears to be hidden; that blaming God is at best spiritually immature and at worst blasphemous; that God should be praised despite appearances to the contrary?

It has been suggested that it is more "mature," spiritually, to praise God apart from what God seems to be doing in relation to one's circumstances, to praise God *for who God is* rather than *for what God does* for us. Some have even argued that embracing physical suffering unquestioningly is the only route, in fact, to a perfect love of God.[55] This essay is not refuting the validity of such religious experiences, but suggesting that they are not always more faith-full, nor for everyone the best route to communion in the context of the God/human relationship. The petition of the psalmist was in fact the vehicle that enabled him to move to a posture of non-blaming; if blaming had been precluded in his conceptuality, how would he have reached the point of praise? To say that the new perception of the psalmist is in any sense the "goal" is also not to imply that wherever there is praise there is a greater spiritual maturity connected with it than wherever one finds blame. On the contrary, praise offered by one who has never struggled with why a powerful God does not eliminate oppression and suffering has little to offer to those who value human life and human living.

The psalmist who praises, further, is not one who suddenly ignores the reality that he worships a God who is a liberator in a context in which God has not liberated. God will liberate, the psalmist proclaims, still aware that there are those who need to be fed (v. 26) and those who will need to be told the message of deliverance (v. 31). The psalmist's awareness of the oppression which surrounds him is evident in the very fact of his anxiousness to praise and to keep his vows and to live for God; the psalmist seems to believe that his actions are integral to the divine deliverance. Rather than feeling powerless in relation to this oppression (e.g. vv. 14–18), then, the psalmist has clearly come to understand that he has power in relation to it (e.g. vv. 22, 25). Rather than waiting in isolation for the Liberator-God to intervene and alter his circumstances, he has come to see that the God who liberates is a God who respects his subjectivity by refusing to manipulate circumstances. The psalmist's belief in a God he can blame and trust makes it possible for him to realize that he can act in relation to the events and circumstances of life. Thus here we see an instance in which belief in a transcendent God promotes, rather than inhibits, human agency.

---

55   Cf., for example, the works of Simone Weil.

III. Theological Reconstruction: The Possibility of an Empowering Transcendence

My objective in this paper has been to respond to the concern that belief in a transcendent God bridles human agency by considering the phenomenon that oppressed persons are, in fact, often empowered by their conviction that God is a liberator. Because I am committed both to challenging convictions that perpetuate oppressive power relationships and to respecting religious beliefs that "make and keep human life human;"[56] because I believe that God has called human beings to be genuine, contributing partners with God in the ministry of reconciliation,[57] it is important to me that I learn to discern when and how belief in divine power is held at the expense of human power and when and how such belief enhances human power.

After examining contemporary and biblical examples of oppressed persons who are empowered rather than disempowered by belief in a transcendent God, and after considering these examples in relation to the process by which human beings can move from understanding themselves as powerless to understanding themselves as power-full, I am now in a position to make some distinctions between different types of transcendent beliefs. To distill the exploration pursued in this essay, I offer four criteria for self-discovery from my discussion of "dangerous memory," using these criteria to assess when transcendent beliefs are detrimental to the work of social liberation and when and how they, in fact, propel such work.

I have explained that dangerous memory accomplishes the following: (1) it enables the remembering individual to understand herself as a subject in relation to the events of her life; (2) it allows the remembering individual to realize that she or he has been violated; (3) it gives the remembering individual permission to feel pain; and (4) it empowers the remembering individual to resist further oppression.

In relation to these four criteria, it has been suggested that notions of transcendence are detrimental to the work of liberation: (1) when humanity is understood to be insignificant in relation to divinity; (2) when God is understood *only* to liberate, so that remembering events of violation is not a possibility; (3) when, because remembering is not permitted, pain is not allowed to be felt; and (4) when resistance is forgone in lieu of an "eschatological 'Day of the Lord'" when all things will be made right.

I have argued, through examination of Psalm 22, that belief in a transcendent God can function to foster human agency: (1) when it enables an oppressed person to understand herself or himself as a *subject* in the context of the divine/human relationship; (2) when it

---

56   This is a phrase that was frequently used by Christian ethicist Paul Lehmann.

57   Cf. II Corinthians 5 and Barth, *CD* IV/2, esp. 1-11.

permits this person to blame God for not liberating and to choose to trust God to liberate, so that she or he is free to remember incidences of violation and to recognize her agency in relationship to life-events; (3) when, because violation can be acknowledged, pain and joy can be felt; and (4) when such a belief empowers an individual or a community to work for social justice in the present.

For those who are interested both in retaining notions of God's transcendence that are empowering and standing prophetically against the oppressive ends that an emphasis on divine transcendence has too often wrought, attention to these distinctions is critical.

Implications For Power, Powerlessness, and the Divine

This essay has focused less on constructing a new way of speaking about God and more on exploring how God is talked about by oppressed and suffering people in their particular *Sitze im Leben*. I have identified an understanding of the relationship between divine and human power that already exists, but which I think has not been adequately considered by those committed to addressing issues of social justice because of the cogent reality that belief in a transcendent God often serves to perpetuate oppression. I have argued that belief in a transcendent God is not inherently disempowering or inevitably associated with an abuse of power, offering one possibility for how it can, in fact, enhance the power of human subjects.

In the conceptuality I have examined, power is not a commodity that is exchanged back and forth between God and human beings, something that God has most of and that humans hope to gain some of. Rather, power is centered precisely in the relationship between the human being and God, in the honest cries of forsakenness or praise that insist on the Liberator's involvement and yield actions that are not divinely-powered *or* human-powered, but empowered by shared participation in the stuff of life.

While the paradigm I have been discussing rests in the conviction that God is a transcendent, distinct subject who has the power to liberate, consciousness of the divine power in this case promotes, rather than inhibits, the realization of human power. Conceptions of the divine transcendence which ultimately render human beings powerless are not acceptable; belief in a God who has all the power, who robs human beings of their subjectivity, must be challenged. By contrast, I have attempted to show one way in which belief in a transcendent God can actually nourish human agency and so promote the work of human liberation. We are selves because God is a liberator; God liberates when we are selves.

6

Power and the Agency Of God

William Schweiker

⌘

In an age of technological power and radical moral diversity among peoples and cultures, it is not surprising that theologians and moral philosophers are exploring the complex relation between beliefs about the world and specifically moral norms and values.[1] How a culture or community conceives of the values and norms that ought to direct human conduct is intimately related to some construal of the world in which human beings act and suffer. Stated differently, at the root of all cultures and communities is some moral ontology, some construal of the moral space in which human life takes place and how persons and communities are to live in that space.[2] The *Sitz im Leben* of this paper is the search in a technological age for an ethic capable of directing human power in the project of respecting and enhancing the integrity of life on this planet.

I intend to undertake this search by comparing the contemporary moral outlook with the biblical construal of the world, which, I argue, pivots on the idea of the agency of God. What can a biblically informed

---

[1] This essay originally appeared in a slightly different form in *Theology Today* 52:2 (1995), 204–224.

[2] On the idea of a moral ontology and what it means for ethics see Charles Taylor, *Sources of the Self: The Making of Modern Identity* (Cambridge, MA: Harvard University Press, 1989). Also see William Schweiker, "The Good and Moral Identity: A Theological Ethical Response to Charles Taylor's *Sources of the Self*" in *The Journal of Religion* 72:4 (1992): 560–572.

moral ontology contribute to moral reflection in the present time? That is the specific question I seek to answer in the following pages and, in doing so, to make some small contribution to the larger agenda facing ethics.[3]

The Lines of the Argument

I intend to compare dominant features of the biblical construal of reality and the moral ontology of post-theistic, technological societies.[4] This form of reflection presupposes that it is possible to compare moral beliefs across time and culture based on an important, but modest, claim about the nature of human existence. As Charles Taylor has recently argued, human beings exist in a moral space of life constituted by questions about how to live. What is more, we orient ourselves in life with respect to some implicit or explicit idea of the good. The place of human existence is always a space defined by questions about how to live and commitments to what is and ought to be valued in human life. The commitments and values persons and communities hold, no matter how divergent and different, provide a framework within which questions about how to live are assessed, criticized, revised, and, finally, answered. Without those commitments and our interaction with others it is not clear that we would have any sense of who we are. This seems

---

3   While the focus of my attention in this paper is on Christian discourse, I understand the task of theological ethics to be that of understanding and providing direction for the lives of agents, that is, beings who face the problem of how to direct their lives.   The perspective from which moral discourse is undertaken is theological in character; the basic fact of human existence for theological ethics is that we live, move, and have our being in God.   But this perspective is one within moral inquiry and, thus, the focus of concern is not simply the Christian life but human moral existence.   In this respect, longstanding divisions between moral philosophers and theologians is of less significance than usually thought.   Contemporary theologians are less likely to make appeals to special moral knowledge or special revelation in their ethics; many moral philosophers now realize the ways in which moral discourse is situated within moral communities and traditions.   The fact that theologians draw on the resources of the Christian tradition cannot mean that they are barred from the general task of moral inquiry.   And philosophers might find within this tradition of thought resources for their task.   In this context, it make sense to speak once again of the task of Christian moral philosophy.   It is this mode of inquiry which I undertake in the present essay. For a fuller statement of the argument and method of this essay see William Schweiker, *Responsibility and Christian Ethics* (Cambridge: Cambridge University Press, 1995).

4   Of course, a post-theistic age does not mean that our time is necessarily post-religious.   The contemporary interest in forms of spirituality and also the worldwide fundamentalist movements are evidence of the importance of religion in the postmodern context.

to be true of all human existence. The wild diversity of moral outlooks on this planet does not negate this modest, formal claim about human life.

Given this fact about human beings, we can isolate features of a moral ontology, that is, features of critical reflection on the moral space of life aimed at providing direction for how to live. First, a moral ontology presents a picture of the moral space of life, that is, it provides a generalized description of how a community or society understands the domain of human life and how to orient life within it. This feature of a moral ontology is, properly speaking, an act of metaphysical reflection. The purpose is to provide an account of reality and the place of human beings and moral values in reality.[5] In this respect, any culture will be characterized by some implicit or explicit metaphysical beliefs. In what follows, I intend to focus on the connection among agency, power, and value in beliefs about reality found in technological societies and the biblical texts.

Second, a moral ontology is also the analysis of the basic structure of the moral space of life. The concern here is not to develop a generalized "picture" of reality, but to analyze what is presupposed in moral existence as its basic elements. This is, strictly speaking, the work of ontological analysis. The elements of the moral space of life, I contend, are (1) human beings as self-interpreting, social agents, (2) patterns of interaction between persons and their world(s) including different modes of being in the world(s), and (3) the mediation of self-understanding and, thus, the identity of persons and communities, as well as beliefs about the "world" in which one lives, by values and norms, and the sensibilities and affections these involve, used to orient human existence. The fact that these elements are basic is shown by noting that cultures always picture human agents in some world, we always act and exist "somewhere," and we exist and act in that place with respect to values, symbolic resources, and norms that guide our lives. A moral ontology provides an analysis of these elements of the moral space of life aimed at understanding the moral meaning of our existence as agents.

These features of a moral ontology, what we might call the acts of articulation and analysis, mutually entail each other. How one pictures reality must meet the test of analysis; examining elements of existence is always in the service of deepening our insight into the reality of our lives and our world.[6] Third, then, these features of a moral ontology inform

---

5   On the importance of this in ethics see Iris Murdoch, *Metaphysics as a Guide to Morals* (New York: Penguin Press, Allen Lane, 1993). Also see *Iris Murdoch and the Search for Human Goodness*, eds. Maria Antonaccio and William Schweiker (Chicago: The University of Chicago Press, 1996).

6   For an example of this form of inquiry see William Schweiker, *Mimetic Reflections: A Study in Hermeneutics, Theology and Ethics* (New York: Fordham University Press, 1990).

the normative claims of an ethics, that is, claims about how we *ought* to live. Accordingly, these aspects of moral inquiry (articulation, analysis, prescription) guide the argument of this paper as I compare the moral outlooks of the technological world and the biblical text. The crucial point of comparison is the place of power in a moral ontology, the relations, as it were, among agency, power, and value in finite existence. I want to show that power is basic to the moral ontology of a technological age, whereas a biblical construal of the moral space of life centers on the transvaluation of power.

The implicit moral ontology of late-modern societies is one in which human agents exert power through action in an otherwise value-neutral, materialistically conceived universe and, thereby, constitute the value of their world. This is, at one level, hardly a novel insight. But what has not been explored is how morally and ontologically basic the connections among agency, power, and value are to the contemporary understanding of reality and human existence. As we will see, late-modern societies dominated by technical rationality operate with two overlapping principles for understanding the moral space of life: (1) that the human agent, or communities of agents, is sovereign in the creation of value through the exercise of power, and (2) that value is not ontologically basic for understanding reality; reality is the scene for the human creation of value. The conjunction of these two principles means that the technological world is one in which the maximization of power is the primary good of life. Power does not serve a value beyond itself, because it is believed to be the source of value.

If the above is at all correct, then the moral ontology of contemporary societies has, in principle, no norm for evaluating the moral rightness of creation versus destruction or preferring viable future life over present interests as long as in any particular action or policy—even destructive ones—power is maximized. And given this, it is hardly surprising that late-modern societies are dominated by economic conceptions of value, strongly individualistic ideas of the self, the constant threat of meaninglessness and alienation from the value-creating centers of the culture, unending conflict over access to social, political, cultural, and economic power, and increasing violence and the glorification of destruction. This is because the value and meaning of human life are thought to rest in the exercise of such forms of power.

The late-modern view of the world and human life is at odds with the biblical construal of reality. Admittedly, it is difficult, if not impossible, to speak of "the" biblical view of reality given the immense variety of biblical strands of thought. To account for some of this diversity I will further explore cultic, prophetic, and legal discourse with respect to the question of the direction of human power. Each of these forms of discourse helps to circulate within a society a construal of reality that centers on the agency of God and thereby structures or forms the moral self-understanding of that society. In other words, these divergent forms of discourse are deployed to enable a community to understand itself through a theistic vision of the world. The agency, power, and value connection remains basic in biblical thought, but it is, in principle, internally transvalued. How is this so?

The distinctiveness of a biblically-informed moral ontology is that to identify ultimate reality as an agent (for example, 'God'), that is, to specify the inner meaning of ultimate power as an identity bearing actor, is to assert a value that transcends natural, social, and political power, namely, the value of a commitment to respect and enhance identifiable agents and the conditions necessary for ongoing action. That is to say, the name 'God,' and its polymorphic expression in divergent forms of discourse and symbolism, expresses the transvaluation of power; the name 'God' specifies power as the *origin* of value, but, importantly, does not instantiate it as the sole *content* of value.[7] This is, for instance, the moral significance of God as creator; it is also the meaning of the Christian claim that God is love. Love and creation are instances of power in which power generates value. That is, power (creation; love) bestows value on another, but power alone does not define value. What is then basic to understanding the moral space of life from a theological perspective is not a materialistic account of reality or human capacities for creative action, but the transformation of power in which power binds its identity to the worth of finite existence.

From this perspective, one does not see the world simply as a web of interdependent processes nor as so many historical monuments to human civilization and barbarism. Rather, the world is seen as a field of action composed of diverse struggles to transform relations of power for the sake of respecting and enhancing the integrity of life. Identifying or naming ultimate power "God" entails, then, a construal of the world, or a moral ontology, and a set of moral commitments that necessarily focus on the a transvaluation of power. This is so because any affirmation of and fidelity to an agent, for example, faith in "God," in understanding the world in which one lives, entails a commitment to the well-being of agents and the necessary conditions for action, that is, natural, social, political, economic, cultural, and interpersonal conditions necessary for agents to act. Social and political institutions as well as interpersonal relations and moral aspirations are judged right or wrong with respect to the demand to respect and enhance the integrity of life.

My contention, then, is that in spite of their diversity, the biblical texts assert that the question "Who is acting?" is basic in a construal of

---

7   On the relation between naming and thinking God, see David Tracy, "Literary Theory and the Return of the Forms of Naming and Thinking God in Theology," in *The Journal of Religion* 74:3 (1994): 302–319.

the world, in a moral ontology. The basic questions in asking about the meaning of reality are not about the structure and dynamics of natural processes. They are questions about who is acting, who is responsible, and what is going on. While this line of thinking has often been used to explain and even justify human suffering and misfortune through ideas of retribution, punishment, divine intervention, and so on, something else is actually at stake. What is at stake is how persons (or communities) understand the moral space in which they exist and thus how they ought to live.

My argument centers, then, on the *moral* and *hermeneutical* import of claims about divine agency. This means two things. First, I am not trying to denote a literal, individual acting being, as in traditional theism, with purposes, intentions, and acts of will who is (or is not) causally responsible for bringing about events in the world. It is also the case that I am not making an argument for God as the inclusive individual, as some process theologians do, nor, for that matter, exploring how the biblical narrative renders an agent, as many so-called narrative theologians argue.[8] Rather, I am exploring how the construal of ultimate power as an agent constitutes an individual's or community's understanding of the meaning of life in the world, how it entails *in nuce* a moral ontology. Stated differently, I am concerned with the practical status of theological discourse with respect to the moral life

---

[8]   There have been a range of theological responses to the modern criticism of agential conceptions of God. Without examining these options in detail in this paper, let me mention some of the most prominent. First, theologians like Paul Tillich argued that religious symbols, like "God," point to the depth structure of the self-world relation. Second, through the Word of God or through the use of the category of narrative some theologians, like Karl Barth, have attempted to understand all of reality within specific discourse about God. Third, there are theologians who attempt to demythologize biblical discourse with respect to basic existential questions or understand claims about God as imaginative constructions for the purposes of orienting and guiding human action. These theologians, like James Gustafson, Sallie McFague, and Gordon Kaufman, seek to accommodate non-theological construals of reality while designating the unique function of theological claims. Next, there are theologians influenced by process metaphysics who understand the divine as internally related to the world. This means, as Schubert Ogden puts it, that "God interacts with all, not only acting on them but also being acted on by them." See Schubert Ogden, *Is There Only One True Religion Or Are There Many?* (Dallas: Southern Methodist University Press, 1992), 49. Finally, liberation theologians seek to understand the presence of God in solidarity with the oppressed and the struggle for liberation. Here an understanding of the social world is dependent on the perspective of the interpreter, and, so the argument goes, the theologically valid perspective is one in solidarity with the oppressed. Clearly, the question of agency and interpretations of reality is one point, and I think a crucial point, at which reflection on divine power and powerlessness intersects with consideration of human existence and action.

rather than offering a theoretical argument about God in God's self. Questions about the *aseity* of God are simply beyond the scope of the present inquiry.

I also want to show, second, that from the perspective of theological ethics claims about the divine are needed in ethics in order to affirm the value of existence as such. These claims are validated insofar as they help articulate and analyze what must be affirmed in order to hold the moral commitments that already define who we are as well as the commitments we must adopt in order to have a viable future on this planet. In this respect it is proper to say, borrowing from Paul Ricoeur, that, in theological ethics, we invent in order to discover. We construe the world theologically in order to discover our own most basic moral affirmations. An affirmation of the right of finite life to exist and make a claim against ultimate power, rather than valorizing finite existence in terms of power, is at the heart of a theological ethical worldview and interpretation of the moral life. This means that we are to respect and enhance the integrity of life and this endorses a project of actively seeking to transform oppressive and destructive structures and relations.

With these matters in mind, I want now to provide a brief interpretation of our contemporary context as the *Sitz im Leben* of theological ethical reflection. This is the next step in undertaking an inquiry into power and moral agency since it will further clarify the current criticism of traditional theistic beliefs. Following this I will explore resources within biblical texts and ancient ethics in order to advance the claims made in the previous paragraphs. The essay concludes with directions for constructive theological ethical reflection. That will return us, via an engagement with traditional and contemporary modes of thought, to our current situation.

An Interpretation of Our Situation

Several factors in our current world situation are of special importance for theological ethics. The first is the moral outlook of post-theistic societies. These are societies in which there is the widespread loss of any sense that fundamental norms and values concerning human well-being and justice are consistent with or dependent on beliefs about God. A post-theistic society is one in which, practically speaking, beliefs about the God of traditional theism do not motivate or empower persons to live by the norms and values they hold. Persons and communities are motivated by moral or purely prudential considerations and religious claims are interpreted in their light. These are societies in which the context of human action, the "world," is not understood by appeal to God, that is, to creation, providence, or judgment. A post-theistic society holds that nature is not to be understood as creation and thus dependent on a transcendent source of value; the dignity of human life is not dependent on the human reflecting the divine as the *imago dei*. It is also a society in which the meaning of social and historical existence is not to be grasped by appeal to divine providence. This means that human beings, or human collectives, are seen as the sole agents in reality. Again, in these societies the theistic conceptual framework within which the moral life has been understood by most, if not all, Western thought is simply no longer integral to the actual, practical beliefs by which persons live.

The second factor confronting contemporary ethics is the radical extension of human power through technology. This power alters our understanding of reality as much as it confronts us with new and different degrees of responsibility. Thinkers like Hans Jonas see this change in human action ontologically, as a change in our understanding of reality itself.[9] For instance, we can now change the genetic structure of future generations and thus alter the human species. As Paul Ramsey once noted, this reveals the odd and troubling fact that those who come after us might not be (biologically) like us.[10] What then is our moral relation to those in the future? What is our responsibility for respecting and enhancing the conditions necessary for there to be viable future life on this planet? The manifold questions that surround technological innovation have led some thinkers to claim that previous moral and religious beliefs are simply unable to meet our ethical questions because of the account of action and view of reality they entail.

This brings us to the third factor confronting current ethics. John B. Thompson is correct that contemporary societies are increasingly dominated by mass communication and the circulation of symbolic forms.[11] In this situation, as Thompson notes, meaning is in the service of power, that is, in the service of forms of domination. Given this, we

---

[9]   See Hans Jonas, *The Imperative of Responsibility: In Search of an Ethic for the Technological Age*, translated by Hans Jonas and David Herr (Chicago: The University of Chicago Press, 1984), 81.   For Jonas's metaphysics see his *The Phenomenon of Life: Towards a Metaphysical Biology* (Chicago: Midway, 1982). Also see his *Philosophical Essays: From Ancient Creed to Technological Man* (Englewood Cliffs, NJ: Prentice-Hall, 1974). For critical responses to Jonas's ethics see William Schweiker, "Radical Interpretation and Moral Responsibility: A Proposal for Theological Ethics" in *The Journal of Religion* 73:4 (1993): 613–637, Karl-Otto Apel, *Diskurs und Verantwortung: Das Problem des Übergangs zur postkonventionellen Moral* (Frankfurt: Suhrkamp, 1990), 179–218, and Wolfgang Huber, "Toward an Ethics of Responsibility" in *The Journal of Religion* 73:4 (1993): 573–591.

[10]   Paul Ramsey, *Fabricated Man: The Ethics of Genetic Control* (New Haven: Yale University Press, 1970).

[11]   John B. Thompson, *Idealogy and Modern Culture: Critical Social Theory in the Era of Mass Communication* (Stanford: Stanford University Press, 1990).

must consider the "circulation of symbolic forms," such as legal, political, and economic discourse, if we are to understand questions of human agency and thereby respond to the plight of oppression and the struggle for liberation. This is because moral knowledge is bound to the forms of discourse, the symbols and narratives that are found in a society. As I noted above, a basic element of a moral ontology is the belief and discourse about values that mediate self-understanding and a construal of the world. The symbolic forms of importance for this essay are beliefs about "agents" and the "world," especially within cultic, legal, and prophetic discourse, around evaluations of power.

I am suggesting, then, that in order to forward an adequate interpretation of our situation we must address the question of agency with respect to claims about reality and the symbolic forms which circulate in a society in order to legitimate structures of power. We can thus deepen our interpretation of the contemporary situation by exploring first the relation between accounts of moral agency and worldviews and, then, by turning to the question of the circulation of symbolic discourse. That is, we can now examine in greater detail the elements of the moral ontology of technological, post-theistic societies.

It is not difficult to grasp the conceptual relation between some construal of reality and beliefs about the nature of agents. By definition, an agent always acts in some situation and at some time. We are always acting somewhere. The situation in which an agent or community acts can sustain or impede human action. Political and economic situations of poverty and oppression, for instance, radically impede the possibilities for persons to act. In this respect, every human action—and thus all human suffering as well—attests to the relation between an agent (or community of agents) and the world in which the agent(s) act(s). Given this, a view of reality is at least implicitly entailed in beliefs about moral agents, that is, some construal of the spatial and temporal situation of life and action. Of course, there can be wildly divergent ways of construing the world. For instance, apocalyptic language pictures reality differently than the machine of a deistic conception of reality; contempt for the world warrants different patterns of life than an affirmation of worldly existence. These different ways of picturing the world bear on human action, enhancing or impeding it. Similarly, there are different ways of being *in* the world (however that world is pictured). Being in the world as an agent can be characterized by hope, fear, struggle, compassion, courage, and what have you. But in each case this is different than being in the world as an object (for example, a tool) or simple chemical processes. Agents (however understood) always act in some world (however understood) in terms of different *modes* of being *in* that world, modes that, for agents, always have an evaluative character. That is, contempt, courage, fear, faith, and other beliefs, attitudes, and feelings that characterize the lives of agents express evaluations of the world in which the agent lives.

Given this, any comprehensive construal of the situation of life, or a moral ontology, is dependent on symbolic forms. Since we have no perception of the "whole," the totality of what is the context of existence and action can only be conceived and spoken about through symbolic or metaphorical means. Indeed, even to speak of the "world" as the place of human action is to use a symbolic discourse open to a variety of interpretations.[12] For example, is the world "fallen," as in traditional Christian belief? Is it an expression of the creative grace of God? Is the world a complex of natural and social processes? In this light, a crucial feature of technological societies is that they picture human agents as acting in a value-neutral time and space. The modern world, as scholars note, is disenchanted. The "whole" in which human beings act is pictured as a complex interacting matrix of natural processes. Moral values and norms are not written into the fabric of the world but are human creations to serve specific needs and purposes, often the needs and purposes of the powerful.

The defining characteristic of the late-modern Western moral outlook is that it pivots on the metaphysical proposition that humans are the only agents in the world. Value is dependent for its existence on the power of human beings to act and create their world; the greater power human beings have, the greater they can and will endow their world with value. Because of this, all worldviews, and the values they endorse, are necessarily seen as nothing but human constructs and serve human purposes. And the first imperative of such a outlook is to acquire power in order to create value. This worldview is anthropocentric and the value of human purposes is written onto a value-neutral time and space. Beliefs about the world must be explained in terms of their social, psychological, or political utility for human beings.

The relation between human agents and the value-neutral environment in which we are condemned to create value has been given expression in two seemingly competing positions. First, work in the natural and biological sciences as well as evolutionary forms of thought in other disciplines have attempted to explore the emergence of human agents from natural reality. Human beings are to be understood as a subset of a comprehensive account of the natural world. In their capacity to act in the world, human beings are the leading edge of the material universe—the emergence of freedom in reality. Second, this account of the emergence of human freedom amid a value-neutral background exists alongside modes of thought that begin with our experience of

---

12   For a fuller account of this point see William Schweiker, "Understanding Moral Meanings: On the Use of Philosophical Hermeneutics in Theological Ethics" in *Christian Ethics: Problems and Prospects*, eds. Lisa Sowle Cahill and James Childress (Cleveland: Pilgrim Press, 1996).

being agents. Since we exert force on the world in such a way that we have some self-conscious apprehension of ourselves as agents, it is possible to construct a plausible interpretation of our being in the world from that fact. Forms of idealism and existentialism attempted just that enterprise. Jean-Paul Sartre, for instance, insisted that "man being condemned to be free carries the weight of the whole world on his shoulders; he is responsible for the world and for himself as a way of being."[13] From this perspective, the reality of the acting subject is the condition of the possibility of making claims about the meaning and value of reality. In an act of freedom the agent transcends natural conditions of life to constitute her or his own identity and to create value. Self-transcendence, rather than emergence, is the character of the relation between human beings and their natural and social environment.

The usual assessment of modernity by theologians sees materialist and existentialist arguments as radically opposed and thus posing different challenges to Christian faith. Theologians then take up the challenge of "religion and science" or matters of "faith and meaning." But these trends in modern thought are, in fact, interlocking features of one comprehensive moral ontology that characterizes the distinctiveness of human beings by the power to create value within a value-neutral universe. In spite of differences, "transcendence" and "emergence" as ideas or symbols for articulating and analyzing human being *in* the world specify human power as the origin and end of value. It is also important to grasp that each of these positions conceives of the future as the "space" upon which the value of freedom must be projected and realized. Freedom must emerge into an open future from natural processes; in the act of choice, the self stands out, transcends its present self, into a future it creates. Thus, not only is natural reality understood in value-neutral terms; the future, as the crucial condition for human freedom, is also conceived as empty and waiting for the work of human power to fill it with value. This is, I judge, what defines these modes of thought as thoroughly modern in character.[14]

Each of these positions is necessarily post-theistic. On the grounds of a materialistic theory of reality, claims about God or the agency of God are rendered meaningless and void in any account of the world. Appeals to God do not "explain" anything, except, perhaps, the psychological needs of those who continue to believe in God. One does not need the concept of God to understand the structure and dynamics of natural processes. The idea of God is metaphysically void; it has no

---

13   Jean-Paul Sartre, *Being and Nothingness*, trans. by Hazel Barnes (New York: Washington Square Press, 1966), 707.

14   For the classical statement of this position see Friedrich Nietzsche, *The Birth of Tragedy and the Genealogy of Morals*, trans. Francis Golffing (New York: Doubleday Anchor Books, 1956).

descriptive force in understanding the world. Conversely, from an existentialist reading, human freedom is not genuine if it is dependent on a power other than self, on the divine. Theological claims seem to violate the conditions necessary to grasp the meaning of our being in the world, that is, that we are free self-constituting agents, and so do not aid in analyzing the structure of life. Theistic claims can then be decoded as symbolic expressions of our freedom where we act *as if* our moral duties are from God, as Kant said. More likely, religious beliefs, as Nietzsche insisted, feed a slavish mentality that is destructive of real human vitality and flourishing.

Let me summarize the argument thus far. I have argued, first, that the current criticism of traditional theistic ethics centers in part on the moral ontology those moral beliefs entailed. I have further shown, second, that a post-theistic social milieu backs that criticism given basic suppositions about the relation (emergence; transcendence) between human beings as agents and the spatial-temporal nature of reality. Yet however that relation is understood, the origin and content of value are understood in terms of power. Thus, third, I have argued that the moral ontology that backs late-modern societies is one in which reality is understood in value-neutral and materialistic terms while the distinctiveness of human existence is our capacity to exercise power (freedom) in the creation of values (i.e., values specified through law, art, morality, economics, and the like) in an open future. What is basic to this moral ontology insofar as it is concerned with values we ought to seek is then power itself. Only through access to power do agents or communities of agents endow their world with meaning; only through the exercise of power, the capacity to change the world for human purposes, is the distinctiveness of human life to be found. The technological age is merely the working out and institutionalization of this moral ontology.

Thus far I have been exploring in some detail the moral ontology implicit in late-modern technological societies. I wish now to compare this ontology with the moral outlook of biblical texts. Put as a question, if it is one of the central claims of biblical thought that God "acts" in some fashion, and if mythic modes of interpreting the world think in agential terms about deities, how, if at all, are we to make sense of biblical claims once we grant, as I think we must, the contemporary criticisms of agential accounts of the world? In order to address this question we must now explore strands in biblical thought and also developments in the history of ethics. This is a necessary step on the way back to the contemporary situation.

Biblical Thought and the History of Ethics

In order to link our discussion of biblical thought with the contemporary moral outlook, we can consider a text which centers on the exercise of power in the creation of value. The text is the story of the Tower of Babel.

(v.1) Now the whole earth had one language and the same words.

(v.2) And as they migrated from the east they came upon a plain in the land of Shinar and settled there.

(v.3) And they said to one another, "Come let us make bricks and burn them thoroughly." And they had brick for stone, and bitumen for mortar.

(v.4) Then they said, 'Come, let us build ourselves a city, and a tower with its top in the heavens, and let us make a name for ourselves; otherwise we shall be scattered abroad upon the face of the whole earth.'

(v.5) The Lord came down to see the city and the tower, which the mortals had built.

(v.6) And the Lord said, 'Look, they are one people, and they have all one language; and this is only the beginning of what they will do; nothing that they propose to do will now be impossible for them.

(v.7) Come, let us go down, and confuse their language there, so that they will not understand one another's speech.'

(v.8) So the Lord scattered them abroad from there over the face of all their earth, and they left off building the city.

(v.9) Therefore it was called Babel, because there the Lord confused the language of all the earth, and from there the Lord scattered them abroad over the face of all the earth.

(Genesis 11: 1–9 NRSV)

This well-known narrative is often seen by scholars as an etiological explanation of different nations and languages. It also is the climax of the prehistory of humanity introducing the age of the patriarchs. The subtlety of the narrative is that the motive for the building of the tower "lies within the realm of human possibility, namely a combination of their energies on the one hand, and on the other the winning of fame, i.e., a naïve desire to be great." And this further means that "God's eye already sees the end of the road upon which mankind entered with this deed, the possibility and temptation which such a massing of forces holds. A humanity that can think only of its own confederation is at liberty for anything, i.e., for every extravagance."[15] The city of Babel arises as a sign of self-reliance, the work of civilization, while the tower is a testimony to their fame. God acts punitively, but also preventively, by confusing tongues and scattering peoples. The text inscribes divine action as setting limits on human possibilities with respect to the *future* viability of civilization, or, to put it differently, there are limits set on the unification of power as the precondition of building a civilization with respect to future possibilities and intentions. There is no question about the centrality of power to value; the question is whether or not there are limits on future expressions of human power other than the simple exercise of power.

Several of the features of the text stand out for the purpose of our present inquiry. First, the narrative focuses attention on the culture-creating power of human beings bound to technical capacities to build, centralize political organization, and produce material conditions for civilized life. This is linked, second, to fundamental motives: the drive to be great, to make a name for themselves, as the unifying force of a civilization ("they are one people," the text says). The motive is the exercise of power in order to accomplish values that seem dependent on that power, the values of unified political existence, the goods of civilization (the city) and the establishment of cultural greatness (the tower). This motive, third, is against the backdrop of the fear of chaos and social anarchy ("otherwise we shall be scattered abroad"). Thus the problem of social unity—and with this peace and stability—is linked in the text to the exercise of power in building a civilization. Yet, fourth, the actions of people do not take place within a value-neutral space and time, nor are human goods defined only through the exercise of human power. Rather, the lord "came down" to "see the city and the tower." Human civilization, and thus the exercise of power in the creation of distinctly human values, transpires within a context defined by the action and vision of God. God's punitive action has the effect of overturning the supposition that *solely* through human power is the unity and greatness, and thus coherences and peace, of a civilization to be found. The narrative intensifies the alienation of the human from God (Gen. 3:22–24) and from others (Gen. 4:1–16) by portraying the alienation of all society from God and from other peoples. The answer to this alienation must be a reconciliation between peoples, the divine, and even society and the divine.

The problem of what grounds the unity and greatness of human civilization as well as the limits on human power is answered within the

---

15   Gerhard Von Rad, *Genesis: A Commentary*, translated by John H. Marks (London: SCE Press, 1961), 145.

narrative once the link between the prehistory and the age of the patriarchs is seen (Gen. 12ff.). While the "mortals" tried to make a name for themselves, Abraham, who will be the father of many nations, is named by God.[16] Likewise, the nation of Israel will be one nation, a holy people, defined by its relation to the transcendent source of existence amid the dispersion of peoples resulting from the drive of human power in the creation of civilization. The text does not entail a denigration of human capacities for action nor demean the significance of the creation of culture and thus the great task of civilization that befalls the human species. Rather, the text suggests that the fundamental problematic of human civilization is how to make right contact with power(s) other than the human in and through the exercise of power. What is at issue is charting the inner-limits of human possibilities in the creation of a viable social world. This is because, we might say, outside of contact with this other power, with the divine, the value of human existence becomes dependent solely on the mechanisms of human power with all the dangers that entails. The basic human problem is not that of exercising power in the creation of civilization, but, rather, fidelity to a power that grounds and limits human power—the divine. This is a problem endlessly examined throughout the biblical texts.

The parallel between Genesis 11 and the contemporary moral worldview as I have specified is perhaps too obvious to elaborate. Of more immediate importance it is the need to examine the moral ontology implicit in the text. As we have seen, the question of human agency is unavoidably bound to how a culture, or individual, understands the nature of reality, to its worldview. If we take this text as emblematic, it is a safe generalization to say that for the ancient world human beings are not the only agents active in the world. That is to say, in a mythic construal of reality human beings encounter other powers—whether conceived as deities or not—that act on and in human existence often determining human destiny. The context of human action—the very structure of reality—and human action itself are understood as intimately bound to the question of other operative forces or agencies. As Walter Wink has noted, within the modern materialistic conception of the world, we "do not have categories for thinking of such Powers as real yet unsubstantial, as actual spirits having no existence apart from their concretions in the world of things."[17] How are we then to make sense of these ancient texts? Is it enough to say that we must demythologize them? Are there resources in these ancient modes of thought for considering the meaning of human freedom in the world?

---

16   See Samuel Terrien, *The Elusive Presence: The Heart of Biblical Theology* (New York: Harper & Row, 1978), 72–76.

17   Walter Wink, *Naming the Powers: The Language of Power in the New Testament* (Philadelphia: Fortress Press, 1984), 4.

In classical thought the operative power(s) other than the human might be understood through the idea of "fate," the actions of the gods, demons, the furies, or the divine lordship. But in each case, reality cannot be totally explained through a model of natural causation and the uniformity of natural processes even as human action itself cannot be understood simply with reference to human creative capacities. One sees this, for instance, in the biblical context through the ideas of election and also the charismatic power of the prophets. God speaks through the prophet. God and the prophet act, each is accountable, in one and the same action. More graphically put, non-human powers take possession of persons and direct their actions (see the betrayal of Judas in John's Gospel). And even Paul can state that it is not he but Christ in him that is crucial to the life of faith. We might speak of these as examples of the phenomenon of dual agency. Clearly it is not, as critics argue, simply an example of heteronomy; that is, the prophet's or demoniac's action is not simply defined and motivated by some external authority. Yet it is also not an act of brute autonomy. Rather, we have something like what Paul Tillich and others called "theonomy."[18] The point, I take it, is that human responsibility is not believed to be violated when it is asserted that a power or powers other than the human are operative in human action.

Interestingly, there is a conflict between naturalistic and non-naturalistic construals of reality seen in Greek and Roman thought different than seen in the biblical texts. Pre-Socratic thinkers questioned the validity of mythic and agential, especially retributive, visions of reality out of concern to give a naturalistic explanation of the universe. Even Socrates, in the attempt to bring philosophy down to earth, is concerned to grasp the distinctive character of human action and the principle for right action (see *Euthyphro*). His claim that knowledge is virtue means that the operative power (*arete*) of human action is knowledge. While scholars such as Donald Wiebe disagree, this shift to understanding human agency in its own distinctive light is shared with Socrates by Plato and Aristotle.[19] However, this does not deny the fact that for Greek and Roman thought the character of human action is not understandable outside of its relation to non-human powers or reality. Moral action entails some right relation to these other powers. The Epicureans, for instance, related ethics to their physics, even though they held the gods unconcerned with human flourishing. The Stoics, in arguing that virtue is happiness, insisted that one must live according to nature, a nature permeated by *logos*. In spite of the grave differences

---

18   See Paul Tillich, *Morality and Beyond,* The Library of Theological Ethics (Louisville, KY: Westminster/John Knox Prsss, 1995).

19   See Donald Wiebe, *The Irony of Theology and the Nature of Religious Thought* (Montreal & Kingston: McGill-Queen's University Press, 1991).

between these moral systems, there was a shared assumption about the fact that the moral life strikes the very core of reality. The debates in ethics, accordingly, were at bottom debates about the nature of reality.

Seen in this light, the moral problem for biblical thought is how to discern or judge which powers *ought* to be operative in human life and then how human beings or communities *can make right contact* with them, be morally empowered by them, in and through the exercise of power by human agents. We can see the social means for practically answering this problem by isolating diverse forms of biblical discourse and practice. First, in cultic practice contact with divine power is through the ritual act. Cultic activity re-enacts in time and space the fundamental structure of reality (whether cosmogonic and/or historical) and thereby stabilizes the present social order. And it valorizes the ritual object not simply through the exercise of human power, but in relation to the divine. Next, in prophetic discourse, contact with the source of empowerment is in moral action, in seeking justice, loving mercy, and walking in humility with God (Micah 6:8). The community is charged to understand itself, to interpret its existence, with respect to norms and values that are to be endorsed in all actions. The appropriate worship of God, and thus contact with the source of empowerment, is transformed beyond previous cultic and sacrificial means to include matters of justice and mercy. In a word, a construal of reality and its ritual reenactment in cultic practice and an account of just and merciful social relations are symbolically mediated by prophetic discourse.

There is then a concern in cultic and prophetic discourse to make contact in action with power(s) other than the human. This is further elaborated in legal discourse. Through the structure of law, what came to be called by Christian theologians the moral, civil, and ceremonial law, there is increasing differentiation of types of actions and norms for conduct with respect to the ongoing life of the community. This structuring of life is against the backdrop of the cultic need to re-enact the structure of reality and the prophetic claim about the values that should inform and guide self-understanding and action. This is why the manifold forms of action mediated by legal discourse are seen as basic to the formation of human identity. We might go so far as to say that a community's identity, its "name" (to recall the text from Genesis 11), is enacted and constituted through a host of types of action and their legal mediation. These types of action are in the service of power and contact with power(s) other than the human, that is, the power of the divine rule, covenant fidelity, the eschatological presence of the divine, as well as the exercise of human power.

My concern is not to trace the development of divergent strands of biblical thought and discourse, a task, quite frankly, beyond my scholarly abilities. Yet it is also not to enter more deeply into ancient ethics although these are matters closer to my expertise. The point to grasp is that for much ancient ethics, and certainly all Christian theological ethics, the most basic moral problematic was how the agent or community was to relate to some source of power other than itself and yet empowers the self or community to act. In Christian thought, this "source" was conceived in agential and personal terms ("God") and this provided the grounds for a construal of reality, an understanding of the origin and status of moral norms, and also proper moral motivation. This source of value was, furthermore, depicted in polymorphic forms of discourse that served to structure the identity of persons and the community. This form of moral identity entailed the endorsement of beliefs about reality that asserted that the context of human action is not value-neutral. And it also implied a commitment to respect and enhance the conditions necessary for human action. In my judgment, these beliefs and commitments are the hermeneutical point of biblical and Christian agential construals of reality.

Much modern ethics, as we have seen, has tried to show how the self acts out of its own freedom, and this has made power central to an account of the human. This has meant the attempt to reduce an account of the moral space of life to a theory of the emergence of freedom from matter, or, conversely, existentialist accounts of the transcendence of freedom over matter. In this light, the moral ontology found in the biblical texts is surprising complex. It does not reduce the moral space of life to the interaction between autonomous agents seeking power and value-neutral matter understood simply in terms of either emergence or transcendence. Rather, human beings act in a moral space defined not solely by their own power; action is mediated by forms of discourse and practices that reinforce the moral order (cultic action); human freedom is directed to the ends of justice and mercy (prophetic discourse); and the social system is differentiated into interacting domains of activity (legal discourse). Most importantly, human power is not definitive of value even if diverse forms of power are the origin of value. Human power is exercised for good or ill within a horizon of value symbolized through the divine and mediated by different forms of discourse. Surprisingly, the biblical texts taken in their diverse strata seem truer to the actual complexity of the moral space of life than the forms of conceptual and axiological reductionism characteristic of modern philosophy and theology.

The great danger of biblical and Christian thought is when contact with this other power becomes the warrant for the establishment of a "Christian civilization" that shifts the question of value back to the domain of human power now sanctioned by ostensively divine commands. Such developments, which, we must note, mark the whole of Western history, violate the best insight of the moral ontology articulated through the complex forms of discourse seen in the biblical texts. And this is why theological ethics must articulate, critique, and revise prevailing discourse and patterns of action both within and outside of the religious community. Mindful of the real and present danger of biblical thought, the orienting question of this paper returns: What, if anything, might theological ethics contribute to contemporary thought?

The Transvaluation of Power

I have been arguing that we must explore the biblical texts in search of symbolic resources capable of transforming our perceptions of power and thus endorsing a moral commitment to respect and enhance the integrity of life on this planet. In light of our discussion, the most important resource seems to be found in the dialectical relation between cultic and prophetic modes of discourse for conceiving how persons and communities make contact with the source of value. Cultic practice, as we have seem, re-enacts the moral order of reality and, when mediated by the name "God," asserts that value is not dependent solely on human activity. In terms of the basic elements of a moral ontology, cultic actions enact a "world" in which the exercise of power, the cultic act, actually transvalues power through the symbol "God." However, while cultic action can stabilize the community or culture, it does not necessarily specify principles for moral action *in* the actual social — as opposed to ritualized and symbolic—world. Prophetic discourse provides those principles for existence *in* the social world (justice, mercy, humility) which are then to structure the self-understanding of persons and communities. As a basic element of a moral ontology, prophetic discourse provides beliefs about the meaning of our existence as self-interpreting agents. Prophetic discourse circulates in a society to test, transform, and radically to interpret social mechanisms and relations operative in that society. It endorses the demands for mercy and justice within a commitment to an inclusive moral community depicted as the reign of God, a community defined by a commitment to respect and enhance the integrity of life. Thus, prophetic discourse works to transform the ritualized "world" of cult in terms of the demands of justice and mercy even as its seeks to apprehend the work of social justice as a "cultic" means for contact with the divine.

Cultic discourse and prophetic discourse express two elements of the biblical moral ontology (that is, world enactment and moral agency). They provide a view of reality (cult) and human, social agents (prophetic discourse) that are then further mediated by legal discourse aimed at social interaction and, thus, the exercise of power. When the complex relations among these practices and forms of discourse are severed, there is a degeneration into brute moralism, self-legitimating sacrificial mechanism, and barren legalism. This is because a discourse and practice for enacting a symbolic world (cult) is severed from a discourse uniquely concerned with moral norms for human action (prophetic) and the means for structuring social interaction (legal). In this case, power fills the void as the basic value. The fact that this possibility is examined in the biblical texts themselves—such as in the case of the Tower of Babel—is a testimony to the fragility of this moral ontology and its capacities to shape and direct human life.

Thus, I have examined the moral ontology of a technological age and shown how it centers on power as the origin and content of value. With this we have seen how depictions of our being in the world in terms of emergence and self-transcendence specify the spatial-temporal conditions of life as value-neutral. I have also explored the moral ontology of the biblical texts in order to clarify (1) symbolic means and forms of practice for transvaluing power, but also (2) how this too can devolve into a reduction of value to power. Given these results of our inquiry, how might a thorough understanding of the contemporary moral outlook and the complex relation between the modes of action and discourse that circulate in the biblical texts help address contemporary theological-ethical questions? What has our work in comparative moral ontology shown?

A central moral and religious problem in contemporary life is the degree to which the possibility of viable life on this planet in the future entails imperatives for action. This means that moral character and conduct must now be defined through the imperative that persons and communities understand themselves as agents who respect and enhance the conditions necessary for the continuation and flourishing of life on this planet. Further, the world we are *in* must now be conceived in terms of the *temporal* arena or horizon of life, that is, the possibility of future life on this planet. In the light of our inquiry, we can say that technological societies are characterized by a form of "cultic" action, that is, ritual acts aimed at enacting a "world," in which the future is defined in terms of efficiency based solely on the exercise of human power. Possibilities for future life are to be sacrificed for the sake of present empowerment and control. It is hardly surprising, then, that the future, as the horizon upon which we project a construal of the world in which to act, must be seen in value-neutral terms in post-theistic societies. To speak of the moral standing of the future is nonsensical within the context of purely technical rationality and the moral ontology it entails. And this is because technological action does not re-enact a moral order or re-direct the exercise of human power under norms to protect the powerless.

Criticizing the technical rationality that characterizes post-theistic social life does not entail a romantic longing to return to a supposed pre-technological state. Such a state has never and will never exist. It is axiomatic of human existence that we are technological beings. This is seen in the text from Genesis 11. Human beings face the great task of civilization and the exercise of technological power because of the fact that we are instinct-poor. The point I am making, then, is that the technological outlook must be criticized and limited by the circulation of another form of discourse in the social order, specifically, prophetic discourse.

What does that mean? It means that from a prophetic stance the future is not conceived in value-neutral terms but with respect to the symbol of the reign of God. This symbol, which, we must see, defines an evaluation of the world with respect to the affirmation of reality by an agent, potentially reconstitutes an understanding of time and history as the context for human action. That is, prophetic discourse charts the limits of human possibilities and powers in terms of the annunciation of a future, just, and merciful condition (the reign of God) placing a claim on the present for its realization. This ethical-religious outlook asserts that moral integrity is determined by an orientation towards that inclusive community characterized by justice and mercy rather than with respect to sources of immediate empowerment that negate possibilities for real future life. And this stance further means that human agents make contact with the source of empowerment, and thus the divine, by dedicating themselves to respecting and enhancing the integrity of life. In other words, prophetic discourse functions to constitute communities that seek to re-enact this claim as basic to their own identity. That is because this symbolism helps to specify why finite existence matters on grounds other than utility by defining it in terms of a future condition of justice and mercy. This articulates a root affirmation of finite being as good in its very finitude, an affirmation basic to the moral viability of post-theistic culture itself.

What I am arguing is that in a post-theistic context we must understand biblical, agential construals of the divine and reality in hermeneutical and practical terms. We can explore how that discourse circulates in Israelite, biblical society to reconstitute the self-understanding of individuals and communities in their construal of the world and also to guide action. The importance of the biblical texts is that through prophetic discourse, cultic practices are reconstituted as the means for contact with the source of empowerment. This has the effect of morally transforming power in the social order because it endorses an inclusive moral community characterized by justice and mercy as that which persons and communities can and ought to respect and seek in all their actions. This is the case, because to identify ultimate power as an agent (God) is to assert a value that exceeds power, namely, the value of a commitment to respect and enhance identifiable agents and the conditions necessary for ongoing action. This follows since, as we have seen, to specify any agent is also to affirm some construal of the world. The insight of biblical discourse is to identify or name ultimate power in such a way that the affirmation of the value of finite being (the world and future life) is entailed in that identification, and, given this, fidelity to God requires a commitment to respect and enhance the integrity of life. To interpret one's own life or the life of a community from this perspective has the effect, I am suggesting, of transforming assessments of power, personal and social, and thus the origin and content of value. And it is a small—yet crucial—step to realize that this specifies the empowerment of the powerless to be active, identifiable agents in history as a basic moral and political requirement. Only in this way can we make sense of the right of the future of life on this planet to exist, a claim that must surely be binding on all of us.

The validity of this theological perspective for ethics must be demonstrated hermeneutically and practically. That is to say, this perspective must demonstrate its capacity to isolate and answer problems found in rival ethical accounts for how we should understand human existence and the world with respect to guiding action. In this essay, I have attempted this demonstration along two lines. First, I have tried to show that the contemporary moral ontology constricts our moral outlook with respect to the demand that future life ought to exist by focusing on the maximizing of power. This constriction of our moral outlook manifests itself, I believe, in the indifference found in current technological societies to these matters, even though an open future is seen as basic to human freedom. Second, I have also tried to show how a moral ontology centered on power alone cannot specify whether or not there are limits on the exercise of power and thus is unable to provide the means to distinguish morally between creative and destructive expressions of power. Since power serves nothing beyond itself—since it is, as I have put it, the origin and sole content of value—all that matters is the maximization of power. In this respect, the theological-ethical perspective outlined in this essay provides resources for articulating an imperative for present action, critically assessing current modes of thought, and also specifying a revised understanding of Christian faith. The question that necessarily remains open is the extent to which this ethical-religious outlook can actually empower human life.

Conclusion

In this essay I have tried to practice a mode of theological-ethical reflection that can at one and the same time engage the biblical texts and also debates in contemporary thought and society. Yet the questions that surround our ideas and beliefs about the meaning and significance of human agency are not merely academic. They touch on the most basic matters of human life. The responsibility placed on theological ethics in an age of human power is to bring its resources to bear on these basic matters in order to provide some guidance for considering how we should live. The present essay has been in the service of that larger, if more complex, enterprise.

7

Reconstruing Transcendence:
A Response to Welker, Keller, Rigby, and Schweiker

David E. Klemm

⌘

I should like to begin my response with an expression of gratitude to the conference organizers for raising in a purposeful way the question concerning the relationship between Bible and theology—a question which points to a plethora of biblical and theological traditions. For too long, biblical scholars and theologians have worked in separate compartments, and these papers represent an important effort to establish a working dialogue across disciplines.

The four papers to which I am responding are explorations in a new paradigm of theological reflection whose structural outline is sketched out in the introduction to this volume. The new paradigm distinguishes itself from the older "mono-systematic" approaches to thinking, approaches which assume that the biblical text has a singular meaning to which all subsidiary meanings can be reduced and that theological science has a singular principle to which all derivative concepts can be reduced. By contrast, the new "multi-systematic paradigm of thinking" announced in this volume strives to be capable of identifying, diagnosing, and prescribing cures for the systematic distortions resident in our post-modern or post-theistic societies and cultures, dominated as they are by an emerging multi-centered awareness of pluralism, limits, local knowledges, and marginalized particularities on one hand, and a countervailing emergent awareness of ever-unifying global order, expansionism, technical rationality, and irresistible universalizing or leveling of social forms on the other hand.

The question confronting this group of authors is this one: Can reflection on the diverse strata of biblical and theological materials contribute anything of substance to a much-needed clarity about the grave and urgent moral and spiritual problems confronting us—a clarity that is potentially transformative of our socio-historical forms of life? The focus for this multi-sided reflection is the grand topic of power, powerlessness, and the divine. In the following response, I shall focus on the way the relationship between Bible and theology is figured with regard to the topic of power and powerlessness. I hope to isolate the contribution each author appears to propose to the audience. I should also like to put a question or two to each author, and I ask the authors from the outset to correct and to forgive any systematic distortions that I might impose in my response on their otherwise unencumbered agencies.

Michael Welker addresses the pressing problem of the powerlessness of moral communication in a time of global crisis. It is dusk, and yet the owl of Minerva sleeps on. Why does not theological-ethical discourse have the power to awaken decisive action? Offering a partial explanation, Professor Welker first analyzes a signal condition of such moral incapacity to be the phenomenon of the *market constitution of morality.* Society in our time devolves into different subsystems of economy, politics, law, education, religion, and family, each of which articulates a different discourse with different moral criteria for granting or withdrawing recognition or respect, and so create different publics within a poly-centric whole whose constitution is inherently unstable and marked by accelerating flux. No wonder moral appeals to the "whole" or to the "common good" inspire no wisdom: they simply cannot be heard or assimilated as such. In his analyses of Hans Küng and David Tracy, Michael Welker shows how theological discourse ought *not* to proceed in this new situation.

According to Welker, Küng proclaims the need for a fundamental consensus on the unconditionality and universality of ethical obligation by reaffirming God as "the primal ground, the primal support, and the primal goal of humankind and the world." Welker argues that Küng's effort to overwhelm a new systemic problem with an old theological idea smacking of metaphysical hierarchy and teaching authority inherently misses the mark, however, because any mono-systematic answer today is immediately received within competing subsystems under their own criteria as a particular voice contending for power.

Likewise David Tracy's project fails, in Welker's judgment, in spite of its more sophisticated grasp of the polycontextual situation in which we think. Tracy's mystical—prophetic blurring of distinctions on behalf of the poor and oppressed fares no better in meeting the necessary condition of moral communication today. The essential condition is to articulate forms of moral discourse which themselves consciously adopt a pluralistic approach without blurring distinctions, addressing both continuities and discontinuities among societal subsystems. Such moral discourse is aware of its own susceptibility to distortion and error and so can be vigilant against distortion and error elsewhere.

Michael Welker finds a model for such moral discourse in the new Biblical theology, which takes different *Sitze im Leben* seriously and so resists the temptation to unify emergent processes that are in fact diversifying themselves. Michael Welker's contribution to moral communication takes the form of articulating the intrinsic connection between God's power and powerlessness that is multi-valently expressed in the image and concept of the *Spirit of God.* This enormously rich idea serves as a common principle of this group, when properly understood. How so? God's Spirit is itself in the nature of the case both *one and many.* It is one precisely in its pouring out into manifold and discontinuous situations, where it preserves rather than cancels differences, transforming powerlessness into power. Professor Welker cites the Pentecost story, which is itself in consonance with Isaiah 42, in order to make his point. Hope for renewed moral communication today rests not a metaphysical theology of primal ground, or a mystical-prophetic theology of differentiationless abyss, but with a theology of the living Spirit of God viewed in creative tension with the justice of God, according to Welker. The capacity of the spirit of God in the suffering Messiah and the crucified Jesus to communicate differently and effectively within different contexts of life gives living testimony to this hope.

In Welker's presentation, as I understand it, theology relates to the Bible as a multi-layered but systematic thought-pattern relates to a diversified source. In Welker's practice, both the Bible and theological science are one and many in their deep structures. Theology has the task of reflecting in conceptual form the meaning of the central image of the biblical narrative, thus articulating its coherence and rationality. In Welker's analysis, that central biblical image is the dynamic image of the Spirit of God, whose creative, sustaining, and culminating power is manifest in the interactions between power and powerlessness across diverse social strata. The idea of the Spirit of God provides an articulation of the first and final principle of thinking and being that is at once unified and diversified. God's Spirit preserves its identity precisely by manifesting itself differently in different situations and circumstances. Theological reflection should attend to transformation patterns, as found both in biblical narratives and in social reorganization, in order to trace and understand the dynamic process of God's self-manifestation.

I have two short questions for Michael Welker's excellent paper: 1) Is it so evident that power in contemporary society is differentiating itself into discontinuous albeit related subsystems of economy, politics, law, education, religion, and family, as Welker suggests? Rather, is it not increasingly be the case that the competitive global system in which we live is increasingly dominated by just one of these sub-systems, namely, economy? In my view, the system as a whole increasingly can be grasped as law-governed, and the law of the system is an economic one: *Maximize one's economic benefits*. Human motivations, decisions, and actions are increasingly generated with reference to market exchange because those who obey that law flourish and those who do not obey are pushed to the margins. The law constrains human actions such that all moral communication is increasingly measured by that law, thus the otherwise most well-intending polities, legal institutions, educational institutions, religious bodies, and families are increasing bound by a single necessity. The collapse of communism exacerbates the situation, for capitalist market exchange is now the only game in town. Isn't the question today precisely how to challenge the emergence of a new economic determinism and with it a new and unanticipated form of social Darwinism? Michael Welker's own use of the metaphor of moral markets would suggest so.

This leads to my second question: 2) Is the biblical image of the Spirit of God directly usable by theology, or must not theology reflect on the ontological structure revealed in this diverse-yet-unified image? And if it must, then does not theology once again become mono-systematic, perhaps in the best and highest sense possible?

I turn now to *Cynthia Rigby's* provocative paper on "Divine Power and the Self-Recovery of the Oppressed." Cynthia Rigby responds to the oft-cited claim that belief in a transcendent and omnipotent God constrains and distorts human agency; thus visions of divine power renders people powerless. Rigby claims that when belief in a transcendent God pacifies people into passively waiting for that "someday" of liberation, it must be rejected. But she cautions that belief in a transcendent God can also have the opposite effect to function to empower human agency. Her account, which runs in the direction of religious psychology, shows how some oppressed people are motivated actively to resist oppression rather than passively to suffer it precisely by the God-talk that sets them free to wrestle with God, to blame God, to whom is attributed the power to liberate although God does not in fact liberate. How does this empowerment occur?

To answer this question, Rigby brings together biblical image of God as Liberator, such as she finds in the language of Psalm 22, with the psychological exploration of the dangerous memory by which the self may be restored to itself. According to Rigby, imaginative reconstruing of painful repressed events gives vivid presentation of the ultimate standard of moral evaluation by pushing into consciousness the recognition that people *ought not* be treated this way! Awareness of the ought, the moral law, is empowered when it is accompanied by the "I can resist" of a resolute will set free through catharsis and an angry "Where were you?" directed to the God who in principle can liberate but in fact often does not. A conversion occurs when the remembering subject realizes both that by not acting God respects free subjectivity, and that in the presentation of the "ought," God does liberate, for genuine freedom is awoken only in appropriation of the moral law.

How does Rigby figure the relationship between Bible and theology with reference to power, powerlessness, and the divine? I believe she would say that adequate theological reflection requires attention to the rich ambiguity found in biblical texts such as Psalm 22 with its apparent contradiction between "God liberates" and "God does not liberate." Theological interpretation of biblical texts ought not to reduce that ambiguity to univocity, she implies. Theological interpretation ought instead to develop a concept of God that can hold together both sides of the contradiction in a rich and productive tension, much like Paul Ricoeur analyzes the metaphorical meaning as it arises out of the productive imagination spurred by a formal contradiction to generate new concepts in the synthesis of the heterogeneous, a synthesis that does not annihilate distinctions but brings them into fruitful interaction.

Cynthia Rigby's point is that theological thinking borne by biblical interpretation should have less to do with metaphysical products of synthesis (meanings, conceptually expressed) than with psychological processes: to know God's power in powerlessness is to undergo an event in the inner life of the soul through the courageous act of remembering, an act in which dawns an authentic spirituality lived not for the sake of the inner life of the soul but for the communities in which one is always already embedded. The awakening of spirituality is the awakening of power within powerlessness, a power turned outward to a world in which oppression exists and in which oppression can be resisted.

My question to Cynthia Rigby, whose posing of the issue of spirituality interestingly interacts with Michael Welker's contribution concerning God as spirit, is quite simple: What is the difference between theology and spirituality or religious psychology? It seems to me that it is one thing to reflect on the effects that the image of a transcendent God may have on certain individuals and it is another thing to reflect on the conceptual content of the God of traditional theism. Is there anything ingredient in the *idea* of God that necessarily entails either assent to human freedom as a basic principle or denial of human freedom? Is the idea of God arising from the correlative reflection between biblical texts and psychological experience different in kind from the God of classical theism such as we would find in Thomas, or even in Schleiermacher, or Tillich? Does the idea of God provide a standard for measuring "liberation" or is liberation meant in a purely socio-psychological sense?

Catherine Keller addresses the rhetoric of divine power by examining the reflection on power represented by major strands in theological thought today: namely, liberationist, feminist, postmodernist, and process conceptualities. Her paper aims at determining what divine power *is* and what it *is not*, by following the "power-lines" extended through these conceptualities into complex and polyrelational social locations defined by race, gender, class, nation, religion, species, and so on. Catherine Keller's intention is both critical and constructive: she exposes systemic distortions in thinking about power within each of the four conceptualities she examines, and she discloses a vision of divine power as relational presented not in the triumphant mood of a major key but in a humble and contrite spirit of a minor key that is nonetheless capable of transforming received positions which differently mediate the opposition between divine power and powerlessness. Moreover, Catherine Keller articulates her vision with respect to the Book of Revelation, a work marking the "limit" of the Christian rhetoric of power. Can a revisioned idea of "God" make a difference for social justice?, she asks. Let me briefly reconstruct Catherine Keller's critical reflection through four moments.

1.   *Liberation theology* invokes divine power in opposition to worldly powers within an apocalyptic temporal framework that is open-ended and sustained by the promise of a coming reign of God. The rhetoric of liberation tends to reify an opposition between divine omnipotence viewed as ultimately in control of history and an oppressive social situation that is not God's will. This trope of antithesis may lead the oppressed to emulate the image of divine omnipotence through the revolutionary movement and thereby to marginalize certain other groups—women and indigenous peoples, for example.

2.   *Feminist theology* addresses and resolves the dualism inherited from liberation theology between divine omnipotence, evaluated as domination, and the social condition of oppression within the people's movement that is inherited from liberation theology. In contrast to liberation theology, feminist theology reconceives power in non-hierarchical fashion as *relational:* power is not unidirectionally exerted *over* some one or ones but is relationally exerted with and *through* the many individuals who collectively constitute a group. Power is dynamic

interactive pattern and its measure is mutuality. The idea of power as relational is the lasting contribution of feminism to the discussion on power, but the rhetoric of feminism brings forth a new dualism, the dualism of gender.

3. *Postmodern thought*, such as in Michael Foucault, illuminates the way in which power is both self-determined in freedom and determined by the other's act of resistance. Power involves both initiating agency and resisting agency: this insight presents a theoretical capacity to undo binary oppositions, including the dualism of gender bequeathed by feminist thought, while demonstrating that resistance to power is not in the nature of the case transformation of power. Postmodern or poststructuralist thought, however, still leaves open a serious reflection on what power is and in what sense we can speak of divine power.

4. *Process thought*, according to Keller, can provide the means to conceive power more adequately than its predecessors through the distinction between divine final causation and effective or mechanical causes. The process conceptuality of inter-relational causality or relational power brings clarifies the sense in which power is never uni-directional but always mutually exerted. This point Keller finds illustrated in the Book of Revelation, which she develops into a theologically transformed apocalyptic vision of the all in all: omnipotentiality, omnincarnation, and omnirelationality embodied into a just community of mutually shared potencies.

As I read her paper, Catherine Keller figures the relationship between the Bible and theology as one between rhetoric and reflection. Theological reflection finds itself in a determinate social space shaped in part by its reception of powerfully persuasive biblical texts. Reflection has the task of dislodging the immediate impact of persuasive discourse and grasping what is presupposed by the rhetorical situation itself, namely, mutual relationality. How so? In rhetorical discourse, the speaker or writer is influenced by the audience and the concrete situation into which she speaks or writes just as the speaker attempts to influence the audience. Theological reflection grasps the meaning of biblical rhetoric as inter-relationality—an ontological fact of spiritual life that is rendered ethically good by the measure of achieved mutuality. Study of biblical rhetoric persuades the theologian that her reflection is similarly rhetorical. The lesson is that theological reflection, informed by its newly found principle of inter-relationality, should use its own rhetorical power to transform the misconceived win-or-lose structure of inherited rhetorics into a working vision of the mutuality of social justice

My questions to Keller ask for elucidation and clarification: exactly what is the final concept of relational power she advocates? What is it, and what is it not? And how should we think of divine power as fully relational power?

William Schweiker accomplishes some fundamentally important work in his comparison and contrast of the moral ontology found in the biblical construal of reality with that found in the post-theistic technological societies. According to Schweiker, the post-theistic societies are marked by a moral ontology in which human agency encounters no countervailing divine agency and is therefore free to exert power in a value-neutral world by positing value as a product of its unconstrained positing activity. Such a vision is not new—it is shared by Callicles and Thrasymachus in their debates with Socrates. New is the awesome extension of human power through technology and the proliferation of symbolic forms through which power is manipulated. In such a situation, all things are possible—not, as Kierkegaard meant it, for God, but, as Nietzsche meant it, for the all-too-human. The will to power is the all-determining reality in the post-theistic societies.

By contrast, the biblical construal of reality posits the agency of God as a power that really limits human power. In the Tower of Babel story, which Schweiker interprets, humans act as if they were the sole agents in a value-neutral world until confounded by the Spirit of God who confuses their language and scatters them over the face of the earth. Schweiker proposes that viewed hermeneutically and practically, the divine agency manifests itself by setting limits on human possibilities with respect to the future viability of civilization. To view nature as creation, the human as creature, and history as purposive is to grasp divine agency not as one agency among others, as one more competing and jealous or forgiving power, but rather as the first and final principle of agency itself, the infinite agency making possible the finite structure of human agency in relation both to the natural world and to other finite human agents. A human agent is a finite origin point of action, circumscribed somewhere and at some time. Divine agency is the origin point of that structure, and its disclosure in the biblical construal of reality limits the arbitrary exercise of power in principle. Humans construed in relation to God are construed as absolutely dependent on a power which grounds, guides, and limits human power. Human power is necessarily construed as responsible, i.e., answerable, to that principle as both source and final purpose or highest good. Being as being is intended as good through divine agency.

How does William Schweiker figure the relationship between Bible and theology in this paper? It seems to me that for Schweiker the Bible is a source for theological interpretation as a second-order reflection on the first-order biblical language. In this paper, however, God-talk both biblical and expressly theological, as well as its displacement in post-theistic discourse, also serves as a source for reflection on the moral ontology implied within these systems. Theological discourse for Schweiker is always ethical discourse; ethical discourse is always theological. Following that line of thought, Schweiker asserts that the power of both biblical and theological discourse about divine agency is measured by its capacity both hermeneutically to disclose a worldview that is centered on human responsibility to divine power and ethically to measure and evaluate the creative and destructive uses of human power.

William Schweiker's contributions are manifold, but perhaps most important is his willingness to make a formal claim about the nature and structure of human existence: Humans are selves in a world manifesting a spiritual identity through diverse forms of purposive action all oriented toward a single final purpose, an idea of the highest good. Bravo!

I have many questions to ask of Schweiker's outstanding essay, perhaps the most pressing for me returns us to the programmatic concerns announced in the introduction to the volume. The introduction claims that Western theism is all too often reductionistic ("mono-systematic") and oppressive ("In classical theology and its impression on all Western thought, the act of thinking the being of God is thinking the unity of all that is, the coherence of reality, from the perspective of dominating power operative outside of relation to other social powers"). The papers in this volume attempt to explore a new paradigm of thinking that breaks free from that of the classical theistic one.

My question to Schweiker's eloquent paper is this: Does this paper not take the biblical construal of reality as a *theistic* construal? In other words, is there not a presupposed identity in conceptual content, if not in form, between the image of an acting God, say in the Tower of Babel story, and the idea of divine being in classical theism? If so, the paper implies that under at least one version of the theistic picture (namely, this version) human responsibility is not violated when divine power and agency is asserted, but is rather affirmed and preserved in its integrity by a setting of limits. How, exactly does this version of theism differ from earlier reprehensible classical versions? Did they really view God as "removed from the conflict and process of transformation in social—historical reality"? Did they really engage in "the systematic reduction of complexity to a single principle" any more than this version does? If not, what is wrong with theism or even the great idea of a highest good? Why are we biblical scholars and theologians associating theism with oppressive domination as if in the nature of the case? Is Schweiker really abandoning the classical paradigm of theism, or is he rehabilitating it?

I cannot help but wonder aloud whether the papers as a set do not misidentify the problem. Is classical theism the source of systematic and systemic distortion of power? Or is the failure to understand classical theism the problem? If the idea of God in theism was systematically distorted in its social-historical institutionalization and reception, should we continue systematically to distort that great idea in our own academic—ecclesiastical discourse?

Part Three

—SOCIAL-EXPERIENTIAL INQUIRIES—

⌘

8

A New Thing In The Land
The Female Surrounds The Warrior

Rita Nakashima Brock

⌘

The modern period, marked by Enlightenment influences, has come under intense scrutiny through that amorphous group of theories called post-modern, including post-colonial, deconstructionist, and feminist theories. Many of the forces that have given momentum to modern Western culture, its converging vigors, as well as the energies generated by binary, oppositional powers, are seen as either too weak or too destructive to continue. The romantic idealization of progress and the last four hundred years of modern history have been unmasked as legacies of North Atlantic hegemony, including the ensuing centuries of wars of increasingly destructive magnitude. The U.S. has not been immune to the global forces of destruction that have taken 100 million lives since the end of World War II—it has added its own contributions to those forces.

As the world faces continuing civil wars and internally fomented forms of terrorism, we have to ask what will stop the destruction. The conflicts of post-modernism, with its deconstructions of power—of race, class, and gender privilege—have also entered the current fray. With challenges to Eurocentric and androcentric theologies, works from alternative perspectives have argued for the validity of ideas emerging from underneath those hegemonic structures.

New voices have challenged the notions of canon, orthodoxy, tradition, and universality. These new, alternative reshapings of Christian theology emerge from voices nurtured by a process of "hearing into speech," as Nelle Morton put it—a process by which those who suffer speak in their own voices in a context of listening that encourages the telling of truths heretofore silenced. Through such telling, analyses of power and oppression are developed into subversive discourses.

Subversive discourses emerge every time a community of solidarity in suffering emerges. That new theologies have begun to emerge in the last two decades indicates histories of formation; for they have not suddenly found voice *ex nihiloi*[1] They emerge as structures of power shift. Democratic ideals, revolutionary and popular movements, widespread education —ideals of modern liberalism—have provided means for marginalized groups to make their voices heard.

These new voices have created at times a symphony of justice and at times a cacophony of competing demands for visibility and credibility. Listening to their analyses of power is crucial to the creation of redemptive theologies for our contemporary world. At the same time, these voices often make conflicting claims, and one group may find itself at odds with another, an adversarial network that has been created by intent by the dominant economic, racial, and gender structures of capitalism.[2] The conflicts may lead us to the creation of a more just society or to the destruction of the social fabric necessary for the maintenance of community and humane life in the U.S.

If we are to maintain social fabrics from which to create justice, competing groups must learn how to negotiate relationships with each other as well as with the dominant society—and we would do well to be suspicious of the dominant American society's economic and social values and behaviors as a guide. Those structures do not understand the distinctions between structures of oppression and difference that are

---

[1]　This discussion of the domination which silences voices is partly informed by James C. Scott's *Domination and the Arts of Resistance: Hidden Transcripts* (New Haven: Yale University Press, 1990). Scott discusses the existence of dissident discourses within long-standing communities which nurture such discourses, a nurturing without which articulate speech could not so readily emerge.

[2]　Ronald Takaki in *Strangers from a Different Shore: A History of Asian Americans* (New York: Penguin Books, 1989) provides several examples of how Asian immigration was controlled by whites in Hawaii and California who used one ethnic group to control another, including the use of Chinese in the south against freed slaves. See also Gary Okihiro, *Margins and Mainstreams: Asians in American History and Culture*, (Seattle: University of Washington Press, 1994).

potentially escapable, such as poverty, and those that are virtually inescapable, such as race, gender, and sexual orientation. At the same time, we must be careful that the politics of identity (as important as those are) do not simply replace conversations about ethics.[3] The religious communities of our society, especially at the grassroots levels, are one arena in which we can have such cross-cultural conversations about identity and justice, about individual integrity in community.

The relativizing of any particular perspective has raised the question of how claims to justice can be made, especially among groups differently oppressed or marginalized. Authority, truth, and identity have undergone scrutiny as new perspectives emerge. In a shift of focus toward such perspectives, we have begun to create new angles on theology and hermeneutics. Even as the current fundamentalist emphasis shifts toward convergence—toward more singular and clear sources of authority and truth, the post-modern impulse has been to move toward multivalent divergence—toward a more fluid and contextual understanding of identity, authority, truth, and power.

This divergence is not the total relativizing of truth, but an affirming embrace of difference and an acknowledgment that truth is contextual, provisional, and need be neither universal nor final to be efficacious. As marginalized voices have emerged, the voices of hegemony have also changed, as men, heterosexuals, and whites have begun to examine the cost of maintaining dominance; and a new conversation is taking place as voices of dominance speak in ways that do not protect power. Conversations among various contextualized understandings of truth make connections that both challenge hegemony and shape empathy, community, and mutuality instead of walls of difference. This essay focuses on the arena in which our understandings of conflict and identity and our capacity to make connections are learned: families.

In many societies, the moral guidance and psychological and physical nurturing supplied by families, which are the bedrock of livable societies and which form capacities for empathy, have been seriously

---

3 Charles Taylor discusses the nature of multicultural inclusion thus: "There must be something midway between the inauthentic and homogenizing demand for recognition of equal worth, on the one hand, and the self-immurement within ethnocentric standards, on the other. There are other cultures, and we have to live together more and more, both on a world scale and comingled in each individual society" [from "The Politics of Recognition," in *Multiculturalism and the Politics of Recognition,* ed. Amy Gutmann (Princeton: Princeton University Press, 1992), 72].

Cornell West also raises a question about public discourse that places the politics of race over discussion of ethics in "Black Leadership and the Pitfalls of Racial Reasoning," *Race-ing Justice, Engendering Power: Essays on Clarence Thomas and Anita Hill,* ed. Toni Morrison (New York: Pantheon Books, 1992).

eroded by a complex series of forces created by modern urbanization, industrialization, and capitalist competition. Yet, outside feminist and conservative circles (i.e. what is commonly called the "religious right"), theology has, until recently, largely ignored what has been happening to domestic life. Domestic life has been used in its metaphorical functions to define divine paternal power, not as a source of theological construction and knowledge.[4] Most public U.S. discussions of families are influenced by the conservative perspective, a perspective which focuses on the maintenance of a nostalgic status quo founded in traditional biblical paradigms and a false view of American history. The conservative nostalgia ignores the uses and misuses of power embedded in traditional ideologies of the patriarchal family, ideologies crucial to the maintenance of today's capitalist nation-states. The religious right has used an ideology of family to further a political agenda that is pro-military, anti-woman, and economically anti-family. The conservative approach uses a picture of the nuclear family that was never the most common form of American family, except for a brief couple of decades following World War II, and virtually ignores the current economic, architectural, and political destruction of communities and families.

Both liberationist and mainstream forms of Christian theology have had little to say about the family, which has allowed the right to dominate public discourse with rhetoric about "family values." Theologies based on the *experiences* of domestic life, rather than on traditional family ideologies, are in short supply. The Christian tradition has long used a model of power in the domestic sphere as a mirror of the hierarchical structures of patriarchal militarism—political systems that inform the cultural and social context of power and its historical development. Both biblically and theologically, Christian theologians have appropriated the patriarchal and military power systems of their day as metaphors to create a transcendent structure of power to challenge earthly political powers. They describe the power of God in parallel terms of power that join family structures to human empires focusing on control, obedience, competition, and triumph. Theologians do this even as they mean to be different from and critical of human political powers. This hierarchical value system is still firmly in place in the West socially, economically, legally, and theologically. These

---

4   Bonnie Miller McClemore in *Also a Mother* (Nashville: Abingdon Press, 1993) argues that the theological neglect of family and childrearing issues is a product of the sexist structures of academe in which those who work must leave such concerns behind to be considered professional and serious. She asserts that feminism itself has had to cope with this dichotomy between public and private at great psychological cost to women. Renita Weems in *Battered Love* (Minneapolis: Fortress Press, 1995) discusses the metaphorical use of marriage and violence in Hosea, Ezekiel, and Jeremiah.

polarized and hierarchical constructions of political power use gender to subordinate all aspects of domestic life through the subordination of women.

Deconstruction of the patriarchal family and its structures of authority is crucial to understanding the nature of power in its most intimate manifestations and in the theological resonances that emerge from our earliest experiences of power in families, even when theological systems ignore these earliest forms of power. Feminist perspectives provide this deconstruction, a deconstruction that unmasks abuse and oppression.[5] With that analysis we can begin a constructive proposal that does not simply accept hierarchical gender polarizations characteristic of North Atlantic societies.

We need, I believe, alternative ways to understand power and values that enhance community, healing, and justice—that unleash the life-giving energy necessary for just and sustainable life in human communities and on the earth. In analyzing power, we often focus on domination and subordination and on oppression and victimization: on power and powerlessness. These analyses are extremely helpful for revealing the exploitation, alienation, and violence of fixed hierarchies, but they do not point us much beyond reversals of power, conflicts of power, balances of power, or condemnations and avoidances of hierarchical power, typical of polemics. In fact, societies conceive of power in many different ways, and new understandings may help us see beyond deadlocks in our own views.[6]

To shift the conversation about power and values into a third alternative, I am proposing a paradigm of taking responsibility. In such a paradigm, we must be willing to acknowledge power inequalities and their devastating consequences, but our focus shifts to questions of agency and its consequences within unequal structures. In looking at both/and forms of power, I want to direct our attention to sources of renewed personal agency for change and for personal accountability for all who live within hierarchical structures. Perhaps such a paradigm may move us into a different discourse than the common hierarchical comparisons of the severity of oppression and competing claims for justice among groups differently oppressed.

In searching for a way to negotiate such new relationships, I will reflect on how several feminist analyses of power and relationship lead

---

5   Cf., for example, *Christianity, Patriarchy, and Abuse*, eds. Carol Bohn and Joanne Brown (Cleveland: Pilgrim Press, 1989).

6   Shelly Errington discusses cross-cultural nuances in understanding how power is described and imaged in "Recasting Sex, Gender, and Power: A Theoretical and Regional Overview" in *Power and Difference: Gender in Island Southeast Asia*, eds. Jane Monnig Atkinson and Shelly Errington (Stanford: Stanford University Press, 1990).

us to biblical texts that offer alternative models of power to the traditional ones, models that may better present us with ways to envision creating community amongst a diversity of interests and demands. The biblical text of Jeremiah 31 seems suited to this inquiry because it also emerges during a major crisis in a civilization, when the exile had brought Israel face to face with the loss of its king and temple cults. The prophetic texts of that period experiment with new religious paradigms and theologies for restoring life to a devastated people.

I find feminist/womanist/mujerista analyses helpful because women's voices are layered in among other marginalized voices. In every oppressed group that has structures of male dominance, women represent more than one marginalized voice. In addition, some women belong to groups who have dominance, even if they themselves have little power within their own subclass. Belonging to a variety of groups, both oppressed and dominant, has led many women to negotiate forms of power while seeking to maintain connections.[7] These layered complexities may be helpful experiential guides toward new ways of seeing power and identity as intricate, fluid, and contextual. In seeing identity as less fixed and locating personal power in a fluid identity, we may be able to root both ethics and spirituality in paradigms that encourage the taking of personal responsibility and the enabling of accountability to relationships of care.

Looking at the experiences of various women is crucial because the domestic worlds and work of women have remained outside traditional understandings of power, except as women were used symbolically to serve masculine functions and the domestic world was modeled on the hierarchical political one. Outside these metaphysical and patriarchal systems to which women were expected to be subject, we have been regarded as problematic, polluting, or evil. Physical matter, the body, and the natural world, which are closely associated with women, have been, until recently, relegated to the status of passive, conquerable, or invisible objects to be used to serve progress, success, control, and domination.[8]

I will be using analyses of power presented by Alice Miller and Nel Noddings, especially as power is used and understood in domestic

---

7   See Henry Louis Gates, *Reading Black, Reading Feminist: A Critical Anthology* (New York: Meridian, 1990), Trinh T. Minh-Ha, *Woman, Native, Other: Writing Post-Coloniality and Feminism* (Bloomington: Indiana University Press, 1989), and bell hooks, *Ain't I A Woman: Black Women and Feminism* (Boston: South End Press, 1981).

8   Cf. chapter two, Rita Nakashima Brock and Susan Brooks Thistlethwaite, *Casting Stones: Prostitution and Liberation in Asia and the United States* (Minneapolis: Fortress Press, 1996), for an analysis of the subordination of women in Christianity and Buddhism.

relationships. Because I believe our earliest experiences with power and its uses underlie both what we find compelling in divine images and how we live out uses of power in private and in communities, I will use this analysis of power to examine abusive images of divine power. I will then explore the strategy of moving from a paradigm of power and powerlessness to one of taking personal responsibility, which involves examining uses of power when one is between levels of power —both powerful and powerless at the same time, an analysis found in Sara Ruddick's work on maternal thinking.[9] Finally, I will present biblical images that challenge and undermine paradigms of the abuse of power and present us with new images of hope.

My interest in the theological implications of power in domestic relationships was born out of my growing awareness of what people are capable of doing to children, an awareness that has come from personal experiences with a wide variety of adolescents and from women's sharing and writing about domestic violence. My particular focus rests upon the harm done to children through misuses of power by adults and the need to reflect on the consequences of such misuses. Behind my preoccupation with domestic relationships also lie the writings of many Asian American women, which address the ambiguities and challenges of living in families and communities caught in cross-cultural riptides.[10] Their writings reveal the multilayered, complex voices that make up an individual's identity. In addition, I have been transformed by the pioneering work of Alice Miller on child abuse.[11]

---

[9]   While all three of these particular theorists are white, middle class women, my original insights about the issues raised by victimization and innocence came from my readings of the work of Asian American women, which are discussed in my essays, "On Losing Your Innocence but Not Your Hope," *A Feminist Ethical Commentary*, ed. Elisabeth Schüssler Fiorenza (New York: Crossroad Press, 1993), "Dusting the Bible on the Floor: The Loss of Innocence and the Power of Wisdom in Asian American Women's Writing," *Humline Review*, 15 (Spring 1991), and "On Mirrors, Mists, and Murmurs: Toward an Asian American Thealogy,"*Weaving the Visions: Patterns in Feminist Spirituality*, eds. Judith Plaskow and Carol Christ (New York: Harper & Row, 1989), 235-243.

[10]   Cf., for example, *Making Waves: An Anthology of Writings By and About Asian American Women*, Asian Women United of California, ed. (Boston: Beacon Press, 1989), Maxine Hong Kingston, *The Woman Warrior: Memoirs of a Girlhood Among Ghosts* (New York: Vintage Press, 1976), Joy Kogawa *Obasan* (Boston: David R. Godine, 1982), and Amy Ling, *Between Worlds: Women Writers of Chinese Ancestry* (New York: Pergamon, 1990).

[11]   Especially through her books *The Drama of the Gifted Child: How Narcissistic Parents Form and Deform the Emotional Lives of Their Talented Children* (New York: Basic Books, 1981), *For Your Own Good: Hidden Cruelty in Child-Rearing and the Roots of Violence* (New York: Farrar, Straus, & Giroux, 1984), and *Thou Shalt Not Be Aware: Society's Betrayal of the Child* (New York: Farrar, Straus, & Giroux, 1984).

Adults are rarely held accountable for inflicting the equivalent of torture on the most helpless and defenseless members of families, an impunity aggravated by the private, isolated, and unsupported nature of parenting in American society. These structures create the potential for great evil to be done, an evil identified as soul murder by Morton Schatzman.[12] Evil occurs with chilling regularity, finds innocuous and banal private forms, and is deeply embedded in the most intimate corners of human life. Mechanisms for social accountability in minimizing such evil are scarce in U.S. society, and the legacies of such evil are long, running for generations.

On the other hand, human beings are remarkably resilient and drawn to goodness. And goodness also occurs with regularity, is ordinary and banal, and is deeply embedded in the intimate corners of life. Human beings have intense drives to be healthy. We yearn to reach out to each other, and our passions for integrity and wholeness are strong, even when we carry within ourselves enormous legacies of pain. These reservoirs for wholeness are the roots of personal and spiritual power. But their resources can be severely tested by abuse.

Poisonous Pedagogy

Alice Miller develops her analysis of child abuse in *For Your Own Good*, which gives accounts of several cases of severe abuse in Europe and its destructive consequences for adults. Miller argues that child abuse and its consequences involve a reversal of values that has serious negative consequences for both individual victims and for societies characterized by this complex system she calls "poisonous pedagogy."[13] Miller believes poisonous pedagogy structures human behaviors, social interactions, and religious attitudes. The system's core reversal in values is that between parent and child—between stronger and weaker. Within the framework of poisonous pedagogy, children, who are more dependent and vulnerable, are expected to serve the wishes and needs of parents, who are stronger and more self-sufficient.

Through discipline, positive reinforcement, manipulation, deceit, entrapment, and punishment, children are expected to love, respect, obey, and serve their parents—to fulfill their caretakers' desires. These methods of shaping children, argues Miller, relativize all values except the value of being stronger—of having power, authority, and control—

---

12   Morton Schatzman, *Soul Murder: Persecution in the Family* (1973), as discussed in Miller's *Thou Shalt Not Be Aware.*

13   Alice Miller, *For Your Own Good: Hidden Cruelty in Child-rearing and the Roots of Violence* (New York: Farrar, Straus, and Giroux, 1985). Cf. 59–60 for a summary of the basic principles of poisonous pedagogy.

which are the only absolutes upheld by the power to control another's behavior. Values such as respect for others, nonviolence, honesty, bodily integrity, intimacy, and self-awareness are relativized by their violation. When they betray humane, ethical values, the stronger party blames the weaker for the betrayal. Those with greater power often rationalize their misuse of power as being for the good of those more vulnerable, who are expected to bear the negative burdens of the system of power established by the stronger. Miller points to many obvious biblical images of God depicted in this abusive mode.

Through the system of poisonous pedagogy, care and protection are reversed, and the needs of the vulnerable are exploited by those with greater power. The weak are abused and are blamed for their abuse. This process undermines their sense of personal agency and power; they forfeit an awareness of themselves that gives them confidence in their own feelings and perceptions; and they become increasingly isolated in a private world of guilt and suffering.[14] This pattern manifests itself in a variety of dimensions in intimate relationships.

The extension of this system of abuse into the larger society means the vulnerable and less powerful are forced to accept responsibility for the actions of the more powerful, an acceptance which leads to the abrogation of personal, moral responsibility by the powerful. Discourses of power are structured by images of domination and subordination. Stronger parties have the authority to violate any values and use any means necessary to achieve their own objectives. Victims are expected to feel guilty for having caused their own suffering.

When victims of abuse are made responsible for the behavior of their abusers, the actions of the powerful are placed in the hands of their victims or scapegoats, who control the abusers' actions. Those who abuse others blame their behavior on those who provoke their actions, so that they can see themselves as victims of the misbehavior, seductiveness, or willful contrariness of those they abuse.[15]

Abuses of power and authority by the powerful are often accompanied by an illusion of passivity or helplessness and the absence of a sense of personal responsibility and power. The powerful believe their behavior, even when it is excessive, is "caused" by the perverseness of their victims. This insidious aspect of poisonous pedagogy creates victims but no perpetrators—all motivating power is external. Hence,

---

[14] Judith Herman discusses the psychological traumas associated with extreme forms of intimate abuse in *Trauma and Recovery: The Aftermath of Violence—From Domestic Abuse to Political Terror* (New York: HarperCollins, 1992).

[15] It is interesting that the defense in the 1992 Rodney King police beating case in Los Angeles argued that King controlled the behavior of the police officers, who structurally and physically had a great deal more power than he.

we are left with the paradox that the more destructive the abusers, the less personal power the abusers believe they possess, i.e. they believe their behavior is in the hands of misbehaving victims. The more the abuse of power, the more the illusion of powerlessness, at the same time that authority and power are reinforced. Scapegoats then become the target of projections of anger and outrage and are blamed for being targets because of who they are. Blame and punishment become the focus of controlling behavior.[16] And only the ability to control provides the return of a sense of power.

Miller is unequivocal in her assertion that any use of pain and/or emotional manipulation to control the behavior of children is not benign. Because the male-dominant and hierarchically structured North Atlantic societies Miller discusses have preferred to defend authority and power, few avenues exist for the reclamation and integration of pain and anger at abuse. Public discourses are oriented toward the maintenance of dominance and subordination. Hence, through repression and rationalization, what a person pretends to be becomes more important than who that person is and how s/he feels.

Because pain and anger in victims must be denied, they are used in an unrecognized process of self-destruction or projection onto others, or both. Children, women, Jews, ethnic minority groups, racially darker groups, gays and lesbians, the elderly, the mentally or physically disabled, prostitutes, and other such groups have functioned variously in Christian cultures as scapegoats, as targets of community hostility and divine wrath. The abuse of scapegoats by the powerful is justified by stereotypes about their "evil" natures, which make the abusers the victims of those they abuse.[17] This mentality of victimization is heightened when those who are oppressed challenge or protest their abuse, such that those with greater power may depict themselves as victimized by those with less power.

Another way that those with power maintain a victim's identity occurs through a strong identification by abusers with innocent victims,

16   In April of 1994, an American teenager in Singapore confessed to acts of vandalism. Part of his sentence was to be struck six times by a cane, a bloody punishment that slices the skin and often leaves permanent scars. Newspaper letters to the editor and radio talk shows revealed an overwhelming public support of Americans for the caning, an act of brutality and torture not allowed in the U.S. system. What is astounding is the extent of support for punishment, if one accepts the premises of punishment as necessary, that seems disproportionately severe to the nature of the crime involved, if he actually committed it, which is under some doubt.

17   James G. Williams in *The Bible, Violence, and the Sacred: Liberation from the Myth of Sanctioned Violence* (New York: Harper Collins, 1991) examines the scapegoat motif and its institutionalized violence in the biblical text, as well as the countervoice of innocent victims found in the text, especially in the story of Jesus.

those whose abuse is undeserved and on whose behalf those with power act. With innocent victims outrage about abuse can be unequivocal (and, of course, the more innocent someone is, the more easily s/he is victimized). Innocent victims make the malevolence of the abuser unambiguous because innocence implies helplessness or powerlessness. When malevolence is clear, righteous anger is unleashed. Righteous anger can function as an indirect means by the powerful for catharting their unresolved anger at earlier abuse. Their anger and pain about previously having been victimized are experienced, then, through an identification with innocent victims, those who suffer undeservedly, a process of identification that Barbara Deming has called anger by analogy.[18] Any evidence of moral ambiguity or personal agency in victims becomes grounds for the loss of help and protection and the revisiting of abuse. This paternalistic system of identification with innocent victims and the avoidance of moral ambiguities continues to locate responsibility for abuse on the victims of the system, and perpetuates abuse by deflecting attention away from the root causes of abuse, thereby sustaining abusive power structures.

The moral force of innocence is a passive goodness, not an active agency and accountability. Obedience and disobedience are cast in life or death terms, and in order to identify scapegoats and differentiate those who are just from those who deserve blame and punishment, clear moral lines must be drawn between the innocent and guilty. Those with the power to enforce their own will on victims must blame those groups for their abuses of power to avoid moral ambiguities. Because the focus of the cause of the abuse is misplaced, there is little means to redirect our attention to the fundamental realization that abuse is wrong, not because victims are innocent, but because abuse, even by "good" people for a "good" cause, is a misuse of power and dehumanizes abuser and abused.

Ethical Terror

The religious aspects of poisonous pedagogy for Christian fundamentalists are poignantly spelled out by the historian Philip Greven, who notes their authoritarian use of the Bible, their obsession with apocalyptic thinking, and their belief in an omnipotent god who crushes evil and rewards good.[19] His psychological studies of religious child rearing provide devastating evidence of the abusive norms that

---

18   Barbara Deming, *We Are All Part of One Another: A Barbara Deming Reader* (New Haven: New Society Publishers, 1984), 206–217.
19   Philip Greven, *Spare the Child: The Religious Roots of Punishment and the Psychological Impact of Physical Abuse* (New York: Alfred A. Knopf, 1991).

permeate conservative Christian models of the family. The leaders of these religious groups, not coincidentally, are the most resistant to feminist ideas and the most comfortable with militaristic images of God.

Poisonous pedagogy did not, however, originate in conservative Christian circles but permeates the entire history of Christian thought. It is not just fundamentalists who use a canon and theology permeated with images of God as poisonous pedagogue and abuser. In its Augustinian traditions, Christianity continues polarized dualisms that dichotomize the ideal and real, the concrete and abstract, sin and salvation, and good and evil. Caught within the conflicts of these dualisms, human beings must conform their own wills to that of the superior, ideal, transcendent divine will. Disobedience is the sin that brings suffering caused either by divine punishment or the inherent consequences of sin, which separates people from God.[20]

Nel Noddings calls the theological use of poisonous pedagogy "ethical terror."

> Since God, who clearly has the knowledge and power to do otherwise, inflicts or allows the greatest of suffering, the infliction of pain cannot be a primary ethical abuse... Our thinking, then, is distracted from the loving parent's attitude that would relieve and eliminate suffering to a long and perhaps hopeless quest to be justified in God's sight.[21]

Where a tragic view of life developed by those with power, it is used to justify the inflicting of pain, rationalizing "the tragic necessity of doing evil and accepting evil rather than a sustained commitment to stand against it."[22]

Ethical terror is a system that upholds theological rationales for fighting evil by inflicting suffering and attributing such behavior to God. Acting according to the divine will then becomes a mandate to do the same, so that evil is projected onto scapegoats who must be punished. Good and evil are dichotomized as warring powers, warfare in which human beings are expected to take sides and to seek to dominate, defeat, and/or control evil. All authorization for the power to control evil comes from God, an external source, and structures of domination and subordination remain firmly in place.

---

[20]   In a previous work, *Journeys By Heart: A Christology of Erotic Power* (New York: Crossroad Press, 1988), I discussed how child abuse haunts christological doctrines, especially various doctrines of the atonement.

[21]   Nell Noddings, *Women and Evil* (Berkeley: University of California Press, 1989), 20.

[22]   Noddings, 33.

Through the model of warfare and conflict, ethical terror aggravates human pain and suffering by basing admirable behavior on the desire to dominate and control. The creation of the need to conquer evil ratifies the use of control through torture, war, and punishment. The structure of conflict and victory and the resulting values of domination and control increase human helplessness, intensify pain, and destroy bonds of interdependence and nurturance—and it is these latter that Noddings identifies as the greatest evils in human life. Hence, the dualistic structure that identifies the evil to be defeated itself creates greater evil by aggravating pain, helplessness, and separation. This production of evil transmutes the poisonous pedagogy of domestic life into the ethical terror of theological systems and religious institutions, much the way the prophet Hosea transforms his domestic violence into divine judgment.

The Augustinian doctrine of original sin is supposed to free us from an obsession with perfect performance and the fear of punishment. We are to be saved without the necessity of being innocent and free of sin. As James G. Williams argues, atonement christology ought to free us from the need for scapegoats.[23] The freely given grace of God is supposed to be accepted through faith and only this is required for entry into salvation. But if that freely offered grace is not accepted, the threat of consequences lingers as a coercive wedge. The salvation offered by faith which delivers us is achieved by the unilateral power of God acting in Jesus Christ. We cannot take responsibility for rectifying our sinful natures, but are shielded under the paternalistic protection of Jesus who is the ultimate, unambiguous victim, the innocent scapegoat, and shield from divine punishment. While the death of Jesus would seem to eliminate the need for scapegoats once and for all, this structure of salvation creates an idealized structural paradigm to be repeated. The virtue of suffering for another and of self-sacrifice are Christian ethical norms, especially for women. Woman's only moral claim, like children's, comes from innocence and silence, as Williams argues is the case for all good scapegoats and victims.

If we maintain that disobedience must be punished, we must identify who is to blame for evil. Through the hidden assumptions of ethical terror, we perpetuate mechanisms of domination and oppression, which are not seen as inherently wrong, but as serving the protection of goodness, and we defend the divine mandate and the duty of the powerful to punish the wicked, no matter what structures and methods do this.

To create models of personal power, the appropriate uses of power, and the taking of responsibility for both good and evil in

---

23   Cf. *The Bible, Violence, and the Sacred: Liberation from the Myth of Sanctioned Violence* (New York: Harper Collins, 1991).

ourselves, we need, as Noddings suggests, to redefine evil, so that evil becomes whatever increases human helplessness, reinforces intractable pain, and creates separation from relationships of love and nurture.[24] This redefining undermines structures of domination and subordination with regard to evil. Ethical agency becomes the attunement in context to acts of healing and loving care.

We can perhaps say that those who know inescapable oppression experience evil as pain, separation, and helplessness, and, given the limits of human power and the ambiguities of our lives, such evil permeates human life inevitably to some degree. Hence, to cope with evil, we might examine what strategies and behaviors increase or decrease the amount of evil in our lives, rather than what forces defeat or end evil. The redemptive task is to minimize evil in human life, to the best of our ability, by increasing human efficacy, enabling ethical action, alleviating or preventing pain, and increasing and strengthening caring relationships. This shift in defining evil helps us move beyond the polarized power dichotomies of innocent victims and evil oppressors to more nuanced and ambiguous alternatives that help us to understand power and our uses of it.

It may help us to begin with the understanding that virtually no one is totally innocent of the power to make another helpless, to inflict pain, or to destroy relationships just as no one has the knowledge and power to prevent all occurrences of helplessness, pain, and separation in human life. Hence, to behave ethically requires self-respect and critical self-awareness, as well as patient discernment of our own contexts of power and privilege and of our potential for misusing power. The misuse of power destroys fabrics of human community by creating webs of denial, deception, scapegoating, and demands for obedience to a goodness defined by the powerful for the purposes of control.

Taking Responsibility

Most adults struggle in-between structures of power. Western societies and their justice movements tend to give moral voice to those who claim victimization and innocence. The importance of this mentality is not something I want to minimize. It stands in a long and noble

---

[24]   This nondualistic approach is not an attempt to eliminate our capacity to make distinctions and to identify what might be evil in human life. It is rather an approach to such questions that does not structure reality as a conflict between polarized and reified forces of good and evil which must result in the unambiguous triumph of the forces of good. Good and evil are seen as more fluid realities in which what may appear as the power of good has the capacity to become evil in shifting contexts.

prophetic tradition. The concern for victims, "the widows and orphans" has enabled women, the disabled, the poor, and people of color to demand justice. I suspect that this mentality is rooted both in the prophetic tradition and in christological doctrines of the atonement, but they have permeated the secular culture. Paying attention to victims of oppression has been and is a major contribution of Judaism and Christianity to the consciences of many, including the powerful. I am not arguing that those subject to abuse do not have a unique lesson to teach others, especially about how oppression affects those hurt by it most, but we must remember that the prophetic voice is often a paternalistic one, which can become abusive, as in the case of Hosea, Ezekiel, and Jeremiah, as Renita Weems notes in *Battered Love*.

What brings us to a point from which we are able to see the power we gain from the hegemonic structures of status-oriented societies? What shows us the ways we may misuse our own power? How can we see that our domination has silenced others? Without such awarenesses, it is difficult for us to see how we misuse the power we have.

A great deal of energy can be generated from a morally unambiguous sense of outrage at abuse and injustice. At times, such energy and outrage are important and necessary for fueling social change. But we should be clear that such energy is reactionary. As reactionary energy, it can imitate the power it opposes; its oppositional nature means its terms are limited by what it opposes; and it can carry serious misuses of power because it cannot admit an understanding of the ambiguities within which people live their lives. A sophisticated understanding of exploitation and a willingness to stand up to and condemn oppression does not automatically translate into behavior that is liberating of others. For example, the failure, until recently, of male liberation theologians to take gender oppression into account, the extent of racism in white feminism, or the amount of domestic violence in the homes of peace activists point to how easily oppressive behavior is perpetuated.[25] Reactionary energy does not automatically lead us to examine the complex relationships through which we build understanding and coalitions among differently oppressed groups. It is too polarizing.

Something is missing in the public discourse about justice, something beyond moral proclamation and denunciations of oppression—beyond domination and silencing—something that opens

---

25   See *Against Machismo* by Elsa Tamez (Oak Park, IL: Meyer Stone Books, 1987) for a discussion of gender issues among liberation theologians. The initial failure of liberation theologians to discuss women's oppression (with perhaps the exception of Rubem Alves) is telling, given that Marx and Engels discuss the oppression of women and that the Chinese revolution also paid attention to gender issues (albeit imperfectly).

doors of conversation, especially among groups differently oppressed or victimized. Moral high ground tends to be given either to authority figures with power or to innocent victims, a ground from which victims can make demands, but which allows little agency to make change. There is a danger to oppressed groups in this structure of morality. If a victimized group defends its innocent status and then can be proven to lack innocence, the implication is that the group no longer deserves justice. Any hint of moral ambiguity or the possession of power and agency throws a shadow across one's moral spotlight. To seek to protect or idealize innocence is to continue the dichotomizing of good and evil, the structures of domination and subordination, and the reinforcing of ethical terror. To move beyond poisonous pedagogy, which is obsessed with guilt and innocence and with blame and punishment and which carries the voice of reactionary self-righteousness, we must be willing to identify the antidote.

Alternatives come partly, I believe, through the acceptance of multiple selves, or complex chords of voices within ourselves—the acknowledgment that identity is multivalent. As adults, we include within ourselves not only the experiences of our childhood, which we must not ignore, but also the strength, knowledge, and status of adult life in all its stages. A dialogue among the voices may help us recognize the ways (perhaps even as children) we used what power we had to minimize our own helplessness, to avoid pain, to maintain connections to those we loved, and to control people, to hurt others, and to alienate friends. The adult voice, in listening to the hurt child, may be better able to avoid inflicting such pain onto others. This recovery of early trauma is a necessary, but not sufficient, means for coming to terms with the complex and difficult relationships of power and love in which we find ourselves enmeshed and which we find mirrored in the biblical texts. Sufficient means would include our attention to a multiplicity of voices that allow us to see where we are accountable and can take responsibility. Sufficient means might enable us to use our voices strategically for change while doing less harm.

Maternal Thinking

To begin the discussions that will move us politically and theologically beyond poisonous pedagogy and ethical terror, I suggest we rethink good and evil and moral agency. Sara Ruddick, in her work on mothering, explores the shifting sands of such complex experiences from her life as a middle-class, well-educated white feminist. In her discussion, Ruddick is careful to note that mothering is a highly sophisticated skill that must be learned in relation to social role, not an innate, essential capacity of women. She reflects on what the learned experience of mothering can teach us about those who straddle worlds between the helplessness and suffering that come with attempting to nurture children in male-dominated societies and the immense potential for power and control that resides in nuclear family structures that give mothers virtually sole responsibility for caring for children. She proposes necessary elements of a nurturing, empowering pedagogy. Her ethical principles are grounded in an acknowledgment of the ambiguity of parent-child relationships and the necessity of maternal self knowledge, honesty, and moral reflection.[26]

Ruddick argues that mothering skills gain efficacy through experience, practice, and reflection. The implications of her thesis are that the responsibility for nurturing children and the values and skills of mothering are available to all persons in society and that everyone must learn such values and skills. The limiting of mothering to women is part of the problem and dilemma of the nuclear family that Ruddick examines. However, she chooses to use the term maternal to highlight what traditional gender socialization has devalued as female work that was viewed as unreflective and instinctive. Mothering is work that has had no measurable value or quantifiable productivity, and, since it cannot be measured in economic theories, it has no value beyond sentimentality.[27] In combining the term maternal with thinking, Ruddick creates a cognitive dissonance that destabilizes those assumptions, since thinking and mothering are rarely regarded as belonging together as an activity of reflective agency. To avoid the use of the term maternal in favor of a neutral term masks the feminist commitment to revaluing women as crucial to the formation of humane societies. Maternal thinking and mothering are terms that describe reflection on experience, virtues, and ethical values associated with the care of children. By extension, the work of mothering provides a potential ethics for our participation in unequal relationships in which we hold power and responsibility for others. The term maternal thinking is an attempt linguistically to identify moral forms embedded in our common culture that are hidden behind domestic walls.

Ruddick seeks, not to set up a moral code of mothering, but to explore the experiences, actions, and thinking behind adequate mothering for their messages about ethical adult behavior. Important to Ruddick's analysis is its feminist commitment, which includes an awareness of the dynamics of power. She refuses to accept the

---

26   In *Maternal Thinking: Toward a Politics of Peace* (Boston: Beacon Press, 1989).

27   Cf. Marilyn Waring, *If Women Counted: A New Feminist Economics* (San Francisco: Harper & Row, 1988), for a feminist analysis of the problems with economic theory and World Bank policies.

privatization of child care as trivial "women's" work, and she reflects on her own experiences of mothering as part of the work of making justice. Ruddick notes rather unsentimentally that there is much about children that provokes anger, and maternal feelings about children involve a great deal of ambiguity. Some children are far more difficult to nurture than others, regardless of the reasons why. Mother and child relationships are often highly charged, and self-control is crucial in mothers since so much mother-child interaction takes place in private isolation within post-industrial capitalism. In using examples of the moments mothers feel rage or despair, Ruddick discusses appropriate uses of power and authority to preserve through love, to foster growth, and to teach conscience.

Ruddick is not concerned with the guilt or innocence of children. She understands that even tiny infants make demands that are often quite difficult to meet, especially in a society such as ours which gives so little support to mothering, even as it expects too much of mothers and disempowers children. Infants are capable of provoking highly ambiguous feelings in their caretakers, even in those who love them deeply. Instead of focusing on the nature or state of children, Ruddick explores the responsibilities of the social role of mothering. She argues that, regardless of the behavior of a child, mothering requires certain commitments that must be held even under the most trying of circumstances and even through the most conflicted feelings.

One of those commitments, which is highly ambiguous, is to nurture willfulness, to create the capacity in a child to gain the knowledge and self-confidence that enables her/him to assert her/his will in the world, sometimes in opposition to a parent's desires. The paradox of mothering is to have used one's power to nurture an individual who becomes independent of that power and to take satisfaction from having used one's power to increase the power of another. In this paradox, to be happy, a child is not always "good," and instead sometimes acts willfully against a mother's wishes.

Ruddick describes the irony of parenting that is trustworthy so that a healthy suspicion of authority is encouraged.

> If, when their mothers fail them, as they inevitably do, children deny their hurt and rage so that they can continue "trusting," they are in effect giving up on their mother. By contrast when they recognize and protest betrayal, they reaffirm their expectation that their mother has been and can again become worthy of their trust. . . .Proper trust is one of the most difficult maternal virtues. It requires of a mother clear judgment that does not give way to obedience or denial. It depends on her being reliably good-willed and

independent yet able to express and to accept from her children righteous indignation at trust betrayed.[28]

Such willfulness in trusting is enhanced, not by attempting to maintain innocence in children, but by encouraging them to gain greater knowledge of both good and evil in others, including their own mothers, and by mothers supporting the right of their children, at times, to be disobedient.

The care of children has been assigned virtually solely to women and then regarded as biologically automatic, unreflective behavior, as Noddings also argues. Ruddick contends that when a mother's behavior is loving, caring, and ethical, it is actually complex, imaginative, intellectual, and active—behavior which involves self-knowledge and the ability to accept personal responsibility for one's behaviors because one pays attention to the conflicted feelings and concerns mothers feel. In addition, mothers are haunted by hope, by an imaginative vision of what they anticipate for the future of their children which is embedded in the relationships they manage on a day-to-day basis. Mothers who are good nurturers learn to manage their behavior, through ethical reflections upon their deepest commitments and hopes, in the midst of a series of competing voices. Noddings insists that maternal choices are highly sophisticated decisions involving both attention to feeling and intense intellectual thought.

Maternal thinking opens doors for examining the multiple voices that allow us both to identify with those who are vulnerable and to accept responsibility for our power. This multiple consciousness happens because those who mother sit on the fulcrum of power and powerlessness, of domination and silence, of hope and despair, and of abuse and empowerment. The ambiguities of maternal thinking allow for greater honesty and accountability, as well as for the dynamic dialectical processes of creative disruption and recreation. They lead us to relational and dynamic understandings of power and its uses, even as they acknowledge that many human relationships involve unequal forms of power.

Maternal thinking gives us a clearer picture of how poisonous pedagogy and ethical terror can be counteracted. Ruddick demonstrates how persons in hierarchical power systems might learn to respect the power of others, even when the choices of those they respect are frustrating. She discusses how it is possible to allow the greatest possible freedom to choose for everyone within the limits of what is safe for all when that can be determined. While Ruddick is careful not to recommend maternal thinking as a model for all human relations because adults must often relate as peers, she argues that the values and

---

28   Ruddick, 118-119.

practices maternal thinking teaches are crucial to the creation of just and peaceful societies (this is also a primary concern of Miller and Noddings). Ruddick's analysis is helpful because she breaks open the dilemmas of the choices that face us when we are both subject to oppressive powers and possess the power to hurt others. She provides an ethic with the goal of equalizing unequal power as much as possible, rather than protecting status or control. The ability to pay attention to both aspects of power in our lives is a key to moving beyond thinking in terms of dominance and oppression. If we can hold to a commitment to refusing to be abused (where possible), and refusing to cause abuse ourselves, we may move away from poisonous pedagogy and ethical terror. I find a similar emphasis on maternal ethics in Jeremiah 31:15–22.

Paradigms Of Taking Responsibility

> Rachel is weeping for her children; she refuses to be comforted...[God replies] Is Ephraim my dear son? Is he the child I delight in? As often as I speak against him, I still remember him. Therefore my womb is moved for him; I will surely have compassion on him. . . For the Sovereign One has created a new thing on the earth: a female surrounds a warrior.
>
> —Jeremiah 31:15b, 20, 22b

This text depicts a time when the old Deuteronomic ethics of obedience/reward and disobedience/punishment were collapsing under the overwhelming destruction of Judah at the hands of Babylon. The text appears in a longer chapter that proclaims profound hope for the future of Israel, a future in which the people will be restored and made whole. In its conclusion the chapter moves toward a recapitulation of creation, an affirmation of the creative, life-giving power of God.

The depth of the people's suffering is presented in this section through several voices: the prophet who announces the sayings of God; the voice of God comforting Rachel, the mother; the repentant people of Israel personified in the wayward son Ephraim; God again as the mother Rachel; and finally a word of instruction and hope from the prophet. Each represents an angle on the tragedy befalling the nation.

While the mother Rachel's inconsolable grieving is the framework of the text and its emotional centerpiece, the divine voice speaks in her stead. God calls attention to her suffering and offers a word of hope as divine compassion and maternal love reach out to the wayward people. The people are heard in the pleading of Ephraim who wants to return home. Ephraim has repented from youthful undiscipline; he has experienced the suffering of his life as punishment for his misbehavior, strikes himself, and is ashamed. His remorse is a point of turning back, of seeking the maternal comforts of home.

The answering voice of God both acknowledges the failures of Ephraim and reasserts the indissolvable maternal bonds of compassion that are the source of divine delight and mercy.[29] In recognizing the errors of her son, God rejects judgment and places remembrance and love at the heart of her relationship with her people.

The text presents a complexity of voices that confront profound suffering. The voice of Rachel the mother is one of unrelenting and inconsolable sorrow at the loss of her children, the voice of one powerless to save them. Ephraim is the voice of obedience and disobedience, reward and punishment, the voice of repentance who experiences his suffering as a deserved penalty. The suffering of the people is surrounded by maternal feeling, first through Rachel's loss and grief, and at the end by the divine assertion of compassion instead of judgment. Hope is given in the midst of despair. The mother is hope's central paradigm in this text.

After the divine mother offers compassion and merciful grace, the prophet's voice returns with instruction about how to return home. To receive divine love, the people must know what to do. So the prophet commands the child who, once a son, has now become a virgin daughter. Jeremiah is instructing the daughter homeward, as God instructed Rachel not to weep. The virgin daughter (the image of innocence) is silent, but she is given the final word of hope—God will create a new thing in the land: a female surrounds the warrior.

This final line presents hope in the transmutation of traditional values of power and conquest. The line has baffled commentators in the past who tend to neglect it, to say that the meaning is obscure and difficult to comprehend, or to see it as a simple role reversal of power in which the woman takes on the power of a man.[30] Phyllis Trible's work, however, points to how it can be quite clear, not as a simple reversal, but as something more. The activity of God is indicated by the same word for creation as Genesis 1, creation on the earth, *ereṣ*, the holy land. The female who surrounds the warrior is the same category of being,

---

[29] Phyllis Trible explains in *God and the Rhetoric of Sexuality* (Philadelphia: Fortress Press, 1978) that the roots of the words for mercy and divine compassion in verse 20c indicate the maternal images in the Hebrew *rḥm* (womb).

[30] Cf. William L. Holladay's "Jeremiah and Women's Liberation," *Andover Newton Quarterly*, vol. 12, no. 4 (March 1972): 213–233. I thank Ann K. Fontaine of Harvard Divinity School, who has done extensive research on the history of commentary on this text, for directing me to Holladay's article.

neqeba, created in the divine image in Genesis 1:27.[31] But what she surrounds is not the male created in the divine image, *zakar*. The man surrounded is *geber*, the word associated with the virility and behavior of warriors, the political system that has brought ruin to Israel for so long.

The text acknowledges the destructive power of overblown masculinity and presents motherly compassion as the life-creating antidote, not the acquisition of hypermasculine power by the female. If, as it may well be, this text is a commentary on Hosea chapters 11 and 12, Jeremiah's emphatic use of the maternal and female is even more telling.[32] The Hosea text embeds the maternal images for God within the larger framework of masculine power, marriage, and domestic violence, creating an androgynous image and giving God the voice of the batterer. Through that androgyny, Hosea's God ends with punishment and power, a common fate of androgynous and gender neutral images in male-dominant societies. The destructive marriage metaphors that Renita Weems finds so problematic in Hosea, Ezekiel, and Jeremiah are absent in this text. While Jeremiah uses those metaphors elsewhere, this section stands in tension with those destructive images. Jeremiah's use of Hosea destabilizes the image of God as batterer and proposes a new solution in the land not provided by images of marriage, power, judgment, and dominance. At every point in the text, a female with divine connections surrounds the powers that threaten to destroy life, surrounds not by defeat or conquest, but by loving compassion. Surrounding suggests a new form of power, the power of grief and repentance, of the overcoming of pain and suffering, of neutralizing violence and death, and of transforming defiance and shame through the embracing of—the risking of encounter with—that which threatens and frightens us in our very midst. It is a text that affirms maternal thinking as a paradigm of hope. At a time in Israel's history when traditional politics and religion had failed the people, Jeremiah's experimentation throughout the 31st chapter indicates a disillusionment with traditional forms of power and a reaching for something more forgiving, hopeful and life-giving. He finds it in maternal thinking and in the rejection of traditional notions of power for God. This hope is not thrown into idealized future images of mothers, but is grounded in a strategy that uses familiar images and experiences of maternal activity, as his use of Rachel and allusion to Genesis 1 indicate. His hope is grounded in the new presence of

---

[31]   See Trible for an extended discussion of the Hebrew meanings of this text.

[32]   I am grateful to Dr. Marie-Theres Wacker of Huenfelden-Nauheim, Germany, a feminist biblical scholar, for suggesting this connection between Hosea and Jeremiah.

strategies and values already present in the people hidden in the dominated lives of women.

Conclusion

The hope presented in the Jeremiah text appears in the midst of social breakdown, when a patriarchal military system with huge momentum had reached its dead end. At the end of the twentieth century, post-industrial nuclear military societies such as the United States also confront a crisis in paradigms and values as Cold War politics wane, regional conflicts escalate, and environmental destruction rolls on. We may take the Jeremiah text as warning: if we do not find ways to preserve life, to restore right relationships, and to create structures that do not rely on domination, control, progress, and competition, we will be lost. To return home restored and made whole, we must heed the destructive road by which we wandered into death. On that wayward journey, theology transferred the values of domination and control essential to patriarchal militarism into the domestic sphere without a careful analysis of what is required to nurture life, to enable responsible, ethical, life-giving behavior in human beings, to minimize suffering, and to increase the loving compassion of maternal thinking.

Without the touchstone of values that nurture life, the enabling of the full presence of those marginalized by systems of domination will create a society of armed camps unable and unwilling to take responsibility for the creation of life together. The politics of identity will shout down ethical questions around power and its uses and abuses that must lie at the core of life-giving values. We must take self-critical responsibility for behavior that is manipulative, resentful, domineering, deceitful, and destructive, as well as resist such behavior directed toward ourselves. To enable the taking of responsibility we must create contexts and institutional systems that move toward maternal values and the equalization of unequal power.

Through holding to the values and methods of maternal thinking, we might better explore how the infliction of pain can be avoided and the willful expression of anger at or resistance to pain encouraged as part of our life together. All adults, like mothers, are capable of learning to minimize and manage evil by surrounding it with the nurturing of life forces, by empathetic attunement to the physical and emotional lives of others, by the choosing of cooperation over competition, and by love and compassion. Perhaps then we shall know the antidote to poisonous pedagogy, safeguard ourselves from ethical terror, and find new ways to think maternally. Then, surely, there will be a new thing in the land.

9

The Dying Art of Demon-Recognition[1]
Victims, Systems, and the Book of Job

Kimberly Parsons Chastain

⌘

Introduction: Atrocity and the Bystander God

Judith Herman opens her discussion of psychological trauma in victims of atrocity with these words: "The ordinary response to atrocities is to banish them from consciousness."[2] She is referring not only to the experience of the victim, but also to the response of those who bear witness to that experience: those who see it happening, those who hear reports of it third-hand, those whose help is sought by victims. There is a curious and dreadful lack of response among the witnesses, almost as if, as Renita Weems writes, they "didn't notice." And among those who d o notice, the response is more likely to focus on "disinfecting" the suffering than on healing it.

It is this lack of response that torments the victim of childhood sexual abuse. Less than the problem of righteous suffering, less than the problem of unexplained catastrophe, what challenges the existence of meaning and purpose for these victims is the question, "why didn't anyone help me?" The question of God is posed most starkly by the

---

1   The reference in the title is to a poem by Renita Weems in which she addresses victims of an atrocity, concluding, "The recognition of fools and demons is a dying art." Renita Weems, *Just a Sister Away: A Womanist Vision of Women's Relationships in the Bible,* (San Diego: Luramedia, 1988), 64.
2   Judith Herman, *Trauma and Recovery* (New York: Basic Books, 1992), 1.

abandonment they experience when they seek assistance, rather than by their initial violation. So there remains a great unanswered question in the formulation of traditional theodicies, which is discovered, not through the eyes of the observer, but through the eyes of the victim. The question is not "why do the righteous suffer?", but "why are the good cruel?"

In order to do justice to the experience of the victim, it is necessary to break through the dualism that characterizes most third-person accounts of atrocities, including family sexual violence. The majority of clinical literature and of theological treatments of abusive relationships focus exclusively on the victim-perpetrator dyad, or at best on the "abusive family system." Little attention is given to the social matrix in which the abuse occurs. And yet there is overwhelming evidence that the response of this matrix profoundly affects the degree of trauma experienced by the victim. Sandra Butler (1978) writes of the "second injury" which results from the perceived lack of concern or assistance on the part of the community. Courtois notes that "the lack of assistance when incest is known or disclosed is believed to be more damaging than incest which remains hidden."[3] Judith Herman is even more explicit: ". . . there are only a limited number of roles: one can be a perpetrator, a passive witness, an ally, or a rescuer. . . .The victim's greatest contempt is often reserved, not for the perpetrator, but for the passive bystander."[4] Respect for the victim, then, demands an account of those who are indirectly involved and ordinarily invisible.

This issue is raised, without often being recognized, by the biblical book of Job. From the famous reference to the "patience of Job" in James 5:7-11, to the most recent theodocic reflections in western culture, Job is a figure that dominates the attention of interpreters, and shapes the ways in which suffering is considered. Yet there are few interpretations which read the story as if through the eyes of Job, to discover that there is a problem for Job which defines the problem of his relationship with God, namely, the problem of his friends and interpreters. In spite of the fact that the friends dominate the text for nearly 26 chapters, they are nearly invisible in most interpretations of the story of Job. Within the text, they seem invisible to themselves and to Job as well.

In this essay, I will re-examine these relationships from the perspective of a victim of childhood sexual abuse. Drawing on clinical trauma theory, which illuminates ordinarily hidden social dimensions of traumatic occurrences, I will point to the "second victimization" which occurs when abuse is disclosed. Using Mary Douglas's work on the cognitive drive for coherence within a meaning system, I will discuss

---

3   Christine Courtois, *Healing the Incest Wound: Adult Survivors in Therapy* (New York: Norton, 1988), 116.

4   Herman, 92.

ways in which the "truth" of a patriarchal social system is protected against the challenges of family sexual violence. Finally I will consider the possibilities for understanding divine agency and its relationship to powerlessness within this reading of the text.

This reading accepts a personalist construction of God; God understood as a subject who may act intentionally, with whom individuals may claim or disclaim relationship. It takes for granted that this God may be construed as agent, and that divine activity or inactivity is a problem raised by examples of conspicuous suffering. I have adopted this strategy, first in order to read *with* the narrative of the book of Job, entering its discursive universe. Moreover, I find it illuminating to view the divine as "one among many," as I consider the relationship of atrocity to meaning-system. For this reading, God is not an all-powerful actor before helpless subjects, but an actor-among-actors, whose role in relationship to the victim is brought into question as the community's role is examined. If, as René Girard has argued, ". . .the attitude of men[sic] is responsible for revealing to Job God's hostility towards him,"[5] is it possible to distinguish God's activity from human activity in the book of Job? And what implications will this have for speaking of the divine to situations of victimization and oppression?

Trauma and its Wake: The Victims

An estimated 10–30% of women and 5–10% of men are sexually abused by a family member or friend by the time they reach the age of 18.[6] For more than half of them, the abuse starts before they reached the age of 14. The majority of the perpetrators are male.[7] Each victim feels isolated, cut off from peers and from other family members, trapped by secrecy and shame.

While they are children, victims display many of the symptoms of acute post-traumatic stress disorder. In adult victims, untreated symptoms may have become chronic or given way to secondary elaborations, including chronic depression, eating disorders, sexual

---

5   Rene Girard, *Job, The Victim of His People* (Stanford: Stanford University Press, 1987), 129.

6   There are differing opinions among researchers about what "counts" as incestuous abuse. Browne & Finkelhor (1986) accept these percentages as acceptable parameters. Russell (1986), whose study remains a landmark in methodology and thoroughness, accepts the figure of 25% for girls. There is no similar account of the abuse of boys to date.

7   It is difficult to get accurate statistics on the sexual abuse of boys, because of underreporting associated with shame and because until recently, sexual abuse was viewed as a "women's problem."

difficulties, and revictimization in other relationships.[8] Although only one-fifth of adult victims manifest serious psychopathology, nearly all victims show developmental or psychological impairment of some sort when compared with nonvictims.[9]

Christine Courtois writes,

> . . . the child who is incestuously abused most often suffers chronic inescapable trauma without outside support to either buffer the situation or validate her responses to it. Not only does she suffer sexual intrusion, but it is repeated and escalates over time. . . .The secrecy, silence, and taboo keep her from asking for help and prevent her from getting acknowledgment and validation of her experience. The child's very reality is often negated, leaving her to wonder what is real and what is not.[10]

Chronic inescapable trauma: the phrase is used also to describe the experiences of torture victims, political hostages and prison camp internees. It refers to the shattering of human adaptive capacities through overwhelming, prolonged experiences of helplessness and terror. "When neither resistance nor escape is possible, the human system of self-defense becomes overwhelmed and disorganized. Each component of the ordinary response to danger, having lost its utility, tends to persist in an altered and exaggerated state. . ."[11] For incestuously abused children, the trauma is compounded by the reality of betrayal by one—or more—trusted adults. Accounts of people struggling to come to grips with the effects of abuse repeat the question with agonizing frequency, "If you can't trust your parents, who can you trust?"

Even worse, the betrayal is never unmixed. The father who terrorizes the night is the playful, affectionate father of the morning. The uncle who molests a child on a camping trip is also the bringer of lavish gifts, the genie whose appearance means both happiness and fear. The mother who comforts the terrified child is also the one who responds, "Oh honey, you must have been dreaming," causing the child to doubt her memory and her perception of reality. The people who are supposed to be the main sources of protection and affection for a child—

---

8   "Adult victims" here refers to those who, abused as children, are still suffering from its effects as adults.

9   A. Browne and D. Finkelhor, "Impact of Child Sexual Abuse: A Review of the Literature," *Psychological Bulletin* 99 (1986): 72.

10   Courtois, 8.

11   Herman, 34.

in many cases, the people who *are* the main sources of this nurturance—become the main sources of danger as well.

Children who try to tell someone—overcoming the fear of implied or explicit threats from the perpetrators—often find that the people they turn to for help are unable or unwilling to hear them or to help them.[12] Thus the victims feel ". . . utterly abandoned, utterly alone, cast out of the human and divine systems of care and protection that sustain life. Thereafter, a sense of alienation, of disconnection, pervades every relationship, from the most intimate familial bonds to the most abstract affiliations of community and religion."[13]

Children attempting to cope with this alienation and disconnection develop a remarkable range of adaptive strategies, including walling off their memories, splitting their intellects off from their emotions, sometimes even developing multiple personalities. Many lead productive, "normal" seeming lives, hidden from view by the strategies they have developed. Their depression or dysphoria is never connected to early experiences of violation and betrayal.

For others, the strategies become increasingly maladaptive over time, with social consequences as well as effects on their lives as individuals. Over 90% of prostitutes and a majority of women who have been violently abused in marriages are believed to have been sexually abused as children. Taught that their value as persons is linked to their sexual availability, some become indiscriminately sexual. Children who are taught to disregard their own safety become increasingly vulnerable to revictimization.[14] Adults who were abused as children alternate between anxious overprotection of their own children and indifference borne of the same kind of learned disregard. Boys may learn to re-establish their self-worth by victimizing others; girls will more often internalize the rage and become depressed and passive.

Trauma and its Wake: The Witnesses

"To study psychological trauma means bearing witness to horrible events. . . . At the moment of trauma, the victim is rendered helpless by overwhelming force. When the force is that of nature, we speak of disasters. When the force is that of other human beings, we speak of atrocities."[15] So writes Judith Herman, writing of the impact of trauma, the reality that must be faced by victims on their journeys toward

---

12   Cf. Courtois, 34.
13   Herman, 52.
14   D.E. H. Russell, *The Secret Trauma: Incest in the Lives of Girls and Women* (New York: Basic Books, 1986), 174.
15   Herman, 7 & 33.

survival. She also notes that, "The ordinary response to atrocities is to banish them from consciousness."[16] People do not want to know that such things occur; in a very real sense they *cannot* see or hear when child sexual abuse is revealed.

The inability to hear functions at two levels: the witness's own psychological defenses block this knowledge in the same ways that the victim's defenses block her senses, and the cultural coding of awareness affects the way that the data is received, so that the impact of the information is either muted or distorted. To comprehend what is told or shown is to approach the borders of chaos, to find one's sleep disturbed and one's relationships affected. Ellen Bass describes her experience of editing a volume of stories by survivors of childhood sexual abuse:

> As I read and reread the stories of women who had been raped and abused, there were times when I could not bear to be touched. Too many stories of too many fingers, tongues, penises of adult men slipping into little girls' vaginas made it impossible for me to open my body to a man. . . . I wanted to share intimacy, but when I began to make love, I'd feel the halted breath of little girls trying not to breathe, stiffening, hoping the large invasive hand would disappear.[17]

This is the experience of indirect violence, of second-order trauma. Although witnesses do not go through the destruction of bodily integrity and the awareness of personal violation, they do experience the terror, the helplessness, the sense of terrible wrongness: this should not have happened. Individuals who were in the shock troops that opened Buchenwald at the end of World War II have described years of tormented sleep, of fragments of memory intruding into everyday experience, of joy in life forever shadowed by awareness of what they had witnessed.[18] Police officers who have been involved in hostage, holdup, or kidnap investigations are often haunted by a sense of failure, by the faces of those they could not help. Many police forces now routinely send these officers to counseling immediately, before they develop the symptoms of post-traumatic stress.

I am not saying that the distress of witnesses is equal to or should in anyway be equated with the reality experienced by the victims. I am saying that there is a kind of mystery to atrocity that mirrors the claim made by the ancients about the face of God: it is impossible to look on it

---

16   Ibid., 1.

17   Ellen Bass and Louise Thorton, eds. *I Never Told Anyone: Writings by Women Survivors of Child Sexual Abuse* (New York: Harper and Row, 1983), 50-51.

18   Bettelheim, *Surviving and Other Essays* (NY: Bantam, 1979).

directly and remain whole. Small wonder, then, that witnesses retreat into denial, to paralysis and numbness, to silence and repression. Judith Herman writes of therapists who are working with survivors of trauma that they may,

> . . . defend against overwhelming feelings by withdrawal or by impulsive, intrusive action. The most common forms of action are rescue attempts, boundary violations, or attempts to control the patient.[sic] The most common constrictive responses are doubting or denial of the patient's reality, dissociation or numbing, minimization or avoidance of the traumatic material, professional distancing, or frank abandonment of the patient.[19]

This impulsive, almost instinctive response to the trauma will compound the suffering of the victim and put the observer—by default— on the side of the perpetrator. The unthinkable quality of the experience makes it unspeakable: and the result for the victim is silence, invisibility, stigmatization.

Second-order trauma threatens not only the individual witness, but also the mechanisms of social discourse by which the world is ordered. As Mary Douglas argues, "at any given moment of time the state of received knowledge is backgrounded by a clutter of suppressed information...the information is not suppressed by its inherent worthlessness, nor by any passive process of forgetting: it is actively thrust out of the way because of difficulties in making it fit whatever happens to be in hand."[20] There is a drive for coherence between the received information and that which constitutes the world-as known; when existing "truth" is challenged by the received information, the new knowledge may be suppressed or destroyed in order to maintain the regularity of the world-as-known.

Thus Judith Herman could write of her experience as a psychiatric resident in 1975, "We encountered many incest victims among our first patients . . .In every case the veracity of the patient's history was officially questioned. We were reminded by our supervisors, as if this were something everyone knew, that women often fantasize or lie about childhood sexual encounters with adults, especially their fathers."[21] This belief is more than a misunderstanding in the psychotherapeutic and medical communities; it has been encoded in the culture through

---

19   Herman, 151.

20   Mary Douglas, *Implicit Meanings: Essays in Anthropology* (London: Routhledge, 1975), 3.

21   Judith Herman, *Father-Daughter Incest* (Cambridge, MA: Harvard University Press, 1981), 8-9

legal doctrine, sociological studies, and popular psychology. Children who disclose family sexual abuse are subject to almost intolerable pressure to recant, not only within the family but by others who simply cannot believe what they are hearing. It is easier to believe that a child is lying or fantasizing than to believe that she has been violated.

The myth of the betraying, vengeful child looms large in the public imagination. It is less than a year since I was approached by a pastoral care professor from a major denominational seminary, following a presentation in which I advocated admitting children's testimony as evidence in court cases of child sexual abuse. He wanted to know, "What will happen to all of the good daddies if everything a child says can be used against them? A father's life could be ruined because he wouldn't let her go to a movie or something and she reported him." The man was neither unsophisticated nor uneducated. He was, however, unwilling or unable to take seriously the realities reflected in statistics about reporting of sexual abuse, actual arrests, and convictions of perpetrators: fear of the child loomed too large.[22]

This pastoral care professor is not unique. As awareness of family sexual violence has grown in the past decade, resistance to that awareness has become increasingly sophisticated. A group of respectable, concerned legal experts and (mostly) neo-Freudian psychologists have banded together under large—largely right-wing—corporate funding to form the "False Memory Syndrome Foundation." Its goal is to protect society from women who are led to false memories by their inability to distinguish between fantasy and reality or by therapeutic malpractice. The work of the foundation includes publishing extensive articles in polite language in periodicals such as the *New Yorker* and *Atlantic Monthly*, about false accusations which have torn apart families and destroyed the lives of "innocent" men.[23]

There is every reason to believe that these people, like therapists who attempt to help women accept their "fantasies" as healthy and pleasurable, are well-intentioned and sincere. But they seem to find the severity and prevalence of family sexual violence to be more than they

---

[22]   There is another cultural myth which might be called the "Lolita syndrome" or the "Kinsey myth": the belief that children really crave sexual contact with adults, and that the trauma results, not from violation or betrayal, but from the shame attached to the act.   This myth has been dealt with extensively in Bass & Thornton, Herman (1981), and Russell, so I shall not discuss it further here.

[23]   False Memory Syndrome Foundation, 3508 Market Street, Suite 128, Philadelphia, PA 19104–3311. They publish a quarterly newsletter, and serve as a clearinghouse for articles disputing the reality of repressed memory.   For a disturbing study of the backlash against incest awareness, see Louise Armstrong, *Rocking the Cradle of Sexual Politics: What Happened When Women Said Incest* (New York: HarperCollins, 1994).

can bear, and so they construct an alternative reality which better conforms to cultural myths.[24] The alternative will carry more weight than the truth because it better coheres with the meaning-system of our culture.[25]

Another way for observers and witnesses to distance themselves from atrocity is to demonize the perpetrator. Judith Herman quotes from a Child Protective Services report in rural Idaho: ". . .Most often, the community's response initially is one of extreme anger with frequent comments to the effect that "they should castrate the bastards; they ought to take them out and kill them; they are all crazy and they should be locked up."[26] This approach accepts the victim's testimony about the violation by placing the perpetrator outside the bounds of human community.[27] However, it may deny the experience of the victim, whose feelings about her abuser may include a mixture of love and anger, gratitude for nurture but rage for violation. It is also counter-factual, since many perpetrators are community leaders, teachers, ministers, and doctors; they are thoroughly integrated into their communities, and respected by them.[28] The ambiguity is a reality which the victim must learn to face in order to survive, but it is hard for the bystander to bear.

There are thus two responses to what I have called second-order trauma: both result in declaring the atrocity false to the meaning-system of the culture— either by denying the experience of the victim, or by demonizing the perpetrator. Focus on the individual-as-perpetrator serves the same purpose for the broad social matrix as declaring the traumatic occurence untrue (focusing on the victim-as-falsehood): it protects the social meaning-system at the expense of the individual(s). Knowledge of the abuse is suppressed or recoded: in Mary Douglas's language it is "backgrounded." It is "destroyed by being labelled untrue," by the social matrix; it becomes "too true to warrant discussion" in the psyche of the individual.[29] The experience of victims is "lost", creating

---

24   I am not denying the existence of false accusations, or of incompetent therapists. But the proportion of false claims to the discounted evidence of widespread abuse suggests that what the foundation and related movements are protecting is the meaning system, rather than individuals (cf. Armstrong, 1994).

25   R. Summit, "Beyond Belief: The Reluctant Discovery of Incest," in M. Kirkpatrick, ed., *Women's Sexual Experience: Exploration of the Dark Continent* (NY: Polonium, 1982).

26   Herman, *Father-Daughter Incest*, 130.

27   For example, in New Jersey, a law was passed in August, 1994 mandating notification of community leaders when a convicted sex offender buys or rents a house in their area. One man, falsely identified, has already been attacked and severely beaten as a result of this law.

28   Russell, 105-109. See also Betsy Peterson, *Dancing With Daddy: A Childhood Lost and A Life Regained* (NY: Bantam, 1993).

29   Douglas, 4.

conditions where the trauma is compounded by its hiddenness and its shame and leading to a replication of abusive patterns.

Text and Trauma: Job and the Witnesses

The intersection between the clinical picture and the book of Job comes at the point where the victim begins to speak (cf. Job 2). In both accounts the community's response is to silence the victims, discount their experience, and reassert the fundamental coherence of the meaning system challenged. In order to disclose the essential fragility of this system, however, it is necessary to focus away from the person of Job in a dyadic relationship with God, to examine the social relationships within the text as they reflect human social responses to atrocity. I will give less attention to arguments about thematic coherence or provenance than to the interactive system embedded in the text, returning to the question of God's relationship to, and actions within that system.

The structure of the book of Job is complex: the first two chapters, with chapter 42, form a prose folk tale. Job is a paragon of piety and righteousness, so much so that he captures the attention of the heavenly court. God is pleased with Job; *ha-satan* raises the disturbing question that Job's piety may attach to the material rewards it has brought him. A wager is struck; a series of tests—which for Job, translate into the loss of material possessions, family, home, and health—is begun. Uninterrupted, the folktale would conclude in chapter 42 with the tried-and-true Job receiving double for his losses, living piously to a grand old age, and dying with honor, surrounded by his many descendants.

But the folk tale is interrupted: in chapter three Job speaks in a new way, soaked in all the bitterness of his losses and sufferings. He speaks his innocence, the vast disproportion between anything he could have done and what has happened to him. He proclaims himself a victim, wishes himself un-created in a world where such crimes are visited upon the innocent.

His words unleash a torrent of response from the people who surround him, all of it unsympathetic to his condition or his complaint. For 26 chapters, under the guise of sapiential discussion and with mounting hostility, the friends of Job attempt to shore up the fabric torn wide by Job's cry of dereliction. Their speeches are intended to reassert the justice and simplicity of life, and to return themselves and Job to the piety epitomized in the first two chapters. Job remains as steadfast in his newfound bitterness as he was previously in his contentment.

Another interruption occurs: chapter 28 is a hymn to wisdom, oddly reassuring and refreshing in the midst of the cacophonous, seemingly irresolvable conflicts between Job and his friends.[30] Carol Newsom calls this interlude an invitation, "to return home to the discourse of the prose tale with its vision of moral coherence and order and clarity . . . guided by trustworthy authorities . . .to clear moral conclusions."[31] If the text ended here, the dialogue between Job and his friends would simply be overridden by the recognition that understanding is beyond grasp of mortal beings, the reassertion that submission is the only path to peace. Without changing the fundamental matrix of the meaning-system, this hymn offers an alternative to the standoff between Job's insistence on his innocence and his community's assertion that his suffering proves he deserves it.

But Job rejects the alternative; the argument ends abruptly as Job challenges God to a formal public hearing—what later Judaism calls a *Din Torah*—Job seeks his day in court for the wrongs against him. He is answered—oddly—by Elihu: apparently a late reader of the text who inserted himself as a final advocate for the order so ill-defended by the friends. Job remains obdurate. At last, YHWH arrives on the scene, ready to do battle with this mortal who has dared to assert the world-shattering character of the injustice he has experienced. Newsom comments: "The result of God's speech is virtually to end Job's speech."[32] Job submits, acknowledges that he cannot argue on YHWH's terms, and falls silent.

It remains unclear whether Job is satisfied or merely silenced by the torrent of words which, in tone if not in content, hearken back to the speeches of Job's "other" friends. The grammatical puzzle of Job's submission, which may mean variously, "I despise myself, and repent in dust and ashes," (RSV) or "I repent of dust and ashes," (Janzen) or even "I retract and repent, I am only dust and ashes" (JPS) means that the issue cannot finally be decided.

However, *that* Job submits, on whatever terms, is enough for YHWH. YHWH then turns to the community, vindicates Job (also without explanation), and announces that only Job can restore the friends to right relationship with the God they have maligned, and at his option. Job's fortunes are restored and more, and we are told that Job lives out his years and dies with dignity.

---

30   Some interpreters read this chapter as a speech by one of the friends, or by Job himself. Its mellifluous tone is at odds with the character of the other speeches, however, and forms an inadequate prologomena to Job's extraordinary challenge to YHWH, so I find myself in agreement with those who argue that it is an interpolation.

31   Carol A. Newsom, "Job," in *The Women's Bible Commentary*, eds. Carol A Newsom and Sharon H. Ringe (Louisville: Westminster/John Knox Press, 1993), 131.

32   Ibid., 132.

Rene Girard argues that apart from the prose frame, the book of Job depicts the downfall of a community leader who has become an idol. His reading of the text is reminiscent of the community's reaction to an abuser, especially in the case of a community leader or priest who is "caught" beyond evidentiary doubt. I suppose this is not surprising, since Girard is arguing for a ritual which includes accusations of incest and parricide.[33] The revulsion of the community and the bafflement of the perpetrator at his sacrifice to the meaning-system will follow a Girardian script. The departure from the script, if Job is cast in the role of perpetrator, would come in the amount of talking: the reaction to any disclosure of childhood sexual violence is the move to silence. A confirmed abuser would disappear without long dialogue and without the possibility of protesting his innocence at length.[34] The community does not require of the perpetrator that he acknowledge his guilt in the ways that it will require such acknowledgement from a disclosing victim.

If Job is cast into the role of a disclosing victim, the script shifts in a number of ways. Perhaps the most disturbing is that God becomes the obvious candidate for the role of abuser. The prose frame makes this explicit; God's Dialogue speeches are oddly reminiscent of an abuser's attempt to defuse accusations by the diffusion of information. The lack of real dialogue, the mounting anger of the community, Job's wavering, and even his eventual submission (if that is what it is) parallel what Summit has described as the "sexual abuse accommodation syndrome." In the absence of clear validation and support for a victim's story, recanting is almost inevitable, because even she would rather believe that she is lying, or complicit in the abuse, or mistaken about what has happened, than in her complete helplessness at the time of the abuse. In a situation where no one wants to believe a victim's claims, the claims themselves will wear thin and seem to waver.[35]

---

33   Girard, 35ff.

34   Paradoxically, rendering potential future victims more vulnerable, because the abuser's past is less likely to follow him, since it is "unspeakable."

35   Courtois summarizes a 1983 study by Summit which concludes that unless an offender is immediately forced to accountability following an accusation, and strong support offered to the child who has made the disclosure, the child will retract the accusation in order to restore her life to "normal." She quotes Summit (p. 37):

> This simple lie [the retraction] carries more credibility than the most explicit claims of incestuous entrapment. It confirms adult expectations that children cannot be trusted. It restores the precarious equilibrium of the family. The children learn not to complain. The adults learn not to listen. And the authorities learn not to believe rebellious children who try to use their sexual power to destroy well–meaning parents.

Yet God does not need to be cast in the role of abuser to be implicated in Job's suffering. The relationship of trust is broken: Job, who has lived a life of scrupulous piety and fidelity to God, finds that he is abandoned by that God in his hour of need. Job reaches out for help, cries out for answers, and meets only silence from the divine and silencing from his friends.

Rene Girard notes that readers of the book of Job join the universal doubt of his testimony. "Secretly, we always agree with the false friends who feebly pretend to take pity on Job and treat him as guilty, not only to make him their scapegoat, but also to deny that this could be happening."[36] There is something tiring about Job, about his relentless insistence on his catastrophic pain. It is easy to blame him, because if what he says is true, he is requiring something from us: "All the perpetrator asks is that the bystander do nothing...The victim, on the contrary, asks the bystander to share the burden of pain. The victim demands action, engagement, and remembering."[37] The victim's truth impels us to think differently about the world.

Bruno Bettelheim wrote about the Holocaust that to integrate its psychological impact "would require a restructuring of one's personality and a different world view from that which one has heretofore embraced."[38] It is dangerous to draw parallels between atrocities too closely. And yet his language is apt: the world becomes a different place when one is convinced of the possibility and actuality of atrocity; it means giving up the known world in order to construct a meaning-system which can integrate this new knowledge. To integrate the knowledge is to accept the shock and the pain: they are inseparable from each other. It is, moreover, to examine the very foundations of our culture and our knowledge, opening them to transformation so that the violence can be recognized and cycles of abuse can be broken.

Theology and Trauma: The Problem of God

What, then, shall we say about God? Rene Girard argues for a reading of the book of Job that exposes the "falsity" of the "primitive" God who speaks in Dialogues, whose full revelation comes in the Passion narratives of the Gospels. Job himself is privileged to catch a glimpse of this true God, in Girard's reading of the enigmatic speeches in chapters 16 and 19: "I have a witness in heaven . . .I know that my Avenger lives . . .and in my flesh I shall see God." This is, I suppose, a way to live with his other conclusion, that, "Only Job has spoken the truth about God, by

---

36   Girard, 106.
37   Herman, 7-8.
38   Bettelheim, 33.

apparently insulting him [sic] and denouncing his injustice and cruelty, whereas the friends, who always spoke in his favour, had spoken badly of him."[39] For Girard, the god who speaks in the Dialogues and acts in the prose frame *cannot* be the "God of the victims;" there must be another choice. In this, Girard retreats into orthodoxy in his treatment of God's role in the book of Job, as well as into a religious parochialism which must raise a shudder.

In this he is not alone; in fact, he is joined by the majority of [christian] readers of the book of Job. And yet this reading echoes Girard's own analysis of ideological complicity with totalitarian systems: "...many people are led to minimize what is happening...They are persuaded that the "deviations" will end once and for all on the day when the "good" seize power and chase the "evil" away for ever—in short on the day when the "good" alone will be in charge of the purifying expulsion."[40] It is also oddly reminiscent of the "splitting" that an abused child undergoes to preserve the ideal of a "good" parent, so that the daddy of the daylight is split off from the monster in the closet at night. It answers, but it cannot satisfy.

Nor can I be content with Girard's idea that God explodes the cycle of violence in Jesus by exposing it in his perfect victimization, "He is as innocent as Job and even more so, but by revealing how the world functions, he threatens its foundations more seriously than Job."[41] Neither claim is adequate to the victim's experience of God's silence or inactivity.[42] Whether God is unwilling or unable, for God's own reasons, to offer assistance to the victim becomes irrelevant in the face of clinical findings that the lack of assistance upon disclosure is more traumatic to a victim than is hidden abuse. Whether God is presented as a divine [non]rescuer, or simply as a witness to the abuse, God's role requires an accounting for the believer.

It seems to me, then, that one of the essential components of a theology which takes account of the victim must be a restoration of authentic choice in relationship to God. The survivor of childhood sexual abuse must be allowed to trust her own perceptions, and if she rejects a relationship with God because it has been implicated in her abuse, or abusive of her, that choice should be seen as a real one. The God revealed in the biblical narratives and through the lives of her community may not be adequate to the experience of a survivor, and she

---

39   Girard, 144.

40   Ibid., 119.

41   Ibid., 157.

42   In particular, cf. "Beth's Psalm," in *David Blumenthal's Facing the Abusing God: A Theology of Protest* (Philedelphia: Westminster/John Knox, 1993), 227–232.

has a right to make that determination, without being coerced by threats of hell or persuaded by new metaphors that her perception is flawed.

David Blumenthal, who treats Job in the first book-length attempt to theologize from the experience of child abuse, argues by contrast that a proper theological stance is one of distrust. For Blumenthal, this means one maintains a relationship with God through tradition and liturgy, yet recognising that God has acted, and may act again in ways that must be characterised as abusive. He differs here from Elie Wiesel, whose influence on his thought is marked, in his willingness to theologise (Wiesel refuses to do so on principle) and in his changing of the liturgy itself to acknowledge that abusiveness (a radical move within Orthodox Judaism).[43]

I disagree with Blumenthal's insistence that it is impossible to reject God. I believe that it is possible and perhaps sometimes necessary to adopt a posture of principled a-theism, which acknowledges that God exists without choosing to be in relationship with the divine. This is the true parallel to the therapeutic decision to cut off relations with one's parents, and follows Blumenthal's dictum that "good psychology is good theology, and bad psychology is bad theology."[44]

For many survivors of family sexual violence, christian religious traditions have little to offer as spiritual and theological resources. There are well-documented links between christianity and child abuse, including sexual abuse; between the biblical, patriarchal God and the belief that fathers have the right to control the bodies of their children. (Brown & Bohn; Rush; Bass & Thornton) Victims often feel abandoned or betrayed by God. Still others may feel that they are condemned by God, either for not following the examples of virgin saints and preserving their "purity" at the cost of their lives, or for the hatred they feel toward their abuser.[45] Victims, whether adult or children, who have sought assistance from clergy or religious professionals are often told to "forgive and forget" or to "bear their cross," or worse still are blamed for bringing about the abuse, "leading [the abuser] into temptation." Still others find it nearly impossible to hear the words, "this is my body, broken for you." Stories abound of well-intentioned ministers who have assisted perpetrators to violate court orders forbidding them to see their victims, or have tried to bring premature reconciliation between an unrepentant perpetrator and a still-traumatized victim.

---

[43]   Blumenthal, 1993. This audacious work deserves a more serious response than I can offer in this paper.

[44]   Blumenthal, 201.

[45]   Mary Pellauer in *Lift Every Voice: Constructing Christian Theologies From the Underside* (Fortress Press, 1990), 181.

At the same time, there are survivors who have found meaningful resources within these traditions, and who have chosen to frame their healing in religious terms. Survivors transform religious symbols even as they retrieve them, drawing from their experiences to shape a spirituality that is powerful, transformative, and challenging. Certain themes predominate: healing, the connectedness of all of life, the possibility of transformation, the hope of justice.

It is this final theme which shapes the theological metaphors which I would like to propose as appropriate to describing divine activity in relation to victims on the way to healing, within themselves and within their contexts. Both are present in the book of Job, without stretching the texts or denying God's apparent role in and through the human community: *vindication* and *voice*. Language of finding a voice, or of "hearing each other into speech" has become common since Nelle Morton first used the term. Here God's activity is seen as acknowledging the voice of those who have been silenced, allowing victims to speak and to tell their own stories. Job, apparently abused by God, fights his way to truth, and speaks his pain above the opposition of his community. Even God does not ever allow Job to speak unchallenged. Yet paradoxically, inexplicably, his testimony is finally validated by God, who acknowledges that Job "has spoken rightly of me."

Perhaps, as Jung suggests, Job has brought God to repentance through his refusal to be silenced or stymied. Perhaps it is only when victims begin to speak, to claim their voices and refuse to be silenced, that God is awakened to the need for redemption. Perhaps God joins these courageous ones as they live out their determination that the world might become a safe place for every child, in honor of the countless childhoods lost to family sexual violence. Or perhaps, as Weems suggests, validation comes in the story that remains, so that later generations can weep and be changed by the injustices done.[46]

There are many stories whose redemption is found only in the preservation of their traces in the texts and histories of communities. So we learn, in the biblical narratives, of the rape of Tamar, the exploitation of Hagar, the sacrifice of Jepthah's daughter. These are fragmentary narratives, unlike the exhaustive, and exhausting, story of Job. As Weems reminds us, "The stories *of* these women are rarely stories *about* these women. Their mutilation is often part of a larger story about someone else."[47] We do not understand, and we weep, and we rage at the senseless violence of the stories, but we can also rejoice that the biblical record preserves the memories, even in fragments, of

---

[46]   In the discussion surrounding the poem which gives this paper its title, "A Crying Shame," in *Just a Sister Away,* 64.
[47]   Weems, 65.

those times when justice was denied. It may be that those stories remain as a challenge and a reminder to humanity, as Elie Wiesel has written, that "It is given to man [sic] to transform divine injustice into human justice and compassion."[48]

Perhaps we need to confront this starkest thought: that sometimes God's purposes are worked out at the price of human suffering, and that what is distinctively human is the capacity for this transformation by and through compassion.

Such a confrontation would involve returning to a vision of God as wholly other, even alien from human experience, beyond our capacity to comprehend. Indeed to encounter this God is to come face-to-face with the *tremendum*, to experience humanity as a small part of an intricate creation which is bound to a purpose we can neither fully understand nor control. It is to claim for God a role both greater and more limited in the shaping of individual life; it is to claim for human beings a humbler, but infinitely grander and more complex role within creation. Human beings do not claim co-creatorship with God, nor control over God's elements, but they stand in relationship to each other and the created order as mediators of justice and compassion, healing and hope.

We are not left alone with these tasks. We are given memory, and voice, and vindication when we claim these gifts in order to proclaim our very human outrage at the violence done to each other and to creation. For some, that outrage will find expression in a principled a-theism: the decision to do without a god who has not provided safety, or rescue, or even merciful oblivion. For others, there will be a determination to hold God—and humanity—accountable for the suffering. This will include a re-entering of relationship which recognizes God's role in preserving memory and providing a voice to those who have been silenced. And in the end, God may also offer the vindication which comes to Job, when God acknowledges that, "my servant has spoken rightly of me."

Vindication is that which Judith Herman says survivors need from witnesses: "not absolution but fairness, compassion, and the willingness to share the guilty knowledge of what happens to people in extremity."[49] This is the christian symbol of judgment, conceived not as punishment or condemnation, but as the restoration of balance, the recognition of truth, and the compensation for loss. It is the restoration to a place in the community, not a place of privilege, but one which is cleansed of stigma and which has the same rights of access to safety, trust and freedom as any member of the community. Vindication is not

---

[48] Elie Wiesel, *Messengers of God: Biblical Portraits and Legends* (NY: Touchstone, 1976), 235.

[49] Herman, *Trauma and Recovery*, 62.

vindictiveness, nor revenge, nor even punishment. It is the creation of a place in the conversation for those who have been silenced. In the book of Job, this is seen in chapter 42, where God offers Job the opportunity to sacrifice on behalf of his friends, to restore their relationship to God. By this act, Job accepts a renewed relationship with God and a restored place in the community. His suffering is not obliterated, but he has been vindicated.

Knowledge supressed and memories forgotten in the wake of trauma are not lost. Rather, God works to give back the memory, and the strength to tell, and the healing connections which allow victims to speak, and to hear, and to live out their determination that the world might become a safe place for every child, in honor of the countless childhoods lost to family sexual violence.

10

Divine Power In Powerlessness
The Servant Of The Lord In Second Isaiah

Paul D. Hanson

⌘

The Dialectical Nature of Tradition in the Bible

At the heart of theological tradition lies an inner dialectic. Tradition, first of all, is capable of guiding the life of a community over the span of centuries because it maintains a considerable degree of continuity. What is received from past generations is perceived to have meaning for the present, and for this reason it is re-presented to the religious community and transmitted to future generations, whether in oral or written form. Continuity is thus the first dimension in the dialectic of tradition.

Re-presentation, however, stultifies if it becomes passive and mechanical. As two centuries of philosophical-hermeneutical study have shown, every authentic act of interpreting a monument of the past involves the creative participation of the interpreter and/or interpreting community. In the case of theological traditions, each generation that receives, re-presents, and transmits in turn contributes from its own experience to what is handed down. Creative engagement is thus the second dimension in the dialectic of tradition.

The balance between continuity and creativity in the traditioning process varies from one generation to the next. At times tradition is handed down with minimal innovation. At other times, the creative element is so pronounced as to precipitate an explosion of new meaning.

In dealing with the texts of the Hebrew Bible, it is sometimes possible to reconstruct the historical-political setting within which theological tradition was reformulated. Of particular interest are texts stemming from periods of radical change in the life of the Jewish people, for such periods challenged the spiritual resourcefulness of a religious community as it struggled with problems hitherto unaddressed by the tradition. Rapid social and political change heightened the challenges thrust upon the gathering of the faithful and sometimes abetted considerable experimentation and innovation.

Tradition in Second Isaiah

Second Isaiah addressed the people of Israel at a time of radical change, including destruction of the temple, loss of national autonomy, and displacement of the nation's leading citizens to a foreign land. Could the claim be substantiated that the old traditions still retained credibility? Different answers to this important question emerged.

Perhaps, in keeping with the position of the "friends" of Job, it was a time to build up the community's spiritual defenses in the form of an assertive orthodoxy that dismissed as an egregious form of impiety or even apostasy all questioning of the traditional assumptions arising from the challenges of human experience. Or was it true, as another line of reasoning argued, that the validity of traditional beliefs had been discredited so completely by recent events that it was time to denounce the ancestral god Yahweh in favor of a member of the Assyrian pantheon like Isthar (Jer. 44: 15-19) or the dying and rising god of the ancient Sumerians, Tammuz (viz., Damuzi; Ezek. 8:14-15)?

A third response to the crisis was adopted by a group of leaders who were remembered by later generations as the authentic guardians of the community's faith and whose writings were accordingly preserved and canonized. It was theologically the most demanding alternative, since it refused to adopt either of the simple solutions, i.e., to seek shelter behind a fossilized orthodoxy, or to take flight into the mythopoeic fantasy of a pagan religious system. In their search to reconcile traditional beliefs with the shocking new events of history, these leaders helped shape the dynamic, dialectical understanding of tradition that became the hallmark of the biblical faith handed down to Judaism and Christianity. In this task they were the true descendants of the early Hebrews who had discerned divine involvement in the flight of slaves from Egypt, for they like their ancestors believed that God was encountered in the concrete happenings of this world. Jeremiah, Ezekiel, and the Priestly School all contributed to the developing of tradition in the exilic period. We now turn to another important figure from this period, the anonymous prophet referred to as Second Isaiah.

Facing the assaults of both assimilationists and rigid traditionalists, Second Isaiah sought a faithful response by looking for guidance to the religious traditions of the past while simultaneously searching for lessons among the new events unfolding in the world. As a result, this prophet strikes us both as one of the most faithfully traditional and one of the most audaciously creative of the Hebrew prophets.

Second Isaiah's respect for the theological traditions of earlier generations is evident throughout Isaiah 40–55. The major Yahwistic traditions are all present: exodus, Noatic covenant, promise to the patriarchs, creation, Davidic covenant, and election of Zion. It is equally significant that all of them are formulated in fresh, new ways. The exodus becomes a new exodus out of Babylon, redemption fuses with new creation, and the covenant promises that Nathan had made to David are democratized to apply to the entire nation.

The dialectical nature of Second Isaiah's relation to tradition is expressed nowhere more poignantly than in the following two passages. In 46:8–9 we find this admonition:

> *Remember this and consider,*
> *recall it to mind, you transgressors,*
> *remember the former things of old . . .* [1]

43:18 seems to command the opposite:

> *Do not remember the former things,*
> *or consider the things of old.*
> *I am about to do a new thing;*
> *now it springs forth, do you not perceive it?*

If we are to understand the nature of theological tradition in Second Isaiah, we must grasp the sense behind the paradoxical juxtapositioning of "remember the former things of old" and "do not remember the former things or consider the things of old." But how is this paradox to be explained?

On the surface these two statements seem to create a logical contradiction. And indeed, they *should* be dismissed as merely contradictory, unless, that is, it can be demonstrated that they function together in the service of a truth that intentionally eschews both the Scylla of logical abstraction and the Charybdis of divine capriciousness. But what sort of truth might that be? To answer this question we must fill in some background.

---

1   All biblical citations are from the NRSV.

The heart of Second Isaiah's message is found in the proclamation of release from bondage and restoration to wholeness. It is a message rooted, in the first instance, in divine initiative. Were it not for the fact that God is a gracious God desiring the restoration of the integrity of all people and nations to wholeness within a world freed from the ravages of wickedness and violence, there would be no basis for an announcement of release and healing. But for God's plan of redemption to become a reality in the life of the community, it had to be accepted with openness, trust, and thanksgiving. The twin messages of "remember" and "do not remember" form complimentary aspects of the prophet's appeal to the people to maintain the openness and trust that is receptive to God's saving initiative.

"Remember the former things of old" focuses on the source of the community's essential identity. Memory informs people of faith that their being is rooted in God's release of their captive ancestors and that their identity is realized as gratitude reshapes their human nature into the image of the God who loves them still. From their epic of God's involvement in their history, they inferentially draw forth the attitudes, values, laws, and social structures that preserve the quality of life that is in harmony with God's compassionate justice. The numerous episodes in that same epic describing human rejection of divine grace and its tragic consequences equip them with warnings that futility and despair follow the repudiation of God's love through efforts to construct life on the basis of human resources alone. Memory and forgetting are centrally important in the faith of Israel due to the fact that life is understood on the basis of an ontology that is thoroughly historical in nature. Being human entails a process of becoming within a community shaped into conformity with the nature of God through rememberance of all that God has done. To forget, conversely, is to slip into non-being. Such is the role of memory within a faith embracing an historical ontology. To remember that one is loved is to reclaim the sense of worth that alone can provide a secure basis for life.

Second Isaiah directs the appeal to remember to "transgressors," that is, to those who are abetting the destruction of the future through the denial of the vital connection between past and present. The admonition to remember is thus nothing less than an invitation to reaffirm life as a gift of God. The present generation, despairing as exiles in a pagan land, was to call to mind the story of Hebrew slaves whom God lead out of Egypt to be a free people, for by remembering that tradition their hope would be renewed for their own release from captivity.

In addition to the blessed kind of remembering that liberates and engenders hope and faith, however, is a poisonous kind of remembering that forges a deeper bondage. It grows out of a degraded form of memory, the kind that views tradition not as a dynamic process whose transforming power continues in the present, but as a mythic reality disconnected with the present except as the source of a rigid, closed system that replaces the openness of living relationship with blind submission. Memory, or better, *memorization of* ritual obligations and institutional forms, serves not to tutor the community in a life of responsiveness to divine grace and expectancy of continued growth in understanding, but to bind human consciousness to static structures. That the admonition not to remember is directed at a closed view of history is substantiated by the following clause: "I am about to do a new thing; now it springs forth, do you not perceive it?" (43:19a). The past is to inspire openness to new inbreakings of grace, not slavish imitation of past forms removed from their ontic roots and vulnerable to regressive, elitist myths and ideologies of domination.

The exilic community was thus faced with choosing between two kinds of memory, one that gives life and one that stultifies. Only a clear reaffirmation of her ancestral faith in the God present in history on behalf of the enslaved and oppressed could transform the apparent contradiction between simultaneous commands *to remember* and *not to remember* into a theologically significant dialectic.

Isaiah 40 offers a clue to the nature of that paradox. In verses 7–8, as part of an announcement of God's entry to deliver those in bondage, a shocking metaphor is developed that may seem to nullify the good news of salvation:

> *The grass withers, the flower fades,*
> *when the breath of the Lord blows upon it;*
> *surely the people are grass.*
> *The grass withers, the flower fades;*
> *but the word of our God will stand forever.* (40:7–8)

Can this harsh word possibly form a part of a message of consolation? Only if it is being addressed to a group for whom the message that God is about to level all human structures in an act of purging judgment is good news! And indeed there was in Second Isaiah's world just such a group, namely, the faithful followers of Yahweh living under the absolute authority of the Babylonians. As for those benefiting from the prevailing oppressive structures, they would likely continue to favor maintenance of the status quo as a means of preserving their privileged positions and their control of the masses. But those suffering under the yoke of the oppressor yearn for a divine act that would remove earthly distinctions of power and expose all people to the one decree that transcends mortal corruptibility, namely, God's word of mercy and judgment (cf. Isa. 24:1–3).

Oppressors and the oppressed therefore take opposing positions vis-a-vis the two categories of remembering that we have described.

Oppressors embrace the kind of remembering that freezes the past into a template of mythic/static structures lending divine authorization to their repressive regimes and defining divine power in terms of the absolute power of domination. Through the enforcement of communal memorization of and submission to the official myth, they seek to establish the divine origin and immutability of their regime over against the liberation yearnings of those they exploit. "Remember the former things," they urge, by which they mean all of the myths and legends celebrating the superior wisdom, status, and power of the elite over the subject population. "Remember the former things," they argue, as they point to law codes, social structures, and cultic rites that stratify society according to purported eternal orders of privilege and servitude. At the same time, they oppose the remembering that preserves stories about the liberating God of the exodus who challenged an earlier order of special privilege and invites those living in bondage to project memory into the future by re-presenting the God who liberated in the past as the One calling those in the bondage of contemporary institutions and ideologies to claim their intrinsic dignity and freedom, to renounce oppressive structures and institutions, and to repudiate as distortions all distinctions between entitlement and impoverishment.

From the perspective of the oppressed that comes to expression in the message of Second Isaiah, the two kinds of remembering appear in a very different light from that projected by the ruling classes. To claim as God's will the freedom to reject the kind of remembering that preserves from the past only repressive, hierarchical structures is to be empowered to overthrow the designs of oppressors who identify their human power with divine will and the powerlessness of their subjects with divine judgment: "Do not remember the former things . . ." Affirmation of the kind of remembering that celebrates the God who in every age acts to destroy structures of oppression and to challenge powers of domination nurtures a dynamic, life-giving tradition: "Remember the former things of old . . .My purposes shall stand and I will fulfill my intention."

From the clue given by Isaiah 40:7–8 we are in a better position to understand the process of thought that transforms the two seemingly contradictory statements about remembering and not remembering into a higher paradox-filled unity. It is a unity that is thoroughly dialectical in character. We have already noted that Israel recognized in tradition concurrent dimensions of continuity and discontinuity. Now we need to examine more closely how this dialectical perspective reinterprets the phenomenon of divine power and powerlessness.

The remembering that Second Isaiah repudiates is a remembering subservient to an understanding of divine power as the power of domination, that is, autocratic rule administered on earth by divinely appointed potentates such as kings. The absolute authority of kings over subjects that this understanding assumes requires a myth of infallible certainty, preserved and inculcated by a priestly caste purportedly in possession of divine secrets that are withheld from ordinary mortals. The past is appropriated in the form of a myth of origins that clothes the nation's institutions and social structures with an aura of immutability. The concept of tradition associated with this perspective is the one designated as fundamentalism in modern usage, whereas in the study of ancient societies it is commonly referred to as mythopoeic. It is predicated on a temporal dualism constituted by a golden age of the past and a fallen present era and a corresponding spatial dualism that distinguishes between the eternal splendor of heaven and the bleakness of earth. The aim of religion is defined accordingly, in terms of imitation of the golden age and assimilation to the heavenly order through the power of mythic ritual.

For the power of the patron god and his earthly surrogate to be absolute in the mythopoeic system, the status of subjects must be that of unalterable powerlessness. Assurance of physical subsistence on the part of the latter depends upon complete submission to the social pyramid of the state as the reflection of eternal order. Divine beneficence in this system comes not in the form of empowerment of ordinary citizens to participate in shaping their own lives and their own society but as favors conferred by the king to those who conform to the eternal order. The nature of those favors is determined by one's place in the hierarchy, e.g., land grants to the military officers and nobility, subsistence rations to peasants and aliens.

Against the background of ancient mythopoeic orthodoxy, Second Isaiah's understanding of religious tradition, with its roots in the ancestral experience of defiant peasants and aliens, is revolutionary. It cultivates a new consciousness that refuses to acknowledge an immutable division between power and powerlessness through the ascription of the former to god and king and of the latter to subjects. Rather it views power and powerlessness dialectically as shared aspects within the relationship between God and humans. The deity, traditionally patron of royal power, enters according to the revolutionary new paradigm into solidarity with slaves. This transposition of relationships in turn fosters other changes, all of them contributing to an ontology that is dynamic and open-ended. For example, it connects creation and redemption by replacing the distinction between static material universe established by God *in illo tempora* versus redemption as future hope with an understanding of divine presence as creative-redemptive transformation towards human wholeness and cosmic harmony. It breaks the dualism between pure heaven and sullied earth by infusing political and social structures with God's reforming Spirit, thereby breaking the prevailing linkage of social stability with repression and chaos with change.

The understanding of power and powerlessness in Second Isaiah is thus highly dialectical. It accordingly resists reduction to another common equation, namely, the common pious association of powerlessness with moral virtue and power with corruption. Powerlessness in and of itself is not virtuous, and in fact often leads to despair, while power is good or evil depending on its agency and purpose. The complexity of powerlessness and power can be seen in many different ways. Slavery, though forming the matrix of Israel's origins, is not affirmed as an absolute good, nor is suffering and poverty commended as a special kind of godliness. Those caught in conditions of suffering and poverty that are beyond their control are the objects of divine compassion and blessing. Suffering that comes as the consequence of obedience to God's will in the face of injustice is admired. Yet the blessed era in which all mortals will embrace God's law is described in terms of the absence of suffering.

From the epic account of origins recorded in Penteteuchal traditions, Israel learned that the powerlessness that was to be acclaimed was that which leads to acknowledgment of the vanity of all human pretense and openness to the God who eschews the absolute power of domination in favor of the relational power that enlists humans as partners in the restoration of creation's wholeness. The God of the exodus, as later the God of the cross, exposes the demonic dimensions in coercive power, whether in divine or human form. By entering into the powerlessness of slaves, God transforms power from an instrument of subjugation into one that erases gradations of worth and fosters unity. The dialectic of divine power and powerlessness goes on to reshape the consciousness of the human partners by motivating them to imitate God's governance of shared rule through denunciation of every form of absolute power and domination and through the adoption of laws and institutions that empower and enfranchise the vulnerable and dispossessed. Following the example of the God who entered into solidarity with the powerless, humans enter into the task of constructing a society and world in which mutuality and cooperation become habits of the heart and justice and liberty the marks of human society.

In Second Isaiah we find vivid illustration of how this transformation in the understanding of power and powerlessness generated a rigorous critique of prevailing concepts of rule at the same time that it fostered new models of leadership and governance.

Second Isaiah's Critique of Prevailing Concepts of Power

During the four centuries before the time of Second Isaiah, the Jewish community had lived under a monarchy. In contrast to the period of the confederacy that preceded kingship, the monarchy was characterized by centralization of power within the royal court. Often accompanying the concentration of power in the hands of kings and nobility was its abuse, which elicited the protests of prophets and strategies of defence within palace and temple on the basis of a royal ideology that justified the exalted status of the king by tracing it to divine election and grounding it in a mythologized view of reality.

Second Isaiah's predecessors in the prophetic guild had left behind them a long history of polemic against an understanding of royal power that justified the violation of the dignity and rights of ordinary people by appeal to the divine right of kings. In Second Isaiah's own lifetime the evidence of history added weight to the earlier prophetic indictment: the royal house had fallen captive to the Babylonians, leading to the destruction of temple and nation.

The central tenets of the royal ideology promoted by the protagonists of kingship were the eternal covenant granted by God to David and the steadfast love (*hesed/hasde yhwh*)expressed in the promises that God had vouched safe as part of that covenant (II Sam. 7:12–16 and Ps. 89:2–5). In light of the Babylonian destruction of the royal city and the disgrace that had been heaped upon the last kings of Judah, the divine promises that lay at the heart of temple piety had become an enigma: "And your house and your kingdom shall be made sure for ever before me; your throne shall be established for ever" (II Sam. 7:19).

Second Isaiah's response was in the form of another divine word (55:1–5), one continuous with tradition in that it reaffirmed God's covenant fidelity, but new in that it transferred application from the Davidic King to the people as a whole. In terms of power and powerlessness, it removed the categorical distinction between ruler and ruled upon which kingship was predicated, and by implication, between God and God's anointed king on the one hand and the people on the other. God's presence would not be focused on the glory surrounding one favored family. Through the embodiment of God's covenant fidelity within the community, God's gracious presence would be a reality experienced in the life of every faithful individual:

> *Incline your ear, and come to me;*
> *listen, so that you may live.*
> *I will make with you an everlasting covenant,*
> *my steadfast, sure love for David* (55:3).

The following two verses elaborate on the reformulation of the Davidic covenant tradition. Verse 4 recalls the authority that had been associated with the royal office, while verse 5 goes on to describe the empowerment of the entire people. The seemingly ineluctable tendency towards concentration of power in the hands of the king and court which characterized the entire period of kingship thus meets the challenge of a prophet whose attitude towards tradition is dynamic and dialectical.

The essence of the covenant, its promise of steadfast divine love forever, is preserved. At the same time, a whole new notion of how that covenant will be experienced is introduced. The mythic/static model of absolute power invested by divine decree in the king and the concomitant denial of power to the people yields to a dynamic model of relational power and liberating empowerment. No longer is divine power exclusively yoked to royalty; it is invested broadly in the community. The source of the democratization of power is the same source to which the early Hebrews pointed when they spoke of their liberation from slavery:

> because of the Lord your God, the Holy One of Israel,
> for he has glorified you (cf. 55:5 with Exod. 15:2)

We readily recognize here the creativity with which Second Isaiah, in facing a crisis which shook the Yahwistic faith to its very foundations, reformulated tradition and opened up visions of communal life centered in faith that had hitherto been unknown. The essential verities of Israel's religious traditions were reaffirmed at the same time that they were reformulated with an audacity that broke out of distorted habits of thinking and opened up new redemptive possibilities. This dialectical phenomenon comes to even clearer expression in two other images, "messiah" and "servant of Yahweh."

A Bold New Interpretation of God's Messiah

Second Isaiah's dialectical treatment of tradition becomes apparent in another aspect of his critique of kingship. In the aftermath of the Babylonian conquest, it was inevitable that nationalistic and religious yearnings for restoration were drawn together around the concept of "the messiah," that is, the Davidic King who would be anointed by God to deliver the people. It was a concept intimately related to the royal ideology discussed above. As God had anointed David to deliver the nation from the Philistines, so God would anoint a Deliverer King of Davidic lineage to restore the Jews to their homeland. The techniques that would be used by the king to regain Jewish autonomy were those customarily associated with monarchy in the ancient Near East, those employing the daunting power of domination under divine sponsorship and protection. The anointed one would levy taxes, conscript able-bodied men, restore the glory of palace and temple, and overwhelm all opposition with a superior force. The end result of this centralization of power would be the conquest of foreign nations and the re-establishment of economic, social, and cultic institutions along the lines determined by the royal charter (cf. I Sam. 8:17).

Before Second Isaiah's time the prophets of Israel had already experienced for several centuries the effects of monarchy on the nation. The social stratification and impoverishment of large segments of the population that resulted from the centralization of power in the hands of "the anointed one" had become a central theme in the public utterances of the prophets (e.g., Jer. 22:11–19).

Second Isaiah did not deny that the armies of Babylon posed a real obstacle in the way of the restoration of Jewish freedom. His pronouncements give clear indication that he was acutely aware of international events and their bearing on the destiny of the exiled Jewish community. His political realism and diplomatic acumen infuse the stately pronouncement in Isaiah 44:21–45:7.

In this oracle Second Isaiah turns to Israel's theological traditions as he plots the nation's course through the perils of a changing world. God is Israel's Redeemer (44:24a), God is the Creator of the heavens and the earth (44:24b), God is the One who chose Jacob and Israel (45:4a) and who selected Jerusalem for the site of his temple (44:26,28). God is even the warrior of the cosmogonic myth (44:27). Finally, the tradition of the messiah, the anointed one, is present, albeit with an astonishing twist in which we again encounter Second Isaiah's dialectical approach to tradition:

> *Thus says the Lord to his anointed, to Cyrus,*
> *whose right hand I have grasped . . . (45:1)*
> *who says of Cyrus, 'he is my shepherd,*
> *and he shall carry out all my purposes.' (44:28a)*

We need to stretch our imagination to grasp how these words would have sounded to a people taught by their religious tradition that God had anointed descendants of the House of David to be the nation's kings forever and had endowed them with power to "subdue nations," "strip kings," and "cut through the bars of iron." In the present period of crisis, it was natural for them to look to the House of David for their messianic deliverer. How alien and shockingly offensive Second Isaiah's words must have sounded to those orienting their lives by the compass of traditional Davidic ideology: God was designating a *pagan* king as his shepherd and anointed one and entrusting in his hands God's eternal purposes!

Polemical intent is unmistakable. It is directed towards the same audience Second Isaiah had admonished with the words, "Do not remember the former things . . ." The tradition of God anointing shepherds to carry out his purpose abides, but not in the form that had tied it by an eternal covenant to a particular institution and political ideology (cf. Ps. 89:3–4). God's freedom could not be limited by a mythic/static concept of tradition that had distorted the creative-redemptive vocation of this nation. Tradition, properly understood, tutored the faith community in an attentiveness to the possibility of God's new act, congruous with a divine purpose manifested in past events, but often moving in surprising new directions in its impetus towards wholeness. Second Isaiah's dialectical understanding of tradition was capable of preparing a people to recognize in the Persian king Cyrus the new messiah of God, the shepherd carrying out God's purpose, the one chosen by God to share the power that restores what has fallen and heals what has been broken. This dialectical approach to tradition opened history and the entire cosmos to God's "new thing," God's drawing all agents of justice into a solidarity of purpose, respecting neither national boundaries nor the limits of imputed status, but committed alone to the construction of a just and humane world inclusive of all peoples.

The Servant of Yahweh as a Metaphor of Divine Power and Powerlessness

Having considered the dramatic effect of Second Isaiah's dialectical approach to tradition on the concept of "the anointed one," we are prepared to deal with an image that presses the dialectic further than any other, that of "the servant of Yahweh" (*'ebed yhwh*).

In Second Isaiah's vision of the restoration of the Jewish community, we have seen his reaffirmation of the promises of the Davidic covenant and his extension of those promises to the entire nation. We have seen the exercise of military might transferred from the Davidic king to a foreign ruler. There is no sign in Second Isaiah of divine intention to re-establish sacral kingship as the form of governance for the restored nation. But how was the community to be organized? What model of leadership could replace the traditional model of a divinely designated king? While Second Isaiah does not explicitly address these questions in the way, for example, that Ezekiel does in Ezekiel 40-48, we find in the so-called Servant Songs a pattern of themes pointing to new possibilities.

The first Servant Song (42:1–4) opens with a divine appointment. The choice is not determined by dynastic principle. It is not based on human qualifications. It is guided by the free choice of God ("in whom my soul delights"). But it uses language that creates unmistakable connections with the anointing of David described in I Sam. 16:13: "I have put my spirit upon him"(42:1bα). Moreover, the servant's assignment certainly is of the scope normally associated with royalty in the ancient world: "he will bring forth justice to the nations"(42:1bβ) But the divine freedom to choose one from the ranks of the people that characterized the stories of the judges is also reflected in the servant's appointment.

Once again we witness Second Isaiah's dialectical appropriation of tradition at work. Israel will not be left without divinely appointed and spiritually endowed leadership in the new era. But that leadership will be transformed in a manner drawing from, but not confined to, forms of the past. The relational dimension of divine power comes to vivid expression here. God is personally involved in the life and vocation of the Servant. In looking upon the Servant, one sees the qualities that characterize the Creator of the universe! And those qualities stand in marked contrast to the style of absolute monarchs with their governance through coercion and control by virtue of the daunting power of domination. The gargantuan mission of establishing justice on the earth in fact will be accomplished by the Servant in such a gentle manner as to introduce an alternative to worldly conventions of power. Justice would be established by inspiration and example rather than by force (42:2–3). What ultimately makes this alternative style of the Servant possible is expressly stated. The Servant is not relying on personal power or worldly wisdom, but on the strength and spirit of God. The common human pattern of amassing power is not necessary for the one filled by God's spirit and committed to God's purpose. Without the flash of arms or the display of deadly might, the Servant can quietly administer justice, with a confidence arising from the God who upholds him, in order that "he will not grow faint or be crushed until he has established justice in the earth"(42:4a) The amplification of the Song in verses 5–9 gives even a fuller description of the relational quality of the Servant's style of leadership. Accompanied by God, the Servant goes forth to restore the wholeness of the human community.

The second Servant Song develops further the theme of divine power coming to expression in apparent human weakness. The first three verses of Isaiah 49 identify God's call as the basis of the Servant's identity and the glorification of God as his life's purpose. But the Song is candid in admitting the Servant's sense of powerlessness (verse 4). Yet the human perception of inadequacy does not nullify a deeper sense of quiet confidence, confidence not in self but in the abiding presence of the One who both clarifies direction and assures fulfillment:

> *Yet surely my cause is with the Lord,*
> *and my reward with my God.*

The Servant's confession of power in the midst of personal powerlessness culminates in the fourth Servant Song, a composition replete with mystery and ponderous symbolism. Framed within a description of the Servant's final vindication (52:13–15 and 53:10–12),we find a portrait of one subjected to profound innocent suffering (53:1–9). It is a portrait that goes beyond the earlier descriptions of a faithful individual accepting God's alternative power in powerlessness to establish justice where the power of domination had failed. It goes further first in describing the extent of the Servant's afflictions: ". . . no form or majesty, nothing in his appearance that we should desire him, despised, rejected, suffering, acquainted with infirmity, one from whom others hide their faces, despised, held of no account, stricken, struck down, afflicted, wounded, crushed, bruised, oppressed, by a perversion of justice taken away, cut off, crushed with pain, anguished, poured out to death, numbered with transgressors." All of this the Servant has endured in spite of the fact that "he had done no violence, and there was no deceit in his mouth"(53:9b).

Innumerable have been the attempts to identify the historical entity thus described. All such attempts are doomed from the start, since they confuse poetry with biographical prose and thus miss the essential point. In creating a metaphor too vivid to forget, Second Isaiah heaps up practically every word available in Hebrew to portray suffering and powerlessness. This in turn creates the opportunity prepared for by all of the Servant Songs and all of the paradoxes running through Isaiah 40–55, the opportunity to describe with consummate sharpness the nature of the power that *God* was introducing into the world: "Through him the will of the Lord shall prosper" (53:10bβ). In what is the least likely place to find success, according to worldly standards, we here encounter the instrument through which God's plan for universal peace and justice would be fulfilled.

What new thing is this? What are the ingredients in this proposal?

(1) Interpreted within the context of Second Isaiah's message as a whole, the fourth Song clearly is denouncing the customary coercive applications of the power of domination to achieve order in the world. The Song opens with a description of the masters of worldly power—kings—now made speechless by the spectacle of this unlikely leader. With the royal title removed from the House of David and placed upon Cyrus, the way is cleared for a redefinition of indigenous leadership and power.

(2) The redefinition, however, does not move in the direction so often taken by people who claim to be following a biblical understanding of power and powerlessness, namely, the path of willing suffering as a proper preparation for heavenly bliss. The Servant does not offer a model of acquiescence to the oppressor, but empowerment. "The righteous one, my servant, shall make many righteous..." (53:11). Righteousness is not a submissive quality. Righteousness is a power-sharing, community-restoring, society-constructing, world-healing,

universe-building quality! As the prophet declared God's intent to impart the covenant promises of David to the whole people, so too here the Servant becomes the agent through which that which alone can build universal peace and justice is imparted to the many, that is, righteousness. In place of elitist forms of governance with their concentration of power and privilege in the few, the Servant becomes God's channel for the empowerment of all citizens.

(3) The path to restoration is not one of comfort and ease, but one that acknowledges realistically the formidable obstacles that stand in the way of compassionate justice. Infirmity, iniquity, disease, sin... such are the qualities that characterize the life of the community that has turned away from God, its source of life. No facile solutions can whisk away such fallenness. Trust must be placed in the willingness of the Servant to reject the temptation to use righteousness as a means to immediate, personal reward and to find in it instead the invitation to submit in obedience to God. But here the paradox of the Servant reaches its apex. Submission is not loss of selfhood, but restoration to wholeness. For God is not a tyrant establishing rule through the power of domination, but through the sharing of power, through the empowerment of the lowly. The Servant, in being drawn into a cause larger than the individual, is both vindicated and empowered to become an agent of healing on behalf of others.

How did Second Isaiah come to this audacious proposal? I suggest it was through a profound experience of solidarity with the people, an experience involving both remembering and forgetting, that made the prophet keenly conscious of God's presence. Second Isaiah remembered the suffering of the people, beginning with their slavery in Egypt; remembered the courage of Moses and Miriam and the Hebrew wetnurses; remembered the rebelliousness amidst trials in the wilderness and the mixture of repentance and sin as people heard and then rejected the prophets. As the many allusions to Israel's traditions running through all sixteen chapters indicate, Second Isaiah took the courageous path of dangerous remembering, and thus was prepared to project memory of human sinfulness and divine forgiveness into a daring vision of the future.

Second Isaiah was equally emphatic in forgetting, forgetting all of the false promises to fulfillment, promises of royal splendor that would make Israel the envy of the nations, of daunting military power that would cause the enemies to cringe, of easy divine blessing that would grant peace while simultaneously smiling on iniquity. Second Isaiah could distinguish between redemptive remembering and seductive remembering because he was mindful of the role of both truth and distortion in human consciousness.

The remembering and not remembering that preserved the hard-won truths of the past and preserved openness to the new thing God was about to do tutored Second Isaiah for the task of imagining an alternative to the forms of governance that distort justice and the powers of domination that destroy human society. The alternative was the way of the Servant.

Divine Power in Powerlessness: Biblical Tradition and Contemporary Experience

As we look to biblical tradition from the vantage point of contemporary struggles with issues involving power and powerlessness, the easy road of drawing absolute answers from the text is blocked by the testimony of the Bible itself. This is not to say that it is not a road well-worn by religious persons in search of meaning for their modern lives and for the society and world around them. The easy road is the one that derives direct solutions from a Bible that serves as a manual of God's answers to current events. Within Second Isaiah, religious tradition did not function in this facile manner. Patterns of kingship recorded in earlier writings could not serve as a blueprint for God's future. The temple architecture could not merely be copied in the new generation of believers. The faithful had to be open to the new thing God was about to do.

This is not to say that tradition was ignored. Second Isaiah is steeped in tradition. But tradition functioned in a different way from the uni-referential one used by fundamentalist proof-texting. Tradition provided something other than convenient molds into which new situations could be fit. Religious traditions pressed into such service were torn from the dynamic epic heritage of early Yahwism and forced into the static worldview of myth, thereby threatening the historical ontology that characterized Israelite thought and the accompanying reordering of power structures and transvaluating of concepts of human worth.

In traditions like the creation of the heavens and the earth, the ancestral tales of promise, the exodus pageant of empowerment and deliverance, and the drama of guidance in the wilderness, Second Isaiah found traces of the God present still with the people in their new and uncharted situation in Babylon. The easy road of fundamentalistic transfer was rejected by Second Isaiah. To those insisting that old structures of thought would solve all contemporary problems, Second Isaiah simply replied, "Do not remember the things of old." But what was the nature of the new thing that would guide the people in reconstructing their broken world, and how was it to arise?

A clue is found in Second Isaiah's application to the new situation of a central concept of biblical faith, *mišpaṭ* that is, "justice." Like every other central concept of the Bible, *mišpaṭ* cannot be reduced to a simple definition. Its multivalence extends to moral virtue, social justice, legal contract, divine justification, and cosmic ordinance. In the writings of Second Isaiah's mentor, Isaiah of Jerusalem, *mišpaṭ* revolved primarily around matters of social justice, since the prophet was struggling with leaders who were neglecting their responsibilities on behalf of the people and exploiting the powerless and the poor. Second Isaiah found the Jewish community in a different situation. Distinctions of status had been leveled within the sociology of captivity.[2] *Mišpaṭ* came to focus on a new issue, whether Israel's God was any longer an effective agent in relation to the victorious gods of Babylon. Second Isaiah therefore describes God's defense, "a law will go forth from me, and my justice (*mišpaṭi*)for a light to the peoples" (51:4b).

From this adaptation of the important concept of *mišpaṭ* to a new situation, we see that tradition was not regarded as a rigid template. It was a dynamic instrument of God's Spirit operating through an audacious faith committed not to self-preservation of a cult but to transformation of distortions and brokenness into truth and wholeness on behalf of all creation.

To be sure, it was precisely in crises like Babylonian captivity that the easy road of imitation of the past became sorely tempting. When social and political foundations have crumbled, the old institutions and customs look irresistibly attractive. O for a new Davidic king to "fight our battles for us," a new Zadokite high priest to order our spiritual life. Let new leaders modeled after our leaders of old rebuild our armies and reconstruct our altars and prescribe the rituals and beliefs that we are to follow. But the prophet interrupts nostalgic ruminations and denounces the easy way of imitation: "Do not remember . . ."

The remembering Second Isaiah commends instead is something vastly different from mindless imitation. It is memory placed in the service of courageous reaffirmation of the central confessions of the faith and construction of new social forms and political institutions that release the creative-redemptive power of God into human history. Imitation of past forms, while giving the appearance of faithfulness to tradition, can in essence be an act of betrayal. The revelatory impact of the harsh new experiences of the Jewish community in the sixth century was to expose distortions of Israel's religious ideals that had developed and become lodged at the heart of the nation's social structures and institutions. What the new period of crisis demanded was reexamination of all forms received from the past and a stringent critique and courageous re-envisioning that could describe to a new age the meaning of living in covenant with the God regarded not only as

---

2   I am drawing here upon the research of Harvard doctoral student, Thomas L. Leclerc, M. S., whose forthcoming Th. D. dissertation will trace the development of *mišpaṭ* within the Isaiah corpus.

Creator of every human but as defender of the dignity of persons regardless of the relative degrees of status attributed to them by society.

Second Isaiah was audacious in critique and re-envisioning. From the religious heritage this prophet received not a fixed blueprint but a model of active engagement with life in partnership with a God remembered for a passion for justice. Second Isaiah's question was not, "How can we reestablish Davidic kingship?" but rather, "How can the steadfast love of God expressed in the covenant promises made long ago to David come to expression in the new circumstances of the present?" Some startling answers grew out of the intersection between Second's Isaiah's dynamic understanding of tradition and the new context, answers having to do with a Persian messiah, a Servant of Yahweh, and a nation empowered with the covenant promises earlier conferred upon David. These answers pointed the way towards a radical re-ordering of society and world that replaced powers of domination with relational powers, elite structures of privilege and exclusion with inclusiveness and shared responsibility, resolution of conflict through coercive force with persuasion and example.

There are significant ways in which our situation is similar to that of Second Isaiah. While the modern world is vastly different from that of Second Isaiah, we feel drawn to that world in search of insight into our own crises. If we are prepared to learn from this prophet, we must first realize that the easy road of direct answers via imitation is a dead end. A more difficult path must be taken, the path of searching for transcendent Reality that informed the prophet's engagement with tradition and guided the prophet's critique and re-envisioning within the context of rapid change. The search of the believer attempting to relate the Bible to contemporary life is of course even more difficult than Second Isaiah's. Tradition has continued to unfold for over a score of new centuries, increasing both the richness and the complexity of our religious heritage. And the complexity of our biblical heritage is matched by the complexity of the world we seek to address. There is no denying the fact that the effort to enlist the Bible for contemporary theological discourse is an arduous one, not free from hazards.

Specifically in relation to Second Isaiah, though, we can even here draw certain lessons. There is a persistent theme in the Bible that at the center of life a God is present who transforms structures built by powers of domination into structures dedicated to power that is shared by all for the benefit of all. Implied is struggle, for the powers of domination are notorious for their resistance to challenge and their cunning in persuading their victims that their enslavement is benign and intended by God. And unfortunately the religious record of our tradition is not free of distortions that can be cited as proof for the argument of oppressors.

Struggle is also inevitable in the model commended by Second Isaiah of shared leadership and inclusive covenant. The community cannot simply rely on the big chief to do the difficult work of critique, discernment, and society building. Not even a Big, Big Chief like a patron deity can be summoned. And this is the main point in Second Isaiah. The universe does not have located at its center a Power exercising dominion by brute force. Biblical tradition is not lacking allusions to the divine warrior of myth who unilaterally imposes a heavenly archetype on human society, but traditions like Second Isaiah and the Gospels that subsequent generations have held as hermeneutically significant in interpreting the whole canon provide bases for unmasking the inadequacy of the image of God as the Enforcer of hierarchically-ordered structures of domination. The lesson of the Servant of the Lord and the Messiah on the cross is a lesson in a God eschewing daunting power in favor of solidarity with the powerless. Yet this lesson does not lead to a romanticization of powerlessness, but to a clarification of an alternative definition of power. Divine power is shared power, power-with rather than power-over, patient power rather than power of imposition, persuasive power rather than power of coercion, luring rather than forceful power. And is this not, after all, an infinitely more enduring power than the one applied by dictators and armies?

Lasting peace arises where humans are drawn to compassion and justice due to its attractiveness. This is why the biblical tradition of swords melted into plowshares can be embraced as normative and the image of plowshares being beaten into swords as a distortion. Efforts to repair the world through force will finally lead to greater destruction. Certainly there are a sufficient number of crumbled walls covering the face of the earth to prove this. The only question remaining then is this: how can humans finally learn the patience that allows the lure of shared power to work its magic?

Here is the most unpopular aspect of all in the biblical proposal: only in submission to God can the necessary patience and perseverance be gained. Blocking this step is the fear of submission to a force that finally obliterates human dignity. But this fear is predicated on a gross misunderstanding of the core of Second Isaiah's understanding of alternative power. The God to whom the faithful submits is not a God of coercion or domination, but a God of empowerment of the dispossessed and oppressed. By submission to this *empowering* Power the human discovers the basis for human dignity that no tyrant can take away, while at the same time preserving safeguards against the temptation to use newly-found power to exercise domination over others.

Corporately, moreover, there is no other possibility available to humanity to transcend the conflicts predicated on partisan self-interest.

Granted, the human race stands far short of recognizing this truth. So a poignant opportunity for exercise of the virtue of patience and humility presents itself. In our own limited spheres we can begin the gracious exercise of abdication of the power of domination and the corresponding exercise of discovering the new forms of community that assure every human an equal place. *Tiqqun`olam*, the concept of repairing the universe through acts of loving kindness taught by Jewish rabbinical tradition, is not a task reserved for the Messiah. It is the vocation of every friend of mercy and justice that strengthens the partnership between God and humanity. In this relationship alone lies hope for a more peaceful and humane future.

11

Power and Ambiguity
A Response to Brock, Chastain, and Hanson

Flora A. Keshgegian

⌘

I begin with a deep appreciation for these papers and for the interests and commitments that underlie them. Our presenters ground their own biblical and theological reflections and constructions in concrete historical conditions and in human concerns of suffering. They ask that the biblical witness and theology not only be meaningful and make sense of the historical circumstances with which we humans contend, but that they make a difference and be effective in those circumstances. Thus, human suffering must be addressed practically. All three presenters want to change, or at least challenge, historical circumstances of suffering, caused by injustice and/or violence. They are motivated in these endeavors by a redemptive ethic which seeks to uphold human agency, to create and sustain community, and to enable faithfulness, healing, empowerment, and/or vindication. I share such commitments and relate them to an understanding of theology as a strategic practice, intending liberation, redemption, and transformation. Such intentions are made concrete for me in a particular historical commitment and interest: namely, to enable those who have been victimized not become victims; by which I mean that the circumstances of victimization not become the conditions of revictimization or the forming of a victim identity. I think that interest is shared by our presenters and so I will come back to it as I consider their proposals.

I will, however, first highlight some contributions. Brock, Chastain, and Hanson have presented us with rich, complex and provocative papers. Each intends, as I have indicated, to hold the feet of the biblical and theological traditions to the fire of human suffering and to honor the human quest to go on living with commitment and hope. I would like to underscore one or two particular ways in which each deals with the problematic of suffering.

Rita Nakashima Brock has helped us to see that the category of victim is a complex one, and a political one. It is an identity, which in today's marketplace of identities, is major currency. Being a victim is "in," so "in" that everyone is claiming to be a victim in one way or another. Identity politics has become the playing field of competing victimizations. Therefore, it is necessary to address the politics of victimization and to problematize and deconstruct the identity of victim. A key aspect of that identity, notes Brock, is the claim to innocence; a way to proceed, then, is to reconsider notions of innocence. Brock points out that such a claim to innocence may protect a victim from blame, but it also undercuts her or his agency and obfuscates power dynamics. To make one's innocence be the measure of whether another's behavior is to be regarded as abusive skews our understanding of abuse and evil. Instead, Brock argues for a "paradigm of taking responsibility" that focuses on human agency and action. Such a paradigm requires that we reconsider our understandings of power and identity and see them as fluid and contextual. Empowering action is to be understood as a practice, yoked with responsibility, which seeks to construct new forms of relationship and new concepts of God. "Maternal thinking," as advocated by Ruddick, is an example of empowering action which, Brock suggests, has the potential for encircling violence and transforming relationships. Both Brock's problematization of the idea of innocence and her advocacy of the need for more fluid and contextual understandings and images of power are key and important contributions of her paper.

Kimberly Parsons Chastain also turns our attention to notions of innocence, innocent suffering and scapegoating. She would especially have us attend to the dynamics of denial which accompany our inability to face the suffering of the innocent or of those who are abused and oppressed. Using the story of Job as a model, she insightfully suggests that it ought not be understood as a dyadic encounter between Job and God, but must be understood in a social context. The dynamics of denial need also to be so understood. Chastain helps us to see how denial functions as a defense mechanism not only for those who are victimized and traumatized directly, but also for those who are traumatized indirectly by being witnesses to atrocities and violence. Such denial functions, both personally and societally, to enable the maintenance of world view and culture. To take in the violence is to have to rethink the given reality. Two manifestations of denial—namely, rejecting the experience of victims and demonizing perpetrators—serve to distance oneself from the trauma and to protect the social order. Not surprisingly, Chastain also draws our attention to the importance of witnessing as a remedy for denial and as a way to create a space for victims to find voice and vindication.

Paul Hanson turns to Second Isaiah as a text about Israel finding voice and vindication in new concepts of the divine and of the divine/human relationship. He focuses especially on the Suffering Servant as a redemptive image. The creativity of Israel, as demonstrated in Second Isaiah, is in its ability to develop, within a historical context of defeat, exile and powerlessness, a new way to understand itself in relation to God and a new way to understand power and powerlessness. The figure of the Suffering Servant is meant to show that righteousness, exhibited in suffering, makes righteous and is powerful; good power is that which empowers. This power does not come to Israel by virtue of its election; rather, Israel must demonstrate its ability to embrace a new self-understanding and so be empowered. In making his argument, Hanson astutely reminds us that tradition is a process: it is "traditioning." Such traditioning is about memory. As someone whose own theological work attends to memory as a theological category and to remembering as a way to name the dynamics of salvation, I appreciate this connection. I especially appreciate that Hanson draws our attention to the *dynamics* of remembering. He suggests that remembering and forgetting are dimensions of a dialectical process of making sense of historical circumstances. Authentic memories, true memories, he argues, are those which empower in changing historical circumstances. Forgetting allows such true memories to take shape and hold. In the dialectical play of remember/do not remember, Israel remembers anew in a way that allows it to go on.

It is that "going on" which is a goal for each of our presenters: alternatively stated, each is concerned with what it means to embrace life, to claim power, to be empowered and empowering, in historical circumstances which seem designed to thwart life. Their responses range: Brock calls us to take responsibility, Chastain to bear witness, Hanson to engage in a process of remembering authentically. There is much at stake, they contend. Not only is our ability to go on with life at stake, but and the moral, social, and theological order is at stake, as well. Yet these two stakes may be at odds. It is in relation to that potential opposition that I would pursue my exploration in three directions: by revisiting the idea of innocence, by probing further the dynamics of remembering and forgetting, and by examining the positioning of witnesses.

While Brock addresses innocence most directly and intentionally, it is a theme in all three papers. The presumption is that the suffering being addressed, whether it is the suffering of those who are abused or oppressed, or of Job or of the Suffering Servant, is innocent (which means it is undeserved). Those who suffer are not to blame. Such innocence is connected to powerlessness. There is thus a corollary presumption that if one has power in the situation, one is not fully innocent. The righteousness of the Suffering Servant is related to its powerlessness and its innocent suffering, the same with Job. This connection is precisely what Brock sees as problematic. If a claim to innocence requires powerlessness, then what price is paid for it by the disempowered? Meanwhile, the powerful can claim or assign innocence as a way of masking the dynamics of power.

I agree with Brock that innocence is a problematic category. But I would highlight and underscore a particular dimension of innocence which attenuates the problem: namely, naiveté. While innocence points to moral status, naiveté suggests an innocence of knowledge. Those who are victimized in this world and seek to resist cannot afford to be naive. Along with a paradigm of taking responsibility, I would offer one of critical and committed knowing, which employs a critical consciousness and a hermeneutics of suspicion, engages in political analysis, and practices deliberate partiality. This type of knowing has to extend fully to our use and appropriation of biblical and theological resources. Indeed, we need to cultivate epistemological approaches that see knowledge and truth not only as perspectival and socially constructed, but as discourses of power which arrange, reveal, and mask particular social relations.

For example, Chastain asks us to consider the story of Job in its social setting and not just as a dyadic encounter between God and Job. When I do so, when I consider the social and political dynamics of the narrative, I begin to wonder if anything really is different in the end, except perhaps that God's power is more absolute. Job is after all restored to his wealth and position. One could argue that both God the patriarch and Job the patriarch emerge from the story affirmed. Those who challenged them are dismissed. God prevails over the divine testers. And Job, by not giving in to the advice of his friends, maintains his position. Nothing is presumably lost, except the lives of those originally in Job's household, who but function as pawns in this narrative. The patriarchal order withstands challenge and even total disaster. The effect of vindication can be read as a reaffirmation of that order.[1] What is reinforced is God's power and righteousness, despite circumstance, and Job's alignment with God's order. While Chastain advocates holding God accountable and rejects Girard's dismissal of the

---

[1]   I am grateful to Carole Fontaine for pointing out that, at the end of the story, Job does behave differently in a way that is counter to the patriarchal order. When Job is blessed again with family and fortune, the text reads that he gave his daughters "an inheritance along with their brothers" (42:15). This was not customary practice.

Joban God as false and primitive, I would ask whether she offers a fully political reading.

Relatedly, one dimension of the Christian practice of naiveté, as I understand it, has to do with affirming God's power as able to restore and vindicate. This affirmation functions to obscure or mask what has been lost. I find this affirmation problematic because it is counter to the experience of those who suffer, who need to accept that there are losses which are not redeemable. For example, in the case of the sexual abuse of children, there is irretrievable loss: namely, the loss of childhood as innocence and naiveté. There is no restoration or vindication that can make up for that loss and the harm done against the child. There is no resolution that can erase it. Similarly, with other instances of evil, especially massive evil, such as the Holocaust or other genocides, nothing, absolutely nothing, can make up for the losses.

The moral, social and theological orders are ruptured in these instances and any seeming resolution rests on an unstable fault line. This is not to say that we can no longer claim meaning and order and so embrace life; but it is to say that any world view has to be cognizant of the instability, contingency and ambiguity contained in all affirmations of reality. For those of us who live on this fault line, which I would argue is all of us in the post-modern Christian west, there is no insurance against the potential of eruption and chaos. There are, however, precautions and practices which will help us to live with the instability and ambiguity and to go on. To play with the metaphor a bit more: while we cannot prevent earthquakes, we can build structures that are flexible enough not to shatter and be destroyed when the earth erupts.

One precaution we can take is to remember. Not "remember" and "forget," but rather "remember in a complex way." The admonition to Israel not to remember the former things, because God is doing a new thing, makes me nervous. It didn't used to. In fact, I, as an advocate for change, used to point to it, as Hanson does, to underline that our understanding of ourselves in relation to God and our views of tradition are dynamic and changing. Now I react differently, not because I am against change, but because forgetting is fraught with danger. Hanson himself warns us that forgetting implies non-being. I would extend his notion to suggest that by forgetting the monarchy, Israel may forget part of its being and its history: namely, how it abused power against others and sought to dominate other lands and peoples. Rather than forgetting, I would advocate a stance toward the past that includes mourning irretrievable losses, acknowledging and repenting of complicit actions, and letting go of the dominance of these pasts, but not of the memory of them. Mourning, which may be accompanied by repentance, includes recognition of irreplaceable loss and harm. Remembering is pledge of that recognition. So rather than the directive, "do not remember the former things," I would suggest, "remember all that has happened to you and all you have done." It is important to remember faithfulness and faithlessness, victimization and agency, not because there is some essential and true identity in the past that must be retrieved, but because our fluid and multiple identities are constituted by all of these things.

Such remembering is an ongoing act of witness. Chastain especially points to the importance of witnessing for healing. I would, however, have us consider further what we mean by witnessing. I understand witnessing to be an act of solidarity, being with, "with-nessing." As such it may be understood as a strategic action designed to counteract an opposing tendency, that of splitting.

Splitting is a defense mechanism often used by those who are abused. In splitting, the abused person cuts the actions of the abuser off from awareness so, for example, a child being abused may talk about disappearing into the lamp or floating along the ceiling. In the moment of violence, splitting can be a protective move so that while the abuse happens to the child, she does not feel it. However, the continued practice of splitting or the dissociation that accompanies it means that the child is not living her life; she is not connected with all parts of herself.

While splitting may thus be a "helpful" move in a situation of trauma, it is not helpful toward wholeness or redemption. A form of splitting, a related strategy, is also used by perpetrators and bystanders. As Chastain indicates, the action of denial is a way to separate oneself from a reality one does not want to face or accept. Both splitting and denial warrant witnessing, but the movement of witnessing is different in each instance. To witness with the abused is to recall them from dissociation and to ask them to stay connected and present. To witness with perpetrators and those complicit in abuse is to challenge their denial and to recall them to the actuality of what they have done or allowed.

To further generalize from these dynamics, I would suggest that there are forms of splitting and denial operative within moral and theological categories. Brock, for example, points to the problematic nature of the splitting of power and responsibility in systems of poisonous pedagogy and the various manifestations of splitting that are at the core of dualistic systems. I would suggest that we need to explore further these dynamics of splitting and denial as operative in our theological formulations and in relation to the biblical materials. For example, the Suffering Servant passages may be read as a splitting off of what is too painful for Israel—namely, its own powerlessness—onto a figure it can both identify with and see as separate. To the extent that the Suffering Servant is a spectacle, we are in some sense split from it, as is God. It functions as an object of our attention which deflects our attention away from other things.

My intent here is not to psychologize theology. Nor am I suggesting that we ought not use this image of the Suffering Servant or that it is an invalid way of relating to God. Rather, I am arguing against naive uses of images and concepts which do not take into account the ways in which they have been used to oppress as well as to liberate. We need to analyze our images and categories from all angles, to make ourselves more aware of what they allow us to see and what they hide, and how they structure and deploy power. For me, such analyses would be guided by my interest, namely, that those who have been victimized not continue to be victims. Thus I would align with and bear witness to those uses which do not reinforce oppressive arrangements of power that split powerlessness, innocence, and naiveté from power and so obscure the relational and contingent dynamics of power.

Such an approach calls for an epistemology of ambiguity, which helps us figure out how to live on the fault line. This epistemology would require something other than attention to systematic distortions, a term which to me suggests that if we find the right lens or lenses, be they bifocal or multifocal, we can correct our vision. Rather, I am suggesting that any lens, any perspective, distorts even as it enables us to see. And so we need to remain aware of the limitations and ambiguities in our vision, as well as in the vision of those we seek to examine, critique or correct. I end these remarks then with the humble recognition that such advice applies also to my thoughts and perspectives. As we embrace such instability of vision and power, however, I hope and I wager that we will learn alternative practices of power. These will enable different discourses and relationships which might resist splitting, innocence, and naiveté. Potentially they may do less harm and be redemptively effective.

Part Four

—INTERPRETATIONS OF THE BIBLE IN TRADITION —

⌘

12

Woman Wisdom and the Strange Woman
Where is Power to be Found?[1]

Claudia V. Camp

⌘

But where is wisdom to be found?
And where is the place of understanding?
Job 28:12[2]

It is no doubt a mark of our time and situation that for me the quest for wisdom has become a question about power. A question of finding it, to be sure, but also a question of defining it and our relationship to it. I choose two figures from the book of Proverbs—the personifications of Wisdom and Strangeness—as guides for the quest, partly because of my long scholarly acquaintance with them, partly because of the current controversy about Sophia in the Protestant churches. As female images constructed by men, they are in one sense inherently disempowering for women; they inhibit our ability to name and shape ourselves by telling us in advance who we are and may become. On the other hand, as *powerful* female images they tantalize the female questor/questioner of

---

1   This essay was first published in *Reading Bibles, Writing Bodies*, ed. T. K. Beal and D. M. Gunn (London: Routledge, 1996), 84–111. I thank Routledge for permission to re-print.
2   All biblical citations are taken from the NRSV unless otherwise indicated.

power. Could there be an imagistic surplus of power available here that is not under the control of the fashioners?

In its broadest sense, this is an essay on *language as power*. I am interested in how language works: how it is manipulated and by whom, and how it shapes our situation beyond any conscious intent. To speak of language and power means, inherently, to speak of specific social-historical contexts. Thus, this paper begins and ends with reflection on such contexts: first, the post-exilic situation in which the book of Proverbs, with its female imagery, approached canonical status; finally, the contemporary firestorm provoked by the purported worship of the "goddess Sophia" at the Re-imagining Conference in November, 1993. In each case, I ask the questions of who uses the female imagery, and to what ends, with particular attention to its effect on women's power. In each case, we shall find that power is a multi-faceted force, that the power and powerlessness mediated through female imagery cannot be seen as simple opposites, but must be sorted out in varying degrees and kinds.

The middle two sections of the paper deal with metaphor and (metaphorical) theology. They provide transition between the ancient and modern contexts, in several ways. First, metaphor's attention to similarity and difference generates a constructive play, and thereby a hermeneutical bridge, between the expectations and associations of the two historical eras. Metaphor theory thus helps us articulate and address the challenges of theologically appropriating an ancient text—whose original "power lines"[3] may have been quite different—in the modern context. Second, and relatedly, because metaphor is a way of speaking theologically, it bridges the enterprise of understanding the Bible's theology, which is often metaphorically expressed, and that of constructing theology from the Bible, a task in which the appropriators of Sophia are actively engaged. Finally, analysis of metaphors in terms of their sublimation of meaning allows us to dis-cover the (also powerful) "unsaid" suppressed by powerful manipulations of language. Such discovery is crucial to understanding how language works as power—and as theology. In particular, attention to the unsaid may illuminate the vicissitudes of power—its shifting margins and centers—in the days of the life of Sophia and her traditioners.

Women and Wisdom in Proverbs: A Case Study on Power and Powerlessness in Ancient Theological Discourse

One way to approach the question of power in these texts is to think historically. What, in heaven's name, are they doing in the Bible?

---

3   A phrase conveniently at hand from Catherine Keller's paper in this volume.

Who wrote them, read them, preserved them? And, in particular, what do they tell us about women's power in that society?

Female Imagery and the Structure of Proverbs

Female images function meaningfully in the structure of the book of Proverbs. Scholars often think of the book in three parts. The central section (chapters 10–30) comprises collections of short sayings that modern readers usually connect with the term "proverb." Chapters 1–9, however, are longer poems, either instructional in nature or reflective on the idea of wisdom. It is here that the figures of Woman Wisdom and Woman Stranger are developed in quasi-mythical terms. Chapter 31, the book's final chapter, is made up of two poems, one an instruction to an unknown "King Lemuel" by his mother and the other an acrostic paean to the "woman of worth." Female imagery thus dominates the beginning and ending of the book of Proverbs, serving in effect as the main structural supports for the book as a whole. Whereas Wisdom and the Strange Woman are almost mythic figures, however, the women in chapter 31 appear more "real-to-life," however idealized they may be. Nonetheless, abundant similarities in vocabulary establish a relationship, especially between Wisdom and the worthy woman.

Female Imagery for Wisdom in Proverbs 1–9

Proverbs 1–9 uses a multiplicity of images to develop the Wisdom figure. In Proverbs 1:20–33, the image of the prophet, who calls out in public places to chastise a sinful people, is woven together with vocabulary ("reproof," "simple," "scoffers," "fools," "counsel") typically identified with the wise sage or teacher.

> Wisdom cries out in the street;
>> in the squares she raises her voice.
> At the busiest corner she cries out;
>> at the entrance of the city gates she speaks:
> "How long, O simple ones, will you love being simple?
>> How long will scoffers delight in their scoffing
>> and fools hate knowledge?
> Give heed to my reproof;
>> I will pour out my thoughts to you;
>> I will make my words known to you.
> Because I have called and you refused,
>> have stretched out my hand and no one heeded,
> and because you have ignored all my counsel

> and would have none of my reproof,
> I also will laugh at your calamity;
>   I will mock when panic strikes you,
> when panic strikes you like a storm,
>   and your calamity comes like a whirlwind,
>   when distress and anguish come upon you."
>   (1:20–27)

Importantly, although Woman Wisdom uses the stock phrase "fear of the Lord" (1:29) as the object of her teaching, she also speaks very much on her own authority. Actions elsewhere identified with God she here takes herself, pouring out *her* thoughts, calling and stretching out *her* hand. One seeks and finds *her*; listening to *her* assures security and ease (1:33). There are a number of associations to human women implicit in the poem: to the mother as teacher, regularly referred to in Proverbs (e.g., 1:8; 31:1, 26); to female prophets like Huldah (2 Kings 22:14–20); to the lover who "seeks and finds" her beloved in the Song of Songs. Nonetheless, the Woman Wisdom of chapter 1 is also a transcendent figure.

Proverbs 4:1–9 and 7:1–5 are both instructional poems in which wisdom is first identified with the father's teaching and then personified as an independent entity.

> Listen, sons, to a father's instruction,
>   and be attentive, that you may gain insight.
>
> Get wisdom; get insight:
>   do not forget, nor turn away from the words of my mouth.
> Do not forsake her, and she will keep you;
>   love her, and she will guard you.
>   . . . .
> Prize her highly, and she will exalt you;
>   she will honor you if you embrace her.
> She will place on your head a fair garland;
>   she will bestow on you a beautiful crown.
>   (4:1, 5–6, 8–9)
> My son, keep my words
>   and store up my commandments with you;
> keep my commandments and live,
>   keep my teachings as the apple of your eye;
> bind them on your fingers,
>   write them on the tablet of your heart.
> Say to Wisdom, "You are my sister,"
>   and call Insight your intimate friend . . .
>   (7:1–4)

In these passages, Wisdom is depicted as lover and wife: "sister" is a term of endearment, as we learn from the Song of Songs, and Proverbs 12:4 tells us that "a good wife is the crown of her husband" [cf. 4:9]. These ideas are reminscent of Proverbs' expectation of the sexual enjoyment (5:15–19) and the economic bounty (31:10–31) a man can expect from his wife. This wife is one "given," furthermore, under the father's authority, and she has a protective function. The ensuing verses in chapter 4 (10–27) show the young man's need of protection from "evildoers," while 7:5–27 identifies the "strange woman" as the danger from which Wisdom will shield her lover. Similarly, the love poem in 5:15–19, which refers to a real-life wife, becomes a warding against this strange woman in vv. 20–23.[4]

Chapter nine also presents images of wifely provisioning and protection against the strange woman (here Woman Folly, 9:13), but adds to them a transcendent strength. Wisdom has not only "slaughtered her animals . . .mixed her wine. . . [and] set her table," but

> Wisdom has built her house,
>   she has hewn her seven pillars.
>
>   (9:1)

While the reference to "her house" is thrice echoed in the poem on the good wife (31.15, 21 [twice]), the reference to "seven pillars" (not to mention her "hewing" them!) sounds as much like a deity building a temple, perhaps even the cosmic temple, the earth supported by seven mountains.

Chapter eight's wisdom poem contains the most dramatically transcendent imagery in Proverbs.[5] It begins similarly to the poem in chapter 1, with Woman Wisdom crying out in public places, offering words of truth worth more than earthly treasure (see also 3:15). Then, however, she asserts herself as the power (not so very far!) behind the throne:

---

4   Carole Fontaine notes the coincidence of many of these features with the folklore type of the "sought-for person," or princess-bride, bestowed by her father on the hero after a set of trials, who provides both good counsel and material blessings, and who must be discerned from the "false bride" ("Proverbs," in *Harper's Bible Commentary*, ed. James L. Mays [San Francisco: Harper and Row, 1988], 502–503).

5   This imagery is anticipated in Prov. 3:13–18 and 19–20. Although these two brief units in chapter 3 were no doubt originally independent, their contiguity in the book of Proverbs is telling, and surely related to the chain of associations made in chapter 8. In 3:13–18, Wisdom is better than earthly treasure, though she offers that, too, as well as life (cf. 8:10–11, 18–21, 35–36). She is to be laid hold of (*hzq*), a verb used elswhere of intimate embrace (7:13). Vv. 19–20 shift suddenly to YHWH'S wisdom by which he founded the earth (cf. 8:22–31).

> By me kings reign
> > and rulers decree what is just;
> by me rulers rule,
> > and nobles, all who govern rightly.
> > > > (8:15–16)

Although the context may alter the connotation here, it is interesting to note that these verses are followed immediately by a return to the "wifely" images of love and prosperity:

> I love those who love me,
> > and those who seek me diligently find me.
> Riches and honor are with me,
> > enduring wealth and prosperity.
> > > > (8:17–18)

Verses 22–31 provide the biggest surprise of all. Although certain vocabulary is curiously ambiguous in meaning, Woman Wisdom is depicted as present with God before and during creation, and then deciding to take her place on earth with the human race.

> YHWH conceived (*or*: acquired) me at (*or*: as)
> > the beginning of his way,
> > > the first of his acts long ago.
> Ages ago I was installed [in office] (*or*: woven [in the womb]),
> > at the first, before the beginning of the earth.
> When there were no depths I was labored forth,
> > when there were no springs abounding with water.
> Before the mountains had been shaped,
> > before the hills, I was labored forth.
> > > . . . .
> When he assigned to the sea its limit,
> > so that the waters might not transgress his command,
> > when he marked out the foundations of the earth,
> then I was beside him like a master artisan (*or*: darling child);
> > and I was daily a delight,
> > > rejoicing before him always,
> rejoicing in his inhabited world,
> > and my delight was in human beings.
> > > > (8:22–25, 29–31)

Wisdom then offers life and favor from YHWH to those who watch at her gates, and wait beside her doors (vv. 32–36). In these last few verses, however, the voice of Woman Wisdom once again blends with the voice of the teacher (perhaps a mother here?) in the address to "my sons." If female imagery in the preceding poems has served to make the quest for wisdom an attractive one to the young male student, chapter 8's dramatic elevation of this imagery adds as well a ringing note of authority to the teacher's instruction.

Female Imagery for Wisdom and Women's Power in the Post-Exilic Period

What does this overview of the wisdom poems tell us in terms of our questions about women's power? Two considerations operate in tension with each other around this question.

First, I see little doubt that a certain kind of woman was empowered by these texts. The wise, hardworking wife who could counsel her husband astutely and teach her children well is given enormous pride of place. She is not celebrated for meek obedience, moreover, but for energetic industriousness and management skills that take her into public places as well as the home. It is even possible that a mother's teaching rather than the father's lies behind certain texts (Brenner and van Dijk-Hemmes propose chapter 7;[6] I would perhaps also add at least the last few verses of chapter 8).

Although Israelite household stability and prosperity always relied on the wise wife and mother, this need was particularly keen during the post-exilic period, as the returned exiles attempted to re-establish a society whose basic form of political organization—the monarchy—had been shattered.[7] This context may have provided the impetus for binding the more predictable adulations of the wise wife managing "her house" together with the striking depictions of Woman Wisdom as source of all government and builder of the ritual or cosmic "house." Powerful, divinely authorized Woman Wisdom functions in part as a symbolic replacement for the lost king, becoming one of the first of the idealized mediator figures that would populate Jewish religious thought in ensuing centuries.[7]

There is another symbolic issue at stake as well, related to the structuring of the book of Proverbs by means of female images, as noted above. The book was edited during a time when written texts were rapidly becoming a definitive part of the religious tradition, although

---

6   Cf. *On Gendering Texts* (Leiden: E. J. Brill, 1993).

7   See my *Wisdom and the Feminine in the Book of Proverbs* (Decatur: Almond, 1985); and, for further considerations on contextualizing these texts, "What's So Strange About the Strange Woman?" in *The Bible and the Politics of Exegesis*, ed. D. Jobling, P. L. Day, and G. T. Sheppard (Cleveland: Pilgrim Press, 1991), 17–32.

7   Cf. Burton Mack's essay in this volume.

that tradition was still heavily influenced by orality. The enclosing female images seem not only to give structure to a largely unstructured collection of proverbs, but also to provide an authorizing *voice*, not simply to wisdom teaching in general but to this book, *qua* book. Indeed, Skehan provides a convincing structural argument that at least one metaphorical referent of Wisdom's house in chapter 9 is the book of Proverbs itself, "built" by her.[8]

The question of why a *woman's* voice was chosen for this authorizing function then becomes important. I would suggest, first, that men's experience both of their mothers' instruction and the good wife's love, counsel and support created the possibility of a female voice. Their experience supplied, in other words, the affective grounding that is necessary for a symbol to be embraced as constitutive of reality. But what makes this possibility achieve realization? One answer lies, I believe, in the contingencies of the social situation described above, and which will receive further elaboration below: in the post-exilic period conditions were right for women's on-going contributions to society to be noticed consciously and even found desirable of further authorization. At one and the same time, this recognized status lent authority in turn to the concept of wisdom it embodied.

A second reason may lie in another of Israel's symbol traditions, namely, the tendency to personify the community (usually, though paradoxically, defined as the *male* members of that community) as female. This typical prophetic device (but see also Numbers 25:1) usually works itself out in the marriage metaphor, with Israel as the adulterous wife who "plays the harlot" with other gods and YHWH as the betrayed husband who punishes (and sometimes forgives and restores) her. Female personification is also at work in Proverbs, but with two key differences. First, Proverbs' Woman Wisdom combines transcendent qualities with her earthly ones; second, she is powerful and righteous rather than ripe for punishment.

What can we make of this similarity and difference? I turn again to the relationship of the book of Proverbs to the wisdom tradition, of which it is both product and paradigm. The wisdom tradition in Israel was essentially a human tradition. Although never conceived antithetically to Yahwistic faith, it was nonetheless basically comprised of the teachings of the mothers and fathers of Israel. In an era when books were beginning to be perceived as loci of divine revelation, however, the editors of Proverbs clearly sought a higher level of authorization for the tradition it represented. They achieved this through the use of the female Wisdom figure, a figure present with God

---

8   "The Seven Columns of Wisdom's House" in *Studies in Israelite Wisdom and Poetry*, J. A. Fitzmyer, ed. (Worcester, MA: Heffernan, 1971) 9–14; and, in the same volume, "A Single Editor for the Whole Book of Proverbs," 15–26; "Wisdom's House," 27–45.

during the most crucial acts of ordering creation, yet not quite identical with God. Not identical in part because she is female to YHWH's male. On analogy with the prophetic personification of the human community of Israel as female, this gendering of Wisdom suggests her on-going identification with the wisdom tradition as product of that community. I propose, then, that the sages, perhaps hesitant to fully equate a human tradition with the voice of the male God, did the next best thing in imagining Wisdom's persona as transcendent, but female. If so, they drew on the tradition of female personification of the community, but also shattered it with their previously unimagined characterization of a woman both powerful and righteous.

With respect to women's power, however, there is a second consideration, with a contradictory force. It is clear that, precisely as products of a patriarchal society, part of the very purpose of these powerful female images was to define and control female identity. We must therefore consider the inherent limitations in the symbol of Woman Wisdom with respect to real women's power. First, Brenner and van Dijk-Hemmes have argued that at least chapters 7 and 31 of Proverbs represent female traditions of instruction. If this is true, the point certainly reinforces what I have said above about the power of a certain kind—the "right kind"—of woman. But it also shows the over-reaching power of patriarchy: the women who speak with the fathers' voice are the women who have a place, and they are divided off from other women who refuse this allegiance. Second, Carol Newsom[9] has argued that these texts represent not only gender struggle, but generational struggle; that is, the fathers are attempting to control their sons, as well as their wives. This argument would explain the unusual (for the Hebrew Bible) expression of concern for husbands remaining sexually faithful to their wives, as well as vice versa, while also illuminating the patriarchal manipulation of the Woman Wisdom image.

These observations come into focus when we attempt to account not only for the presence of exalted Woman Wisdom in these texts but also for her opposite, the Strange Woman. The presence of female personified evil alongside woman as the perfect embodiment of righteousness is a sure tip-off to the gender reality of the ultimate purveyors of power in Proverbs. Examples abound in history of this imagistic either/or, one of patriarchy's favorite symbolic games. Yet there is still, I believe, something to be learned from studying the particulars of the figures in Proverbs. Let us, then, consider the Strange Woman in terms of imagery and socio-historical context.

---

9   Cf. "Woman and the Discourse of Patriarchal Wisdom: A Study of Proverbs 1–9," in *Gender and Difference in Ancient Israel*, ed. P. L. Day (Minneapolis: Fortress, 1989), 142–160.

The Strange Woman

We have already noted the oppositional conjunction between Woman Wisdom (along with the beloved wife) and the Strange Woman: one of the major functions of the ideal female is to protect her lover from this particular danger. But what is the exact nature of the danger? Much hinges on how one understands the two terms, typically used in parallel structure, that designate the negative female. Although the word pair most often comes into English as something like "loose woman/adulteress" (still so even in the NRSV), the Hebrew terms *zara* and *nokriyya* represent most literally the feminine forms of "stranger," "foreigner," "outsider to the family," or "other."[10] Thus, while the ensuing characterization of this figure is one of sexual looseness—she is indeed the "other" woman in our modern colloquial sense—the terms themselves are broader in meaning.

From a literary point of view, there are two features of Proverbs' Strange Woman important to our purposes here. First, like Woman Wisdom, her portrait is multi-dimensional and thus difficult to channel into a single meaning. Second, in spite of the apparent opposition between Woman Wisdom and the Strange Woman, there are in fact many fascinating literary linkages between them.

The multi-dimensionality of the Strange Woman derives in part from attempting to articulate an answer to the question: In what sense is she strange?[11] The first inclination is to assume that she is a foreigner, a non-Israelite. Closer analysis reveals that her ethnic status is not the first consideration.[12] Rather, strangeness of a sexual sort looms large, though this is metonymically paired with religious "infidelity" of some sort. Thus, the young man who finds wisdom

> . . .will be saved from the strange woman,
> from the outsider with her smooth words,
> who forsakes the partner of her youth,
> and forgets her sacred covenant.
>
> (2:16–17)

---

[10]   The two terms overlap in this range of meanings, though they are not absolutely identical.   *Zar*, for example, has two connotations apparently not available in *nokri*: it can mean, specifically, an outsider to the Aaronid priestly family; more generally, it can also simply mean "not oneself, another."

[11]   See my "What's So Strange About the Strange Woman" for a detailed discussion of the dimensions of strangeness in Proverbs.

[12]   This point is arguable, and has indeed been much argued. Even if I am wrong in my judgment, the multiplicity of meaning in this figure does not allow a limitation of the Strange Woman's significance to this connotation.

In a curious layering of sexual perversions, the adulteress—whose husband is away from the marital bed on a long journey—dresses and acts like a prostitute, seeking and boldly propositioning her customer out on the streets (7:10–12). What's more, this prostitute-adulteress also manages to choose a time for her activities, during the days of peace-offering sacrifice (7:14), when sex is ritually forbidden (Lev. 7:11–21). Thus, improbably, yet a third layer is added to her sexual offenses. The punishment for this ritual offense is, moreover, precisely that threatened by the Strange Woman: Leviticus 7:20 prescribes that offenders shall be "cut off from their people," while those who dally with the Strange Woman will be "cut off from the land" (Prov. 2:22) and "in utter ruin amidst the assembly" (Prov. 5:14).

Based on the preceding observations, I would suggest that the Strange Woman does not represent any particular real women or class of women. Rather, the layering of different kinds of sexual misbehavior, as well as ritual offense, generates a portrait of idealized evil in its multiple dimensions. With this in mind, we can re-consider the notion of ethnic foreignness that is a primary connotation of the terms *zar* and *nokri*. I do not believe that this connotation can ever be removed from the force of these terms. Whether or not the authors of Proverbs are concerned with foreign women in a literal sense, it lurks always as a powerful part of the system of commonplaces associated with the metaphor of strangeness, and adds yet another horrendous dimension to the portrait of Evil inscribed in the Strange Woman.

From a social-historical perspective, the characterization of this female figure as "strange" to the point of death takes on special power in the context of Israel's on-going struggle to define itself over against those foreigners in their midst, the Canaanites with whom they had so much in common. At least by the time of the Deuteronomist, the danger of marriage to foreign women, who contaminate Israel with worship of foreign gods, had become part of the cultural polemic.[13] Even beyond this, biblical rhetoric often so mixes the language of female sexual impropriety with that of foreign worship that the two components are inseparable. At least echoes of this metaphorical convention are at work in Proverbs.

Consideration of the post-exilic context may nuance this picture further. Women were important in this period not only in their on-going roles as household managers and educators of children, but also, through advantageous marriages, as a means for gaining and sealing

---

13   This polemic against foreign wives may, in fact, be no older than the (late seventh century) Deuteronomist. Biblical scholars, observing that there are no differences at the material level between so-called Israelites and Canaanites, increasingly tend to view intermixing as the norm until relatively late in the biblical period, citing Josiah's nationalistic reforms as the likely origin of the Bible's polemic.

land claims among Jews returning from Exile. "Foreign" women were dangerous not only as potential conduits of foreign worship into Israelite families, but also as representatives and mediators of the claims that non-Jews—or the "wrong kind" of Jews—might make on the land. This last qualification is an important one for, in this period, Jews were divided in a contentious struggle to define the nature and control of the community itself, and especially the norms of right worship. They faced, in other words, a most devastating psycho-social reality: the "foreigner" could be another Jew. In this context, the layering of many sorts of "strangeness"—ethnic and sexual, moral and cultic—onto a single figure produced a powerful symbolic touchstone against which to assert one's own claims to orthodoxy. The fact that this figure was female is hardly an accident. Woman, the quintessential Other, was the perfect embodiment of the full-orbed Strangeness that tormented post-exilic Jews in Palestine. What we have in the end is a quasi-mythic figure, whose dangers are conceived not merely in the material terms of separation from land and people, but in terms of death itself. Thus, the young man is warned that

> . . . many are those she has laid low,
>   and numerous are her victims.
> Her house is the way to Sheol,
>   going down to the chambers of death
> (7:26–27).

To bring this consideration of the Strange Woman to a close, we must return once more to her alleged opposite, Woman Wisdom. There can be no doubt that, on one level, the text presents an absolute dichotomy here, one that confronts the reader with a forced choice between good and evil, life and death. Yet there are numerous items of vocabulary and imagery in Proverbs 1–9 that connect the two figures as well. Encounters with each involve "embracing" and "grasping." Both are found "in the street" and "in the marketplace." Both invite followers to their respective houses; both offer bread and beverage. With either the Strange Woman or his wife, a man can "fill himself" with "love" or "her breasts" (the latter two words are quite similar in Hebrew: *dodim/dadeyha*). Aletti[14] suggests that the editor of Proverbs, through this ambiguous use of vocabulary, has created a deliberate confusion between Woman Wisdom and the Strange Woman in order to stress the difficulty and importance of discerning true speech. The effect of this ambiguity within a contemporary discussion of power and powerlessness will be taken up in subsequent portions of this paper.

---

[14]   "Seduction et Parole en Proverbes 1–9," *Vetus Testamentum* 27 (1977): 129–44.

A Metaphorical Perspective

The Concept of Metaphor

These historical observations on the use of a female image, however righteous and powerful, by men for their own ends confronts modern readers with a hermeneutical dilemma: will reference to Woman Wisdom empower women today, or will it not? What are the advantages and dangers of appeal to this biblical figure?

I have argued elsewhere[15] that there are a number of advantages for the reader who, in effect, disavows the image's ideological history, its patriarchal source and manipulation, and thinks, instead, in terms of metaphor. One way to theorize this intellectual process is to distinguish between the functions of metaphor and those of symbol, the term I have up to now been (loosely) using to refer to Woman Wisdom. McFague[16] argues that a symbolic view of the world tends to be static, by virtue of its stress on the similarities and harmonies between things. It also tends to be hierarchical: the substance of the symbol is valued primarily in terms of its divine referent. Thus, according to various interpreters, Woman Wisdom may symbolize the wisdom of God, the wisdom tradition, the order of the world, the book of Proverbs, etc. We notice two things here. First, the significance of the symbol seems to pale beside what it symbolizes. Second, in every case, the *female* element in the symbol—its unconventional element—is thoroughly suppressed in favor of the male-determined referent. This is certainly one way to view Woman Wisdom, but it is not the only option.

To personify as female an abstract concept like wisdom is, in effect, to create a metaphor, "Wisdom is a woman." Now the second term is not only noticed; it is also highlighted as crucial to understanding. While it is possible to create such a personification and leave it at that (think, for example of the Statue of Liberty), the Proverbs poems go on to carry through the metaphorization process with their varied allusions to different roles of human women. Certain relevant historical associations of "woman" have been discussed above: in Israel, woman was wife, lover, provider, prophet, counselor, etc. Such images constitute what Max Black[17] calls the "system of associated commonplaces" evoked by a metaphor.

---

15 "Woman Wisdom as Root Metaphor: A Theological Consideration," in *The Listening Heart: Essays in Honor of Roland E. Murphy*, ed. K. G. Hoglund et al. (Sheffield: JSOT Press, 1987), 45–76.
16 Sallie McFague, *Metaphorical Theology* (Philadelphia: Fortress Press, 1982), 10–18.
17 Max Black, *Models and Metaphors* (Ithaca: Cornell University Press, 1962), 38–44.

A metaphor with a wide and powerful range of such associations falls into the category of "root metaphor," one that goes beyond mere symbolic representation or condensation of ideas and actually carves out the conceptual and affective space in which we live. Root metaphors create reality. I believe that the metaphor of Woman Wisdom in fact functioned as a root metaphor historically and has the potential to so function again in current Christian religiosity.

A metaphorical perspective has at least two advantages for a theological discourse centered in biblical texts. The first is related to the notion of metaphor as expressive of a system of associated commonplaces, or, perhaps better, the interaction of the systems of commonplaces associated with each of its terms. If an historical understanding of "Wisdom is a woman" requires elucidation of those systems entailed by "wisdom" and "woman" in post-exilic Israel, it is equally true that the contemporary reader can hardly approach these terms without what is commonly denigrated as "our own cultural baggage," but which here might be more usefully framed as our own systems of commonplaces. A hermeneutical bridge between past and present is constructed as we play with—and meet the challenges of—the similarities and differences not just between the terms of the metaphor, but also between the eras. The role of the reader in generating meaning from texts is thereby acknowledged, but not at the cost of repudiating all possibility of historical meanings.

Secondly, a metaphorical approach is advantageous insofar as metaphor functions by means of sublimation.[18] That is to say, metaphors operate as much by suppressing and concealing meaning as by overtly creating it. With Bal, one must ask "the question of what the metaphor makes unspeakable." Let us consider, then, the spaces carved out and concealed by Woman Wisdom.

Wisdom and Language as Metaphor

Wisdom thought is deeply concerned with language, a concern that Proverbs clothes in female garb. Based on the number of proverbs that address proper and improper speech, we can assume that the traditional sages were much interested in both the efficacious and truth-telling aspects (not always identical!) of language. Language itself, with both its positive and negative aspects, is personified in Proverbs 18:21:

> Death and life are in the power (lit: hand) of the tongue,
> and her lovers will eat of her fruit.

---

18   Mieke Bal, "Metaphors He lives By," *Semeia* 61 (1993): 205–6.

Woman Wisdom, of course, represents the claim to truth and life, and makes these available to her lover:

> Hear, for I will speak noble things,
>> and from my lips will come what is right;
> for my mouth will utter truth;
>> wickedness is an abomination to my lips.
> All the words of my mouth are righteous;
>> there is nothing twisted or crooked in them.
> They are straight to the one who understands,
>> and right to those who find knowledge.
>> > (8:6–9)

Death, however, also embodied in female form, is the end to the devious user of language, and to one who is taken in by it. Nowhere is this point clearer than in Proverbs 9, where the Woman of Folly echoes, but subverts, the words of Woman Wisdom. Wisdom says,

> "You that are simple, turn in here!"
>> To those without sense she says,
> "Come, eat of my bread
>> and drink of the wine I have mixed.
> Lay aside immaturity, and live,
>> and walk in the way of insight."
>> > (9:4–6)

Folly parodies:

> "You who are simple, turn in here!"
>> And to those without sense she says,
> "Stolen water is sweet,
>> and bread eaten in secret is pleasant."
> But they do not know that the dead are there,
>> that her guests are in the depths of Sheol.
>> > (9:16–18)

Three features of the space of language may be discerned in Proverbs' assertion that Wisdom is a woman. First, by locating truth in human speech, Woman Wisdom locates a divine immanence within this essential human attribute. God's presence is found in the world and, particularly, in women's world: the world of relationships in both home and marketplace, in the private and the public domains. Second, by embodying Language itself, as well as Wisdom, in female form, this essential human attribute is identified as female. Third, the embodiment of Language's deception, as well as its truth, in female form gives rise to a double vision. On the one hand, this dualistic linguistic embodying represents the (male) need to divide and conquer both women and language by distinguishing Wisdom from Folly, *the* truth in the midst of lies. Thus also, however, an appropriate reservation is articulated against all assertions of absolute truth; attention is called to the ease with which language becomes deformed. The possibility of a critical approach to these texts is embedded in the material itself.

Re-reading Women's Roles

Analysis of Woman Wisdom as a metaphor allows for more empowering readings of the Bible with respect to women's roles, readings that move beyond some of the more detrimental possibilities of the text. Disconnected from the first nine chapters of Proverbs, for example, the closing poem on the woman of worth can easily be read as a license for slavery: the good wife is one who works her fingers to the bone night and day so her husband can parade around like a prince at the city gates. Alternatively, but relatedly, we have already noted how the opposition of Woman Wisdom and the Strange Woman may appear as the woman-negating "virgin/whore" dichotomy. While it is important for the sake of honesty not to deny these spaces in the texts, there are also others.

The closing poem by itself presents a "dead metaphor," the terms of which are taken literally and for granted: the good wife is wise. This is a space in which we live, but one that we no longer see as such.[19] The good wife has "mastered" her wisdom, just as her *ba'al* (= husband, master, v. 11) has mastered her. The book's opening chapters, however, turn the metaphor around. Now Wisdom is the good wife. And mastery she has! She does not simply "keep" her house; rather she builds it. And her house is not simply the family dwelling; it is the community, the cosmos, the written revelation of God. She is not mastered but sought and embraced.

If we could go no further than to say that this portrayal of Woman Wisdom valorizes traditional women's work, we would have said something important, but not sufficient. Hitler used a similar ploy. We must rather extend our analysis of the roles of women and wisdom to the mode of relationship involved. Wisdom as woman and the wise woman stand together at the nexus of at least two relational polarities. The first is that of the public and private spheres of social existence. Social-historical study alone would show us that these two spheres were not divided in ancient times in the same way or extent that they are today. The family household was the basis of societal formation both

---

[19]   Cf. the analysis of "metaphors we live by" by Lakoff and Johnson in their book by that title (Chicago: University of Chicago Press, 1980).

materially and symbolically. Thus it should not be at all surprising that the woman of worth operates in the domain of public economic activity, bringing food "from far away," buying and financing the cultivation of a vineyard, selling to merchants the garments and sashes she produces (31:14, 16, 24). If she, with her transcendent counterpart, is not merely "home-maker" but also "house-builder," then she is responsible for the interface between these two arenas. Her power is public as well as private, while at the same time investing the public realm with the relational values of the household.

As builder of the cosmic house, as well as of the family household, Woman Wisdom stands at the juncture of the divine and human realms as well. This is a location we shall explore further below. Here I shall simply note the wonderful immanence of the divine expressed through this figure, now in body as well as in language. And in choice as well as in body. The woman who originates with God, who plays with God, decides of her own volition to reside and play with human beings (8:30–31).

Re-reading Sexuality

Before considering Wisdom as goddess, there is one further observation to be made in regard to the metaphor "Wisdom is a woman." We highlight here the association of woman to sexuality: Woman Wisdom is a lover. As with other dimensions of this figure, this one is both problematic and salutary. In all probability, the sexually embodied aspect of Wisdom as woman is more surprising to a modern sensibility conditioned by later Greek influence than it was to the ancient Israelites. Let us accept our surprise gladly. Whatever negative opposition is constructed in these texts between the good woman and the bad, it is *not* an opposition based on sexual experience versus its negation. If some version of the "whore" is in a sense on one side of Proverbs' polarity, it is curiously not the "virgin" on the other. Proverbs 1–9 is remarkable for bringing the vocabulary and forms of the Song of Songs into its portrayal both of Woman Wisdom and of the beloved wife. The former is to be sought, grasped, loved, prized, spoken to with terms of endearment, waited for at her gates and doors. Similarly, the latter should be faithfully attended to and rejoiced in as the source of emotional and physical pleasure:

> May her breasts satisfy you at all times;
> may you be intoxicated always by her love.
> (5:19)

The liberative potential of this valorization of sexuality in a religious context comes under the double-barreled fire of patriarchy and heterosexism. Although the "good" female here is not a virgin, she *is* a wife. Her job is to protect her husband from the Strange Woman, while at the same time avoiding "going strange" herself, a possibility imagined in 2:16–19 and 7:10–20:

> You will be saved from the strange woman,
> from the outsider with her smooth words,
> who forsakes the partner of youth
> and forgets her sacred covenant. . .
>
> (2:16–17; see also 7:10–20)

Sexuality is celebrated, but only if it is properly controlled.

Sexuality is also assumed to be heterosexuality. Indeed, nowhere in the entire Bible is it more obvious not only that a man is writing[20] but that a male audience is intended. Who else would say to Woman Wisdom, "You are my sister" and call Insight "intimate friend" (7:4)? Who else indeed? But this literary display of the audience pushes the readers of every new generation to the foreground as well. Can we identify? What will we do if we cannot? How delightfully shocking to insist that women today should read this text literally, to insist on our right to be the audience of the text, to feel its call to intimacy with Woman Wisdom, to speak to her words of love, to identify each other with her, and be intoxicated always with that love. The text's unmitigatedly male discourse provides the implement for its own un-manning.

A Theological Perspective

As we turn to consider the explicitly theological dimensions of this material, we will leave behind neither the historical nor the metaphorical perspectives introduced above. To assert that "Wisdom is a goddess" is to make the same sort of epistemological claim—one of metaphorical naming—that was made with "Wisdom is a woman." And the "ess" suffix assures that considerations of femaleness cannot be outside the picture, even as its absence subverts rather than supports claims of gender-neutrality. The two metaphors are metonymically linked. Reflection on the metaphor "Wisdom is a goddess" entails again both recurrence to historical-literary considerations and reference to contemporary usage. The latter has been dramatically limned as a

---

[20]   It may be, as Brenner and van Dijk-Hemmes argue, that a mother actually delivers some of these teachings, but even they do not attempt to dispute the fact that it is patriarchal ideology we hear.

power issue since the Re-imagining Conference in November of 1993. The possibility of owning Wisdom as goddess has generated a crisis, a term rendered (so I've been told) in Chinese script with the characters for "dangerous opportunity."

Wisdom: God and Goddess

The goddess elements in the figure of personified Wisdom have always been a matter of dangerous opportunity. The creation of this figure in the first place depended in part on language and imagery drawn from Egyptian, Canaanite, and Mesopotamian goddesses.[21] This co-opting of foreign traditions was commonplace in the development of Israelite religiosity, but always entailed a risk. These elements had to be integrated into the orthodox tradition in such a way that they were ultimately marked as "us," not "them." In the case of Woman Wisdom, I have argued that it was precisely the concomitant reliance on human female imagery and the experience of real women that mediated in this process. Thus the Woman Wisdom of Proverbs is, as demonstrated above, an amalgamation of the traits and roles of real women with a transcendent aura.

But was she, or should she be, regarded as a goddess? Historically, in Proverbs, my sense has been that she was understood as essentially what she appears to be: an act of theopoetic imagination that reflects claims about and for the wisdom tradition in its social context as much or more than claims about the nature of divinity.[22] This way of thinking about the figure begins a trajectory that culminates in Ben Sira's identification of Wisdom with Torah, about 180 BCE. Only a poetic image whose meaning was open and polyvalent could support such a fresh moment of inspiration.

On the other hand, "life and death are in the hand of the tongue": the rich fruit of poetic language can easily take on a life of its own. In hindsight, who can gainsay the fact that Proverbs 8 seems to portray a living being with divine powers, whether or not we choose to use the loaded term "goddess"? Thus the tradition seems to have noticed. As Cady, Ronan and Taussig argue in their book, *Wisdom's Feast*,[23] by the time the Wisdom of Solomon was written (either first century BCE or CE), the ambiguously divine Woman Wisdom of Proverbs had become a

---

21   See Fontaine, "Proverbs," 501–502, for an overview of the data.
22   A new analysis by Judith McKinlay will likely lead to further nuancing of this assessment. McKinlay not only proposes Asherah as a meaningful element in Wisdom's ancestry, but also argues that the Proverbs poets systematically suppressed the goddess through increasingly domesticated images of Wisdom. *Gendering Wisdom the Host* (Sheffield: Sheffield Academic Press, 1996).
23   San Francisco: Harper and Row, 1989.

more fully-fledged divine figure, not an independent goddess, but rather a way of talking about, of relating to, YHWH and "his" works. This particular naming of divinity (not only of God but also, in the New Testament, of Jesus as well) has more recently been taken up in the feminist context, for example, in the worship elements introduced by Cady, Ronan, and Taussig in their pastorates and study groups; in the more academic theology of Elizabeth A. Johnson's *She Who Is*;[24] and by the liturgists of the Re-imagining Conference.

While I can only affirm this liberating use of long-neglected Scripture, there are some underlying issues that need attention, spaces hidden, if you will, by the metaphor "Wisdom is a goddess." If we begin from Bal's perspective that metaphor works by sublimation, by making certain things unspeakable through its "cover-up" language, we might notice that the most important thing that "Wisdom is a goddess" makes unspeakable is itself. That is, none of the scholars and churchpeople just mentioned actually wants to *say* "Wisdom is a goddess." In the current denominational political climate, none of them *can* say it even if they want to. Thus, the only people saying "Wisdom is a goddess" are those who construe that statement as a heresy charge against those who cannot or do not wish to say it.[25] What's at stake here?

Feminist theologians deny the practice of "goddess worship" insofar as this suggests an entity over against the biblical God rather than simply a re-naming of him. Ah, yes, but there you have it or, rather, there you have "him." In a language that distinguishes gods from goddesses, if you cannot use the latter word, have you not merely folded the female into the male, allowing him to co-opt her? It is certainly accurate to say that these feminist theologians are not calling for "goddess worship" in the sense of imagining a divine figure apart from the biblical god. However, to say, in a way truthful both to the biblical tradition and to the impulses of feminist theology, that *Woman* Wisdom (or "Sophia," as many prefer) names God, we must be also able to say that God is Goddess. In this sense, the self-styled orthodox have called the results of the game correctly, though using the wrong rules.

Wisdom: Truly Woman and Truly God/dess[26]

Now, this proposal that Sophia-God names God as Goddess has a problem of its own, namely, that goddesses don't always help real

---

24   New York: Crossroad, 1992.
25   I allude here to the controversy surrounding so-called "Sophia worship." See below for further discussion of this debate.
26   For want of other options, I shall resort to Rosemary Radford Ruether's writable if not readable designation for divinity that both incorporates and transcends all aspects of human sexuality. *Sexism and God-Talk* (Boston: Beacon Press, 1983), 46.

women. History is replete with societies that acknowledge strong female deities and yet are also politically male dominated. This is very obvious in the ancient Near East, and should give the lie to any attempt to blame Israel for patriarchy. What became orthodox Yahwism may have made an unprecedented attempt to kill the goddess, but women's lives did not much change, at least at the political level.[27] The role of the Virgin Mary in Catholicism is similar: the Queen of Heaven may be a comfort to women, but is hardly a standard-bearer for women's power.

Even more to the point is the case of Woman Wisdom herself, and I think there's a multiplex paradox here yet to be accounted for by Sophia-logians. I have suggested above a development in the portrayal of Woman Wisdom from the more earth-bound characterization of Proverbs to the divine being of the Wisdom of Solomon.[28] This development coincides, however, with an apparent de-valuation of human women in the texts and, to the extent we can tell, of real-life women in society. Proverbs not only casts Woman Wisdom in human female images, but also sings a hymn to the woman of worth. Ben Sira, perhaps a couple centuries later, continues to use female imagery for wisdom, but the language becomes more formal and abstract. His Wisdom is a rigid disciplinarian, a role more like a male teacher than a woman, and he ultimately identifies "her" abstractly with the Torah. This author has much to say about human women, but virtually all of it is negative, and virulently so. Wives and daughters are a constant threat to male sexual and economic honor; indeed, in Ben Sira's view,

> From a woman sin had its beginning,
> and because of her we all die.
> (25:24)

The Wisdom of Solomon gives us divine Wisdom, but no human women at all. Instead of the intoxicating love and breasts of his wife, here the sage's fantasy is uncoupled from living flesh and real relationship:

---

[27] In response to the conference presentation of this paper, Carole Fontaine appropriately called for a nuancing of my implication that the presence of goddess worship makes no difference to women if the society is socially and politicallly male-dominated. In fact, women can be profoundly empowered at the spiritual level, with all the attendant ramifications thereof, by goddess-piety. Fontaine's own historical research gives a fine example of this in the case of the Hittite queen Puduhepa's worship of the Sun-goddess Arinna ("Queenly Proverb Performance," in *The Listening Heart: Essays in Honor of Roland E. Murphy*, ed. K. G. Hoglund, et al. [Sheffield: JSOT Press, 1987], 95–126). Carol Christ makes a similar argument for contemporary goddess-worship in "Why Women Need the Goddess," in *Womanspirit Rising*, ed. Carol Christ and Judith Plaskow (San Francisco: Harper and Row, 1979), 273–87.

[28] See further my "The Female Sage in Ancient Israel and in the Biblical Wisdom Literature," in *The Sage in Israel and the Ancient Near East*, ed. J. G. Gammie and L. G. Perdue (Winona Lake: Eisenbrauns, 1990), 194–203.

> When I go home I shall take my ease with [Wisdom].
>   for nothing is bitter in her company,
> when life is shared with her there is no pain,
>   gladness only, and joy.
>
> (8:16)

Well, if a man had a wife like Ben Sira's this would be quite a relief. But does this goddess empower women?

We encounter, then, what I would submit is a crucial theological problematic. We know that control of language, especially the key metaphors that name ultimate reality, can be a powerful force for change, as it has been a powerful supporter of the status quo. Feminists have long assented to Mary Daly's dictum that a male god in effect makes men gods. Yet, we know historically that the mere presence of female deities does not make women goddesses. Specifically, we see that the presence of Woman Wisdom may or may not do much for women. The question, then, is: when does the metaphor God is Goddess or, specifically, Wisdom is God/dess, make a difference and when does it not? My reflections thus far suggest at least a tentative part of an answer. This metaphor holds power when it is not allowed to conceal another metaphor, namely, that "Wisdom is woman," with its entailment that "God/dess is human."

Now, this proposal is either extremely radical or highly orthodox. If I say that "God is known through the humanity of Jesus Christ," I have said at least part of what I mean, and few Christians would argue. If I say "Goddess is known through the femaleness of human women," I would have said another part of what I mean and opened myself to heresy charges. What is the real difference between these two statements? The male vs. female difference of course leaps out, but it is matched by another of equal importance, namely the particularity of the singular Jesus vs. the universality of human women. It is not just that Jesus is male, it is that Jesus is *the* (one and only and therefore) *perfect* male. Human women are never that. It is precisely at this point that I return to Proverbs to highlight another element of paradox that illuminates both its patriarchal conservatism and its openness to radical re-reading.

Wisdom: Good God or Strange Woman?

Imperfection is the issue here. Yes, even evil. We have noted Proverbs' good-woman/bad-woman dichotomizing. Already this would seem to be a problem for a Sophia-based theology. It would seem to raise a particular problem for precisely that element of Proverbs' theology that I praised a moment ago: the book that highlights and supports "real" women also uses female imagery to create a symbol of deadly evil in the Strange Woman, which is absent in both Ben Sira and the Wisdom of Solomon.

We have a couple of options here. We can, on the one hand, ignore and suppress the Strange Woman texts, as most contemporary Sophialogians have done. Why deal with her when we have the Wisdom of Solomon's goddess to worship? Just let one metaphor erase the other, as the tradition itself did. If "Wisdom is God/dess," why bother with "Woman is the Stranger"? We must bother because, of course, the tradition did not erase the latter metaphor at all. It persists in the canonical state of Proverbs and it persists, poisonously unspoken, in social practice. What happens if we take another option, and bring "Woman is the Stranger" to speech?

One thing we notice is that "Woman is the Stranger" conceals another metaphor under the surface of the tradition, namely, "the Stranger is God/dess." As it does with the transcendent Woman Wisdom, Proverbs endows this negative figure not only with attributes of human women, but also with divine ones. And, as with Woman Wisdom, the result is the creation of a dramatically new theological motif with long-lasting implications. My point of reference here is a comparison of language used for the Strange Woman with that used for God, specifically in Isaiah 28.

Outstanding among the numerous items of vocabulary and imagery connecting Proverbs 1–9 to the Isaiah text[28] is the reference to YHWH's works with the same word pair that repeatedly limns Woman Stranger. YHWH will rise up

> to do his deed—strange (*zar*) is his deed!
> to work his work—alien (*nokriyya*) is his work!
>
> (Isa. 28:21)

In this same chapter, Isaiah also ascribes to God several terms used by Proverbs of Woman Wisdom. In Proverbs, Woman Wisdom offers her follower a fair wreath and beautiful crown (*'at eret tiph'eret,* Prov. 4:9); in Isaiah, YHWH will be to his people a "glorious crown" and a "beautiful diadem" (*'ateret-tsebi/tsephirat-tiph'arah,* Isa. 28:5). Similarly, just as Wisdom gives strength (*geburah*) to give to those who judge rightly (*shophet tsedeq,* Prov. 9:5, ET 8:14–16), YHWH is a spirit of justice to the one who sits in judgment (*yosheb 'al hammishpat*) and strength (*geburah*) to warriors (Isa. 28:6).

Remarkably, the positive and negative attributes that are *combined* in the prophetic depiction of YHWH are *divided* in the sage's

---

28   See "What's So Strange About the Strange Woman" for further examples and discussion.

rendition of the two female characters. But both sets of attributes remain fundamentally *divine* attributes. The Strange Woman is shaded no less with this transcendent aura than is the Wisdom Woman. The enduring import of this figure lies in its personification of a divine power of evil over against a God who is now unstained by death-dealing qualities. If God is Goddess, Devil is also Woman. It's not just that women are not perfect, it's that Woman is Death. Now, there's an enormous amount of power at stake here, but what do we want to do with it?

Power, Powerlessness and the Divine: A Case Study on the Bible in Contemporary Theological Discourse

Let me turn first to what it seems *has* been done with it in the context of the Re-imagining Conference, which produced considerable conservative reaction within the mainline denominations that supported it.[29] It may first be worth noting that the conflict aroused by this conference was anticipated by several years in a similar reaction of conservative Methodists to Cady, Ronan and Taussig's book, *Wisdom's Feast* (1989). Cady and Taussig, both Methodist pastors, were threatened with a heresy trial for this work. What was the problem? The book is a fine piece of both historical scholarship and liturgical creativity. It is actually composed of two parts. The first part is an historical look at the figure of Sophia in Jewish and Christian scriptures, which had in fact appeared three years earlier as an independent monograph (titled *Sophia: The Future of Feminist Spirituality*). To the best of my knowledge, there were no significant criticisms in relation to the earlier publication. It was the second half of *Wisdom's Feast* that generated the heat. Here the authors offer Bible studies and liturgical elements that were actually used in churches and that were intended for others to so use. Quite an example of how little scholarship matters until it involves praxis! By the same token, I would argue that the Re-imagining Conference would not have created a blip on the conservative radar screen if it had just been theologians reading papers

---

29   Readers wishing to track the debate are referred to several denominational publications, dating from just before the conference and for close to a year after it. The *United Methodist Reporter* and the *News of the Presbyterian Church* are the official organs of their respective denominations. The *Prebyterian Layman*, *reNews* (a publication of Presbyterians for Renewal) and the Methodist *Good News* are conservative publications that published virulent attacks on the conference. More recently, the ecumenical periodical *The Christian Century* has published critical (though not negative) assessments of both the conference and of Sophia-centered theology. See J. D. Small and J. P. Burgess, "Evaluating 'Re-Imagining'" and L. D. Lefebure, "The Wisdom of God: Sophia and Christian Theology," both in vol. 111 (1994): 342–344 and 951–956, respectively.

to each other; surely nothing was said there that has not been said at the AAR/SBL or in many published feminist works for years. The difference at the conference was that there were not just scholars in attendance and that what was said intellectually was also ritualized.[30]

I believe that understanding the prior Methodist uproar over *Wisdom's Feast* is one crucial element in understanding the fall-out of the Re-imagining Conference. If all one had was the record of the conference, one would have to ask why so much attention has been paid in the conservative denominational presses to Sophia. This figure actually received little reflective time in the overall conference, though she was invoked at certain ritual moments: in a brief litany that preceded each speaker's presentation, although *no* speaker actually talked on Sophia, and in a liturgy that celebrated Sophia as creator alongside aspects of women's embodiment in the context of a "milk and honey" meal that closed the gathering. The latter usage was anticipated by, if not directly drawn from, *Wisdom's Feast*. But, more than this, *Wisdom's Feast* and the worship experiences that generated this book created the conservative awareness of Sophia that, in spite of the infrequent conference references, led to headlines like *Christianity Today's* "Fallout Escalates Over 'Goddess' Sophia Worship."[31] One of the most-quoted blasts against Sophia—retired Methodist Bishop Earl Hunt's statement that "no comparable heresy has appeared in the church in the last 15 centuries"—was, by his own account in the *United*

---

30   There was, of course, denominational money involved in putting on the conference and sending delegates to it. Particularly in the United Methodist and Presbyterian (USA) churches, some outcry has centered overtly on how such funding decisions are made. I would argue, however, that the funding issue is a smoke-screen. Denominations spend infinitely more money year after year supporting colleges and seminaries where these theologians teach and write. Although there are a few seminary professors (notably Tom Oden of Drew; see his "Confessions of a Grieving Seminary Professor," *Good News* [January/February 1994]:10–13) attacking the issue at this level, this is not the dominant discussion, as can be seen in the resolution of the Presbyterian General Assembly on funding decisions. There is little hue and cry about money, as long as those feminist theologians are off doing their thing in the ivory tower. The problem arises when church people are confronted with the possibility of putting the ideas into practice. Although I formulated this analysis independently, I thank Cynthia Rigby for sharing a paper that supports it, though from the other side! "An Open Letter to Presbyterians," by Diogenes Allen, et al, states: "Had the Re-imagining Conference been nothing more than an exercise in theological experimentation, there would be less cause for complaint. Little was said there which had not already been said many times over in books written by the Conference speakers . . . But the Re-imagining Conference was much more than an exercise in theological brain-storming. It was a worship event—indeed, an event in which the deities worshipped can only be judged (in light of the New Testament and the Confessions of our church) to be idols."
31   *Christianity Today* 38 (1994): 74.

Methodist Reporter, prepared *before* the conference took place. I can only assume that its impetus was *Wisdom's Feast*.

The larger point to be taken here is that Sophia becomes a problem when the church is forced to notice her, specifically, in a worship context. Left to her own devices in the Bible, she can be safely ignored. So ignored, in fact, that Susan Cyre, in the *Christianity Today* article just cited, credits the Bible's statements about Sophia to the conference organizers: "Organizers *claimed* Sophia is the embodiment of wisdom, found in the first nine chapters of Proverbs. Sophia, *they said*, was with God at the Creation, and she is 'the tree of life to those who lay hold of her'" (emphasis mine). The quotation in the last phrase (from Prov. 3:18) provides an ironic comment on Cyre's attempt to blame contemporary feminists for these ideas!

There is another point as well that requires attention, one that is articulated clearly in another paper by Catherine Keller.[32] As part of the system of commonplaces contemporary Christianity associates with female deities, Keller points to the conference critics' conflation of "heretical" worship with "feminist-womanist-lesbians," terminology that appeared on a tear-out postcard provided by the conservative Methodist magazine, *Good News*, for the convenience of those who wished to mail in their protest to the U. M. C. Women's Division of the Board of Global Ministries. This conflation reveals a metonymic link between the notion of religious apostasy and what is regarded as aberrant female sexuality. "Aberrant," we might note, applies any time women have control over their own sexuality.

This figuration has, again, a paradoxical quality when it comes to feminist theologizing with respect to the Bible. On the one hand, Sophia is *there*, and it may well be regarded as miraculous that she is. The attempt to implicitly deny Sophia's biblical basis by those who rant about heresy shows how deep the cover-up has been. On the other hand, it is problematic for those who wish to claim the Bible's Sophia tradition as authoritative, for the tendency to metaphorize apostasy as female sexual aberration is also precisely a biblical one. The Bible can hardly speak of non-monotheistic worship without the language of non-monogamous behavior. Metonym becomes metaphor as aberrant female sexuality comes to name the heresy: false worship *is* adultery and fornication. As we have seen, moreover, Proverbs takes a step beyond even this languaging to constitute Evil itself as the woman who is sexually strange. What kind of authority, then, is the Bible for us here? When we go to the Sophia image for power, what exactly are we doing? How can feminists claim Sophia without automatically authorizing that other element in the tradition that spearheads the attack? Or, to frame

---

[32]   "Power and the Politics of Heresy: A Case Study." Quotations are from this unpublished paper, a portion of which was published as "Inventing the Goddess," *The Christian Century* 111 (1994): 840–842.

the question as I shall take it up here: on what basis can feminists claim authority for and from Woman Wisdom, while ignoring the Other Woman—the Strange Woman—beside her?

It would be remiss to imply that these questions have gone unnoticed in general, even though they have not been applied to Sophia in particular. Christian feminists have long struggled over the question of biblical authority, and appeal could easily be made in this instance to ideas like "usable tradition" (see, e.g., Letty Russell) or to the authority of the biblical people to proclaim the life-giving elements of the tradition, while refusing to acknowledge the revelatory nature of the rest (see E. Schüssler Fiorenza). What makes such hermeneutical moves difficult in the case of Sophia is the profound rhetorical linkage that Proverbs creates between what feminists would regard as positive and negative imagery for women. I would like to conclude by pressing further on the paradox of this linkage.

What Proverbs has joined subtly, by means of common vocabulary and imagery, the critics of "Sophia worship" have joined perversely, by re-configuring the Bible's own valuations. Keller appropriately describes this move as "the hereticizing of Sophia," but I would suggest that the biblical imagery lets us sharpen the point even further. Rather amazingly, by making Sophia the object of the contemporary equation of aberrant sexuality and false worship, *the Sophia critics have in fact turned Woman Wisdom into the Strange Woman.*

As I have stressed, what the defenders of Sophia have to contend with is the fact that the possibility for this move is implicit in the linkage created by the text. Keller has pungently noted how "[t]he lurid accounts of the *Good News* writers rip image after image [from the Re-imagining liturgies] out of context, yoking together the most sensuous metaphors in order to create an aura of pornography." The hands-down winner of the Most-Quoted Line Award in the conservative denominational press is extracted from the Conference's liturgy celebrating women's embodiment: "We are women in your [= Sophia's] image. With nectar between our thighs, we invite a lover, we birth a child." Keller notes that similar sentiments are celebrated in the Song of Songs, but I would also recall the Strange Woman's invitation to her prospective lover:

> . . .I have come out to meet you,
>   to seek you eagerly, and I have found you!
> I have decked my couch with coverings,
>   colored spreads of Egyptian linen;
> I have perfume my bed with myrrh, aloes and cinnamon.
> Come, let us take our fill of love until morning;
>   let us delight ourselves with love
>   (Prov. 7:15–18).

This, precisely, is the sensibility with which the conservatives calumniate Sophia and her "worshippers." And, to an extent, biblically speaking, they are right: to the extent that Woman Wisdom and the Strange Woman share a female embodiment, to the extent that they share the language of seeking and finding, and, through the beloved wife, of sexual delight, there is latent in this common imagery an understanding that *all* women, even Woman Wisdom, are Other.

But in Proverbs this understanding is rendered ambiguous by the contradictory willingness to affirm a powerful and empowering goodness in women, a goodness that in some sense represented the very core identity of "Us" as well. Such redemptive ambiguity is lost to the Sophia-critics, at least in part, because they do not realize how the they have twisted the text to produce their invectives or, more precisely, how the text's own rhetoric turns its surface message on end.

For feminists who are conscious of the powerful work of metonym and metaphor, another shaping of the linkage of Wise and Strange is possible. Regarding the two Women of Proverbs as unified, rather than opposed, has generated for me the beginnings of a fruitful meditation on the relationship of the power of the center to the power of the margin.[33] Here we read against the surface grain of the text, with its power to pit one woman against another. We read rather, to use an image from folklore, as tricksters, those two-sided characters who appear both as creators and disruptors of social order, whose flaunting of the boundaries of social convention is embraced as part of the life-giving fabric, whose strangeness is acknowledged as part and parcel of their wisdom. We read as Strange Women.

The textual dialectic of wise and strange, surely intended by its authors to remain a polarity, creates its own semantic energy, forcing itself beyond the bounds of its original historical context into a hermeneutics of power. The power manifests as deadly venom when anti-Sophia polemicists channel all its dialectical energy into strangeness, laying patriarchal claim to the center and consigning all dissenters to the Sheol outside the community's circle. Keller has powerfully analyzed the ideological force at work here as one of racism and sexism, framed in ancient rhetoric.

> The rhetoric of heresy and apostasy armors [the ecclesial right] in the battle against the new abomination they have now managed to name feminist/womanist/lesbian goddess worship. Only by achieving this particular configuration could they hope to sidestep charges of racism regarding

---

33   For further discussion, see my "Wise and Strange: An Interpretation of the Female Imagery in Proverbs in Light of Trickster Mythology," *Semeia* 42 (1988): 14–36.

actual womanists, charges of gender competition in relation to white women, and the disinclination of half the [Methodist] denomination to bash gays and lesbians. By erecting the goddess Sophia as the idol of their opponents, they have constructed a "heresy" which. . .functions to disqualify every feminist/womanist experiment in God-language, and therefore to de-legitimate the "subordinated knowledges" whose insurrection in the churches has begun . . . .to gain institutional power.

The hermeneutics of power generated by Proverbs' dialectic of wise and strange also manifests as the rush of the Spirit for Christians who re-imagine the biblical deity as Sophia, and I have tried to argue that there is nothing to be gained in pulling our theological punches as we name God Sophia. Granted that all attempts to speak of the holy are partial and metaphorical, there are metaphors and there are metaphors. To call God Sophia is *not* on the same level as calling God a mother hen. Sophia is a powerful naming, a root metaphor, that names God with the same fullness as the name Jesus Christ. Indeed, though we have not pursued the New Testament data here, it is clear that many early Christians—*orthodox* Christians, I hasten to add—named Jesus Sophia as well.

But this latter move is also one that channels a dialectical energy into a single course, albeit one of powerful goodness. It empowers us: it affirms our identity as the center. But it also shapes God/dess in our image; it disallows the existence of evil in our midst. The paradox of divinity and humanity, of the goodness and evil that infuses both, is denied; something of reality slips away. Again, Keller's analysis is most helpful. She contrasts "the language of heresy-charges [that] always sought to enclose a domain of orthodoxy pure of mistakes" with the reality of power as "something intrinsically amoral [that] fuels both sin and grace." "Power," she says, "is first of all life-force, energy, circulating freely through networks of relationship." Power, I would say, is both wise and strange, and the deification of Woman Wisdom without attention to her Strange companion risks the denial, the sublimation, of those aspects of power we have difficulty seeing or do not care to see, whether the unconscious striving toward a claim to orthodoxy in ourselves, or the various forms that resistance to oppression might take.

Again we take up the struggle to stay inside the space of paradox, to live the tensive relationship of the liminal to the center. Woman is One: patriarchy has made of each and all the Stranger. Woman is not One: we have not all been equally on the outside and Sophia does not move us all equally to the center. As we live inside the paradox, the whole notion of center and margin shifts and shifts again. The center of what and of whom?

Through Sophia, the power of female liminality is drawn into and re-invigorates the center. There is a danger of patriarchal co-optation in this move, however. The dynamic is only effective for women if Sophia remembers her connection to the Stranger. In Proverbs, Sophia lent power to the good wife, but that power was controlled and channeled to the support of a patriarchy that divided woman from woman. We are no doubt more sophisticated now, more resistant to being manipulated by the existing power structure. Perhaps the fact that women are using the Sophia metaphor for ourselves will liberate it, and us, from the trap of co-optation.

Yet all naming entails a kind of reification. Making Deity female, making Deity Other, will fall into the same absolutizing traps as all other theologizing unless we remember that Otherness itself is multiple, unless Otherness itself remains at some level yet Strange, even to us strange women. The memory of Strangeness inhibits Wisdom's turn to imagining herself One, "centered," perfect.

Who owns the center, who the margin, and where is power to be found? The center has long been held by men, but never without the help of their good wives. In small circles over recent years, and in a large circle that November, the center was claimed by those long regarded as strange. Yes, call us by our proper name: feminist, womanist, lesbian, Goddess worshiper. Yes, call us by our proper name: Christian. But where is the margin now? Does it fall along the pew where the good wife sits each Sunday? Is it marked by a strand of rosary beads that comforts an abused woman? Is it stepped out in the notes of a spiritual sung in a blighted city or in the hymns of a dying prairie church? How will the wise and powerful women with the bold imagination to call forth blessing on the nectar between our thighs continue to speak to strangers like these? The memory of the Strange Woman forbids a claim to the center, even by Sophia. The mistake made by the men who wrote Proverbs was to see this denial as the source of death. To the contrary, precisely through her representation of the ever-shifting margin of power, the Strange Woman—like Wisdom and with Wisdom—promises life and favor from the unnamable I AM.

Conclusion

In what is surely one of the world-class examples of academic overkill, I have been writing on the female imagery in Proverbs for fifteen years. My own powerful attraction to this material has for most of that time seemed one of those scholarly idiosyncrasies. Repeatedly I have asked myself whether this language, these metaphors with their curious and tensive twists and turns, would ever make any difference to anyone, empower anyone, but a few lonely souls in their ivory towers. The current Sophia controversy, beginning with the publication of *Wisdom's Feast* and coming to wide public attention with the Re-imagining Conference, has begun to answer that question loudly! Where a few women have caught a vision of Sophia, a rampaging right wing, gathering momentum from a well-meaning but uninformed middle,[34] have made her a cause. Most strangely of all, they have done so by making Woman Wisdom out to be a Strange Woman.

This inversion points to another underlying issue as well, namely, the power of the Bible itself. It is curious that the Bible suddenly makes such a difference in this particular way. I expect lines to be drawn over whether to "believe" the Bible or not; over whether to take it "literally" or not; over what to do with its problematic stances on issues like homosexuality. I do not expect to see bombs bursting over people just accepting what it says about God. It must be hard to be one of "them" right now, desperately trying to re-cover (the contradictions of) the Bible's metaphorical power.

---

[34]   As I prepared this paper, I learned that Chung Hyun Kyung, one of the thealogians who did not speak about Sophia at the Re-imagining Conference, had been engaged to speak at the Women's Quadrenniel of my denomination, the Christian Church (Disciples of Christ). Publication by the conservative Methodist and Presbyterian presses of a radical snippet or two from one of her earlier addresses provoked one of my fellow Disciples in Fort Worth—a man with a long-established liberal reputation on most matters—to write a protest letter to the Department of Church Women, and send copies to many associates at least around this city, if not further afield as well. The letter was an excellent example of the hysterical linkage of references to foreign goddesses (in this case Korean), Canaanite fertility worship, and Sophia which Catherine Keller analyzes so well. After actually seeing a videotape of Chung's address, the letter-writer had the good grace to send another, recanting his worst objections to her appearance before Disciples women. Still, the ability of the right wing to whip a relative liberal to action by appealing to these fears was a mighty evidence of their power.

13

Power, Purity, and Innocence
The Christian Imagination of the Gospel

Burton L. Mack

⌘

I present a meditation on the notion of power in the Christian imagination as a contribution to the topic of "Divine Power and Powerlessness." I choose to focus on the term "power," bracketing the term "divine" until I develop my thesis on the way in which power is construed in the Christian gospel. I avoid the term "powerlessness" as a secondary consideration of interest to theological concerns with contemporary sociological issues. Understanding power is the fundamental challenge, not only for Christian theology, but for theories of religion and society in general. My thesis is complex. One axiom is that power and purity were fundamental notions in the social contractions of the ancient Near East, and that they formed a complementary pair of opposites. Another is that power and purity were collapsed in the early Christian portrayals of Jesus. And a third is that, in the process of early Christian mythmaking, the narrative gospel construed the encounter of this Jesus with the social and political powers of his world under the rubric of innocence and guilt. Thus: power, purity, and innocence in the Christian imagination.

The outline will unfold in six sections as follows: A social theory of power and purity with application to Second-Temple Judaism; Jewish reconfigurations of the temple-state as social model during the Greco-

Roman age; Conceptions of the *polis* during the Greco-Roman age; The early Christian notion of the kingdom of God; Purity, power, and innocence in the Gospel of Mark; and Innocence and power in contemporary Christian imagination.

A Social Theory of Power and Purity

Jonathan Z. Smith has turned my head with his theory of religion and society, best laid out in his book, *To Take Place: Toward Theory in Ritual*.[1] In it he draws upon a canon of intellectuals in the fields of ethnography, cultural anthropology, and the history of religions, including Hume (for the rational and empirical foundations), Dumezil (for the discovery of patterns of myth and social structure capable of cross-cultural comparison and historical modulation), and Levi-Strauss (for the integration of social structuralization with the fundamental logic of human thought as articulated in systems of dual classification). Then, with a little help from Kant, Dumont, Wheatley, Boas, and Geertz, Smith formulates his own theory of society, religion, and thoughtfulness, and applies it to Ezekiel's visions of the new temple in Jerusalem.

Smith finds that Ezekiel's visions accord with the model of the temple-state as honed to perfection during the previous three or four thousand years of ancient Near Eastern civilization. This model consists of two systems of social stratification governed by the notions of power and purity. A king occupies the apex of the system of power—the organization of labor, the authority to tell people what to do, the ability to get things done. Thus power is executive and filters down through a hierarchical stratification of control in which all members of the society have their place. All power is derived from the king who is sovereign, and whose power determines that he be regarded as the locus of the sacred. Purity is the notion that governs a second system of stratification concerned with the order and stability of the society as an organic unit of human activity and social well-being. Priests preside over a system of temple sacrifices designed to rectify things that go wrong or get out of place. At the apex of this system in which everyone and everything has its proper place, the high priest represents sanctity or holiness. The two systems are merged in such a way that everyone knows his or her place in relation to both authority (power) and purity. But the two systems also work as binary opposites, in that the king is highest in power, lowest in purity (by virtue of his function as warrior and "executioner"), while the high priest is highest in purity, but lowest in power.

---

1   Jonathan Z. Smith, *To Take Place: Toward Theory in Ritual* (Chicago: The University of Chicago Press, 1987).

The importance of Smith's work is enormous, not only as an explication of the social logic invested in the Jerusalem temple of Greco-Roman times, but also as a social theory of religion in general, and as a research method that calls for the construction of axioms by careful attention to description.[2]

Jewish Reconfigurations of the Temple-State

Jewish literature of the Hellenistic age reveals an overwhelming fascination with the image of the temple at Jerusalem, as well as a deep concern for its fate in the cross-currents of the political and cultural histories of the times. The temple was understood on the ancient Near Eastern temple-state model, and that model was assumed as the right way for Jews to imagine themselves structured as a people whose destiny was storied in the epic of Israel. But most knew that the Jerusalem temple-state was in serious trouble, and many felt that the trouble was due as much to the Hasmonean dynasty (unclean priests) as to the occupations of the Seleucids and Romans (foreign power). Thus, there were many attempts to research the epic, analyze the recent social history, identify the core loyalties that defined Jewishness, and rethink the shape of Jewish society. The temple-state model loomed in the background as the ideal standard by which to judge the current state of affairs and imagine what must happen to secure a Jewish future. However, depending upon where a Jewish intellectual stood in relation to the plural forms of social life characteristic for the times, and in relation to judgments about the political and cultural state of affairs, the temple model itself was scrutinized. Many reconfigurations of the temple model were produced as one of the ways in which Jews seriously engaged the questions of their place in the larger scheme of things and their destiny as a people. One might illustrate the variety of (temple and social) reconfigurations by reference to the conclusion to Ben Sira's poem in praise of the *hasidim*, the organization and ideology of the Qumran community, Philo's projection of the temple liturgy onto the structure of the cosmos, the daring meditations on Jerusalem and the land of Israel in the first century B.C.E. Psalms of Solomon, the cosmic order of wisdom liturgy in the Wisdom of Solomon, the tragic view of the epic's end in Josephus and the apocalypse called 4 Ezra, and so forth. What I would like to do is suggest that three other characteristics of the literature of the time (in addition to this basic fascination with the

---

2   See my review of Smith's *To Take Place* and his more recent book, *Drudgery Divine: On the Comparison of Early Christianities and the Religions of Late Antiquity* (Chicago: The University of Chicago Press, 1990), in *Numen* 39/2 (1992): 225-33, titled "After *Drudgery Divine*."

temple image), usually interpreted in other ways to be sure, are also best understood as intellectual labor in the interest of temple-state reconfiguration (i.e. rethinking the social shape of Israel).

The first characteristic is the presence of ideal figures, sometimes decked out in the most extravagant, bigger-than-life imagery. Many of these have traditionally been understood as "messianic" figures, and taken as evidence for a wide-spread Jewish expectation of "the" messiah, a promised king in the line of David. However, recent attempts to actually document such an expectation have failed. I refer, among other studies, to the Princeton Symposium published as *The Messiah* with James Charlesworth as editor, and a collection of papers edited by Jacob Neusner in *Judaisms and Their Messiahs.* A better designation for this phenomenon, studied from a slightly different perspective, is *Ideal Figures in Ancient Judaism*, the title of a set of studies edited by George Nickelsburg and John Collins.[3] My own view is that these figures functioned as symbols for a social construct. Instead of describing the structure of an imagined society as a whole, and detailing the complex interrelationships among its various layers, fabrics, and boundaries, these Jewish authors worked out the essentials of the society they idealized by projecting a single anthropological image. This agrees with the way in which abstractions were achieved in Hebrew thought, and especially with the way in which single figures (such as Adam, or Israel) were storied as individuals but understood as social symbols. If so, it is of extreme importance to notice that the fantastic portrayals of human figures in this literature condense and combine the attributes that belonged to the social roles of structural significance for the temple-state model and its epic history: king, priest, prophet, and the patriarchs. Their stories were understood to be about the covenants that guaranteed the eventual establishment of the temple-state in Jerusalem.

A second characteristic of this literature is the way in which the story of Israel was treated as an etiological epic for the temple-state in Jerusalem. In this case, the questions raised by the troubled times had to do not only with the significance of the founding events for the shape of the temple-state in Jerusalem. They were also about what went wrong to account for all of the disasters befalling it. Epic revision is a perfectly understandable mode of mythmaking. It consists of a search for the elements essential to the promise, ideal, or logic of a people's history (as epic) and society (as culture). This ideal is frequently found toward the beginning of the history, or in some golden age of the past. Seen clearly once again, the ideal image can be set in contrast to the present state of

---

3   James Charlesworth, ed., *The Messiah* (Minneapolis: Fortress Press, 1992); Jacob Neusner, ed., *Judaisms and their Messiahs* (Cambridge: Cambridge University Press, 1988); George Nickelsburg, ed., *Ideal Figures in Ancient Judaism* (Chico, California: Scholars Press, 1980).

affairs as a standard for judgment, instruction for repair, or as a projection of hope for future resolution. One might think, given the traditional Christian interpretation of the Hebrew scriptures and the customary view of Jewish messianism at the time of Jesus, that the golden age of David and Solomon would automatically have been in everyone's mind as the ideal image of theocracy. To be sure, there were a few flirtations with that era of the epic as ideal. The author of Chronicles took a turn at portraying David as the ideal king. The Hasmoneans thought of themselves as recapturing the extent of his kingdom. And the notion of a Davidic messiah did pop up again, it seems, in the Bar Kochba resistance to Rome. But most intellectuals looked elsewhere, for the Hasmoneans had tarnished the Davidic ideal. And besides, a realistic assessment of the time made the warrior king model look silly. None of the kings of recent history had fit the model. The foreign kings were wrong because they were foreign (Ptolemies, Seleucids, Herodians, and Romans). And their own kings were wrong because they were first and foremost (illegitimate) high priests who then proclaimed themselves as kings as well. What to think and do? The answer for most was to look elsewhere in the epic for the promised ideal.

Ben Sira imagined the covenants with the patriarchs as the foundation for the ideal temple-state governed by a high priest. And he wanted very much to see Simon II's priesthood as the realization of that ideal. He did acknowledge that Israel had had three "good" kings— David, Hezekiah, and Josiah—but each of these were important for reasons other than their royal power. In Sirach's view, their kingdoms were part of the history of struggle, on the way to the Second Temple; they were not the ideal. Philo zeroed in on the life and writings of Moses where he found the constitution for the *diaspora* synagogue as a perfectly proper way to be Jewish and worship in God's cosmic temple. There are only two mentions of David in twelve Loeb volumes of Philo's works, and one of those occurs inadvertently in a scriptural citation. Qumran focused on the prophets as a wedge driven between archaic priestly ideals (as in Leviticus), and the present temple establishment, a wedge of divine oracles that promised an eventual purification of the temple system. The Psalms of Solomon are a precious documentation of some group of pious Jews who were forced to re-conceptualize the shape of Jewish society in Palestine by painfully relinquishing the Jerusalem temple to the past, putting a "king" in the place of the high priest, and then portraying this king as a teacher of *torah* wisdom. Is it any wonder that the Jews had had their fill of kings and finally found a way to live without one? One can trace the moves from Second Temple Judaism to Rabbinic Judaism as a marvelous revision of epic history. Not David, the king with power, nor Aaron, the performer of sacrifices, but Moses, the teacher who understood what God really wanted, captured the Jewish imagination. Philo had idealized Moses as prophet, priest, and king. But he was "king" by virtue of "legislating" the law (a wonderful twist on the Hellenistic concept of the king); "prophet" by virtue of receiving the law as revelation from God and seeing the meaning of history from creation to the land (a very clever subversion of both Greek and Jewish notions of the prophet); and "priest" by virtue of writing the five books as textual mystagogue for the instruction of Jews of all times wherever their synagogue might be.

A third important feature of Jewish thought toward the end of the Second Temple period was a heightened concern for purity. Purity was sometimes expressed as righteousness (having learned about such from the Greeks), and sometimes as loyalty to torah or "the traditions of the fathers." Deuteronomistic theology was also at work to underscore the serious consequences of failure to keep (observe) the commandments, and the word that marked the contrast to piety in this case was "sin." But the more significant development was the way in which the priests (such as Ben Sira), the Pharisees (in Jerusalem), and the leaders of synagogues (in the diaspora) redefined the laws of purity. Following the archaic model, the laws of purity were articulated in the temple system of sacrifice (and Leviticus appears to have been a basic handbook). What happened was a resignification that dislodged the significance and observance of these codes from the system of sacrifices. None argued against the temple liturgy, leaving it in place as a very important actualization of Jewish presence in the world. But all developed alternative and substitute ways for being a pious and observant Jew. Ben Sira used life-wisdom to turn torah and the observance of temple sacrifices into an all-encompassing ethic. Philo "spiritualized" the "special laws" by using allegory to develop a Jewish ethic of intention and behavior that could be lived even in Alexandria. And the Pharisees actually produced a small code of rituals that anyone could perform in the course of the daily and weekly round (prayers, fasting, washings, tithing, and family taboos). These counted as standards for Jewish purity and became the basis for the later Rabbinic elaborations. These are remarkable developments. They should not be misunderstood as quests for personal piety, religious experience, or salvation. They were the products of intellectual labor in the interest of redefining Jewishness and Jewish society in the pre-shadow of the temple's demise.

The upshot was that Jews decided for purity and against power. After the destruction of the temple, as the shift was made from the Pharisees to the Rabbis, it was not forgotten that the notion of purity was rooted in the temple-state model. But the model was now imagined with God as the only king. Priests were still in the picture as the rabbis thought things through, but the priests and their sacrifices now took place only in an imaginary temple. In their stead, teachers and their laws of ritual purity sanctified the life of Jews who gathered in *diaspora* synagogues. How did they do that? By *halakah*, an elaborate hermeneutic that transformed the *torah* written by Moses from temple charter into codes of purity. Purity, not power, would define the ethos of *diaspora* Judaism.

The Concept of the Polis in the Greco-Roman Age

The ancient Near Eastern temple-state was not the only model of society haunting intellectuals during the Hellenistic period. The Greek *polis* (city-state) was also firmly in mind, an ideal state where a *demos* (citizens) had freedom and autonomy to govern themselves by legislating their own laws. In the minds of some intellectuals, the *polis* might have room for a "king," but only for a philosopher-king whose wisdom gave guidance for wise legislation. This model, born during the classical period, played an extremely important role in shaping society during the Greco-Roman age. Cities were founded everywhere in the wake of Alexander as the vehicle and expression of Hellenistic culture. Thus Hellenistic culture was a culture of the city. But there was a problem. The model did not fit the form and function of the cities founded in its name. To the peoples of the Levant, the Hellenistic *polis* was a vehicle of colonial imperialism in control of disenfranchised natives. The *demos* consisted of foreigners (Macedonians, principally, but also other "friends" of the Ptolemies and Seleucids), and the power to govern was in the hands of kings who ruled by force, not wisdom. Even intellectuals in the several school traditions of Greek philosophy could see that. So something had gone wrong.

The response of the philosophic schools was a major shift in focus, away from the classical model of the "democratic" city-state, and toward the imagination of an ideal kingdom. Treatises were written on the topic of "kings" (good) and "tyrants" (bad). The ideal king would be the embodiment of (moral) law (an *empsychos nomos*). As for the law (*nomos*), traditionally understood as "convention" rooted in democratic legislation, it was now imagined as ideally rooted in *physis* (the "natural" order of the cosmos). And as for "virtue" (*arete*), the Greek ideal of personal character achieved by learning and discipline, it was now defined as living "in accordance with *physis*." An older mimetic hierarchy of *cosmos/polis/anthropos* was transformed to become *physis/nomos/arete*. An assessment of real society (where tyrants governed cities and empires) forced the elision of the *polis* in the archaic model, put *anthropos* in direct relation to the cosmic order, and encouraged the reduction of all images of sovereignty to symbols of personal virtue. As the Stoics said, "Only the wise man is king." Or, as

Epictetus said, the Cynic's staff was his "scepter."[4] Thus the language of rule or kingship came to be used as a metaphor for personal self-control. The term king no longer had to refer to an actual ruler, and kingdom no longer had to refer to a political domain. "King" became a metaphor of a human being at its "highest" imaginable level, whether of endowment, achievement, ethical excellence, or mythical ideal. "Kingdom" became a metaphor for the "sovereignty" manifest in the "independent bearing," "freedom," "confidence," and self-control of the superior person, the person of ethical integrity who could "rule" his "world" imperiously.[5] Of course, no one was fooled about real kings and their real power. Stoics knew that real kings were dangerous, and that an outspoken philosopher could be banished or executed. The author of the Wisdom of Solomon knew that the righteous were being killed by the rulers of the world. And the Maccabean historians, fully aware of the problem with kings, had to turn their heroes into martyrs under a despicable ruler in order to find some way to eulogize them. Real kings were tyrants; real kingdoms had no soul; and real power was brutal. So pensive people looked to the cosmos on the one hand, and turned inward on the other, to find a way to survive with integrity in a world where violence had become banal.

The Greek analogue to the Jewish notion of purity was honor. Honor and shame provided the codes that structured society in layers and governed one's place in the whole. During the Hellenistic era an important thing happened to the notion of honor. Honor was tied to virtue, and the example supreme of an individual's virtue came to be the noble death. To endure unto death and die as a martyr for one's teachings was considered the ultimate display of one's virtue. Thus the tyrant's power had become the standard for judging the integrity of virtue, even though the standard for virtue itself was the "law of nature" (*nomos tes physeos*). The logic of the noble death was the logic of martyrdom. One "died for" personal integrity, a philosophy, a people, land, or righteous cause. Note the element of strength in "weakness." Endurance unto death at the hands of those in power was not considered weakness. It was the ultimate display of sovereignty. No priest. No purity. Honor. As the sayings went, "Living well is to practice dying"; "Your cross will come to you."

To be sure, I have overdrawn the importance of the philosophers and their ideas in describing the tenor of the times. Life went on in the society at large with its loyalties to those in power, honors traded on the conventional model of patronage, and energetic scurrying on the part of most to take advantage of the large and messy mix of peoples for

---

4   Epictetus, Discourse III, 63.

5   I have cited a few lines from my book, *The Lost Gospel* (HarperSanFrancisco, 1993), 126.

personal gain. And yet, I find no evidence for public enchantment with the kingdoms of the *diadochoi* or the empire of the Romans. And every traditional culture, with its land, people, and social institutions, had been disrupted. The suddenly-expanded horizon of the world, now ruled by a single king, was no substitute for the smaller, organic societies that had sustained a fully-orbed life for their people. Peter Brown and Jonathan Z. Smith have emphasized the experimental nature of social and religious activity resulting from the fragmentation of traditional societies.[6] Associations, cults, networks among households, schools, shrines, and enclaves document the interest in closer-knit, smaller societies in which to live. So the philosophers were not wrong in their assessment of the larger social scene as problematic for human well-being, nor in their attempt to understand how one might nevertheless become a citizen of the whole world (a cosmopolitan). Their contribution to the emergence of Christianity is basic. They introduced an ideal king into the city-state model of society, expanded its horizons to cosmic proportions, and transferred the whole to what Philo called the noetic world (from *noesis*, meaning "thought" or "intelligence"), an ideal archetype of the world "below," a world known only to the mind, yet held to exist as the fundamental order of things. From the Greek point of view, an ideal king had to be in the picture to counter tyranny, the inexplicable curse that troubled actual societies. It was the tyrants of this world who had caused all the trouble.

The Early Christian Notion of the Kingdom of God

Early Christians were fascinated with a social vision they called the kingdom of God. It was their own social vision, stemming from Jesus and his teachings, and it soon became a distinctive concept that merged the social anthropologies fundamental to both the Jewish and the Greek cultural traditions. On the one hand, it was rooted in the Jewish notion of theocracy and the corporate concept of the people of God as a family. On the other it drew upon the Greek notion of the individual living in accordance with nature, participating in a "kingdom" that was, in effect, an order of things prior to, displaced from, and in contrast to the kingdoms of the world. It was not at first thought of as a temple-state. Jesus may well be credited with the genius of this combination, but the scholarly analysis of his teachings does not indicate that his challenge was grounded in more than a vague vision of the kingdom of God. He

---

6   Jonathan Z. Smith, "The Temple and the Magician," in *Map is Not Territory* (Leiden: Brill, 1978; Chicago: The University of Chicago Press, 1993), pp. 186–87, with reference to Peter Brown, *The World of Late Antiquity* (London: Thames, 1971), 102–3.

did not imagine a program or start a mission on the basis of the novel idea. And he did not think of himself as a king. The vision, however, together with the challenge, created its own attraction, combining as it did the heady notion that any individual could "belong" to the kingdom and so become a "child" of God. This combination of individual affirmation with the paternalistic notion of divine sovereignty was a winner, especially when experienced in the formation of groups that found themselves, quite by surprise, I think, no longer defined along traditional lines. I have in mind Clifford Geertz's "primordial ties": blood, kinship, ethnos, land, language, etc.[7] At first it was enough to think of individuals catching sight of the kingdom and behaving in ways that manifested its call to alternative life-styles (as in Q and the Gospel of Thomas). But it was not long before the kingdom of God became a self-designation for the Jesus movement, and the groups that formed began to think of themselves as (fictive) families whose social relations represented the kingdom of God in the real world. And then, two big ideas clicked. Under the pressure of working out their social salvation in contrast to the kingdoms of the world—voilà—members of the Jesus movement began making the claim to represent the people (Israel) of God. That was a very large claim, and it introduced one of the major tasks for early Christian biblical theologians—revising the epic of Israel so as to end with Jesus and the Christian's kingdom. That task was not completed until the fourth century. On the other hand, the cosmic horizon of God's kingdom opened up to encompass all other kings and their kingdoms. That also was a most audacious idea. Nevertheless, the so-called Christ hymn in Philippians 2 is clear documentation that the congregations of the Christ had actually entertained the daring thought of allegiance to a king whose kingdom was destined to subsume the kingdoms of the world. Jesus had become Lord, and the congregations of the Christ became a network of social units destined to challenge the Roman order. The speed at which this change took place, from alternative life-style to alternative society, the complexity of the conceptual and mythic logics that had to be packed into the new self-understanding, and the extravagance of the claims implicitly made, all bear witness to the attraction of the new social vision and the excitement created by those who came together to explore its possibilities. The combination of the two big ideas, constituting both (the new?) Israel and the ultimate kingdom, must have been very heady indeed. And Jesus was now the Lord of this kingdom, a kingdom imagined to encompass the whole world.

The story of mythmaking in the early Jesus movements and Christ congregations, or how Jesus the teacher became Jesus Christ the Lord

---

7   Clifford Geertz, *The Interpretation of Cultures* (New York: Basic Books, HarperCollins, 1973); see index, "primordial attachments," 467.

and Son of God, is much too complex to unravel here. I have worked out the logic of much of that early history in *A Myth of Innocence* and *The Lost Gospel*.[8] The main point is that mythmaking à la a social theory of religion does have its logic in relation to the social and intellectual labor involved in the construction of societies, and all of the many "views" of Jesus cast up by the early Jesus people and Christ people do make sense in relation to the many experiments in social formation these movements represent. For our purposes, it is enough to note that all of the "christologies" that eventually took their place as the standard designations of Jesus in the prevailing orthodox theologies were terms of sovereignty. Christ, Lord, Son of God, Son of David, and the Great Shepherd of the sheep, were all royal titles. Kingship was the common denominator. Jesus became the king of the kingdom of God he envisioned.

What happened to Jesus as teacher and prophet? What about Jesus as priest? One was erased and the other eschewed in the exaltation of Jesus to Lord. I have described the erasure of Jesus as teacher in *The Lost Gospel*. Here I must take note of the fact that Jesus was not mythologized as the great high priest. The book of Hebrews is the only evidence for an attempt to imagine the Son of God as the heavenly high priest, but it ruined the martyrology of the *kerygma* to which it was indebted, and it was viewed by the "orthodox" with great suspicion during the next three centuries. As it turns out, it is still an anomaly in the New Testament, for we do not know where to place it in any of the many early Christian traditions about which we have some knowledge. That may seem strange, given the fact that the temple did begin to pop up as an appropriate image for the Christian kingdom, given the fact that Christians did want to lay claim to the Hebrew epic which was an etiology of the Jerusalem temple, and given the incidence of sacrificial terminology in the myths and rituals of the early Christ cult. But much of the sacrificial terminology used to explicate the "saving significance" of the death of Jesus, though derived from and intended to allude to the sacrificial temple cult, actually served to elaborate another, more fundamental, notion of sacrifice. The sacrifice that provided the fundamental logic of the Christ myth (or *kerygma*, e.g. 1 Cor. 15:3-6) was a martyrdom, the noble death of one who dies for his teaching at the hands of those in power who are threatened by his teaching. Jesus' teaching was about the kingdom of God, and the logic of the *kerygma* was that he "died for" (the Christ congregations as) the people who belonged to the kingdom of God. The logic was that, if God "regarded" Jesus' martyrdom as justified, the cause for which he died was also

---

8   Burton L. Mack, *A Myth of Innocence: Mark and Christian Origins* (Philadelphia: Fortress Press, 1988); *The Lost Gospel: The Book of Q and Christian Origins* (HarperSanFrancisco, 1993).

justified (Rom. 3:24–26). I know, I know, the temporal displacement of the "cause" makes it an odd argument. But that is the way they worked it out. Politics, virtue, honor, and vindication were the basic ingredients of this "death for" the kingdom, not a vicarious "sacrifice," not the rectification of wrongs that needed to be set right.

And that introduces the question of what happened to the notion of purity. In some ways this question is the most difficult of all, namely why early Christians rejected such a fundamental concept. Part of the answer is that some did not. Peter, the Jerusalem "pillars," some of Paul's Jewish-Christian "opponents," and the entire Jewish-Christian movement that lasted for centuries, all accepted purity codes pretty much on the Jewish model. And part of the answer is that the codes of purity shifted when interpreted by the teachings of Jesus (as in the Gospel of Matthew) and that the concept of holiness changed when applied to the new congregations of the Christ, as in Paul. But the debate with the Pharisees in Q and the pronouncement stories of the Gospel of Mark, as well as the issues of law, ritual, piety, table fellowship and the circumcision of the Gentiles in Paul and other early literature, together with the long history of *adversus iudaios* literature characteristic for patristic theologies, are more to the point. As the pronouncement story in Mark 2:15–17 lets us see, eating with tax collectors and sinners was just what the Jesus movement was about. Yes, they were unclean. But it was OK. The Jesus people were saying that they were the "clean unclean." And as the Christ cult concluded, they, including their Gentiles, were fully "justified" not to demand that they all live like Jews. So the Christian kingdom, of mixed and spirited constituency as it became, was bound to be in trouble with its ethical codes. Jewish codes of purity would not do for Gentiles, and the Greek standards of virtue and honor were also not quite right. (Though they were used as a matter of course for centuries, the Christians having only a few new ethical "values," of the kind that Paul said could not be legislated.) The vision of the kingdom of God apparently called for another kind of standard. Paul took a stab at it with his "law of Christ" and "mind of Christ"; Mark turned discipleship into a mimetic following of Jesus to the cross; and it wasn't long before the "witness" supreme was located in the martyrdoms of the apostles and bishops of the flock. Loyalty to another sovereign was the real code, a sovereign not of this world. And the sovereign? Jesus the Lord, or Christ the king, a symbol of the kingdom in which purity was subsumed in the concept of his rule.

It is important to note that early Christians symbolized Jesus and conceptualized his kingdom by merging Greek and Jewish thought, even while carving out a place for themselves that was bound to compete with both Greek and the Jewish culture. The mythology of Jesus as Lord, the preferred epithet for God in the Septuagint, was a revision of the Israel epic of astonishing affront to Jewish sensibility. The collapsing of purity and power in the conception of divinity was a challenge to Greek conceptuality as well. The historical significance of the early Christian turn to symbols of sovereignty, in contrast to the Jewish turn to symbols of the priestly teacher, and in contrast to the Greek symbols of personal virtue, all as responses to the breakdown of societies in the Greco-Roman age, is therefore very great. It was this fascination with sovereign power that predisposed Christians to cozy up to Constantine which then set the pattern of relationship between the scepter and the staff for the next one thousand year.

Purity, Power, and Innocence in the Gospel of Mark

Mark set Jesus in opposition to the Pharisaic laws of purity and the sacrificial system of the temple cult. He also portrayed Jesus and his message without recourse to the Greek notions of virtue and honor (except for the implicit honor attached to his noble death). And he did not pick up on the notion of righteousness as developed in the Christ cult, even though he took from it the concept of martyrology basic for the Christ myth and ritual. In Mark's depiction, Jesus represented power, sheer power, the power of God in confrontation with the power of the Jewish high priest, the power of the Jewish king, and the power of the Roman empire. Jesus' power was pure, but it was a kind of purity other than assumed by the temple system. Jesus was pure, not because he resided at the pinnacle of priestly activity, but because he was the (royal) Son of God by virtue of an anointing with the holy Spirit from God. The holy spirit in Jesus was out to route the unclean spirits in control of the worldly kingdoms. This was a new notion of purity, a union of sovereign morality and priestly holiness. As much it violated both the temple state model's bifurcation of purity and power, and the Greek ideal of sovereignty grounded in virtue. If one sets the temple-state model in the background for comparison, one could only imagine such a combination at the level of the divine itself where God ruled over both the king and the high priest. Thus divine power and purity collapsed in the singular figure of the Christian's king. What a symbol.

How and why Mark achieved this characterization is a very important question. That is because his narrative, the first one to be written, became the basis for the other New Testament gospels. It therefore marks the moment when the Christian gospel was composed. It created the picture of Jesus and Christian origins that everyone still has in mind. I have told the story of Mark's accomplishment in *A Myth of Innocence*. It has to do with the way in which Mark combined earlier Jesus traditions with the essential logic of the Christ myth (a martyrology) by using the wisdom tale of the innocent righteous one. It was the wisdom tale that provided the pattern for his composition of the passion narrative. In the Christ cult, the *kerygma* was purposefully not placed in an historical setting where motivations other than those of God and Jesus would have to be supplied. In the transition from the kerygma to the narrative of the passion, however, where the "tyrants" were named and motivations had to be spelled out for everyone participating in the event, the questions of innocence and guilt were unavoidable. (Apparently, Mark did not mind.) This means that Mark's gospel introduced the notion of innocence to the characterization of Jesus as the man of power and purity. What a man! Jesus became the Christian symbol of a social anthropology in which power, purity, and innocence implode in the moment of violence.

Briefly, Mark took the sign of power implicit in the miracle stories and displayed it as the exponent of purity in a cosmic battle between good and evil. He therefore preferred exorcisms over healings, for they could be used to define Jesus' exercise of power as legitimate, that is, pure, setting up the contrast between unclean spirits and the holy spirit that Jesus brought into the world. Mark then combined this notion of power with that of Jesus' authority taken from the pronouncement stories where Jesus always had the last word. The formal combination of miracle story with pronouncement story is absolute and programmatic in the first action of Jesus in the synagogue at Capernaum, and in the first set of stories in Mark 2:1–3:6. In this set of five incidents, Jesus encounters the bad guys and exhibits his power and purity. His weapon is now his word, and the leaders in league with the temple establishment make the point by charging him with blasphemy (Mark 2:7).

One can trace the escalation of this conflict in the design of the first five stories, and then throughout the gospel. In the story of Jesus' first appearance in the synagogue (Mark 1:21–28), the scribes are not present, but they are mentioned by the people as those whose authority was not like that of Jesus. At the healing of the paralytic (Mark 2:1–12), the scribes are present and murmur about blasphemy. In the next story about eating with tax collectors and sinners, the detractors are identified as the "scribes and the Pharisees" and are brought to silence (Mark 2:15–17). The Pharisees question the disciples in the next story about fasting (Mark 2:18–22), then finally address a question to Jesus himself in the story about plucking grain on the Sabbath (Mark 2:23–28). In the last story of the set, another combination of miracle and pronouncement story, Jesus directly confronts the Pharisees with his program and the Markan plot is set. The Pharisees go out to hold "counsel with the Herodians against him, how to destroy him" (Mark 3:1–6). From that point on, various combinations of Jewish leaders show up from time to time in order to track the narrative theme of the plot to its conclusion.

That the man of power gets killed has always been seen as the problem of Mark's gospel. However, such a view overlooks several points. One is that the story time does not end with the plotted time. The story will end in an apocalyptic reversal when the Son of Man and the kingdom finally come with power. This was achieved by setting the gospel story in the larger context of an apocalyptic view of history. Another is that the crucifixion is viewed as a violence perpetrated in the city that thereby sealed its own destruction. This was achieved by relating the crucifixion of Jesus to the destruction of the temple and casting both as the first two battles in an elongated apocalyptic scenario. And the third is that Jesus is portrayed in the passion narrative as the innocent victim of the first precipitating encounter. This was achieved by studied allusion to the old story of the righteous one who is persecuted unjustly. For Mark, Jesus' crucifixion was not a sign of powerlessness, not an event of redemption, and not the end of the story. It was only the first in a series of violent reciprocities. Because they killed him, God would destroy (and by Mark's time had destroyed) the temple, and Jesus would return as the Son of Man "seated at the right hand of power" (Mark 14:62). When Jesus said that, the high priest tore his clothes and called it blasphemy. He was right. Power, purity, and innocence had been collapsed in the single figure of Jesus as the Son of God who, from Mark's perspective, had every right to violate the temple and challenge the sovereignty of the Second Temple state.

If we place Mark in the '70s of the first century, and do a bit of social sleuthing to determine the troubles faced by the Jesus movement for whom he wrote, the strategy is clear. Mark entertained an apocalyptic imagination of the world in order to salvage a social experiment in trouble. The mythic frame was compensation for a social program that did not materialize and a founder figure who should have taken the world by storm, but did not. Not yet.

Innocence and Power in Contemporary Christian Imagination

I have gone to some length in the effort to analyze the narrative symbol at the core of the Christian imagination. I have done so by unpacking it in reverse, that is, by showing how it was put together in the first place. I regard all of the cultural backgrounds, conceptual elements, mythic motifs, motivational assumptions, imagistic facets, and layers of interpretive nuance as integral to the extremely dense symbol Mark created. I know that Christians have subsequently reshaped and redressed the symbol many times over, starting already with Matthew's toning down of the dramatic apocalyptic edge of Mark's story, and that some may see that fact as a reason to discount the importance for our time of the Markan variant of the Christian gospel. I also am aware that our own Christian and cultural contexts are so much different than those of the first century that it is difficult to imagine how some of the facets integral to the symbol at its conception could possibly retain their power. I am thinking, for instance, of the fact that our general acceptance of a postmodern view of the human social enterprise, with its orientation to individualistic anthropologies, social democracies, and critical, scientific thinking, makes it very difficult to grasp the cognitive significance of the symbol's fundamental aspects. We do not automatically imagine that a personal figure can represent a corporate, social construct, for example. And we no longer have much patience with the categories of sovereignty, hierarchy, purity, and honor as fundamental for the structuring of a human society. So some may understand my work to have been in vain, a historian's reconstruction without any relevance for the late twentieth century. And yet, who will say that? The entire enterprise of biblical study and theological hermeneutic would be dispensed with in one sweeping gesture. So things may be more complex than can be addressed by a simple yes or no.

My own suspicion is that the Markan symbol of the Christ is still very much a part of both the Christian and the American cultural imagination of our time, even though we may not be aware of its concentration of values and its power to pattern our ways of thinking. The other gospels did not erase the Markan plot, and the Markan plot at the core of the single gospel story (a story that Christians have imagined by conflating the four New Testament gospels) has frequently resurfaced in troubled times to provide an edge to messianic and apocalyptic programs. I think, therefore, that the narrative symbol Mark created is still very much with us, basic for the Christian imagination of the gospel, even if not consciously in mind. I also think that the Christian gospel has profoundly affected American culture, and that the "hero," in American mentality, owes much to its precursor in the Markan gospel. If so, and I realize that theses such as these require much more argumentation than I can provide here, we may be working unbeknownst with a model of power that is extremely unhelpful, not only for the discussion of power in sociological perspective that is called for in general, but also for the project in constructive theology that has been generated by the topic of divine power and powerlessness. In any case, I would like to present a profile of the American hero in comparison with Mark's portrait of the Christ as a reflection on the construal of power in our Christian culture, and then draw some conclusions about the difficult task we face as theorists in examining the role of power in the construction of human societies.

The Gospel of Mark came to mind as I read *The American Monomyth* by Robert Jewett and John Lawrence.[9] According to Jewett and Lawrence, the American hero is super clean and possesses superior power. According to Mark, Jesus was super clean and possessed of superior power. The question is whether the hero and the Christ are related in any way.[10]

In the first edition of *The American Monomyth* (1977), Jewett and Lawrence traced the profile of the American hero from the popular novels of the late nineteenth century (such as *Uncle Tom's Cabin* [1868], *Buffalo Bill Cody* [1869], and *The Virginian* [1902]); through the radio serials of the '20s and '30s (the Lone Ranger, for example); the comics of the '40s (Superman, for instance); and the dime western, to Playboy, TV serials (with focus on Star Trek), and the cinema of apocalyptic in the late '70s (such as Jaws, Earthquake, and Towering Inferno). Interwoven are vignettes from the daily life of American politics and the articulation of American values by those who momentarily had the public's ear (and then its eye). In the second edition (1988), the list of examples was expanded by including chapters on "Saintly Shootists in a Pop Religion of Death" and "Monomythic Politics: From Star Wars to Olliemania." As one can see, the list of American folk heroes is difficult to place in a single category of fiction. It encompasses real life figures as well as fantastic creations and includes folk heroes and film stars as well as presidents.

The scene is set in the wilderness, whether the dark eastern forests, the wild western expanse, the urban jungle, or the strange and frightening world of galactic adventure. The story opens on a small group of huddled humanity in trouble with some paradisiac vision. This is sometimes cast as the little house on the prairie, sometimes as an enchantment with the pristine beauty of the mountain man's terrain, and sometimes as an edenic enclosure in or near some city, an enclave surrounded by the fright and ugliness of the rest of the world. They are there to find a life better than was possible in the tarnished civilizations they left behind. But they have no plan. The paradisiac vision is not working, and as for the city, the only model available for social construction in mind, it is just the place where the worst evils always immediately cluster. So troubles come, whether in the form of coping

---

9   Robert Jewett and John Lawrence, *The American Monomyth* (Garden City, New York: Anchor Press/Doubleday, 1977; Second Edition, New York: University Press of America, 1988).

10   The discussion that follows is taken from my 1989 address to a joint session of the Society of Biblical Literature and the American Academy of Religion at their regional meeting in Claremont, California. The address was published as an occasional paper of the Institute for Antiquity and Christianity at Claremont, titled *Innocence and Power in the Christian Imagination* (Occasional Papers 17, 1989).

with the wild without, or the sad discovery of conflicts within. Recourse to democratic institutions fails, trust in the law turns to suspicion, and the stage is set for the entrance of the hero.

The hero, for his part, arrives untarnished by the history of troubles. He is selfless, chaste, unencumbered by social entanglements. He is a loner, highly charged with confidence, skill, and impeccable perception. He is able to discern the root of the problem, to locate the source of evil, and give immediate chase. Fortunately for the outcome, the hero also has his hands on the latest technology of destruction. From guns to lasers, we can trust him to use his power for good, for the people's cause is right and the hero is pure. He is the incarnation of altruism, an essentially faceless figure, and even violence at his hands is therefore justified. His shots are straight and his conscience clean.

To take but one well–known example, the good ship Enterprise of the series Star Trek is on a five-year mission to explore the galaxy. The galaxy is the new frontier and the old westward-ho and shoot-out plot are accordingly transposed. Unbelievable power is in the hands of two incarnations of goodness, Captain Kirk and Mr. Spock (a sort of Adam III and Mr. Techne). There was an interdiction from the first against interference in any other culture happened upon, in keeping with the high purposes of the mission. And yet, as we all know, the captain and crew encounter an alien culture in every episode, put it to the test, find it wanting, and demand its transformation. Resistance ends in violence and the trekkies scream for more.

In the Gospel of Mark, Jesus suddenly appears in the world with great authority and power. The world is troubled, full of human illness and the ineffectual powers that be. Jesus' power derives from the spirit God has given him, a spirit which, were we not told, might not be recognized as pristine pure and thoroughly divine. Immediately he announces a new world order called the kingdom of God. He will be the king and he marches into the land to do what has to be done. He enters Galilee, then Capernaum, then the synagogue at Capernaum, and there he confronts the unclean spirit at the heart of the old world's problems. He casts it out, not with a gun, but with a zap nonetheless. The unclean spirit cries out, "What have you to do with us, Jesus of Nazareth? Have you come to destroy us?" The implied answer is "Yes, indeed." The people respond by saying, "What is this? With authority he commands even the unclean spirits." They are fascinated because of the unbelievable concentration of purity and power in the person of Jesus. Later, as the target of his power turns from the demons to the civilization that housed them, we learn that Jesus is not only the man of power and purity, but that he is innocent as well, innocent of the destruction he has caused and will cause, innocent by virtue of his completely altruistic motivations for the people's cause.

There is not a great deal of difference in the story of Jesus and that of the Virginian, or the Lone Ranger, or Captain Kirk, except that Jesus is divine, and he does get killed. To be sure, those differences have always kept the two stories apart in our minds. Don't confuse the Spirit of God with firepower, we say. And don't confuse the sinlessness of the savior with the hero's dedication to his mission. White horses and silver bullets are one thing. Sacrificial lambs another. And let's not talk about purity and power in the same breath. Purity belongs to religion, and power to politics. So let's just say that the Christ is the Christian's savior, and the popular hero a projection of the can-do of the people. That's why the Christ must die in a mission that first fails, and the American hero has to win. The American hero justifies the dominant culture; Mark's story justifies a powerless movement concerned with personal salvation. So how can both stories be related at all?

But can the fact that Jesus gets killed be the redemptive feature that makes the Christian myth a constructive and helpful story for Christians living in a hero's world? What if we notice that Mark part I (the appearance of the man of power in Galilee, chapters 1–8) and Mark part II (from the transfiguration through the passion narrative, chapters 9–16) are actually quite separable scenarios, and that, given a changing social history, now one and now the other may come into more prominent and timely focus for a people? Even the sequence between power and powerlessness, or victimage and victory, or violence and the peaceable kingdom, can shift, depending upon the application of the myth to a social situation and the way in which the righteous ones identify themselves with Jesus, whether as victim or victor. The apocalyptic moment, for its part, also can shift its correlation with social history, depending on the nation's perception of its purity and power. For much of our history America has cultivated a millennial mentality as if, in this land and people, the kingdom has come, is rightly coming, with power. Recently, however, American failures to fulfill its missions have precipitated a sense of power lost, and the apocalyptic vision has been relocated again into the future. When that happens, the tragic, redemptive, anti-hero scenario of Mark part II and beyond finds its fascination.

It is also the case that, as Scott Johnson wrote in the *Los Angeles Times* ("Opinion," May 7, 1985), "The image of American innocence is central to our country's consciousness," and that "Even our failures... seem merely to persuade us that, like all messiahs [we may ask, which messiahs?], we may be at times too good, too eager with our help, and so become the victim of an undeserving or ungrateful world." We may note that, in the shift to an apocalyptic frame for either a reading of the gospel or a re-imagination of the hero, the sign of failure and the sign of victory are identical. The sign is a violent destruction in which victim and victor are simply factors of opposition in an equation of double inversion. The inversions depend on how one assigns the values of innocence and power. Thus, both martyrdom and the destruction of the enemy, whether executed by the righteous nation, the foreign power, or God, can vindicate the righteous cause. "We had to destroy them in order to save them" is the line left hanging in the air from our Vietnam war. With such a symbol imagined at the beginning of the Christian era, and such a sign projected into the future for our eventual vindication, we win either way, violence notwithstanding, as long as we manage the fiction of the man, our man, of power, purity and innocence. It is the concentration of power, purity and innocence in a single anthropological figure, I think, that marks our mythological mentality, and signals to the world our danger. If so, the so-called redemptive feature of the Christian myth only accentuates our affair with the heroic. It is that obsession that seems to be the problem whenever we run into trouble with the use and abuse of power and seek to address it.

Whether a myth's function is to provide a model for social construction, or a constructive escape from the messiness of life in the real world, neither the American hero nor the Christian's Christ appear to be helpful symbols for our time. They do not provide a helpful model for human responsibility and problem solving of the kind required for the social democracies we are trying to construct. They frustrate our coming to terms with post-modern intelligence about the irresponsibility of external authorities and saviors. And they keep us from thinking clearly about power and powerlessness, whether human or divine, as factors to be considered in the construction of societies.

We now know, for instance, that the liberation movements spawned in the last generation organized their ideologies around the topics of power, powerlessness, and empowerment. We also know that powerlessness has been associated with victimage, and that the charge against the structures of power has been that they are wrong and abusive, period. We also know that the charge is most telling when the victims are seen as innocent, and that the discussion of responsibility for situations of abuse has been very difficult to engage. So the myths have set the agenda for naming the problem, but they have not helped to solve it. Victimage may be a basis for rage, but it is not an adequate description of the problem. Powerlessness may be part of the problem, but to leave it there inhibits the critical analysis and constructive proposals needed for assessing systemic structures. And empowerment, with the old model of power in place, is no guarantee against another round of injustices.

Part of our problem, of course, is that we have become a personality driven society where feelings take the place of thinking. But even that may be a result of the way our myths are working. Both encourage personal reenactment. Neither looks to the social arena for help or hope. Neither provides a point of departure for thinking about the many kinds of power that prevail in any given society. The reduction of either the hero or the Christ to an individualistic symbol for personal assessment or reenactment can only frustrate the social analysis called for. We need to understand much more clearly than we do the many structural arrangements of power required in a society that wants to balance powers, limit freedoms, control predation, negotiate interests, celebrate difference, mourn loss, appreciate the everyday, and enjoy one another's foibles. Yes, and delight in the privilege of living in a beautiful and fragile world, so fragile in fact, that the marvels of the human enterprise might be measured, not only by our efforts not to destroy one another, but by our efforts not to destroy the ecology of the natural world that supports us.

Returning now just to the Gospel of Mark, what I suspect is that the theme of divine power and powerlessness is implicitly beholden to the Christian conception of that gospel. Christians have always understood the gospel story to be about divine power and powerlessness, and we have all worked very hard to interpret the powerlessness of Jesus as a sign of divine humility, redemptive purpose, and saving grace. Should we not be impressed with the long history of intellectual labor and mental gymnastic repeatedly required to understand the story of the crucifixion as a powerful, saving event? Of course. But should we not also ask about the continuing value and legitimacy of that theological activity in the light of our contemporary situation? Should we not be worried that so much of our time and energy has been spent in justifying a story of conflict and violence as the singular paradigm for the saving events of divine compassion? Should we not worry that the Christian notion of God's power is derived from that story, and that the story requires both a miraculous resurrection and an apocalyptic display for its vindication and finale? At the very least we should consider the incongruity between the Christian assessment of that death as redemptive and the history of violent killings in our century that have not been.

What if we said that living between a violence and a victory is no longer a helpful way to imagine ourselves in the world? What then might be the relevance of the Gospel of Mark? Should it be the basis for a biblical theology? Could it be an invitation to a critique of Christian culture? Or might it even be a foil for thinking critically and clearly about the chances for constructing a society without Mark's help in which the arrangements of power were subservient to human well-being? Those, I think, are the questions.

14

Contemptus Mundi—Redux
The Politics of An Ancient Rhetorics and Worldview[1]

Vincent L. Wimbush

⌘

I

Harold Bloom is at it again. Convinced that religion is a fascinating intellectual and cultural critical topic, he turns his attention in *The American Religion* to the work he calls "religious criticism." For Bloom, "religious criticism" involves the characterization and criticism of expressions of the religious in American culture.[2] This time he has gone beyond concern about the ancient text "J" and its authorship; this time he has delved into what he understands to be an important aspect of the contemporary American psyche through arguments advanced and assumptions made about aspects of Greco-Roman antiquity. In an effort to account for the origins and orientation of the dominant strand of "American Religion," he has turned to some of the transcendental visions, impulses, and movements of Greco-Roman antiquity, namely, Christianity, Judaism, and Gnosticism.

---

1   This essay is a revision and expansion of my inaugural lecture delivered at Union Theological Seminary, New York City, 22 October 1992. It has been published as "*Contemptus Mundi:* The Social Power of an Ancient Rhetorics and Worldview," *Union Seminary Quarterly Review* 47, nos. 1–2 (1993) 1-13.

2   Cf. his recently published *The American Religion: The Emergence of the Post-Christian Nation* (New York: Simon and Schuster, 1992).

It is one thing to be playful with "J"; it is another to argue boldly, as Bloom does, that the dominant strand of contemporary "American Religion"—other-worldly and radically individualistic, conservative and comprising, well represented by, although not limited to, the circles of fundamentalist Christians—is the ideological heir to the Gnosticism of late antiquity and, to a lesser extent, nineteenth century reactions and adjustments. Bloom, as always, speaks ably for himself:

> Religion, in the ostensibly Protestant United States, is something subtly other than Christianity . . .we are post-Protestant, and we live in a persuasive redefinition of Christianity . . .A blend of ancient heresies and nineteenth century stresses, the American Religion moves towards the twenty-first century with an unrestrained triumphalism, easily convertible into our political vagaries. . . .And the American Religion, for its two centuries of existence, seems . . . to be irretrievably Gnostic. It is a knowing, by and of an uncreated self, or self-within-the-self, and the knowledge leads to freedom, a dangerous and doom-eager freedom: from nature, time, history, community, other selves.[3]

This argument cannot go without a response. Not just because in substance it is a fascinating intellectual argument, but because as a model of "religious criticism" it provides opportunity for the scholar of religion, especially the historian of religion, to reframe normally narrowly focused technical work into reflection upon contemporary issues. The old attitude and claim on the part of the historian of antiquity that antiquity is important in its own right, just because it is antiquity, is naive, and can no longer be defended. Every inquiry into the past is at the same time a quest to understand the present, a statement about the values and prejudices and orientations of a part of the present, certainly, including the inquirer's present. Bloom's provocative arguments make clear that a part of the American present is preoccupied with a part of antiquity (biblical and, therefore, also Jewish, Greek, and Roman) as part of an effort to explain, if not justify, certain contemporary American visions of, and orientations to, the world. Thus, his arguments, whatever their merit on substance, suggest the importance of a different orientation for historical study, especially in the history of religions.

It is difficult for me as an historian of religion to begin historical inquiry at any point other than in *my* present. In scholarly form and in substance, Bloom's work resonates with me. There are few other issues

---

3   Bloom, *The American Religion*, 45, 49.

of greater fascination, heuristic significance, and puzzlement for scholarship (especially in the study of the New Testament and early Christianity, and in the history of religions of late antiquity in general), as well as significance for global socio-political dynamics, than that of the *fin de siècle* resurgence of the attitudes and behaviors described by Bloom.[4]

Yet the most important reason that Bloom must be answered is that on the matter of substance of argument, he is, if not wrong, at least not provocative or radical enough. The dominant strand of American religion, albeit conservative and fundamentalist and obsessively individualistic, should not be argued or assumed to have its origins in— or even to be in fundamental solidarity with—the Gnosticism and/or Gnosis of late antiquity. This is so not only because so much has happened between the two worlds to make any argument for connection other than problematic, but also because contemporary conservatives and fundamentalists in the United States, their ancient Christian rhetorics notwithstanding, are not otherworldly, or anti-worldly, enough—they do not share that comprehensive worldview so fundamental to many Christians and self-styled Gnostics and others of late antiquity. They do not share that "world"—complex, comprehensive and radical in its "outworldly" stance—that is associated with several groups and movements of late antiquity, including early Christianities and, of course, Gnosticism.[5] This difference is important not for the sake of the historian making points at the expense of a literary critic; it is important because although Bloom may be correct in arguing that the contemporary dominant strand of religion in the "religion-soaked," "religion-mad" United States is the type that is obsessed by radical freedom and solitude, it is not at all clear that this modern American defined freedom and solitude should be identified with, or seen to be derivative of, the ancient Gnostics.

At any rate, the matter clearly warrants further examination. But to argue as Bloom does is to fall into the trap of forcing historical connections (origins, influence, etc.) and similarity of worldview on the basis of shared concepts, ideas, and language.[6] It is far better to attempt to account for the "American religion" within the more comprehensive framework of the history of worldview or mentality.[7]

---

[4]   Cf. the multiple volumes of *The Fundamentalism Project*, edited by Martin Marty and R. Scott Appleby, published by University of Chicago Press.

[5]   Cf. Louis Dumont, *Essays on Individualism: Modern Ideology in Anthropological Perspective* (Chicago: University of Chicago Press, 1986) chapter 1.

[6]   Cf. the introduction to Ioan P. Couliano, *The Tree of Gnosis: Gnostic Mythology from Early Christianity to Nihilism*, trans. H.S. Wiesner and the author (New York: Harper Collins Publishers, 1992), for provocative discussion.

[7]   Cf. persuasive arguments of respected historian of religion and practitioner

Contemptus mundi (contempt for the world) is an expression that captures rather poignantly the complex of attitudes, behaviors and rhetorics associated with groups that were part of many different cultures of Greco-Roman antiquity and beyond. An examination of some of the late ancient evidence and the methodological issues involved will afford me the opportunity to engage an aspect of the issues raised by Bloom and may provide a different perspective on American culture.

II

The expression *contemptus mundi* is representation both for a recognized historical literary expression—more broadly, a rhetorics or discursive formation—and a worldview (and associated social formations and orientations). As literary expression (and by extension, rhetorics or discursive formation), it is most notably associated with a certain type of literature that proliferated in the late Middle Ages, especially the eleventh and twelfth centuries, but then shortly thereafter disappeared.[8] As worldview and social orientation, *contemptus mundi* is ancient in origins, dating back to the philosophers and visionaries of the worlds of the Far East and the eastern Mediterranean. Found among many new, interstitial social formations or networks, including the complex of movements that have come to be known as early Judaism and Christianity, it has continued throughout a great span of history to evoke a range of different aesthetic, socio-political and religious responses.[9] Initially appearing and developing "between the cracks" of

---

of "worldview analysis" Ninian Smart in his *Worldviews: Crosscultural Explorations of Human Beliefs* (New York: Charles Scribner's Sons, 1983). Also, re: "mentalities," cf. Michel Vovelle, *Ideologies and Mentalities*, trans. Eamon O'Flaherty (Chicago: University of Chicago Press, 1990).

[8]   Cf. extensive and provocative historical treatment by Jean Delumeau, *Sin and Fear: The Emergence of Western Guilt Culture: 13th-18th Centuries* (New York: St. Martin's Press, 1990); and two classic primary texts in Bernard of Cluny, *Scorn for the World: Bernard of Cluny's 'De Contemptus Mundi,'* ed. Ronald E. Pepin [Medieval Texts and Studies No. 8; East Lansing MI: Colleagues Press, 1991]), and Lothario Dei Segni (Pope Innocent III), *On the Misery of the Human Condition* [*De miseria humane conditionis*], Donald R. Howard (Library of Liberal Arts No. 132; New York: the Bobs-Merrill Company, Inc., 1969). See further recent illuminating discussion re: general European backgrounds and ramifications by Ann Ramsey, "Flagellation and the French Counter-Reformation: Asceticism, Social Discipline and the Evolution of a Penitential Culture," in Vincent L. Wimbush and Richard Valantasis, eds., *Asceticism: Proceedings of an International Conference on the Ascetic Dimension in Religious Life and culture* (Oxford University Press, 1995).

[9]   See V. L. Wimbush and R. Valantasis, eds., *Asceticism* for a number of crosscultural discussions, with historical and contemporary foci; and Hans G.

traditional formations in holistic societies, these formations became reifications of transcendental visions.[10] The philosophers, prophets, sages, seers, and wisdom teachers of the "little societies" stretching from China, India, Mesopotamia, Egypt, Arabia, and all around the eastern and western Mediterranean from roughly 800 BCE to 700 CE[11] came to define themselves as carriers of transcendental visions and impulses over against "the world." The latter came to be conceptualized and problematized as the realm of relations, mores, traditions, and orientations in tension with the new visions or ideals, the newly discovered "world above," or "world to come," the realm of Ideas—and so forth. The rhetorics of the visionaries, to be sure, reflected great differences in cultures, social stations, and psychic states. But they were always oppositional and often hyperbolic, suggesting the problematizing of the world as fundamental or baseline issue.

III

The historiography of (early Christian representations and politics of what is here termed) *contemptus mundi* has tended to attempt to explain it away or apologize for it. This has been due to a rather narrow and negative view of "otherworldliness," with the assumptions that the socio-political ramifications of it are always either slight or negative, and that early Christianity at any rate quickly developed almost inexorably and naturally from a world-rejecting to a world-embracing ethos.[12]

Kippenberg, *Die antike unantiklichen Erlösungsreligionen im ihrem Zusammenhang mit der antiken Stadtherrschaft* (Heidelberger Max-Weber-Vorlesungen 1988; Suhrkamp Taschenbuch Wissenschaft 917; Frankfurt am Main: Suhrkamp, 1991), for discussion regarding ancient Mediterranean cultures.

10   Cf. S. N. Eisenstadt, "Introduction: The Axial Age Breakthroughs—Their Characteristics and Origins," in S. N. Eisenstadt, ed., *The Origins and Diversity of Axial Age Civilizations* (Albany NY: State University of New York Press, 1986), 125; and Michael Mann, *Sources of Social Power: A History of Power from the Beginnings to A. D. 1760*, vol. 1 (Cambridge: Cambridge University Press, 1986), chapters 1 and 2, for discussion of these concepts.

11   This corresponds to K. Jaspers' "Axial Age."

12   Cf. Robert M. Grant, *Augustus to Constantine: The Rise and Triumph of Christianity in the Roman World* (San Francisco: Harper and Row, 1990); and Margaret Y. MacDonald, *The Pauline Churches: A Socio-Historical Study of Institutionalization in the Pauline and Deutero-Pauline Writings* (SNTS Monograph Series: 60; New York: Cambridge University Press, 1988), as examples of fairly typical arguments (although with very different methodological leanings, and one by a very well-known and respected senior scholar, while the other by a young scholar whose work is commanding respect).

But a rather different view is defensible: Ancient Christianity up to Augustine, all of its diversity of expressions and orientations notwithstanding, can be understood as a complex of historical, rhetorical, and social formations governed not by the (sociologically-explained) inevitable turn toward accommodation to the world, but by the problematizing of the world (often discussed in theological circles in terms of theodicy, or the problem of evil). What I am urging here is a different perspective regarding the perspective that I think was dominant among the earliest Christians. The challenge here is to interpret the literary and rhetorical legacy of early Christianity in such a way that the worldview that inspired the continuing problematizing of the world can be surfaced and understood.

The different, even conflicting orientations, and the debates reflected in extant ancient Christian literary sources can be understood in light of the worldview that is *contemptus mundi*. But such a history of ancient Christian *contemptus mundi* requires reconsideration of old interpretive assumptions and schemas: it will no longer do to assume— as does mainstream scholarship on the whole—that ancient Christianity is the dramatic history of the process of "catholicization," "bourgeoisification," or "world-accommodation." An historical-rhetorical reading of the relevant sources suggests that *contemptus mundi* remained a fundamental assumption and ideological touchstone throughout the period of ancient Christianity, in spite of internal differences and external opposition. How to come to speech about it— how on the one hand, to justify it (to radicalize it in defensive response); how, on the other hand, to explain it away (to temper and domesticate it in response to heightened sensitivities about outsiders' reviews)— these would be matters of much debate, thus, impetus for rhetorical experimentation and enormous literary productivity.[13] In essence, then, these matters would shape the history of Christianity—its socio-political orientations in all their diversity—and through it much of the history of the West and the history of the world that the West has determined.

The manifestations of ancient Christian *contemptus mundi* were numerous and diverse enough that a history and taxonomy of early Christian renunciations and of renunciations in the ancient world in general has been thought possible.[14] James M. Robinson thought he had discovered the foundations of a genuine history of understandings of "world" among the early Christians in Bultmann's *Theology of the New Testament*. But this major project Robinson ultimately came to view as

---

13   Cf. Michael Mann, *Sources of Social Power: A History of Power from the Beginnings to A.D. 1760*, vol. 1 (Cambridge: Cambridge University Press, 1986), 303–10.

14   Cf. George H. Sabine's *A History of Political Theory* (3d ed.; New York: Holt, Rinehart and Winston) as one attempt at such a history.

flawed because it was more systematic than historical, ordered according to Bultmann's own prejudices toward the particular understandings associated with Pauline and Johannine theologies.[15] (Of course, one could and should easily extend Bultmann's prejudices beyond the categories of the New Testament and of modern New Testament and theological scholarship to include the modern European, specifically German, world that had shaped him. Could he have understood the New Testament and early Christianity have been understand by him in any other light?)

In a provocative essay published in 1968, Robinson offered his own sketchy outline of what he thought should constitute such an interpretive history of early Christianity in terms of "understandings of 'world.'" He urged the complete abandonment of the history of ideas associated with particular ancient Christian authors for the sake of the more intellectually defensible, comprehensive, and complex "tracing of world as it comes into language," through which one might "trace the historical trajectory to which understandings of existence can be meaningfully related."[16] The term "trajectory" (herein the origins of the concept of and appellation for the *Trajectories* volume that Robinson co-authored with Helmut Koester [1971]) he argued to be the appropriate rubric for the different understandings of "world" that can be associated with the dynamics and orientations of early Judaisms and Christianities. The trajectory ranged on the one end from "loss of world" to "worldly world" on the other. A slightly more detailed charting of the trajectory established the relative nature of "worlds" from the common or baseline perspective of "loss of world." It identified movement from "Jewish apocalypticism" to "Christian apocalypticism" to "Jewish Gnosticism" to "Christian Gnosticism," with different texts and authors reflecting different "modulations" within and between the movements. For example, Paul's differences with the Jewish Palestinian mission was viewed as a more "otherworldly" "world" (according to Paul's perspective) against the more "worldly" concern on the part of some missionaries for comfort and public approbation (cf. 2 Corinthians).

The project Robinson outlined was ambitious, but left unfinished; he turned to other academic agenda. But the challenge he left successive generations of scholars in the field regarding the charting of understandings of "world" in early Christianity through "language" was and remains provocative and unmet. We are still without an interpretive history of early Christianity that attempts to account for its

---

15   Cf. James M. Robinson, "'World' in Modern Theology and in New Testament Theology," in *Soli Deo Gloria*, ed. J.M. Richards (Richmond: John Knox Press, 1968, 88-110), 91–92.

16   Ibid, 104.

different "responses to the world" as reflected through the different types and nuances of its rhetorics and discourses. Robinson's schema for the major early Christian understandings of "world" set forth in his 1968 essay referred to above and developed to a limited degree in the later *Trajectories* volume is a useful beginning that points to some of the significant general methodological and theoretical challenges. But such a schema does not itself go far enough in offering solutions, nor is it comprehensive enough to constitute the history called for by Robinson himself.

In light of the intervening years and developments in scholarship, some of Robinson's arguments—especially his categorizations and descriptions of certain movements—require qualifications, adjustments, and elaborations. And beyond those that Robinson offered, there are theoretical issues and problems galore to be explored. This essay affords the opportunity only to begin some probings into a project.

IV

In the interest of reflecting the greater complexity of the issues, more examples of early Christian expressions of *contemptus mundi* or "loss of world" than either Bultmann or Robinson pointed to or suggested need at least to be broached, and offered as heuristic challenges.

Against the radical renunciations of a minority (the pneumatic elites) in Corinth, Paul's famous and haunting *hos me* (as if not) exhortations, framed by the two "otherworldly" eschatological pronouncements—"the time is short" (*ho kairos sunestalmenos estin*) and ". . . the form of this world is passing away" (*paragei gar to schema tou kosmou toutou*) (1 Cor. 7:29a, 31b)—may actually represent in the context of argumentation I Corinthians 7 a more worldly "world." Notwithstanding the sharp differences in evidence throughout the chapter, it can be argued that all parties in the (reconstructed) debate presume that Christian existence entails, even requires, some sort of renunciation of the world. The real challenge, then, becomes that of identifying, sorting out, and accounting for the different types of renunciations in evidence[17].

The Johannine community, defining itself with the rhetorically dualistic, absolutist, and mantra-like "not of this world," nevertheless

---

17   Cf. V. L. Wimbush, *Paul the Worldly Ascetic: Response to the World and Self-Understanding according to 1 Corinthians 7* (Macon: Mercer University Press, 1987), 6–8, for only a preliminary effort in this direction. Also see Will Deming, *Paul on Marriage and Celibacy: The Hellenistic Background of 1 Corinthians 7* (New York: Cambridge University Press, 1995) for some interesting insights and bibliography.

was the matrix of a history of quarrels between factions representing an actual range of views regarding engagement of the world. From the docetic disgust with association with the physical to the physically graphic imagings and remembrances of Jesus traduced by more "worldly" factions, this loosely defined community represented one of the most histrionic debates about identity and orientation to the world in Christian antiquity. In spite of what in some readings appears to have been a fairly united group in its acceptance of a single *language* of world-enmity and world–renunciation, the actual politics of world renunciation remained rather slippery.[18]

The so-called worldly-defensive, conservative-bourgeois authors of the Pastoral Letters present a rather fascinating hermeneutical challenge. Although their polemics seem to reflect the sensibilities and orientations of acceptance *of* "the world" and acceptance *by* "the world," a second look is warranted. The evidence of the Pastorals themselves and corroborating evidence of near contemporary texts from the same region suggests instead that the authors of the Pastorals and the few individuals who were in solidarity with them hardly gained acceptance by the contemporary world-embracing and established citizens in second century urban Asia Minor. I think they protested too much: they were very defensive and thereby betrayed all too clearly their own "outworldly" sensibilities and the perception of others that they were such. To be sure, the women who had renounced the traditional domestic roles expected of them, including sexual relations and family life, were especially a great shock. But the authors of the Pastorals seemed not to be aware of just how consonant was their general religious worldview—including, for example, the teaching that the end of the world was near—with the responses on the part of the ascetic women and men. In other words, the position espoused by the authors of the Pastorals was itself world-renouncing. The debate that developed was not about *whether* renunciation of the world in general was appropriate, but about which *type* and *degree* of renunciation, in light of prejudices and political power considerations, was appropriate.[19]

The communities behind the apocryphal acts and the complex of "gnostic" documents—arguably the most radical among the earliest Christians in their expressions of *contemptus mundi*—considered their enemies to be all others (including other believers) who had not been initiated into their inner circle, who had not pledged a life of uncompromising solidarity with them, and, of course, who could or did

---

18   See Fernando F. Segovia, *The Farewell of the Word: The Johannine Call to Abide* (Minneapolis: Fortress, 1991), especially chapter 4.
19   See Lucinda A. Brown, "Asceticism and Ideology: The Language of Power in the Pastoral Epistles," in V. L. Wimbush, ed., *Discursive Formations, Ascetic Piety and the Interpretation of Early Christian Literature, Part 1: Semeia* 57 (1992) 77–94.

not demonstrate the appropriate degree of passionate enmity with "the world." Yet it is precisely the politics of their radical asceticisms—the exclusion and elitism, the competition, as well as the liberationist and undertones of status conflict—that reflects the complexity, viz. the politics and hermeneutics of their "worldliness."[20]

Finally, one of the most powerful examples of the complexity of early Christian *contemptus mundi* is Augustine. Usually considered a "worldly" figure by most scholarly interpretive measurements, through a reading of his mature, perhaps most influential work, *The City of God*, he can be better understood as not only advancing but almost defining Christian existence in terms of *contemptus mundi*. Insofar as he encouraged the desacralization and depolitization of the empire that he experienced[21]—in fact, in principle, of every empire or social and political order, whether headed by a Constantine or a Julian!—he encouraged *contemptus mundi*. For Augustine, *pace* Eusebian establishment court theology, the very notion of a "Christian" empire was absurd, a contradiction in terms. The Christian must always be a pilgrim and stranger (*peregrinus*), one who in every social order models *contemptus mundi*.[22]

These examples of *contemptus mundi* raise important issues— about the complexity of understandings and expressions of *contemptus mundi*; about the methodological challenges involved in isolating or charting the course of these different expressions; about the social and political ramifications of such expressions. What follows is an attempt to begin to address some of the pertinent considerations in relation to these issues, and to point toward what might be fruitful directions for a more elaborate research agenda.

V

It needs to be stressed again that all literary evidence suggests that early Christianity represents a great range of expressions of *contemptus mundi*, and with such a range there is an opportunity to explain some of the internal early Christian dynamics and developments and self-understandings. That so much controversy grows out of or

---

[20]   See Dennis R. Macdonald, *The Legend and the Apostle: The Battle for Paul in Story and Canon* (Philadelphia: Westminster Press, 1983); and Karen Jo Torjesen, "In Praise of Noble Women: Asceticism, Patronage and Honor," in *Discursive Formations, Ascetic Piety*, 41–64.

[21]   See Hans G. Kippenberg, "The Role of Christianity in the Depolitization of the Roman Empire," in S. Eisenstadt, ed., *The Origins and Diversity of Axial Age Civilizations*, 261–279.

[22]   Cf. R. A. Markus, *Saeculum: History and Society in the Theology of Saint Augustine* (2d ed.; Cambridge: Cambridge University Press, 1989) and *The End of Ancient Christianity* (New York: Cambridge University Press, 1990), especially I. 4.

Robinson's argument about the need to "trace understandings of world as they come into language" pinpoints one of the major specific methodological challenges to be faced in the effort to account for the complex development that was early Christianity—an analysis of its rhetorics, especially its rhetorics of renunciation. A fathoming of such rhetorics is likely to help greatly in clarifying important aspects of the whole range of dynamics in the diversification of early Christianity. Robinson's call for attention to the manner in which the rhetorics among the early Christians reflect the different "understandings of existence" among them was justified. But he would no doubt be quick to admit that he did not develop or adopt a conceptual model of language and discourse analysis such that the study of early Christian rhetorics and discourses in early Christian texts would make sense in terms of the larger world of language-theory and rhetorical criticism. The examples above are enough to point to the heuristic potential of such conceptualization.

Yet the challenge to investigate the rhetorics of renunciation in early Christianity, important as it is, does not go far enough in terms of comparativist and cultural-critical perspectives. By definition, the worldview that is *contemptus mundi* is cross-cultural. Thus, the study of it should be cross-cultural. So even if focus remains upon historical trajectories and developments in Christianity, it is important that such focus consistently respect the broader histories of religions and histories of cultural formation and development, and draw upon the nuances and variations that such histories will evidence. There are already some exciting advances in this area in the comparative investigation of the origins and worldly-political effect of the transcendentalist impulses and visions.[23]

The pervasive force of *contemptus mundi* within transcendental communities in general, and in early Christianity in particular, suggests that religion can be understood as, among other things, an attempt to realize in social and rhetorical formation particular worldviews. This suggests, in agreement with Robinson, the possibility of a *history* of religions that would focus upon the shifts, the "rising and falling" of "world" of understandings of "world," of world-construction and world-orientation. That a basis for a more consistent framework for the *comparative* study of religion is potential with this scholarly agenda is clear, and should be encouraged for this reason alone.

But beyond Robinson's suggestions, I would argue that with *contemptus mundi* an entirely different set of heuristic categories and typologies suggest themselves in the interpretation of all transcendental religions. With *contemptus mundi* understood as worldview, we might

---

23   Cf., Eisenstadt, ed., *The Origin and Diversity of Axial Age Civilizations*, *passim*.

typologies suggest themselves in the interpretation of all transcendental religions. With *contemptus mundi* understood as worldview, we might discover the necessity of the shifting of conceptual boundaries between and within religious traditions. With worldviews in focus, we might find it intellectually profitable, for example, to associate certain Buddhists with certain Baptists, and find justification in claiming such association to be reflective of a more profound understanding of the religious impulse than the concept of "religion" or the category of "denomination."

So the questions and issues raised above build upon, but also move beyond, the challenge identified in Robinson's work. It is not possible in this paper do much more than to begin their unpacking or elaboration. This beginning will be made by narrowing the scope of concerns and addressing only one issue—that of the social power effects of *contemptus mundi* in early Christianity.

VI

Contemptus mundi had important social power ramifications in the different contexts of early Christian communities and in the Roman empire. The great differences in context and in the range of group-forming conflicts notwithstanding, *contemptus mundi* among the earliest Christians and their contemporaries can be seen as a complex of rhetorical and social formations, a type of "discursive formation," a "matrix of meaning" within which a range of certain sentiments were expressed and practices and relations obtained according to certain shared assumptions. These assumptions constituted an "ideological formation," a set of "ideological relations"—what we have referred to as "worldview."[24] And insofar as *contemptus mundi* represented a worldview, it was worldview in nuanced opposition to both the dominant worldview and social order that was the empire (and all of the contradictions and practices represented in the exercise of dominance), as well as the more local and indigenous power formations and representations, whether religious-cultic, bureaucratic, or military.

Contemptus mundi represented a type of "disidentification" with the reigning ideological formation; it was an act of "unforgetting" the psychic straitjackets normally imposed on individuals by the dominant

---

24   Cf. Terry Eagleton, *Ideology: An Introduction* (New York: Verso, 1991), 195–97; and John B. Thompson, *Ideology and Modern Culture* (Stanford Ca: Stanford University Press, 1990), chapter 6, re: discursive practices. Also see Clifford Geertz, *The Interpretation of Cultures: Selected Essays* (New York: Basic Books, Inc., Publishers, 1973), chapter 5, and Ninian Smart, *Worldviews: Crosscultural Exploration of Human Beliefs* (New York: Charles Scribner's Sons, 1983), re: worldview.

culture. Since the dawn of what is now termed the "axial age" civilizations, this "disidentification" has been accomplished through language or rhetoric, the one common tool or weapon of all those without access to traditional channels of power (viz. political or military).[25] "Disidentification" functioned as "negation," as oppositional "sentiment."[26] It was registered through newly created and often mysterious if not secretive channels of communication in such a manner as to provide a rhetorical and ideological place upon which "cognitive minorities" or "enemies" of the "order" might stand.

Contemptus mundi should not, therefore, be identified as anything simple. It was not mere "otherworldliness." It was not escapism and powerlessness, passivity and victimization, or the idealization of such. It was, instead, a coming into power through an alternate orientation, negation, oppositional speech, a language of critique, one of the "arts of resistance."[27] And even the active mode of the oppositional does not fully explain its social function and power: Its force is double-sided—it represents a problematizing of or critical thinking about the world and worldly existence. The over-against-ness should be seen as part of a strategy in order to gain ground, to seize opportunity for the rethinking and reframing of existence. The rejection of world was not an end in itself, but part of a move to gain perspective for a new prioritization of all that "world" represented.[28]

VII

In *contemptus mundi*, then, might be not only a key to a clearer understanding of a quite popular late ancient rhetorics and worldview, it is also a provocative challenge to modern sensibilities. Ancient Christian texts read as documenting not so much the steady, inexorable development toward world-accommodation or "secularization," but instead the wrestlings over, including the polemicizing and nuancing of translations of transcendental visions and impulses, will put discussions about the appropriation of "Christian tradition" in a different key. Not only must the dominant world-embracing progressive-developmental reading of Christianity (or at least that part of it held to be the major

---

25 See Eagleton, *Ideology*, 221–224; and James C. Scott, *Weapons of the Weak: Everyday Forms of Peasant Resistance* (New Haven: Yale University Press, 1985).

26 See Bruce Lincoln, *Discourse and the Construction of Society: Comparative Studies of Myth, Ritual, and Classification* (New York: Oxford University Press, 1989), 8–11.

27 This is the Language of James C. Scott in *Domination and the Arts of Resistance* (New Haven: Yale University Press, 1990).

28 See Dumont, *Essays*, 50–51.

tributary for the modern West) be challenged, but also some reigning assumptions about the socio-political ramifications of transcendental, so-called "otherworldly" visions and impulses. *Contemptus mundi* can then be argued to be one of the most relevant and provocative legacies of ancient Christianity.

Contemptus mundi remains relevant because it is power—social and rhetorical power to name and define the self and new social formations in different ways, on different (self-affirming) terms, over against the traditional and the customary and the dominant. This power was and is, of course, not specifically or uniquely, Christian. (I emphasize again that the world in which the Jesus movement was begun was full of prophets, sages and seers and philosophers competing with one another over translations and reifications of transcendental visions.)

To focus on *contemptus mundi* is to focus on ethos and worldview, what C. Geertz refers to as the "evaluative elements," the "cognitive, existential aspects," the "tone, character, and quality . . . and mood" of life, a "picture of the way things . . . are" in a particular culture.[29] To focus on *contemptus mundi* as worldview and ethos, then, is not to focus on the history of ideas, or systematic theologies or ethical propositions and moral norms in the study of religion. The study of religion in general should never be *reduced* to the history of ideas. With respect to the study of early Christianity in particular, it can be argued that no continuity in the history of ideas is even possible. Again, there is no getting from the ideas or theology of "Q" to Matthew to the stories of Thecla to Augustine.[30] Religion is not fundamentally or strictly theology, or ideas. It is not even mere ritual. Religion is fundamentally worldview and social force—encompassing and reflected through ideas, ritual, and so forth. The study of religion should reflect as much.[31]

As worldview, *contemptus mundi* inspires and certainly reflects rhetorical and social formations. Focus upon *contemptus mundi* forces attention beyond preoccupation with a particular biblical or early Christian writer's position on certain ethical or theological issues— marriage, law, slavery, women, and so forth. It does not assume that the rhetorics about such are transparent, reflective in any simple way of self-definitions. They are not; particular moral and ethical and other ideas, arguments, propositions, and orientations can have multiple

---

[29]   See Geertz, *The Interpretation of Cultures: Selected Essays* (New York: Basic Books, Inc., 1973), 126–127.

[30]   Robinson's argument in "World," 101–102.

[31]   I am here supported by the arguments of Ninian Smart. See his *Worldviews*, 5–6: "To see how they [worldviews] work we must relate ideas to symbols and to practices, so that worldview analysis is not merely a matter of listing beliefs. . . . In a word, belief, consciousness, and practice are bound together."

meanings, and function quite differently in the same and across different rhetorical formations. No moral and ethical or any other type of discourse can be engaged and accepted unless it is assumed to be part, even a problematic part, of a worldview, a "picture of the way things . . . are." Worldview always governs the particular ethical and moral positions and their discourses and behaviors, notwithstanding the fact that very often particular individuals, communities and rhetorics reflect degrees of contradictory and problematic shifts and modulations of it.

A dramatic example (alluded to above) of how worldview—and the particularity of site of enunciation that it reflects—shapes precepts and concepts and action and not the other way around can be seen in material that has been termed the "household codes" in Colossians (3:18–4:1) and Ephesians (5:22–6:9). These texts have usually been popularly interpreted—whether from the left's horror and disgust or the from the right's transparent reading and simple acceptance—with a view to discerning what are the teachings of the codes regarding such issues as marriage and family life. Scholarship has generally been exorcised over the question of the cultural origins of the codes. At both levels of inquiry what seems to be overlooked is the larger perspective or angle of vision—worldview—by which the teachings of the codes are advanced. They are assumed to be among the earliest examples of the bourgeoisification or world accommodation of early Christianity, often as though they perfectly reflected the ideology and sentiment of the dominant culture. But it is clear that these teachings hardly appeased or convinced outside critics that social formations such as the early Christian communities were world-embracing or respectful of the mores of the dominant culture. In other words, the debate registered by the texts that include the household codes reflect not so much the stark contrast of the world-*accommodating* response over against the world-*rejecting* response, but the range of differences in the process of world-deformation from an "outworldly" perspective

VIII

There are with *contemptus mundi* rather important ramifications for general contemporary cultural and religious understandings and orientations. With respect to western culture and Christian traditions in particular, *contemptus mundi* represents a significant challenge: Our situation in end of twentieth century America, having been defined by transnational capitalism and its power to create and disseminate information and transcultural images and values, reflects enormous shifts and modulations in every facet and sector of existence—and in understandings of existence. And there is certainly great dissatisfaction with—and a falling away from—many forms and expressions of totalizations that accompanied the rise of modernism and industrialism-capitalism, including *religious* and *theological* modernism. The present situation, whether accurately termed "postmodern," or "late capitalism"—perhaps inspired by the weight of the many self-inflicted problems and contradictions of modernity—now seems to reflect among some at least a new leaning toward a relativizing of the modernist penchant for historicist distantiation, a questioning of the typical progressive-liberal embarrassment over and contempt for the peoples, relics and orientations of the past, the pre-moderns, including the archaic and exotic.

These and other examples of "anti-modernism" reflect sensibilities that have inspired "new social movements" that seek "openings" onto forms of "cultural otherness,"[32] relationships with alterities, with differently constructed and oppositional worlds. Such "openings" seek a rapproachment with the "other" in terms of "simulation," or experience, not in terms of the modernist penchant for demythologizations and ritualized "commemoration." (That such seekings can result in both fundamentalisms of the left and right is clear from our history and is warrant for the constant critique of *every* worldview.)

Thus, in the late modern, if not already postmodern era of consciousness—*contemptus mundi* may with some profit be reconsidered. Perhaps, it *must* be reconsidered, on the basis of appeal to openness to the widest possible range of impulses of the cultural critical. As opening onto cultural otherness, *contemptus mundi* stands as powerful challenge and potential social force. Although the rhetorics of *contemptus mundi*, like that of love and art, is hyperbolic, and may at first suggest only the negative, the social and political dynamics and affected consciousness are much more complex. The worldview that is *contemptus mundi* is actually a legacy of critique, of resistance. To be sure, such a legacy has been for the most part without a detailed agenda of world reform. It is only a rhetorics, a complex of visions, constructive of "world." It assumes that no world order can ever be adequate or correct. It represents perennial challenge, perennial review, constant renewal, not the dismissal of and escape from, but the relativization of, the world, an opportunity and a conceptual and psychical field for the re-prioritization, re-hierarchialization of our givens (world). It always assumes the imperative of reform.

IX

Harold Bloom's attempts to link the Gnostics of late antiquity with the devotees of late twentieth century American religion are

---

32   Cf. Frederick Jameson, *Postmodernism: Or, The Cultural Logic of Late Capitalism* (Durham NC: Duke University Press, 1991), 389.

unfortunate. Not only does the linkage smack of exploitation of the Gnostics, viewing them as exotics (an exercise much in evidence throughout history, beginning already in late antiquity). It also represents failure to go beyond the game of solitaire, insofar as the argument abstracts behaviors from worldview. Bloom and others[33] have argued persuasively that American culture in general, including the dominant strand of American religion, is characterized by radical individualism. But the discovery or cultivation of the individual or of radical individualism in the United States or elsewhere does not require late antique Gnosticism as antecedent. At any rate, the Gnostics of late antiquity would be hard pressed to find common ground with modern day Americans, especially with conservative devotees of the dominant strand of American religion. This is so not because of differences in certain notions about the individual, but because of differences in what is more fundamental—"world." Americans would ultimately be considered far too worldly, far too unwilling to level and sustain radical critique against culture and society, to qualify for membership in Gnostic circles.

Bloom's focus upon particular orientations, and the lack of focus upon "world," made his comparison between American religion and ancient Gnosticism provocative but ultimately problematic. Nevertheless—as this essay proves—it provides impetus for a reconsideration of some of the dominant worldviews of our times and of the ancient worldview associated with the Gnostics.

None of us, as is often the case with the engagement of religious traditions at the level of ideas or ethical and moral propositions, can embrace or dismiss *contemptus mundi* easily. It is not a system of thought. It is not a complex of ethical propositions. It is more comprehensive, a rhetorics and worldview, a discursive and rhetorical formation ever productive of new social formations—formations that represent constant renewal, constant reform and social force, a place to stand, from which to shout and constitute and reconstitute the self. The power of *contemptus mundi*, then, lies in what it provides in imagination and discursive formation—"weapons" available to all, even the "weak"—for world reform and renewal. It suggests that only radical, sustained problematization of world provides impetus for world change. If my argument that only the more comprehensive worldviews—not particular ethical proscriptions or exhortations—are important in the interpretation and engagement or rejection of archaic religions, that Christianity as an archaic religion is fundamentally a proliferation of social formations inspired by contemptus mundi as

---

33   I am thinking here particularly of the work of sociologist Robert Bellah and associates. But see also a fairly recent polemical work by Phillip J. Lee, a pastor-theologian greatly influenced by North American neo-orthodox traditions: *Against the Protestant Gnostics* (New York: Oxford University Press, 1987).

worldview, then one of the important questions for our times and situation is not whether, for example, the Pastoral Letters' teachings about slavery are to be embraced, but whether the "outworldly" worldview within which such rhetoric about slavery and other matters is registered is to be countenanced, and whether modern day challenges as important as slavery (modern systemic racism and poverty as examples) are to be problematized and engaged from the same perspective. All our modern theological and religious differences and conflicts notwithstanding, most of us make decisions and live our lives according to an "inworldly," as opposed to "outworldly" perspective. This is the reason for our difficulties with, even embarrassment over, the Bible, our lingering ancient "outworldly" religious text. It is also the reason that the poor and marginal groups engage these texts in spite of our modernist puzzlement and efforts to direct them to more "progressive" "unworldly" agenda and hermeneutics. Such groups, it should be noted, engage these texts not as mere commemorative rhetorics, but as their "world." If my arguments are defensible, the modernists' difficulty with Christianity may be understood as a matter ultimately not of the problem of the anachronism of the primitive and the otherworldly in the modern world, but of fundamentally different worldviews that can be decided for or against. If Christianity can be argued to be one of the many socio-cultural carriers of *contemptus mundi*, and if modern US culture is still very much shaped by Christian rhetorics and worldviews—on this Bloom, I think, is quite right—then what being "Christian" means for individuals and culture explodes into a very wide stratosphere of possible and conflictual meanings, far beyond what Bloom's thesis suggests.

Transcendental impulses and visions translated as *contemptus mundi* can and should be engaged as outworldliness in the world with all the profundity and complexity, with all the potential for good and bad that may be imaginable. They are in fact taken seriously by the powerless and the weak because they represent one of the few remaining channels for the acquisition of power for the weak, for their interests in world de-construction, re-construction, and world-maintenance.

So, in the end, given the perdurance of *contemptus mundi*, in spite of grand historical interpretive and ideological efforts against it, it is very much worth asking—whose texts, whose traditions and religions, are these that lie behind *contemptus mundi*? Understanding of the complexity of transmission and ownership of traditions also represents understanding of the complex dynamics of power in our times—and in times to come.

15

Experiencing the Many
A Response to Camp, Mack, and Wimbush

David Jobling

⌘

Part of the appeal of this project for me is the effort to link biblical studies with theology. I have done all my biblical work in the context of the theological seminary. But even in that context the relation of Bible to theology has gone out of focus. The sense of a common purpose between scholars in these fields is missing in many seminaries. While I do have a sense of commonality with my own theological colleagues, they often have a limited sense of what I am doing in my forays into postmodern literary criticisms, and I do not always do a good job of expressing myself to them in theological terms. Of course, "theological terms" is itself not a static concept. But I don't perceive theology to have been changing as rapidly or radically as biblical studies.

There was another reason why the project appealed to me. As it was presented to me, one of its purposes was to reestablish links between North America and Germany. I was readily convinced of the seriousness of this attempt when I learned that my former colleague Ulrich Mauser was one of the leaders. In the event, I was disappointed with what the 1994 conference could achieve in this area. But I prepared my response with Germany on my mind, and I think this adds a valuable dimension to it. For the relation of North American to German biblical studies has gone thoroughly out of focus. When I began in the field in the 1960s, a stint in Germany was obligatory for the budding biblical scholar. This is no longer the case, and Germany has become a backwater of biblical studies. Since the early 1970s, it is on French thought that I myself have concentrated. But because of that early exposure as a student, German culture and language are really my first love.

It surprised me, therefore, that I, as a North American biblical scholar, was asked to respond to three colleagues who are all in this same category. Where is the voice of the Other? Why not a theologian to respond? Why not a German? Or both? Such otherness as I do bring lies in my being neither by birth nor current residence American. This is sufficient otherness for me to detect in the three essays a certain parochialism, a concentration on American concerns. The essays are not without traces of strain—combat fatigue from the hard battle of trying to promote any kind of humanistic program in the face of US neo-conservatism. Only Mack's essay hints at a view outward, beyond the US, but even he is ambiguous about it. At one point he refers to the Markan myth of innocence as inhabiting "both the Christian and the American cultural imagination." This seems to mean the Christian imagination everywhere equally. Later, though, he suggests that this myth "signals to the world our danger," and the "our" is an American "our," implying not only an acknowledgment of American particularity, but also a desire to address the world, and perhaps even to appeal to it for help.

The US is such an enigma to the view from outside! I shall never forget from my year in Germany, during the Vietnam time, a statement by an evangelical pastor that what he was feeling then was "enttäuschte Liebe an Amerika." He was disappointed because he was full, still, of gratitude for America's role in rebuilding Germany after the war. I find myself borrowing his words, as I read the three essays. They show me different aspects of a war that is going on in America, a *Kulturkampf*, which includes a *Kampf um die Bibel*. As I read, I am tempted to fall into the knee-jerk anti-Americanism which is part of my current Canadian scene. And yet the US—while I long lived there and no less since I have left—has been in a positive sense the context for my whole endeavor in biblical studies, in a way that Germany, or Canada, or my native Britain, simply could not have been. US biblical scholarship has plainly led the world for a generation. And I am grateful.

Each of the essays traces the lines between Bible and theology in its own impressive way. But it seems to me that as much theology is happening in their *form* as in their content, and it is on these implicit theologies that I, in my postmodern way, shall concentrate (though at the end I shall examine one traditional theological theme). In what ways does a piece of writing imply a theology? Theology is implied in its self-referentiality, how—indeed if—it reveals its own investment in that of which it treats. Theology is implied in the degree to which it indicates a pedagogy, that is, carries within itself the evidence of how it intends to make itself available, particularly beyond the professional academy. Theology is implied in how it sets out to engage me the reader, and in how it actually does engage me (not necessarily the same thing). Theology is always implied in the ways we choose to address each other. These considerations will do much to guide my brief comments.

These three essays display different attitudes, or perhaps rhetorical stances, to what I would call the fundamental usability of the Bible in theology. Though Mack does not, in a blanket way, declare the Bible unusable for positive theologizing, he does, I think it is fair to say, declare unusable the part of it which he closely engages. He believes we must "construct a society without Mark's help." I find the rhetorical effect of Mack's essay destructive rather than constructive for a project of collaboration between Bible and theology. Wimbush, on the other hand, comes out saying a general "Yes" to the Bible. Despite a very wide range of stances in the Bible, he finds in it an overall tendency to disaffirm the world, and claims this tendency as a positive theological resource. His is a constructive analysis. Camp's position is in between, or elsewhere. She confronts the Bible as both positive and negative, as a resource for both herself and her opponents. The approach she uses is a variety of deconstruction, the method best adapted, I believe, for avoiding the absolutes of destruction and construction.

These differences seem to me to correlate in a somewhat predictable way with scholarly locations. Though there are numerous exceptions, my experience has been the following. Black biblical scholars are for the most part determined to keep the Bible as a positive theological resource, and the rhetoric of their writing about it is constructive. Feminist scholars occupy a great variety of locations, and include many whose rhetoric on the Bible is largely destructive. But many others, like Camp, convey a sense of needing the Bible still, however fundamentally they critique it.[1] It is white male scholars whom I find most often exerting a generally destructive biblical critique.

There is a correlation here between one's scholarship and the closeness with which one has experienced real social powerlessness. The powerless, and those who write out of experience shared with them, are not prepared to give up the power of the Bible. They need to draw on the Bible's power in empowering ways. It is we white males, socially

---

1   Womanist readings require another set of nuanced distinctions, and I do not hazard a generalization here. Elsewhere in this volume, Catherine Keller suggests a link between womanist readings and postmodernism.

invested with power, who are inclined to assert our power *over* the Bible through a very skeptical critique.[2]

In this respect, Mack's essay was a mirror in which I saw myself. I experience in my own biblical work a temptation to concentrate, as he does, on exposing the harmfulness of internalized biblical myths. I continue to think that such critique of the Bible is utterly necessary. But I find that my work now seems to flow into such a channel almost by its own volition, and I have begun to worry that, as I help my students to take power *over* a Bible which has disempowered and oppressed them, I am denying them access to power *through* the Bible, of which they are much in need. Maybe it's our role—white males are always looking for a role nowadays—but if some sort of division of labor is involved here, we ought to give it hard thought!

I greatly admire the historical part of Mack's essay. Before relating the Markan myth to our own context, he makes its contours in its original context marvelously clear. I experience in reading Mack the power of pure scholarship, so enjoyable, so enviable. This mastery enables him the more readily to persuade me, later, of his main thesis: that, as individuals and as a culture, we are inhabited by biblical myths, often to our hurt.

And I am persuaded. But what are we supposed to do about it? How do we identify these myths, and how get rid of them? It is healing we need, even exorcism. I hope I am not falling into any heroic illusions about my power to perform exorcisms, but I can say without exaggeration that nowadays the *major* goal of my biblical work is to create the conditions for students, for people, to begin a process of exegesis which is at the same time a self-analysis. I want them to confront, and come to healthy terms with, the ways that the Bible has made them what they are. I adapt the famous remark of Itumeleng Mosala about liberating the Bible so that it may liberate us, to suggest that we must heal the Bible, so that it may heal us.[3] But the therapeutic must not be separate from the liberative (a separation which our division in the seminary between pastoral and theology departments often encourages). The two must work together. An enormous proportion of our students come to us out of abuse (most as victims, but some as abusers) sufficient to cause serious psychological harm. The Bible is a factor in much of this abuse. Liberation or healing? The distinction is absurd.

In this connection, I am troubled by Mack's treatment of the liberation theme. He suggests that liberation movements are still fully

---

2   This sort of generalization is supported by Cynthia Rigby's essay in this volume.

3   Itumeleng J. Mosala, *Biblical Hermeneutics and Black Theology in South Africa* (Grand Rapids: Eerdmans, 1989), 175.

caught up in the bad dynamics of the Markan myth. If this makes proponents of liberation do some self-examination, well and good. But should one make such suggestions from a location (at least on the strength of this essay) external to liberation discourse? Not, at any rate, in the form of such apodictic judgments as this one of Mack's:

> We now know . . . that the liberation movements spawned in the last generation organized their ideologies around the topics of power, powerlessness, and empowerment. We also know that powerlessness has been associated with victimage, and that the charge against the structures of power has been that they are wrong and abusive, period. We also know that the charge is most telling when the victims are seen as innocent .... So the myths have set the agenda for naming the problem, but they have not helped to solve it.

I realize that the issue is double-edged. Mack's argument is in itself very similar to ones made by others in this book—Catherine Keller and Rita Brock. But it depends on how the argument is made, and from what location. I want particularly to know from Mack who this "we" is, in whom such knowledge is invested.[4] As an acid test, would he see the other two essays in this section as falling under his generalizing strictures about liberation movements?

One tries first to deal with *one's own* myth-possessedness. Then, if it lies at all in one's power, to create the conditions in which others can deal with theirs (e.g. Brock's "taking responsibility").

Of the three essays, I find Wimbush's the hardest for *me* to respond to. Among the qualities I admire in it are: his insistence that in our biblical work we begin from our own present situation, his analysis of ideology and social power, particularly rhetorical power; and perhaps above all his emphasis—characteristic of all his work—on religion as *practiced*, rather than on theology.[5] I am sympathetic to his view of American culture, and find his rebuttal of Harold Bloom convincing. But I find myself admiring and agreeing with Wimbush in a disengaged kind of way, and I think this has something to do with the lack of any rhetorical indication in his essay, that I can see, of just who is supposed to be included and excluded by the inclusions and exclusions entailed in world-affirmation or world-denial. In and around us, there are all kinds of contempts for all kinds of worlds—world-optimism of any kind is

---

4   It has been rightly said that the ideological analysis of a piece of writing can usually start with how it uses the pronoun "we."

5   Camp gives us a classic example of the appropriateness of this emphasis. She points out that the Sophia debate only got rough when it left the realm of academic theology and entered the realm of liturgy.

scarcely the dominant mood of our culture. But which of these contempts are culturally critical and beneficial, and which are in any sense "Christian?" Are we speaking of a world-disaffirmation that the church as a whole might take up, or groups in the church, or what? Wimbush's discussion of the contemporary scene lacks the specificity of the historical part of his essay, and I have trouble as a reader locating myself in the scene.

The last part of Wimbush's essay goes right to the heart of the issue that I raised earlier, about Mack's treatment of the liberation theme, and the "place" from which one reads.

My basic feeling about Camp's essay is easy to express. I feel invited in, to a feast, to a profitable if sometimes vertiginous read. It is the invitation, perhaps, of Woman Wisdom:

> 'Whoever is simple, let him turn in here! ....
> Leave simpleness, and live . . .' (Prov. 9:4, 6)

I like Camp's theory of metaphor here even better than I have liked her earlier ones, and I relish the metaphoric journey she takes me on in her theology section.

Camp's foregrounding of the Sophia debate I experienced as a breath of fresh air, and I shall say more about Sophia later. One other thing I want to praise in her essay is its *text-centeredness*. This bears on the *mode* of our biblical theologizing. Camp opulently gives me the *words* of Proverbs on which she builds her case. My point is not just a literary-aesthetic one, though it is that—the change of gear the reader experiences in coming upon these indented words of power is important. Nor is it just a tactical point, though it is that too—there is value in knowing the words better than your opponents do. If at the annual denominational convention, as she relates, the opponents can't even recognize biblical words as biblical, you have made a very palpable hit! But my main point is related to the kind of biblical theology for liberation and healing that I discussed earlier. There is no liberation or healing, I become more and more convinced, that does not make a journey through the words, the words themselves. They may be words which one has internalized as rods with which to beat oneself. They may be words never before really heard or read, words which the biblical delivery systems of our churches and culture have distorted, summarized, or translated out of existence. They may be something else. In any case, the way is through the words.

The more traditionally theological problematic that I want to broach in closing is that of monotheism. This has been on my mind since I heard Gayatri Spivak talk about the polytheistic experience (based on some research in her native village in India). She by no means touted polytheism as a cure for the world's ills, but she did suggest how much the West needs the polytheistic experience. What is it like to wake up every morning in a world that is multiply, complexly charged with divinity? I have felt ever since that we could do worse than simply drop our theology for five years or so, and practice the polytheistic experience.

Can divine singleness, for example, cope with Mack's big agenda, "to balance powers, limit freedoms, control predation, negotiate interests, celebrate difference, mourn loss, appreciate the everyday, and enjoy one another's foibles . . . and delight in the privilege of living in a beautiful and fragile world"? There is nothing that encourages me to think so.

On this issue, Camp isn't perhaps quite as bold as she usually is—she seems to show some defensiveness about divine singleness. But she does at the end quote words of Catherine Keller which invite a polytheistic reading: "Power is first of all life-force, energy, circulating freely through networks of relationship." Proverbs 8, for example, is surely (as Camp presents it) about divine relationship—divine relationship between the sexes. Must we conceive of that relationship as one of total harmony and agreement? How are real human relationships helped if we conceive of it that way? May we humans not hear Yahweh muttering, between the lines of Proverbs 8, something like "Women creators! Never could stick to a blueprint"? And Sophia answering, "For God's sake lighten up"?

I have enjoyed in the essays in this whole book the outbreak of mono- and poly- neologisms: "monosystematic," "polycontextual," "polyopsis," and my special favorite, "polydox." What about the Trinity? If the "persons" always work together, why posit them as persons? If Jesus pleads for us with the Father, that's poly, isn't it, rather than mono? Childish questions, but I ask them anyway.

I cannot share Camp's enthusiasm for the Isaiah tradition on this point. I prefer the separations of Proverbs to the unities of Isaiah. I can stomach Isaiah 28, with its marvelously complex and double-edged poetry, though I am already dubious about the one god who takes responsibility for everything. When the same idea gets processed into Isaiah 45:7, God "who makes peace *and* creates evil," I get more worried. And when in the same chapter I read "Turn to me and be saved, all the ends of the earth! For I am God, and there is no other" (45:22), I find myself definitely in the presence of a monotheistic idol, the idol of colonialism, the idol of "globalization" (at least in most of its forms).[6]

---

6 Camp herself refers only to Isaiah 28; the extension of the line of thought to chapter 45 is my own. See further my "Globalization in Biblical Studies/Biblical Studies in Globalization" (a response to articles by D.J.A. Clines, R. Rendtorff, and R.S. Sugirtharajah), *Biblical Interpretation* 1 (1993): 96–110.

I am ready to accept the conventional view that, in the German experience of the Third Reich, what was utterly needed was a Christian witness that was mono. All the bits of Christian divinity, if I may put it so absurdly, had to get together against the devouring idol. But have we since paid a price for this moment of necessary unity, in a neo-orthodox monomania, a mania for the mono? Is this the reason for the mono-methodology which has prevented Germany from sharing in the wonderful multipleness of recent biblical studies? And has the influence of neo-orthodoxy even on this side of the Atlantic (much as it may be on the wane) obscured from us the fact that *our* devouring idol is just the opposite one? Our idol is the divinizing of the One and the Same, the dedivinizing of the Other—monotheism. I would like to echo the comments of David Klemm, elsewhere in this book, on the demonic unity of our moral discourse.

I don't know where these thoughts will lead, how the theological formulations will turn out. No more than Spivak do I want to tout polytheism as a cure-all. But I covet a deep psychological alternative to the biblical/Christian habit of confronting problems of "the One and the Many" with a bias always towards the One. I would like to know how it is to experience the world as a polytheist, how that experience is different from mine, as a way of exorcising in myself perhaps the most potent biblical myth of all.

Part Five

—Conclusions —

⌘

16

Closing Remarks
An Oral Response Presented to the Plenary Attending the 1994 Conference

Patrick D. Miller

⌘

We have had considerable response to the individual papers, so while I will refer to particular papers, I will not try to duplicate the earlier, more specific responses. Instead, I will turn my attention more to the project of the working group as a whole. I will do two things. One is to look at the work of this group as an exemplar of the conversation between Bible and theology, between biblical study and theological study. In this context, I will identify some of the group's contributions to that conversation, as well as some problems; I will also say a little about the relation of process to program. Second, I will address a few specific issues that have arisen either in the papers or in the responses and the plenary discussion.

I

To begin, then, with the first of those items on the agenda: to what extent does this working group engage Bible and theology in ways consistent with what is expected from both ends of the dialogue, with what is expected when the Bible is interpreted and when theology is formulated?

From the Biblical Side

First, from the *biblical* side of that conversation, several things seem to me to be of necessity. One is that the *focus upon texts* is a starting point for most biblical research and an essential part of biblical theology. David Jobling remarked on the strange absence of the texts in the papers of our two New Testament colleagues, but I think a closer look suggests otherwise. What we have are two interpreters who are so at home in the relevant texts (Mark, on the one hand, and the *contemptus mundi* texts from Corinth, the Johannine community, and the pastoral letters, on the other) that they are able to draw in many texts without reference. A careful reader can often recognize specific texts indirectly alluded to. One notes, of course, the rich elaboration of texts in Second Isaiah and Proverbs in the papers of Paul Hanson and Claudia Camp.

What is most interesting to me is the explicit and direct focus on texts of most of the theologians in the enterprise, Schweiker on Genesis 11, Rigby on Psalm 22, Keller on the Apocalypse, Chastain on Job, and Brock on Jeremiah 31:15–22. Welker, like the New Testament scholars, draws on a range of "Spirit" texts, again because this is a textual field with which he is so familiar and also because the manifold manifestations of the Spirit is one of his points.

What is worth noting especially is that in every case, the biblical text is a central part of the theological argument and, though this is not necessary for the point I am making, usually functions in a transformative way as a facet of the stated theological program. Rita Brock takes a long time to get to her text, but her title and the paradigmatic function of the text reveal its formative role.

Second, attention to the *historical dimensions of the text*, where accessible, is expected of biblical research and reflected here in Brock's use of Jeremiah, Hanson on Second Isaiah, and Camp on Proverbs, as well as in the two New Testament essays.

Third, attention to the *larger literary setting or context* comes into play largely in Hanson and Camp, but Schweiker makes a very important tie from the Babel community's thwarted effort to make a name for itself to the divine giving of a great name to Abraham and his seed, an interpretive move I think is absolutely essential for understanding the force of the Babel text.

Fourth, while *attention to questions of form or type* and its *Sitz im Leben* is not generally pertinent or significant for the use of the texts here, Cynthia Rigby's not taking into account the form of Psalm 22:22 ff.

as a psalm of thanksgiving, and her choice of a minority and less plausible reading of the turn at verse 21 against the more likely assumption of an oracle of salvation—which she, of course, is well aware of and does point to as an alternative —leads, in my judgement, to a kind of skewing, if not misreading, of the text that turns it from a classic case of divine power delivering the powerless into prayer as a human empowerment. That, to me, is to be regretted, in part because her fundamental claim in the essay is correct and biblically grounded and there are, in fact, other laments that come closer to demonstrating her point about the power of dangerous memory.

The fifth and last comment from the biblical side of the conversation: Working within the *hermeneutical circle,* that is, attending to the interaction of the part to the whole, of specific texts to larger contexts, and, specifically, to the whole of Scripture, and vice-versa— that is, comprehending the whole of Scripture in the light of the parts— is a critical feature of biblical study. Such a move is an important feature of Bill Schweiker's paper, but I will say a little more about it in relation to complexity and coherence in other cases. For example, in the treatment of Psalm 22, I wonder if attention to the significant use of that psalm in relation to Jesus' death might affect the way in which one deals with and understands the issue of power and powerlessness in that psalm.

From the Theological Side

Now let me look at the results of the work group from the *theological* side and what I judge to be some of the things one would expect theology to attend to in the conversation. First of all, *careful analysis of the human situation* is one of the primary aims and accomplishments of these papers. From the more comprehensive efforts of Welker on the problem of the moral marketplace and Schweiker on the moral ontology of modern technological society and Catherine Keller on the power lines of contemporary world order; to the quite specific analyses of Brock and Chastain of the dynamics of power in the family, to which Keller also speaks; and Mack's brief suggestion at the end of his paper of the necessity to understand more clearly the structural arrangements in a society that wants to balance powers, enhance and limit freedoms, control predation, etc.; the analysis of the human situation is a prominent feature of this conversation.

To be particularly noted (and all of these are simply examples) is Brock's important suggestion that *the reality of sin and evil* may be seen at its most horrific in what families and adults do to children; the domination of the powerful over the powerless. That, of course, is echoed in other papers, but she is the one who lifts this into focus in relationship to the theological understanding of sin and evil. In our time, the paradigm of sin and evil has been the Holocaust. Brock suggests another one that may be as horrible and as banal, as Hannah Arendt noted was the case with that personal representative of holocaustian evil, Adolf Eichmann.

Second, *the role of experience* is also central in the theological work of these papers, indeed, in a large way, in Rigby's reference to the religious experience of the oppressed, as reported to her and observed by her in squatter's communities in the Philippines, African American communities in New York, and economically deprived families in her churches. The experiences of maternity (Brock), of abuse within the family (Brock and Chastain) and, more broadly, of being a woman also come into play.

Third, *the tradition* is less a resource in these papers than is "traditionally" the case in the Christian "tradition" of theology. My word play is intentional, and I am speaking here of the theological tradition, not the biblical tradition. This ambivalence toward the tradition is reflected fairly consistently in the work of the group. One place where this can be seen is in the generally negative view of the tradition expressed strongly in the introduction and found elsewhere in the papers. The primary use of the term "systematic" in these papers is not in its ordering and constructing reference in the term "systematic theology," but in the phrase "systematic distortions," where the enterprise is heavily critical, that is, ideological critique. The playing down of the tradition here also reflects the broad critique of the tradition by the feminist theology operative in the group, a critique one may expect to be to the fore in a focus on power inasmuch as the tradition is generally viewed from this perspective as one large and very long power move.

The tradition is not altogether absent from these papers; witness Michael Welker's engagement of Küng and Tracy, Keller's appropriation of the tradition of process theology, Wimbush's identification of the *contemptus mundi* in Augustine, and even Schweiker's engagement with the Greek and Roman philosophical tradition. But in the project as a whole, theology's history is more a negative reality than a positive one. The rule of faith is not significantly at work as a hermeneutical and theological guideline.

One must ask in all candor if the working group is not in some danger of being hoisted on its own reductionistic petard, if it is not itself engaged in reductionistic and systematic distortion of the tradition it accuses of being reductionistic. This is manifest in several ways:

—In the assumption that a theological emphasis or perspective is a totality, that is, that a particular approach always understands itself as monolithic, or that formal constructs are always "vague ciphers of integration,"—to quote from the Welker/Schweiker essay—as opposed to "a systematically coherent account of the diverse and polycontextual biblical materials." Could not a narrative approach be incorporated into this program? Of course it could, even as process theology, surely one of the more dominating systems of theological thought in our time, is one of the lynchpins of Keller's search for relational understanding of power.

—In the use of language as a weapon against the other, in this case, against other modes of thought. For example, does any defense of the tradition mean that the defender is automatically arguing that God should be seen as some guy up above who should have rescued the victim (as Chastain seems to imply)?

—In the insistence that Christian theism inherently represents an oppressive domination. This is a view that can be argued from Scripture and found in human experience, but also one against which Scripture sets some very profound resistance. In the fear of theological reductionism, are we in danger of reducing God in order to enhance the possibility of complexity, difference, and the human? For example, the view of divine power as spewing up fragments of the vision of the possible—I hesitate to use that one, since it is a part of what I am coming to comprehend as the colorful language of Catherine Keller's theology, all of which always needs to be looked at in a context — still does not immediately remind me of the God I see in Scripture. (I am aware, of course, that Keller would say that is part of the intentionality of her expression). For similar reasons, I find problematic an interpretation of a text where divine deliverance that has implications reaching out to the limits of time and space (i.e., Psalm 22) is turned into the human discovering the power to speak and work for liberation.

Fourth, from the theological side of the conversation, the effort to *order* and, I will risk the term *systematize*, is in fact deeply felt, at least within the Welker/Schweiker essay, although it is not as large a concern elsewhere, and in some papers is even resisted. That effort to order theology (to develop a logic, a sense of the whole) is done in a particular way, however, and this may be one of the chief contributions of the group—i.e., its dialectic of complexity and coherence. Here I expect I detect the voice of Michael Welker luring his partners in the group into a way of perceiving the whole of the theological task. It is appropriate, I think, that his guiding hand be felt at this point, inasmuch as he is as clearly a systematic theologian as the group has. (I say that because I am not even sure whether other theologians in the group would be willing to wear such a rubric.) But he is one whose work has constantly assumed, analyzed, and affirmed the complexities, interrelationships, and interdependencies of the world and the divine. I would like to say a little more about complexity and coherence because I believe that is a major component of the group's work and an important contribution.

It is clear that some members of the group are less comfortable with this theological method than others. I think that is partly implicit by its being less apparent in some of the papers, but some have vocally indicated their resistance to the dialectic. The impetus in the papers, I would observe, seems to me to be more toward complexity than coherence. Nevertheless, there are important instances of a reaching out for a coherence that will not superficially smooth out complexities.

For example, in Welker's paper, where there is a large emphasis on complexity, pluralism, differences and discontinuities, one can nevertheless identify a *formal* principle of coherence, a *material* principle of coherence and an *actual* coherence. The formal principle of coherence is "specific sets of questions about content in boundary situations and relations of proximity uncovered by investigations." One would probably have recognized the source of that quotation, even if I had not told you, by its style, or to use Welker's quote from Polkinghorne in this context, "Questionings that arise from the consideration of particularity gain coherence by the proximity, the boundarying of the particularities."

How this actually works is not altogether clear, but I think the formal principle is there with a high degree of intentionality. The material principle of coherence is God's presence in God's Spirit, and the actual coherence is "God's partiality for the weak, oppressed, and marginalized which serves as the source of unwavering processes for the generation of order and reality, as well as for the transformation of reality." At this point I think Ulrich Mauser is absolutely correct in what he recognized about the paper,[1] and I would like to come back to his observation in a minute.

Continuing still to think about the papers as a reflection of the dialectic, one notes how both Welker and Schweiker (where the dialectic is more evident than in some of the other papers) seek to identify and appropriate primary biblical categories as forms of *complexity* on the way to *coherence*—Welker with reference to the cultic, the legal, and the mercy dimensions of the text; Schweiker with the cultic, the prophetic

---

[1]   *Editor's note:* Miller is referring to a comment made by Mauser in the plenary discussion.

and the legal. The interdependence of these is critical for the possibility of faith and life, and in the case of their particular concerns, for the possibility of value-shaped moral communication and moral ontology in an economic, technological, value-neutral society.

This interplay of cultic/legal/mercy or cultic/prophetic/legal is quite important, both because it overcomes an overly-simplified and reductionistic appropriation of Scripture for theology and ethics, and because it is on the way to a complex coherence. Here the complexity is *material* rather than *contextual*. One would want to bring into such a complex, coherent, material drawing on Scripture the kind of contextual/experiential dimensions that are brought by Camp, Brock, Chastain, Rigby and others.

That such a complex coherence as suggested in the triads that Schweiker and Welker set forth is not a misreading is suggested in two ways: first, in the development of such an analysis in detail in recent works in biblical theology (for example, in Paul Hanson's *The People Called*); second, in the affirmation of this fundamentally Old Testament perspective by one of the chief New Testament voices interpreting the Old Testament—that is, the Matthean Jesus, who rebukes the Pharisees for neglecting the weightier matters of Torah, namely: justice, mercy, and faith. I take it these correspond to what Schweiker and Welker are talking about. It should be recognized that the complexity/coherence paradigm in a slightly different form has already entered biblical theology in the context of J. Christiaan Beker's magisterial treatment of the theology of Paul. In some sense the way is already paved from the biblical side for what this group is talking about.

In this regard, it should also be noted that the group's program is reflected in significant ways not only in its *papers*, but in its *process*. For example, the persistent effort was clearly made to draw into the group voices that would reflect both the contextual and the material complexity of which the introduction speaks. That must not be missed when we observe that they have not fully brought in the contextual and the material. They have nevertheless sought to do that, consistent with the program. (I am thinking here about the actual members of the working group.)

In addition, the program that was undertaken by the working group necessarily created strains and conflicts which you have struggled with over a long time on the way to a working coherence that has not suppressed the complexities and the differences. That is, for the group as a whole, more a methodological or formal coherence than a material one. I think we should recognize, however, that the strains and conflicts your enterprise has evoked—and I think they are intrinsic to the program—have now moved into the plenary discussion, though they may be, as yet, largely muted.

A question: Is not the single respondent at the end a denial of the methodological claims in the introduction, a mono/reductionistic move? Can I get off the hot seat? Or, does it represent the other possibility, that any single presentation is a particular, socialized, potentially insightful, potentially situation-transcending angle of vision? I think that is possible, while at the same time I wonder if an appropriate and happy complexity might have been joined here if my colleague, Katharine Sakenfeld, were up here with me in the response.

II

Let me now move on to three particular issues that have come up that caught my attention, including one to which I have already alluded.

The Reference-Point From Below

The first issue is the question Ulrich Mauser raised about whether there is not in some, if not most of the papers, a hidden "reference-point" from below: justice and mercy for the poor and the oppressed. This is definitely the case, fundamental to the enterprise, and absolutely on target. In this "reference-point" (I'm using Mauser's term now), the working group has put its finger on one of the most critical points of coherence, one that is present from the beginning of Scripture to its end. Without ever referring to it, the work of the group takes cognizance of the fact that the first time human words are lifted to the divine in Scripture, they are in the cry of Abel's blood from the ground, and that cry is heard again and again as a fundamental dimension of the whole biblical project. It is there in the outcry from Sodom and Gomorrah that goes up to the ears of God and is heard by God. It becomes paradigmatic in the Exodus story. It is a major feature of the legal dimension, where the texts say explicitly—particularly at the point of tending to the widow, the poor, the orphan, and the oppressed; or giving somebody's coat back in pledge when you have borrowed it—that if that one cries to me, I will hear, for I am compassionate.

Of course, if this cry of the oppressed were not apparent enough already, it becomes absolutely clear in the voice that cries from the cross. Nearly everything that matters in Scripture— prayer, faith, the reality and nature of the divine, the Trinity, the divine/human encounter—can be brought into the framework of what this working group has identified implicitly and explicitly as its reference-point. In Scripture it is, interestingly enough, explicitly a reference-point *from below*. That is, it is this cry from below that goes up above. In fact, I would deal with the whole notion of the divine anthropomorphisms in this same context, that is, the ears of God that are attuned to hear the cry from below. It is the word from below that brings the divine onto the scene in the biblical story. It is the cry for justice and mercy for the poor and the oppressed.

This, then, is why I do not believe, as some have said, that these papers have reduced theology to a moral concern. The issue here has to do with everything. It has to do with creation, with Israel's understanding of the world and reality. It has to do with the nature and reality of the divine as Psalm 82 sets the very existence of deity and the cosmos entirely around the question of provision of justice for the poor and the weak. It has to do with christology and pneumatology and everything else. All of which is to say that, in my judgment, this group has grasped something that brings the Bible centrally into their sphere of operation.

The Monotheism Question

The second particular issue is the monotheism question. I'm a little hesitant to bring it up; the question was a kind of flyer by David Jobling that may have aroused more reaction than he had expected. It is interesting that it does arouse reaction. Like Bill Schweiker, I am a radical monotheist (and I say it with all the kind of fervor that I think was in Bill's tone of voice as he said it); at the same time I want to remember that fervor seems to be built into the monotheistic position itself, as it is presented in Scripture. I am always interested in Christian theologians who are interested in this question (I started to say "flirting" with polytheism, but "flirting" is a pejorative term). It seems to me that it is possible for Christian theology to contemplate this issue in theory, but I'm not surprised that Camp's students had difficulty engaging the benefits of polytheism,[2] because Christian theology understands reality in a different way.

In this discussion, however, one of the things I miss is the constant indication in Scripture that monotheism is socially complex. One of the governing images in the Old Testament is that of the divine assembly and of the heavenly council. Major things that go on in the Old Testament take place in relationship to this. The whole machinery of divine rule centers around the complexity of this divine assembly, whether in the creation ("Let us make humanity in our image"), in the question of justice and mercy in the divine council in Psalm 82, or in the theodicy issue as it is dealt with in the narrative of Job 1-2. In Genesis 1–

---

2   *Editor's note:* Miller is referring to a comment made by Claudia Camp in the plenary discussion.

11, the place of the human creature is always represented not just vis-à-vis God, but vis-à-vis a divine and complex world (Gen. 1:26, 3:22, 6:1-4, 11:1-9).[3] That this carries on into the New Testament is self-evident. Jobling alluded to the Trinity, but then sort of cast it away; I think, in fact, that this is a fundamental way in which complexity and social interaction are present in the very notion of deity. Clearly, the idea of Trinity is also consistent with depictions of the divine found in the Judaic tradition. So we need to be careful about a reductionistic understanding of the monotheism of Scripture.

Relational Power/Persuasive Power

Finally, I was interested in Keller's discussion of relational power and persuasive power, as well as where she draws upon Brock's book (which I have not read) in raising a question about persuasive power as an adequate replacement for coercive power. I want to stay somewhat with persuasive power, though I want to say more than simply this. While God is not simply "Daddy," it is the case that God knows best— that is my only hope in this world. We can argue about that. But the point is that within Scripture itself this persuasive dimension is a complex phenomenon, and is not singular or moving in simply one direction. That is, you have explicit notions of persuasion present in the biblical texts in the relationship between the divine and the human. But what happens is that the activity of persuasion goes on from both sides.

What I am alluding to is the frequency of the motivational clauses in the Law. That is, right at the point where the community is being told what it must do, it is regularly given reasons and exhortations to persuade and encourage. It allows for the possibility of argument and dialogue. There is one other place in the biblical texts, certainly in the Old Testament texts, where motivational clauses play a very large role, and that is in the biblical laments, where, from the human end of the line, there are all sorts of ways in which human beings are engaged in seeking to persuade and encourage the Deity. I would suggest the possibility that the rhetoric and intentionality in even the very language for prayer suggests that it is to be seen fundamentally as an act of persuasion.[4]

---

3   *Editor's note:* For further discussion on this point, see P.D. Miller, "Cosmology and World Order in the Old Testament: The Divine Council as Cosmic-Political Symbol," *Horizons in Biblical Theology,* 9 (1987), 53-78.

4   *Editor's note:* For further discussion on this point, see P.D. Miller, "Prayer As Persuasion," *Word and World* 13 (1993), 356-62.

Conclusion

In addition to the substantive contributions made by the authors of the essays, I would like to close by commenting on the methodological contribution of the working group as a whole. The group has articulated and demonstrated a way of engaging Bible and theology with each other, and indeed the possibility of the theological enterprise *period.* That is, they have convincingly proposed in a variety of ways that theology can go on in full acknowledgment of the real complexity that is there in the world while struggling to find a coherence - a coherence suggesting that neither faith nor life is wholly chaotic or fully relative.

Contributors

⌘

RITA NAKASHIMA BROCK is Professor in the Endowed Chair in the Humanities, Hamline University. Her Ph.D. from the Claremont Graduate School is in philosophy of religion and theology. She is the author of a number of essays and *Journeys By Heart: A Christology of Erotic Power*, co-author of *Casting Stones: Prostitution and Liberation in Asia and the United States*, and co-editor and contributor to *Guide to the Perplexing: A Survival Manual for Women in Religious Studies* and *Setting the Table: Women in Theological Conversation*.

CLAUDIA V. CAMP is professor of religion at Texas Christian University, Fort Worth, where she has taught since 1980. Her research interests lie in the areas of wisdom literature, methodology in biblical interpretation, and feminist interpretation. Her publications include a book, *Wisdom and the Feminine in the Book of Proverbs*, and she is currently completing another on strange women in the Bible.

KIMBERLY PARSONS CHASTAIN is an ordained minister in the Presbyterian Church, USA and a pastoral counselor in Bound Brook, New Jersey.

PAUL D. HANSON is the Florence Corliss Lamont Professor of Divinity and Professor of Old Testament in the Divinity School and the Department of Near Eastern Languages and Civilizations. He is the author of *The Dawn of Apocalyptic; Dynamic Transcendence; The Diversity of Scripture; The People Called; Old Testament Apocalyptic*; and "Isaiah 40-66" in *Interpretation: A Bible Commentary for Teaching and Preaching*. He is presently writing a book on the Bible and Politics.

DAVID JOBLING is Professor of Old Testament Language and Literature at ST. Andrew's College, Saskatoon. He holds the Ph.D. from Union Theological Seminary, New York. He is the author of *The Sense of Biblical Narrative* (two volumes, Sheffield Academic Press) and *1*

Samuel (Liturgical Press), and is a member of the Collective which wrote *The Postmodern Bible* (Yale University Press). He is a former president of the Canadian Society of Biblical Studies.

CATHERINE KELLER teaches constructive theology at Drew University, in the Graduate and Theological Schools, focusing on the intersections of traditional Christian symbols, feminism, ecology, and postmodern cultural theory. She is author of *From A Broken Web: Separation, Sexism and Self* and *Apocalypse Now and Then: A Feminist Guide to the End of the World*.

FLORA A. KESHGEGIAN is Associate University Chaplain and Adjunct Faculty at Brown University in Providence, RI. She has a Ph. D. in theology from Boston College through the Joint Doctoral Program with Andover Newton Theological School. She is currently writing a book on a theology of remembering for salvation. She is especially interested in relating the construction of memories by and on behalf of those who have suffered, such as survivors of abuse and genocide, to theological practices of memory.

DAVID E. KLEMM is Professor of Religion at The University of Iowa. Among his publications are *The Hermeneutical Theory of Paul Ricoeur, A Constructive Analysis*, editor of *Hermeneutical Inquiry*, vol. 1: *Interpretation of Texts*, and vol. 2: *Interpretation of Existence;* co-editor of *Meanings in Texts and Actions: Questioning Paul Ricoeur* and *Figuring the Self: Subject, Absolute, and Others in Classical German Philosophy*. He is past editor of the *Studies in Religion* and *Reflection and Theory in the Study of Religion* book series of the American Academy of Religion.

BURTON MACK is professor emeritus of Christian origins at the Claremont School of Theology and the Claremont Graduate School. His publications include *A Myth of Innocence: Mark and Christian Origins; The Lost Gospel: Q and Christian Origins;* and *Who Wrote the New Testament? The Making of the Christian Myth*. He is currently involved in several cooperative research projects, including the national seminar on "Ancient Myths and Modern Theories" of the Society of Biblical Literature.

PATRICK D. MILLER is Charles T. Haley Professor of Old Testament Theology at Princeton Theological Seminary. His publications include *Interpreting the Psalms* and *They Cried To the Lord: The Form and Theology of Biblical Prayer*, as well as many articles and edited volumes that are widely used in Old Testament studies. He is also the co-editor of *Theology Today*.

CYNTHIA L. RIGBY teaches systematic theology at Austin Presbyterian Theological Seminary, concentrating particularly on setting Reformed Christian doctrine in conversation with feminist and liberationist concerns. She recently published an article in *Theology Today* titled "Free To Be Human: Limits, Possibilities, and the Sovereignty of God" (April, 1996) and is currently working on a project titled, "The Real Word Really Became Real Flesh: Karl Barth's Contribution To A Feminist Incarnational Christology."

WILLIAM SCHWEIKER is Associate Professor of Theological Ethics at The University of Chicago Divinity School. His publications include *Mimetic Reflections: A Study in Hermenuetics, Theology, and Ethics, Responsibility and Christian Ethics,* and *One World, Many Moralities* (forthcoming, Pilgrim, 1998). He is also co-editor and contributor to *Meanings in Texts and Action: Questioning Paul Ricoeur,* and *Iris Murdoch and the Search For Human Goodness.*

GERD THEIßEN is Professor of New Testament Studies at the University of Heidelberg. His works include *The Social Setting of Pauline Christianity, Psychological Aspects of Pauline Theology,* and *Social Reality and the Early Christians.*

MICHAEL WELKER is the chair for Systematic Theology at the University of Heidelberg where he is also the director of the International Wissenschaftsforum. He formerly served as Professor for Systematic Theology at the University of Tübingen (1983-87) and Professor for Reformed Theology at the University of Münster (1987-1990). He has published 15 books and more than 100 articles and chapters in journals and books, including: *God the Spirit, Kirche im Pluralismus, Creation and Reality,* and *Was geht vor beim Abendmahl?*

VINCENT WIMBUSH is Professor of New Testament and Christian Origins at Union Theological Seminary in New York and Adjunct Professor in the Department of Religion at Columbia University. He earned his Ph.D. at Harvard University. His published works include: *Paul the Worldly Ascetic* (author), *Ascetic Behavior in Greco-Roman Antiquity: A Sourcebook* (editor), and *Asceticism* (co-editor).